# MEDIEVAL KASHMIR

The *Rajataranginis* of Jonaraja, Shrivara and Shuka,
translated into English by J.C. Dutt
under the title "Kings of Kashmira", Vol. III

*Edited with Notes by*

S.L. Sadhu

ATLANTIC
PUBLISHERS & DISTRIBUTORS (P) LTD

Published by

**ATLANTIC**

**PUBLISHERS & DISTRIBUTORS (P) LTD**

7/22, Ansari Road, Darya Ganj, New Delhi-110002
Phones : +91-11-40775252, 40775214, 23273880, 23275880
Fax: +91-11-23285873
Web: www.atlanticbooks.com
E-mail: orders@atlanticbooks.com



Printed & bound in India by Atlantic Print Services

# Preface

KASHMIR has the distinction of having given to the world the *Rajatarangini*, the only history of its kind in medieval India. Kalhana who composed it in Sanskrit verse, spanning several thousand years from prehistoric times, concluded it in A.D. 1149. After about three hundred years Jonaraja, under the inspiration and command of his sovereign Zain-ul-Abdin, undertook to record the events of the intervening period. On the death of Jonaraja in 1459 A.D., the narrative was continued successively to almost the end of the sixteenth century by Shrivara Pandit, Prajyabhatta and Shuka. The work of Jonaraja and his followers embodies the history of nearly five hundred years. They saw with their own eyes some of the most outstanding events, including the resurgence in Kashmir under the benign Zain-ul-Abdin, the heights reached in the land in the domain of art and culture during the reign of his grandson Hassanshah, the civil war following his death that tore the population asunder and the desperate resistance offered by the last independent sovereign Yaqubshah Chak to the annexation of the land by the Mughals.

While Kalhana's work is easily available in English, the works of his above-named successors attracted only one translator, J.C. Dutt, who published the English translation of the Rajataranginis from Jonaraja to Shuka, under the title *Kings of Kashmira* (Vol. iii), in 1898. No other translation has appeared in English since and the book is almost extinct. As a consequence, the history of medieval Kashmir covering about half-a-millennium, recorded by contemporary historians, is not available to English-knowing readers. A serious vacuum is thus created and the layman is no less handicapped than the students of history in various university courses.

This gap cannot be filled by merely reprinting the translated version of J.C. Dutt. The reasons are:

1. Sir Auriel Stein first prepared a critical edition of the Sanskrit work of Kalhana and brought out the English version subsequently. Dutt did not have available to him a critical edition of the works of Jonaraja and others. He probably accepted what appeared to him the best transcript/recension. It is well known that such raw Mss contain numerous errors of calligraphy, omissions, etc. Sometimes distortions and errors crept in inadvertently. Stein, Buhler and many others have shed copious light on the nature of corruption that distorts original texts. The recension made use of by Dutt could not be an exception and the English version has its share of errors.
2. Interested scholars had to wait nearly seventy years till the Visheshwaranand Research Institute of Hoshiarpur, Panjab, brought out in 1967 the critical edition of these texts prepared after considerable labour and study by Prof. Shri Kanth Kaul. A cursory comparison is revealing:

| *(Original) (Dutt)* | *(Emendation) (Kaul)* | *(Original)* | *(Emendation)* |
|---|---|---|---|
| Vartideva (p. 22) | Vantideva | Mahila (p. 26) | Ahala |
| Napalpora (p. 38) | Utpalpora | Snangiri (p. 71) | Jainagiri |
| Vitasta (p. 70) | Pohru (river) | Vatapatha (p. 92) | Avatapatha |
| Chitra country (p. 96) | Land of Chibs | Vipulata (p. 147) | Vishulata |
| Pajabhatta (p. 219) | Najibhatta | Sujya (p. 118) | Khujya |
| Tajibhatta (p. 198) | Pajabhatta | | |

Dutt is not to blame. He has spared no effort in presenting the narrative faithfully but the corrupt forms of words as indicated above create confusion, especially with reference to their context, and the reader is led astray.

3. Dutt was not familiar with the geography of the Valley, especially when the means of transport and communication were primitive. Nor could he be aware of the local traditions. One can list a number of mistakes that crept in on this account:

| *(Original)* | *(Emendation)* | *(Original)* | *(Emendation)* |
|---|---|---|---|
| Sthama | cantonment/camp | mountain that touched the sky (p. 28) | Gaganger |
| a good military road (p. 28) | Tarabala route | heroic queen (p. 50) | Subhatta |
| Lord of Kampana (p. 36) | Commander-in-chief | Lord of Dvara | Commandant of the Gate |
| Durmarga | stiff route | Medavana (p. 244) | Bhedavana |
| estate of Siddhadesh (used as place name | fruitful/correct order | Sagusika<br>Pashupad-ishta road (p. 250) | Gushi<br>goat tracks |

4. Another stumbling block in the way of the reader is that names of the vast majority of places mentioned in the text of Dutt have changed beyond recognition on account of the inevitable tendencies in speech. Thus, when it is said that Mohammad Margesha escaped from the castle in Bahurupa, the place makes no sense for the uninitiate. But when Bahurupa is explained as an earlier form of the name Beeru, a short distance from Tangmarg, a small bell tinkles in the mind of the reader. Examples could be multiplied by the hundred: Andrakotta (Sumbal), Bhimatika (Bren), Jainanagara (Naushehra), Ksipitika (Ka'ta' Kol), Lahara (Lar), Makshikasvamin (Mayasum), Krityaashrama (Kitcahom), Padampora (Pampore), Pradyumna hill (Hariparvat), Pravapura (Srinagar), Samudrakota (Sadrakot), Samudramatha (Sadramar-Haba Kadal), Sikanderpora (Nauhatta), Taksaka (Zevan).....

Unable to link the old place names to the present ones, the reader is likely to give up the attempt in disgust. But when he can locate the spot where a hero was slain, the locality where a battle was fought, or where the troops crossed the river when on the offensive, interest grows vastly and he feels every lane, every street and every stream has played its role in the historical events of the past.

Similar is the case with the names of persons. Suffixes to names of leading personalities who made history, like Margesha, Margapati, Rajanaka, Pratihara and Koshadhiksha, have changed to Magrey/Malik, Raina, Padar and Kuchhai. Likewise Lavanyas, Tantreshya, etc., are no longer in use. The lay reader, as also the research scholar, has to cross the barrier before the chronicles become truly intelligible to him or her.

An attempt has been made to edit Dutt's version of the chronicles entitled *Kings of Kashmira* (vol. iii) with a view to eliminating the hurdles which readers find it strewn with. The 'Notes' have been based on the critical Sanskrit edition prepared by Shri S.K. Kaul and published by the Vishveshvaranand Research Institute, Hoshiarpur. The main text is intact, but wherever Dutt's version is at variance with the critical edition, the latter has been preferred. Likewise the errors and uncertainties referred to above have, as far possible, been set right. Place names appear in both forms in the 'references' and where such names have fallen into oblivion, *e.g.*, Vakpustatvi, or the places are no longer identifiable, *e.g.*, Dvarika, attempt has been made to trace them to their nearest location. Without such editing the work remains unintelligible and even misleading for most readers.

The undersigned lays no claim to a systematic study of history. The provocation for the present venture came from the hurdles with which he himself was baffled and in overcoming which he sought the assistance of colleagues and friends, including scholars with sound knowledge of history. It was their advice and encouragement that drove him to undertake this labour of love. The present work aims at clearing cobwebs spread over the chronicles (as presented in English by the late J.C. Dutt) which are, by and large, as authentic and reliable as the courtier-historians could make them from first-hand knowledge and observation. It presents intelligible and interesting matter to the reader covering nearly five hundred years of medieval history in Kashmir. No attempt has been made to restructure historical events or re-assess the fallout of history in this part of the country. The undersigned would feel his labours amply rewarded if the work helps the reader in deriving greater enjoyment through a study of the chronicles of Jonaraja and his successors.

In its present form the work carries a short introduction,* notes and explanations and an index to facilitate ready reference. Apart from the critical edition of the 'Jainarajataranginis' prepared by Prof. S.K. Kaul, already referred to the undersigned has relied mainly on the following:

---

* It appeared in a partially different form in the *Koshur Samachar*, New Delhi, a few years ago.

*Kalhana's Rajatarangini*, vols. i and ii (Stein)—Motilal Banarasidas *Twarikhi Kashmir* (Pirzada Hassan Shah)— Research & Publications Department, J&K Govt., Srinagar, 1954.
Census Reports—Town and Village Directory of J&K State (years 1941 and 1981).

Reference has been made to other sources wherever possible.

The reader is requested to extend his/her indulgence for any omissions and/or imperfections that may still exist despite the best intentions of the undersigned.

New Delhi. **S.L. Sadhu**

# Preface to the 1898 Edition

It is some satisfaction to the translator to be able to bring his self-imposed labours to an end. In volumes *i* and *ii* of this work which were published in 1879 and 1887, respectively, he completed the translation of Kalhana. Pandit Durgaprasada of Jayapore has published an excellent edition of Kalhana's work, and the translator regrets that he was unable to profit by it as the edition was published subsequent to his translation. The narration left by Kalhana, who may be called the father of Indian history, was taken up by Jonaraja. He again was followed by his pupil Shrivara: and Shrivara's work was continued by Prajyabhatta. It is not generally known that Prajyabhatta left his work incomplete, and that it was taken up by Shuka who brought the account of Kashmira to the time when the country was conquered by Akbar, and it ceased to be an independent kingdom. The works of all these authors have been translated in the volume now presented to the public. To judge from the imperfect texts of these works published by the General Committee of Public Instruction, and the Asiatic Society of Bengal, it seems that the later authors have greatly improved Kalhana's method of writing history. They are clear and perspicuous, and events are narrated consecutively, so that the whole narration runs in one continuous flow. The writer, however, could not forget that they were poets as well as historians, and consequently they interspersed their accounts with flowers of poesy and rhetorical flourishes!

It is to be regretted that the last of the works mentioned above has been very carelessly edited. Portions of the narrative have got inserted in wrong places so as to interrupt the flow of the narrative to render the meaning in those places unintelligible.

The translator has tried his best to put these intruding fragments into their proper places. He has, however, not been able to find the proper place of three unimportant and uninteresting stories which he has put in appendices.

It must be mentioned that valuable as the writings of these authors are from a historical point of view, in the absence of any other history of the country they relate to, we cannot unhesitatingly accept their estimation of persons and events when we remember that they were, what may be called, court *pandits*, and depended on the smiles of kings, whose accounts they wrote, for almost everything they had in the world. It is not unlikely that they often had to read out their writings in court. We almost always find that they begin the account of a king by extolling his virtues to the skies, and we may be sure that they never wrote their censures on any king till he was dead or deposed. As court pandits they had in full measure the vice of such people: fulsome adulation of their patrons. They did not hesitate to raise Mahomedan princes not only above the ancient heroes of their country, whom as Hindus they must have revered, but even above the gods of the Hindus. A strict impartiality of opinion cannot be expected from such writers. A true history cannot be written when the writer has a purpose to serve other than writing a true history. There is, however, no reason to disbelieve the correctness of their accounts, irrespective of the writer's views regarding the events narrated.

No one can be more alive to the defects of the translation than the translator himself. He is, however, the first to translate these valuable records into English, and he hopes that the public will view his performance with the indulgence due to a first attempt of a difficult work. He trusts it will form the ground work for translation which will, no doubt, be more scholarly than his, especially when undertaken by a European scholar like Dr. Stein of Lahore. A European commands much greater resources in this country than what a native of the country may hope to do.

In conclusion the translator begs to offer his best thanks to his teacher Pandit Alokanath Nyayabhushana with whom he read the *Rajatarangini* almost from the beginning to the end. He is also deeply obliged to his brother Mr. Ramesh C. Dutt, C.I.E. for very valuable help rendered in connection with this translation, as in many other things, which the world will perhaps never know.

Calcutta
1st July, 1898

**J.C. Dutt**

# Contents

# Abbreviations used

| | | |
|---|---|---|
| Bla | for | Baramulla |
| BS | for | *Baharistani Shahi* (Persian-ascribed to Mirza Mahdi) translated into English by Dr. K.N. Pandit-Calcutta-1991 |
| dt. | for | district |
| GK | for | *Guldastah Kashmir* (Urdu) by Hargopal *Kaul Khasta* - Sheikh Ghulam Mohammad & Sons, Srinagar |
| Jona. | for | Jonaraja |
| km. | for | kilometre |
| kmr/ksmr. | for | Kashmir/Kashmiris |
| KM | for | *Routes in the Himalayas* by Maj. Kenneth Mason |
| Ksm | for | Kashmiri language |
| mtn. | for | mountain |
| *Nil-n* | for | *Nilamatpuran*—edited and translated into English by Dr. Ved Ghai |
| P. | for | page |
| pb. | for | probably |
| pga. | for | *pargana* (sub-district) |
| PH | for | *Twarikhi Kashmir* (Persian)—by Pir Hassan Shah |
| PP | for | Pir Panchal range of mountains |
| r. | for | river |
| RNS | for | *Rajatarangini* translated into Hindi by Dr. Raghunath Singh—Varanasi |
| RT | for | *Rajatarangini* (Stein) |

| | | |
|---|---|---|
| SK | for | *Rajataranginis* of Jonaraja, Shrivara and Shuka—edited by Prof. Shrikanth Kaul |
| Srgr | for | Srinagar |
| Srv. | for | Shrivara |
| SSC | for | *A Short History of Jammu Raj*—by Dr. Sukhdev Singh Charak - 1985 |
| t. | for | tehsil |
| TA | for | *Tabqati Akbari* by Nizam-ud-Din Ahmad |
| trslr. | for | translator |
| v/vv. | for | village/verses |
| V/Vy | for | the Valley of Kashmir |
| vy. | for | valley |
| Vit. Maham. | for | Vitasta Mahatamya |
| WK | for | *Waqaiti* Kashmir (Persian) by Mohd. Azam Dedamari |
| Z | for | (Sultan) Zain-ul-Abdin |

# Introduction

DEFYING death and oblivion, Kalhana Pandit, scion of a noble family in Kashmir during the 12th Century A.D., conferred immortality on men and women of the ages gone by and resurrected for ever the events they had brought into existence. It is, indeed, a wonder that while mighty edifices in stone, brick and mortar have crumbled or totally disintegrated, men and women continue to breathe and live in the works of Kalhana and others who followed his footsteps. He worked actively at 7826 verses of his magnum opus, the *Rajatarangini*, for two years and brought it to a close in Laukika era 4225 (*i.e.*, 1149 A.D.) while Jaisimha settled down to a peaceful reign after upheavals lasting several decades. Kalhana has thus played his role in *kaalhana*, bridging the ocean of oblivion.

For nearly three hundred years princes and *pandits* enjoyed reading the verses but neither any scholar seems to have thought of emulating Kalhana's example nor did any ruler care to have the events of his own rule recorded. Kalhana's work appears, however, to have retained its interest for readers and it came to the notice of Zain-ul-Abdin who ruled Kashmir for half-a-century, A.D. 1420-70. Known as Budshah, or the 'great king', he was an enlightened sovereign and attracted a large number of scholars and men of attainment to his court. Impressed with the account given by Kalhana of ancient rulers of Kashmir, Zain-ul-Abdin expressed a desire to have the chronicle updated. Says Jonaraja in his *Rajatarangini*:

"The past kings were sunk in the sea of oblivion and Shri Jain-oll-Abhadina wished, out of a tender regard, to rescue them. He employed for the purpose the noble-hearted Shri Shiryyabhatta, chief of all the courts of Justice. I received orders from him, and I have now ventured to complete the story of the kingly line."

Jonaraja thus became the first successor to Kalhana in continuing the story of the kings of Kashmir from where the master had left it in A.D. 1149 in the reign of Jayasimha. He brought it down to his own time and records many interesting facts about his sovereign and patron Zain-ul-Abdin. Jonaraja passed away in the year 35 (*i.e.* Saptrishi/Laukika year 4535 corresponding to A.D. 1459) and the mantle of maintaining the continuity of the chronicle fell on the shoulders of his pupil Shrivara Pandit. The latter survived his patron and brought the account down to the year 4562, *i.e.* 1486 A.D. when Fateh Shah ruled the Kingdom.

Shrivara calls himself a pupil of his predecessor Jonaraja and gave his chronicle the title '*Jainarajatarangini*'. His successor Prajyabhatta took the thread of the narrative from the year 4562 *i.e.* A.D. 1486 and called it 'Rajavalipataka'. By this time leadership in the country was divided among warring camps and the throne changed its occupants frequently. The prolonged civil war provoked very strong partisan feelings and Prajyabhatta felt it unsafe to continue with the chronicle. Says his successor Shuka:

> "Then (in the year 4589, *i.e.* 1513 A.D.) the poet (Prajyabhatta) did not write the account of the kings, owing to the tumults in the kingdom and on account of the fear of the wicked and avaricious..."

Shuka was a contemporary of the later Chaks and the political climate in the country during the period was no better. He was witness to the entry of the Mughal troops into the Valley in 1586 and the loss of independent status held by Kashmir so long. Among the last events mentioned by Shuka is the construction of the rampart round Nagnagri, the township with the Hariparbat as its centre. He also mentions that people made festivities when, under orders of the emperor Akbar, the Mughal troops were asked to vacate the main city and shift their residence to the cantonment inside the rampart. Thus the account of the chroniclers Jonaraja, Shrivara, Prajyabhatta and Shuka comes to a close about the turn of the 16th century.

## II

From the foregoing it is obvious that Jonaraja, Shrivara and Prajyabhatta carried out their respective assignments under the patronage of the rulers and were probably on the payroll of the state. There was, evidently, close contact between the first two and, perhaps, collaboration. Shuka closed his account of events around 1600 A.D. and he could, probably, not have met his immediate predecessor Prajyabhatta who folded up his pen-tray in 1513 A.D. Whether he also was an official chronicler or took up the task as a labour of love worthy of a scholar, even as Kalhana had done, is not clear. But all the four acknowledge Kalhana as their lodestar, admire his role as poet and try to keep close to his style of narration.

Jonaraja and Shrivara were very close to their sovereign Zain-ul-Abdin. Shrivara mentions that the king took him along with Simhabhatta round the mountain lake Konsarnag (altitude 13500 feet) in a boat and that he entertained his liege with the recitation of *Gita Govinda*. Probably he maintained his influence at the courts of Zain-ul-Abdin's successors till he himself passed away. Zain-ul-Abdin and his successors were well-versed in Persian and Sanskrit and enjoyed the company of scholars, poets and men who had attained eminence in various arts and sciences. The chroniclers must have read out their own compositions in the court, or privately, before kings, even as they read out from other works. Under the circumstances it would be expecting too much of them to be directly critical of the king or be absolutely impartial and detached in references to various events or assessment of his policies and achievements. It is, therefore, not at all surprising to find adulatory references to kings and princes interspersed lavishly in the text. Critical comments are also on record but indirectly and in innuendo. For instance, referring to the feelings of Zain-ul-Abdin after a battle with his own son Haji Khan, later Haidarshah (1470-72 A.D.). Shrivara says:

> "He (Zain-ul-Abdin) blamed himself for having cast aside prudence in his kindness, and accused himself as the cause of the mischief."

Shrivara was attached to Hassan Shah (1472-84 A.D.), grandson of Zain-ul-Abdin, from the infancy and when the latter ascended the throne he extended patronage to the chronicler. While acknowledging gratitude to Hassan Shah for his patronage he caustically comments on the shortcomings of his reign. In unequivocal language he calls the king an 'unworthy descendant of Jainaraja' when he caused his uncle Bahram Khan to be blinded.

The king (Hassanshah) and his men while on a deer-hunt inflicted great suffering on villagers and paid no heed to their complaints when his servants 'killed the people in their own houses.' Shrivara remarks:

> "The impotent king heard the people express their wish that he might not come again...If to tie down and kill hundreds of deer, like beasts of sacrifice, be sport, what then is butcher's work?"

While commenting upon the state of affairs towards the end of the king's reign the chronicler says,

> "Accepting bribes was considered by the officers of the State as a virtue, oppressing the subjects was regarded as wisdom, and addiction to women was reckoned happiness. All opposition ceased...."

Hassan Shah died in the prime of his youth. His early death was generally attributed to the use of wine and the company of women. The chronicler puts it in words thus:

> "Those who are attached to this world and enjoy youth and prosperity, and who yield themselves to the love of women, to enjoyments and drinking, they all pass away in a few days...Thus the people said and lamented in the burial ground..."

Tolerance and respect for truth appear to have suffered erosion by the time Shuka assumed the mantle of chronicling events. His comments are obviously less candid and he appears to be writing under a self-imposed constraint.

## III

The chroniclers were orthodox Brahmins and, therefore, generous towards those Hindu and Muslim kings and leaders who upheld the honour and prestige of the Brahmins, the scholarly and the learned. Zain-ul-Abdin, his grandson Hassan Shah and the Mughal emperor Akbar stand prominent as patrons of the Brahmins and the learned. As members of the contemporary society the chroniclers had a stake in good government, administration of justice and survival of the unwritten moral code. They consequently shower praise on those kings, ministers and administrators who were able to maintain peace and tranquility and displayed honesty, loyalty to the land and dedication to duty. As a corollary, they could not applaud those who persecuted Brahmins by imposing poll-tax, by demolishing temples or by resorting to ruthless proselytization. The chroniclers detest leaders and feudal barons *who received pay from both contending parties* or changed sides frequently for selfish ends, thus precipitating conflicts and civil wars which unleashed misery and death. They also cannot conceal their contempt for cowardly rulers who, unwilling to organise defence against an aggressor, quit the country, exposing innocent people to plunder, arson and murder at the hands of merciless invaders.

Appreciation recorded by Jonaraja of the role of Shahmir in defeating the machinations of Achala is genuine even as the condemnation for Sahadeva is. Though Shrivara has an obvious prejudice against the Syed faction during the civil war in the mid-1480s, he very generously praises the valour of one of their heroes Baqir (Bhakeira). The chronicler upheld the cause of Kashmiri nobles against the Syeds during the civil war in 1484 A.D. He, however, does not mince words in expressing disapproval of Kashmiries who organised a mass killing of the Syeds at 'Amrita Park' or Aa'nta Bhavan. Says he,

> "The tree of enmity first grew out of the murder of the Saidas and gradually unfolded its leaves."

The observation is repeated a number of times.

## IV

Zain-ul-Abdin encouraged Hindus to revive their customs and rituals publicly without fear of persecution. He also remitted invidious taxes on them. Some orthodox Muslim historians have disapproved of this policy. Among them is the author of *Baharistani Shahi* which was written long after the end of the dynasty of the Sultans of Kashmir. He also gives interesting details of the conflict between the Tsak or Chak clan of Trehgam (Kupwara) and Sultan Budshah. The Chaks were fierce and desperate fighters but highly self-respecting. When Zain-ul-Abdin constructed the Zainager canal and started building palaces, the Chaks, who appear to have remained untamed so far, apprehended an encroachment upon their liberty and a liability to undertake *beggar* or forced labour for the king and his nobles. They therefore burnt the king's palace and indulged in other forms of protest and revolt. The king was left with no alternative but to crush them. Neither Jonaraja nor Shrivara alludes to these apprehensions of the Chaks. Likewise Shuka lavishes praise on Kanchana or Kaji Chak. Some Muslim historians have represented his administration in adverse colours but the *Baharistani Shahi* eulogizes him on having murdered about 800 'infidels and idol-worshippers' during one night. That Shuka does not mention such a calamity overtaking his relations and friends indicates that intolerance had taken deep roots.

Likewise several other important events have escaped mention by the successors of Kalhana. Lalla Yogeshwari and her younger contemporary Sheikh Noor-ud-din Noorani who flourished in the fourteenth and fifteenth centuries have exercised tremendous influence over life, language, literature, philosophy and culture in the Valley. But they have not even been mentioned by Jonaraja. Other historians state that when Sheikh Noor-ud-Din, also known as Sheikh-ul-Alam, shuffled his mortal coil, the king, Zain-ul-Abdin, personally went to *Tsrari Sharief to be one of the pall-bearers. Jonaraja was alive at the time and should not have missed the important event. Similarly, he makes no reference to the celebrated Mir Syed Ali Hamdani who commands profound respect in the Valley, nor to the saint Bulbul Shah who is said to have inspired Rentchen (1335-38 A.D.) to embrace Islam after the Brahmin leader Devaswami declined to admit him to the Hindu fold.

Shuka who is very particular to impress the reader with his painstaking search for authenticity fails to mention that during the chaotic conditions of 1580s a deputation of Kashmiri elders under the leadership of Baba Dawood Khaki waited upon the Mughal emperor Akbar and persuaded him to annex Kashmir. Jonaraja and Shrivara have given harrowing accounts of famines but Shuka makes no reference to the famine following the Mughal conquest to offset which the rampart of Nagnagri was built. A reference to Haba Khatoon, poetess and queen of song, who was his contemporary and also close to Yusuf Shah Chak, is also wanting.

## V

An interesting episode in the chronicle of Shrivara is the ascendency of the Syeds to power. The Muslim sultanate had been ushered in Kashmir pretty long before the Syeds began to trek in from Central Asia and elsewhere under the onslaught of Taimur. The people of Kashmir have had long experience of sufferings

* The celebrated Sheikh is laid to rest at Tsrari Sharief. Lakhs of people, Hindus and Muslims, pay their reverential homage to the Saint at the mausoleum.

caused by small coteries of outsiders whose numbers proliferated with snowball effect. Such small communities gained control over key posts in the administration and exploited the natural resources of the Valley with a vengeance. In addition, they treated the sons of the soil with contempt and did everything to bar their way to progress.

In their anxiety to secure a homeland for themselves in Kashmir, the Syed immigrants probably did all they could to secure power. For many generations the Muslim kings of Kashmir continued with the old traditions and they also patronized Sanskrit language and learning. The Syeds persuaded the rulers to conform to orthodox Muslim customs, entered into matrimonial relationship with the royal family and managed to seek enviable eminence at the court and in the administration. Patriotic leaders fell into discord under their influence and immense suffering was unleashed for the common people. The resentment of the local people is thus expressed by Shrivara:

> 'The Saidas enjoyed many large estates and by their marriages with the king's daughters had lived like kings for a long time... These foreigners had become rich after coming to this country and had forgotten their previous history... They regarded the people of Kashmir scarcely as grass..."

He graphically describes how under the advice of the patriotic leader Jahangir the king promised to stand firm against the Syeds but

> "When he went to his wife at night he was overcome by affection and he told her all that had been said to him. Whereupon the queen who had espoused the cause of her father's party (Syeds) became enraged, and like a fearful she-serpent sought to injure the Margapati (Jahangir).....Rising from the side of his beloved the king became anxious to favour her party and placed the kingdom in their power...."

Subsequent events narrated by him show how much misery was caused to the people on account of the rivalry between the Syeds and the Kashmiris.

As a patriot interested in the welfare of the sons of the soil, including his own kith and kin, Shrivara expresses strong dislike against the Syeds whose presence in Kashmir gradually strengthened Muslim orthodoxy, thereby causing an emotional shock to the Hindus at the elimination of the traditional customs and festivals accompanied with colourful display and gaiety.

Another outcome—weakening of the authority of the kings—made matters worse for the common man. Persian language dominated the elitist circles and the court, and the Syeds had a mastery over it. The Brahmins found their native prestige and leadership challenged. Further the onslaught on them through proselytization and persecution engineered by Suhabhatta and others decimated their numbers and this was attributed partly to the Syeds. The chronicler also complains:

> "The Saidas had no reverence for Brahmans, and they gave wealth to the Mausalas for the benefit of the king (Hassan Shah) in his final rest."

Hence the bitterness expressed by the chronicler.

## VI

Be that as it may, it would not be correct to charge the Brahmin chroniclers with fanaticism or prejudice against the rulers who from 1339 A.D. onwards were Muslims. Since they enjoyed the patronage of the rulers, they could not afford to be fanatical in their approach. But they, at least the first two, did not hesitate to express themselves unequivocally against policies and deeds of kings and ministers which merited disapproval or condemnation. For instance, writing under Zain-ul-Abdin, Jonaraja condemns the destruction of temples carried out by his father Sikander who is therefore called *butshikan or* iconoclast. In the same breath he bestows the denigrating appellation of 'Turushuka' (Turk) on Harshadeva, a Hindu king (1089-1101 A.D.) who had despoiled temples of their precious images to mint coins to replenish his treasury which had been exhausted on frivolous pretexts. Jonaraja, however, does not fail to acknowledge the administrative ability of king Sikander and partially shifts the blame for iconoclastic fury to Suhabhatta, his minister, who had become a neo-convert to Islam. He also brings into focus the liberal attitude of Shahab-ud-din (1355-73 A.D.) who, even though hard-pressed for money, turned down the suggestion to despoil Hindu temples of their valuable idols to enrich the treasury.

The chroniclers admired kings who patronized learning and arts, who were solicitous for dispensing justice, who could ensure peace and protection to weaker sections and who could keep turbulent elements under strict control. They obviously shared the age-old belief that adherence to one's *dharma* or creed earned one merit which warded off difficulties in this life and the life hereafter. But occasionally political events took an ugly turn and Brahmins came in for bitter persecution, so much so that Jonaraja turns cynical and his lamentation becomes caustic:

> "Where was then their bath, their meditation, their austerity, and where was their prayer?"

These periods of misrule or Brahmin-baiting made sporadic appearance under different kings and apparently all the four chroniclers were witness to suffering and hardships laid upon them or their relations. This, however, does not embitter them against the Muslims as such. The reaction in the mind of Shrivara against the Syeds has been referred to. Nevertheless, without mincing words, he blames his Kashmiri compatriots for conspiring to murder Syeds after the death of Hassan Shah.

During a period of turmoil the Jama Masjid which had been constructed by Sultan Sikander caught fire and the flames engulfed the whole edifice in a short while. Much upset at this accident Shrivara opens out his heart thus:

> "The Masjida was a spacious building, extending on all sides, and was always whitewashed. It was like the embodiment of the fame of King Shri Shekhandera. It was within this building that crowds of worshippers used to fall down and rise at prayers...and looked graceful like the supporters of virtue... Such was the great building which towered to the sky and was decorated with wonderful sculptures...in a moment the fire, all destroying like the fire at the end of the cycle, left nothing of that building but its walls..."

At the back of this outpouring of noble sentiments is obviously a liberal mind with a catholic outlook and profound respect for all the faiths, worthy of the highest traditions in historiography:

## VII

The chroniclers appear to have been familiar with the geography not only of the Valley but also of the outer hilly areas like Poonch, Rajauri, Jammu, Ladakh, the Indus Valley, Punjab etc. Whenever an event is mentioned, the chroniclers give all significant geographical details, even of unfamiliar places like Kalidhara hill and Mangaldevi fort in Bhimber area. This is commendable for scholars at a time when many hazards faced travellers even inside the valley, let alone those venturing into the glens outside infested with desperadoes. Even Stein who knew the topography of Kashmir and the outer hills more intimately then anyone else, has expressed appreciation of the geographical knowledge of Shrivara, in reference to the Kalyanpur-Drabhagam-Bhedavan-Rajouri route.

It has been alleged in some quarters that the chroniclers give an exaggerated account of the military exploits of their masters. Knowing how difficult it is to write objectively on history, especially contemporary history, one cannot be unduly harsh on Jonaraja and his successors. But the writers have actually lived through the events they narrate. The intimate details of geography, deployment of troops and field tactics described by them make it clear that they watched these events closely. Shrivara was an eye-witness to the engagement between Zain-ul-Abdin and his son fought near Mulashul. The accounts of the civil war between the Sveds and the Kashmiris, various encounters with the Kashgaries under Mirza Haider and the engagements between Yaqubshah Chak and the Mughals convince by their details that the writers could understand the nuances of military tactics. Likewise the chroniclers have given minute details of earthquakes, floods, fires, famines and other calamities to which they were witness.

## VIII

Kings and their cohorts, of course, hold the centre stage in chronicles, but the authors' wide perceptions study the motivation provided by elite women to their counterparts. Queens Kota and Mera were the prime movers themselves. The history of the land would have been entirely different if they had been cast in another mould. Among others who played a frontline role was Lasa who brought about an estrangement between Sultan Shahab-ud-din and his principal queen Lakhshmi, who was also her mother's sister, with the result that the mighty king exiled his own (and Lakhshmi's) sons. Neither of them, though alive, could succeed him on his demise, and the throne was occupied by his brother Allau-ud-Din. Other noble ladies are still remembered by their endowments, charities and philanthropy. They include Samudra, Ahala, Lakhshmi, Shaha and Gulkhatun.

Wet nurses are found in all palaces, but rarely have chroniclers projected their diplomacy. King Simhadeva (1286-1301 A.D.) lost his life in one such entanglement. Without mincing words Shrivara has given details of the troubles caused to Zain-ul-Abdin by

Thakuras, the sons of his nurse, who "like unchecked elephants, became the destroyers of the king's joys". The king entrusted to them the bringing up of his sons, and the princes were filled with envy, hatred and enmity for one another. Zain-ul-Abdin did everything for the happiness of his subjects but could do nothing to improve the conduct of the princes who caused him untold sorrow. Alla-ud-Din invited to Kashmir the son of his predecessor (and brother) and planned to make him his heir-apparent. But Loladamara's widow, the wet nurse of Hassan, forged a palace-intrigue to secure the throne for her foster-son. The intrigue came to naught and Udayashri, his palace-patron, lost his head and Hassan once again fled the country. Mohammad Margesha who was imprisoned and chained under orders of Suhabhatta, effected his escape to safety with the help of the sons of his nurse.

Kings and their ministers were required to dispense justice based on laws some of which appear peculiar. According to one such law, enforced in the reign of Haider Shah, debtors were liable to imprisonment and "the friends of a debtor deserted him lest the debt might devolve on them." English writers of the eighteenth century have also left graphic accounts of the humiliation faced by debtor- scribes when state functionaries knocked at their doors to haul them up for indebtedness.

There were also laws to levy fines on householders when the married women of the family were found guilty of immoral conduct. The fine was abolished in the reign of Jayasimha (1128-49), but people guilty of 'carnal intercourse' with dancing girls who had become wedded wives were punished. Simhadeva (1286-1301 A.D.), gratified at the enchanting display of Iddagali, a dancing girl, revoked the order. Five and a half centuries later another dancing girl used her art to move the foremost administrator to throw open the locked portals of a house of prayer to gladden the eager devotees. Allan-ud-Din (1342-55) abolished the evil custom 'under which a childless widow, though unchaste, obtained a share of her husband's property from her father in-law'.

## IX

Kashmir is girdled with ramparts of hills which, it is commonly believed, have conferred peace and tranquility upon the Valley. There is no doubt that the people are peace-loving, intelligent and creatively industrious. But the mountains have hardly ever provided immunity against infiltration, especially when the land was ruled by weaklings. This fact is brought home to the reader again and again in the chronicles. The local politics were dominated by numerous clans including Tantries, Lones (Lavanyas), Chaks, Dars, Rainas, Maliks, Magreys, Nyayaks and Padars. Whoever was cold-shouldered by the ruling party felt no compunction in slipping out of the hills to invite an aggressor. Thus we have had Zulachus, Renchens, Gakkhars, Kashgaris and many others. Internal dissension, as always, caused famines, arson, destruction of works of art and literature, and largescale deaths.

Kashmir and Jammu had close relations during the fifteenth century. Sultan Alishah was married to a daughter of Maldev. Two queens of Zain-ul-Abdin came from the Madra region and his sons and grandsons had maternal uncles among the ruling families there. The Sultan was very friendly with Ajeodeo of Jammu and, according to S.S. Charak, granted an estate in the Valley to Biramdeo, his son. Parashuram, a nephew of Biramdeo was settled on the estate. He and his contingent of troops from *Madradesh* played an active anti-Syed role in the civil war following the death of Sultan Hassan Shah.

## X

The chronicles have been composed in Sanskrit verse and an appraisal in English may not be the right mileu to discuss the peculiarities of the authors' style. One can, however, size up the characteristics of the style of the Sanskritists at a glance. As said earlier, Kalhana regarded himself a poet and probably conceived of his work as *kavya*, a composition in poetry, permeated with *santa rasa*, the sentiment of serenity. Jonaraja, Shrivara and Shuka call themselves poets with some pride and keep close to Kalhana's model. From the reference he makes about himself here and there, Shrivara, appears to have been a man of many talents, a scholar well-versed in the classics, equally at home in *Mokshpaya, Gita Govinda, Yusuf Zulaikha* and Brihatkathat, a courtier, diplomat, musician of high distinction, well-travelled man and something of a soldier too. His predecessor Jonaraja was also a man of high attainments in the court of Zain-ul-Abdin to be able to hold his own against the many peers. The depth of their learning and their eminence in social life urges them to intervene frequently in the narrative to air their own reflections and comments. While the narration of events is in couplets, the chroniclers' comments have been put in four lined stanzas. These last do not always make for heightening of the effect of narration. The poet, in the footsteps of Kalhana, does not feel apologetic but regards his role in this behalf as inseparable from and, in fact, superior to that of a chronicler.

In such instances the chroniclers lay emphasis on the observance of moral principles by kings, nobles and the common people and draw upon the *Ramayana*, the *Mahabharata* and other classics to underscore the point:

Referring to the Nemises that overtook Pratihara Abhimanuyu--he was blinded one year after he had got plucked the eyes of Prince Bahram Khan, grandson of Zain-ul-Abdin—Shrivara observes:

> "On the same day and in the same month of the year in which Pratihara had done injury to the Khanas did he himself suffer injury...The very means which a man adopts for the injury of others leads to his own destruction...."

Shrivara narrates the sufferings caused to the people during the rivarly between Mohammad Shah, son of Hassan Shah, and Fateh Khan, son of Adham Khan (the eldest son of Zain-ul-Abdin).

At the time of their suffering, as at the humiliation caused to the Margapati, or the killings resorted to by the Khasas, he tells people how these are born of the harm caused by them to others.

## XI

A historian studies the interaction of cause and effect on the social and political plane and the chroniclers' observations and comments in this behalf are, therefore, well-advised and close to the mark. But Kalhana often sought refuge in predestination, and even astrological constellations, when faced with tragic events, as the steady deterioration in the conduct of Harsha and his tragic death when he was endowed with intelligence, understanding and love of arts matched with courage and valour. Jonaraja and his successors similarly find solace in fate. Commenting on the defeat of Fateh Khan near Drabhgam (Shupyan-Herapore) Shrivara says:

> "Fate is beyond our comprehension; and though it is not really the cause, yet it is considered the strange cause of events. It casts down, all of a sudden, some person in high places and prospers some who should be cast down...."

It is surprising that Jonaraja who could sum his assessment of worldly affairs in the sentence:

> "Enmity attended with want of circumspection is the first germ of destruction...."

balanced it with another observation in contrast:

> "It was Fate that had killed the one (Bhikhshana Bhatta) by making the other an instrument...."

Probably, like Kalhana, they aimed at giving predominance to *santa rasa* (the sentiment of serenity) and invoked fate and predestination.

## XII

It is not difficult to find various faults with the chroniclers. The narrative is burdened with unnecessary prolixity, reflections, digressions and even exaggerations in the manner typical of the oriental ways of expression. There are, occasionally, poetic flourishes and the chroniclers repeatedly find solace in the use of pathetic fallacy. Every king, with rare exceptions, ushered into the presence of the reader with adulation, makes his exit amidst condemnation. The narrators, obviously, convey their good wishes for an auspicious reign but sum up the king's conduct and achievements or failures towards the end. They also refer to persons by their designations with their modifying forms, such as Margapati, Margesha-Margadhipati, Chakra-Chakresha, Chakradhipati, which creates confusion in the mind of the reader. They have mentioned names of a very large number of participants in different events, especially during factional rivalries, and quite a few of them bear the same or a similar name which naturally strains the reader. Most of the participants belonged to the feudal elite to whose names the suffix Rajanaka is added, and the reader finds endless repetitions boring.

Several references to Syed Hassan and Meya Hassan confuse the reader to infer that they point to the same person. Only in the last book (*i.e.*, the fourth) does one feel satisfied that though appellations Miya, Mira, Mirza and Syed are freely applied to Syed immigrants, the Hassans last referred to are two distinct persons.

On the positive side it has to be stated that the narration of events is enlivening. As the occasion demands, the narrator builds a congenial atmosphere with appropriate details, be it a display of music and acting in the court of Hassan Shah, a confrontation in the field of battle, or a glimpse of the Eternal as on the waves of Kramsaras or Kaunsarnag. Before giving an account of a calamity ominous occurrences in the shape of shooting stars, barking of dogs, untimely flowers, a rain of blood or apparitions are indicated. The severity of a famine is to be gauged from 'a manufacturer of iron utensils killed a barber's boy', or 'people cut off flesh from the Caracas of a dead elephant'. The massacre of the Syeds by Kashmiri nobles and their allies is narrated graphically:

> "They raised the cry 'hala', but the Madras, their hands red with blood, were busy killing them, and moved about like the servants of Death!"

Similarly a dramatic effect is created in giving an account of battles, as between Zain-ul-Abdin and his son Haji Khan, those during the civil war or between the Kashmiris and the Mughals:

> "The battle between the Chakresha and the Margesha ranged round him, and as the combatants fell, there arose the cries of 'come', 'kill', 'stay'....!"

Some competent scholars are of the opinion that despite the pains taken by the translator, the quality of the English rendering does not do full justice to the original Sanskrit and occasionally misses some rare touches of beauty, compactness, vigour and verve.

## XIII

The chronicles project certain stylistic characteristics. Many of the similes have been used with a telling effect:

> "He (Shahmir) frightened the king day and night by holding up Haidera before him, even as one frightens a bird by holding up his hawk."

> "He (Haider Shah) fainted away and lay on his bed, and was like a mirror that did not reflect any image on it."

'Like bees in the month of Magha',...'...hungry even as tanks in hot season...', etc, etc.

A trick frequently met with is the use of parallelism usually with a contrasting effect:

> "Bhikshana and Avatara went into Shahmira, but their protecting deities did not enter with them...."

> "Jamshed had caused a bridge to be built to cross the river at Suyyapora, but did not devise means to cross over his dangers!"

In a narrative teeming with oppression, suffering, natural calamities, betrayals, revolts, invasions and bloodshed there is not much scope for indulging in humour. But folk humour is recorded faithfully as in 'Margesha curry' (*i.e.*, without salt on account of the seizure of the 'salt-route' by the enemy). There is no dearth of occasion for the use of sarcasm:

> "He (Haider Shah) wished to build an edifice by the side of Sheikhenderpuri; it was like the desire to light a lamp under the sun."

## XIV

Place names have undergone a good deal of change in Kashmir between the days of Kalhana and our own. The change must have been on during the period covered by the chronicles, but they offer no clear evidence. The suffixes largely used now, *viz*. 'bal' and 'yar' are nowhere mentioned. The old time suffixes '*-ashram*' (now 'hom') and '*-matha*' (now 'mar') continue in the chronicles. There is no mention of the older bridges Ali Kadal, Fateh Kadal, or Haba Kadal, only Zaina Kadal is mentioned while several bridges of boats '*nava setu*') have been referred to. But names have been in the process of transformation: *Kitsahom* below Baramulla is referred to by its original name, *viz*., *Krityaashram*, but later *Keechashram* is also used.

## XV

The use of the term *mlechha* by the chroniclers is likely to cause some misunderstanding unless it is considered in its proper context. They used the terms Turushukas for Turks, Mughals, Afghans, etc. Sometimes the term *Yavana*, which is believed to have been coined for the Greeks originally, is also used in this behalf: Babar has been referred to as a *Yavana*, so also some other Mughal adventurers and foreigners. On one or two occasions its use covers Muslims also, as when burial is referred to as 'the last rite of *Yavanas*'. He term *mlechha* does not as such connote Muslims for whom the word Mausala has been used as in 'Veda of the Mausalas'. The was named Mohammed Kharrna, a name worthy of Mausalas'... he has very rarely been used for a Muslim, but frequently to connote outsiders:

> "The king of mlechhas (Taimur) had plundered Dilli"
>
> "Dalacha, the king of mlechhas"

> "the mlechha army...", "...a host of mlechhas (invaders)-. "...the enemies and the mlechha soldiers outnumbered the Kashmirian warriors...."; "...how can I (Yaqub Shah) alone cope with the mlechhas?"

On a few occasions it is applied to the rif-raf: those who could be called 'criminal tribes'. A little reflection should make it obvious that the word *mlechha* does not imply 'unclean' or 'low'. It is highly probable that it did not signify 'contempt', 'meanness' or anything derogatory at the time. A clear proof of it lies in that Brahmin chroniclers were in the employ of Muslim kings and who would dare suggest, even by implication, that the patron, or his co-religionist, was 'unclean'? These patrons included not only Zain-ul-Abdin but also his less liberal son Haider, the Syed-dominated puppets, Ghazi Chak who had his own son hanged and other Chak zealots who encouraged Shia proselytization and imposed taxes on Brahmins. The chroniclers could not enjoy court patronage, prestige and respect and yet use derogatory terms for the king, fellow-courtiers and powerful feudal chiefs to many of whom Sanskrit was no alien tongue.

Kalhana regarded himself a poet, which term bore a wider connotation at the time, and the Sanskrit chroniclers from Jonaraja to Suka offered floral tributes to him, each in the true spirit of a disciple acknowledging his master's learning and leadership. Inevitably they share the glory reflected in the well-known verse:

> "Worthy of praise is that power of true poets, whatever it may be, which surpasses even the stream of nectar, in as much as by it their own bodies of glory as well as those of others obtain immortality." (RT.I.-3)

## Jonaraja's

## *Rajatarangini*

# Prologue

ONE HALF of Hara's person was united with one half of Parvati's, as if they had become one through mutual affection. The other halves of their persons, adored in the three worlds, have disappeared as if in sorrow because they could not unite. May the united figure be auspicious to you. May Ganesha with his ample form, dispensing joy and plenty every day to all around, remove all difficulties from your path.

Shri Gonanda[1] and other virtuous and meritorious kings ruled the kingdom of Kashmira from the beginning of the Kali[2] Yuga. But for a long time they were under an evil influence which lasted like the darkness of the winter night, and no one knew of the kingdom, as no sun of poesy arose to disperse the gloom. Then the Brahmana Kalhana with lucid words imparted the freshness of youth to the old accounts of the kings down to the reign of Jayasimha.[3] It is owing to the fault of the country or to the misfortune of the succeeding kings that no one since then has revived the succeeding kings by the nectar-like words of a poet. Now the spotless king Shri Jainollabhadena[4] reigns, and Jonaraja is ready to describe the royal line.

As a tree which promised fruits is planted to remove the wants of the traveller, so is this poem composed to remove the grief of kings lest their glory be forgotten. And as the tree is grown by water, and without any artificial heat, so should this poem be carefully cherished by the good with the cool nectar of mildness. These past kings were sunk in the sea of oblivion and Shri Jainollabhadena wished, out of a tender regard, to rescue them. He employed for the purpose the noble-hearted

Shri Shiryyabhatta[5], chief of all the courts of justice. I received orders from him, and I have now ventured to complete the story of the kingly line. My attempt is not dictated by a desire to obtain the fame of a poet; for, vast is the difference between my words, poor and meagre as water in dried[6] ginger, and the flowing waves of poesy. Can a reed, imitating only the shadow of a lotus, equal the lotus? My poor sense is like a gourd, hollow and light, and relying on it, alas! I am attempting to cross the river of the story of kings. My feebleness in describing the merits of kings should not be blamed, for do not women, devoid of beauty, walk in pride when bedecked with jewellery? My subject, worthy of a poet, sustains and purifies me, even as the water of the Ganges, though it seems but ordinary water, purifies him who drinks it.

I have made only an outline of the history of kings; let the skilful and artistic poets adorn it; a wheel rubs down jewels, it is a finer instrument that can impart beauty to the gems. The good and the noble peruse the works of writers without solicitation; does the moon await solicitation before diffusing nectar on the earth? But the evil-minded, even when propitiated, do not cease to find faults; the charcoal, even when washed by nectar, never attains whiteness. The desire that others should see my work has long departed from my heart, for it is an unworthy desire to wish for the approbation of others. The beauty of a common song and that of the Sanskrita language appear alike to the unskilful, even as the monkey mistakes red seeds for sparks of fire in winter. The ignorant are not affected by listening to poetry; it is those alone who have strength of teeth that perceive the sweetness of the sugarcane in their mouth. Even the pure-minded and the meritorious are filled with thoughts of envy when a composition embellished with sense and sweetness is placed before them. Fate is foremost among those who cannot bear to see the prosperity of others; Fate has stained the moon with spots, and Fate has filled the learned with envy, as with a consuming disease. Fate is therefore an object of reproach. Let my work which is mingled with that of Kalhana Pandita be accepted, for even the water of a reedy marsh is taken for drink when it has mingled with the water of a river.

## Jayasimha

There was a prosperous king, the son of Sussala[7], who delighted the world and respected the gods and the twice-born. Though he was known to ride the elephant alone, yet, O wonderful! Prosperity always rested on Jayasimha. He was brought up by the goddess of learning, as by his mother, and he enjoyed the company of the goddess of fortune. They abided in him together, like a mother-in-law and a daughter-in-law, and did not display hostility towards each other. Once upon a time he received into his court Malla born of the family of Sushramma, the king of Trigartta.[8] Malla had been banished from his country by his enemies, and had come here with a view to obtain a livelihood. Medicinal herbs are ever regarded as mere grass, and jewels as mere stones; and men of merit too, who have travelled in foreign countries, are treated as ordinary men, until they excite the heart of the people by great deeds and distinguished achievements. When the king marched to subdue the kingdom of the *yavanas*[9], Malla became the favourite of the soldiers on account of his great valour. Strong in his courage, Mallachandra[10] went at night to the camp of his enemy in order to ascertain the number of the king of the Turushkas' soldiers that had survived a slaughter. There where even a breath of wind could not enter, where the place was guarded by powerful soldiers, Malla went in among the enemy's troops, no doubt by the force of incantations[11] and charms. But afraid of committing a sin by any hostile act towards those who were sleeping, he did not kill the king of the *yavanas*, but only placed a pair of shoes, marked with his own name, on the head of the king, as his turban. The enemy recognised the shoes, took them with him and went to the camp of the king of Kashmira and surrendered to him his fortune, as if he yielded to him his fame. In the year[12] 30, in the month of Phalguna, on the twelfth day of the dark moon, the king died in the midst of his prosperity, and greatly gladdened the eyes of celestial damsels.

## Paramanuka

Then the indolent people anointed his son Paramanuka, even as the days of the month of Magha which scatter the leaves of trees, anoint the Kunda tree. The king neglected the duty of protecting his subjects and also of making foreign conquests, and he began to accumulate wealth such as would never be exhausted. But the wealth of the king was like that of a Brahmana who follows the injunctions of the Vedas; he could neither give it away to others nor enjoy it himself; and it was robbed by the two cheats Prayaga and Janaka. These men were devoid of truth, and they caused their servants to assume the form of Rakshasas, and night after night they used to frighten the king by strange performances. These evil-minded ministers pretended affection for the king, and induced him to spend his money to save his life from the Rakshasas. On one full moon night in the month of Chaitra, a dependent of theirs was stationed at Bhishayaka[13] dressed as a Rakshasa chief, adorned with precious jewels but covered with grass. And as the signal was given, he stood forth in the presence of men, blessed the king, and took away his ornaments, and retired into the forest by night. Then these two men told the king that since the Rakshasa chief had accepted the king's offerings and had blessed him, his kingdom would be without danger. Thus the wily men frightened the worthless king like a child, and robbed him of his wealth. The king, after reigning for nine years, six months and ten days, died on the eighth bright lunar day of Bhadra in the year 40.

Then his son named Vartideva[14] reigned. He died on the tenth bright lunar day of Bhadra, in the year 47.

## Vopyadeva *elected*

For want of a worthy successor the citizens elected[15] one named Vopyadeva[16] their king. He was like the Rakshasa chief covered with grass, and to him homage was paid. Once the foolish king felt happy at the sight of large blocks of stone, and he ordered his ministers to increase the size of the smaller ones by making them drink the milk of beasts! On one occasion this foolish prince heard of the greatness of the shrine of Sureshvari[17]and, accompanied by his ministers, came there by boat. He made faces on the water arid was angry at seeing his face disfigured in the reflection; and he thereupon struck the water with his palm, so that his jewel-ring fell into the water. When asked where the royal jewel seal was, he pointed to the ripple of the water and said that it was in the ripple. He was the very model of a dunce. He reigned for nine years four months and two and half days.

## Lavanyas anoint Jassaka

His younger brother Jassaka was also a great dunce; and though he did not wish to have on him the weight of the kingdom, he was anointed king by the Lavanyas[18] who wished their own aggrandizement. The parrot which imitates the human voice is caught but not the crow; stony soil is not ploughed and dug like fertile land; and stones are not powdered to dust like rock salt. The very faults of some persons are advantageous to them like merits. There were two Brahmana brothers named Kshuksha and Bhima. By fraudulent means they earned the affection of the king, and then they became disobedient. They thought that as they were rich and powerful, the king would not be able to check them, and so they did not endeavour to strengthen their party by taking in other men. And it was only the power of the Lavanyas, and not any other apprehension, that kept them from attaining the regal state. Alas! that a sweet but unwholesome dish should ever be taken! Alas! that a young but false woman should even inspire love in man by her embraces and her show of affection, for they both bring affliction, and if unchecked, cause death by their poison. The wife of Kshuksha became disgusted with him as he, owing to old age, had lost his vigour; and she killed him by poison and received Bhima to her embraces. Owing to her intimacy with her husband's brother her body came to be marked with white patches; but her sin was lightened by her gifts to Madhava[19] and other gods. The king after ruling the country for eighteen years and ten days died on the tenth day of the dark moon, in the month of Magha, in the year 74.

## Jagadeva

Then his son Shri Jagadeva, who was powerful yet humble, contributed, like the month of Chaitra, to the delight of the people. He looked with an equal eye on the servants of the state who had been contending with one another even as the evening finds the blue and white lotus alike. He was well-versed in science and, as a surgeon extracts a dart, he rooted out the evil laws of the country. He was a person of great merit and penetrated like a dart in the mind of men; but evil counsels prevailed, and he was expelled from the country by the ministers. As Rama received his friend, the king of the monkeys, in the wilderness, so did he in his exile receive his discriminating minister Gunarahula[20]. In the hope of rising again to power, the king and the minister came back to Kashmira like the sun and the moon, and the people wondered at their deeds. Unwilling to relinquish the power they had so long enjoyed, the enemies of the king prepared to fight;

but they fell under the devices ancfthe prowess of the king and his minister, even as the insects fall into the fire. The king conquered the country and enjoyed the fortune that smiled on him and the royal umbrella[21] and the *chamara*; and Shri Gunakararahula also enjoyed prosperity without these royal insignia. The disinterested king built a temple at Rajjupura[22] and adorned it with a silver umbrella. Then the wicked Padma, Lord of Dvara[23], pretending affection for the king, as if he were a friend, secretly gave him poison and killed him. After ruling the country for fourteen years six months and three days, the king died on the fourteenth day of the dark moon, in the month of Chaitra, in the year 89.

## Rajadeva

His son Rajadeva had gone to Kashthavata[24] in fear, but he was brought back by the enemies of the Lord of Dvara. And when Rajadeva had entered a fort named Salhana[25], Padma, of wicked design, surrounded him with troops, even as a serpent is surrounded by a magic line. The Lord of Dvara had in the meantime received a present of a curious pair of shoes, and in his curiosity to see it he was off his guard, and was killed by a *chandala* in a scuffle. Then the Bhattas anointed Rajadeva king, with the sound of kettledrum and conch shell, and innumerable feudatory chiefs bowed to him, and he bestowed favours on servants. The great king apportioned work among the chief men of the Lavanyas in the same manner as before, and they worked like relatives living together.

## Calendar corrected

The powerful Baiadhyachandra[26], lord of Lahara, with his soldiers usurped power over half of Shrinagara, and the king was unable to cope with him. This powerful man caused a *matha* to be built within the city, even like an embodiment of his virtues and marked the *matha* with his name. In the meantime the Bhattas had been insulted by the king, and for a long time they held consultation to find some one with a mild temper among the Khasha[27] tribe whom they would elect king. It was then determined to plunder the Bhattas, and then was heard from among them the cry "I am[28] not a Bhatta", "I am not a Bhatta". At this time, namely in the year 950 of the Saka era, Vimalacharyya[29] corrected the mistake that every 976th month would be considered an unclean month. The disinterested king, Rajadeva, who was like the moon, signalized his prosperity by building Rajapuri and Rajoloka[30]. He died after reigning for twenty three years, three months and twenty seven days.

## Sangramadeva

His son Sangramadeva became the king, and he terrified his enemies as the lion does the elephants. He made his younger brother Suryya his viceroy out of affection, but this wicked conspirator, tempted by the lust of enjoyment, thought of rebellion. Afraid of the king, who had heard of his intention, he entered the territory of Chandra, the lord of Lahara, with a view to rise against his brother. Strange! that at this time when the fierce Suryya joined Chandra, this earthly sun, together with the moon, was eclipsed like the sun in the sky.

Tunga, the lord of Shamala[31], proudly carried Suryya by his side but the king went against him and humbled him. Suryya then went by a road devoid of the sun and the moon and, deserted by his dissolute attendants, was captured and caused to be killed by the king. The sons of Kalhana were evil men, they rose in power, and the king, who was anxious to save his royal state, feared them as serpents. And when the kinsmen of the sons of Kalhana attained power, the king lost all hopes and took shelter with the peaceful lord of Rajapuri[32] When the king had thus retired to a distance, the Damaras[33] began to suck the very lifeblood of the people. Deserted by the wise king and by Brahmanas, the kingdom was for a long time devoured by the Domvas[34], even like food polluted by the touch of low people. The king was sheltered in the kingdom of another, his own country was in anarchy, and no one thought that his reappearance was near at hand. He, however, overcame his enemies, in battle near Rajapuri, but did not kill the sons of Kalhana because they were Brahmanas; and thus he gained his kingdom and attained virtue. At Vijayeshvara[35] the king built a house named Shrivishala, containing twenty-one rooms for the habitation of cows and Brahmanas. But the king was hated by the secret agents of his enemies, the sons of Kalhana, who were intent on plunder, even as a lamp is hated by thieves intent on theft. Beneficent to poets, as the *kalpa* tree with its extended branches, the king was cut down by the evil-minded and wicked sons of Kalhana. Yhshaka, a learned poet, made the king the hero of his composition, and it was like the necklace, an ornament for the learned. The king, who was a benefactor of his country, was slain on the fifth lunar day of Bhadra, in the year[36] 28, after ruling the kingdom for sixteen years and ten days.

His son RAMADEVA then executed the murderers of his father and entrusted the duty of governing the people to Prithviraja. The king built a fort at Sahara[37] on the right side of Ledari.[38] It was marked with his name, and was like a monument of his fame. When preparations were made for the subjugation of Shamala, the temple of Vishnu at Utpalapura[39] had been broken through carelessness. This temple was now renewed. Alas! Vidhata has not given a flower to the sandal tree, nor fruit to the *champaka*; and he gave no off spring to this king. The king adopted as his own the son of a certain Brahmana who inhabitated Bhishayakapura. The strong affection that existed between the king and his adopted child was like that of a father for his own son; even as a good painting is like the object painted. The queen Shri Samudra was like the full blown daughter of the sea, and she built on the banks of the Vitasta within the city a matha[40] marked with her name. The king reigned for twenty-one years, one month and thirteen days, and died in the year 49.

His successor, LAKSHMANADEVA, filled with the lore of the4i six branches of learning, supported with difficulty the weight of the kingdom. A Brahmana by birth, he did not part with the qualifications of his own caste, though he was made a Kshatriya. A painted stone does not take the beauty of a jewel. Mahila[41], his stainless queen, built a new *matha* marked with her name, on the banks of the Vitasta, by the side of her mother-in-law's *matha*. Kajjala[42], a dark and fierce Turushka came to Mandala from outside, and destroyed the king who was the eye of his subjects. He reigned for thirteen years, three months and twelve days, and died at the end of the month of Pausha of the year 62.

Owing to the commotion caused by Kajjala, SIMHADEVA became the king of Ledari only. He was harassed by Samgramachandra, lord of Lahara. When Samgramachandra died, Simhadeva, a lion among men, ruled the kingdom reduced in size, and built a *matha* within the city. The virtuous Simhadeva, during the ascendency of the constellation Leo, associated himself with his religious preceptor and established an image of Nrisimha at Dhyanoddara.[43] The image set up, the king who set it up, the preceptor who helped him in the act and the constellation under which the act was done, all bore the name of lion. One day the king caused the god Vijayeshvara to be bathed in milk purchased with one lakh pieces of gold (*nishka*), and attained purification by his religious act. Shri Sankarasvami was the religious preceptor of the king, and the king gave him, as the fee of his tuition, the lordship over eighteen *mathas*. When the king rose from his bed he always chanted the following verse: "I bow to Sankara the lord of Gauri, whose eyes are pure as fire, whose feet are worshipped by the learned, and who is bedecked with the crescent of the moon." A verse, such as this, smoothed his path to the future world, and like an offering to the goddess of speech, instructed the soul. Once upon a time the king passed orders to punish a man for his daughter's evil character, but revoked those orders at the request of Iddagali[44], a dancing girl.

By keeping company with bad men the king became devoid of his belief in God. His nurse had a daughter who was like the mirror of the god of love, and on this mirror the king's image was reflected! Her husband Darya, with the help of Kamasuha, treacherously killed the haughty king with whom his subjects had now become annoyed. The king reigned for fourteen years, five months and twenty seven days, and died in the summer of the year 77.

Then his brother SAHADEVA, though not of very active habits, subjugated the whole of Kashmira with the help of Kamasuha. Many people came from various quarters and resorted to the king for service, even as black bees resort to the flower tree. Like a second Arjuna, the king established his authority on the borders of Panchagahvara[45], and his son Vabhruvahana built the town of Garbharapura.

Kurushaha was born of the noble[46] family, and the mark of the bow string on his arm, bright as fame, was beauteous as sunrise on the summit of a hill. He had three eyes: it was as if to proclaim to the people that his children, the famed Enamukhi[47] and others, would rule in Kashmira, and that the rulers of that country were a portion of the three-eyed Hara. From him was born Taharaja[48] whose quivering bow string was often pulled to the ear. Then was born Shahamera[49], the ardour of whose prowess was like the summer sun, and the fire of whose valour was excited by the tears of his enemies wives. Once upon a time Shahmera was wandering in a wood, and his eyes were at first intent on game but were eventually closed in sleep. In his dream the great goddess told him in words of nectar that the kingdom of Kashmira would come to his progeny. In the year[50] 89, in the Shaka year 1235, he slowly came into Kashmira. He came with his relatives, and the king of Kashmira greatly favoured him by giving him a salary, even as the mango tree favours the black bees.

## Brahmins fast

At this time Dalacha[51], commander of the army of the great king Karmasena, came to Kashmira, as comes a lion into the cave of the deer. He brought with him sixty thousand mounted force, as if intending to conquer and bestow as many villages to his army. The bad king intended to send back Dalacha by granting him a subsidy and imposed a tax on the people of all castes. The Brahmanas, as if to expiate by the sacrifice of their lives the sin of having received gifts before from such a king, determined to die by fasting.[52]

## Rinchana

At this time the Kalamanya[53] Bhottas (Bhuteas), who had become the enemies of Vakatanya, deceitfully killed him with his friends and relatives, But one of Vakatanya's sons, named Rinchana, respected for his great intellect, escaped the massacre by chance, and was to the Kalamanyas what the fire is to the forest, He joined Vyala[54], Tukka, and others who had combined together in council, and determined to crush the poor-witted Kalamanyas. Rinchana sent word to the Kalamanyas through a messenger that he had been robbed of all his wealth, and asked to be enrolled as a servant of the Kalamanyas. Rinchana, a lion among men, hid his arms in the sands of a river bank, and waited to drink the blood of the Kalamanyas, not to receive their wages, The Kalamanyas came unarmed and Vyala and others, with their fire-like axes which had been hid in sand, destroyed them like grass. Thus having cleansed the treason against his father in the blood of, the enemies, Rinchana came to Kashmira with his friends through fear of the many enemies that yet remained.

## Dalacha's devastation

Dalacha, like a fire-brand, harassed the country and the people of Kashmira became like insects in that fire. Dalacha and Rinchana blockaded the town in the east and in the north, and the people first fled towards the west and then in the direction of Yama (south). Dalacha was like a billow in the water, and on the hill Rinchana was like a tempest, while the chief men in the town, the prosperous and the rich, were struck with fear. As the kite swoops on the young ones of the birds thrown out of their nests, so the swift army of Rinchana seized the people of Kashmira. Rinchana obtained wealth, plentiful as water, from the Bhottas by selling the people of Kashmira and reared himself like a cloud, and covered all sides.

At this time Dalacha destroyed innumerable gods and, afraid of the excessive cold of Kashmira, went out by a good military[55] road. When Dalacha had left the place, those people of Kashmira who had escaped capture issued out of their strongholds as mice do out of their holes. When the violence caused by the Rakshasa Dalacha ceased, the son found not his father, nor the father his son, nor did brothers meet their brothers. Kashmira became almost like a region before the creation, a vast field with few men, without food, and full of grass. Dalacha took away the strong men from the country and Rinchana established his supremacy there; when darkness covers the earth, unchaste women find it to their advantage.

## Ramachandra murdered

The king was now completely freed from the Rahu-like Dalacha, but Rinchana, like the lofty, high-created mountain of the setting sun, sought to block his way. When the people saw the glowing Rinchana stationed on the mountain[56] that touched the sky, no one doubted that the decline of the king's power was nigh. Rinchana intended to pounce upon the city like a royal hawk on a piece of meat, but Ramachandra, the moon of his dynasty, opposed him at every step. In order to destroy the prosperity of Ramachandra[57], who was like the sun on earth in his fullness, Rinchana like a Rahu, was suffered to rise in the blue sky. Rinchana deceitfully sent a few Bhottas every day who came into the fort of Lahara under the pretence of selling clothes. And when the Bhotta people had thus entered Lahara, Rinchana caused their weapons to drink the honey-like blood of Ramachandra. The queen Kota was as the *kalpa* tree creeper in the garden of Ramachandra's household; but now the strong armed Rinchana planted her on his own breast[58].

The king left the city in fear of Shri Rinchana. A Brahmana's curse destroys a race like fire, nor is there a spot where scions of that race can grow. Struck with fear, the king, like a jackal, entered a large cavern in Mandala.[59] How should a sinful man meet death in battle? The cloud-like enemy poured the blood of the king's forces in battle, and dried up the tears in the eyes of the Brahmanas whom the king had fined! This Rakshasa of a king, under the pretence of protecting the country, devoured it for nineteen years, three months, and twenty five days.

## Rinchana assumes control

The country was weary of trouble and disorder, and Shri Rinchana Suratrana[60] gave it rest under the shelter of his arm. When the dark days disappeared, the people of Kashmira witnessed again all the festivities which they had beheld under their former kings. In every place the Lavanyas remained quiet as lamps, but trembled at the power of the king, like lamps in the morning breeze. A division was made among them by the secret devices of the king, even as an arrow is sent into a raft. Strange that the unity among the Lavanyas was thus relaxed. Easily like the birds in the sky, the king roamed in that thorny wood where even the god of love had became bewildered The king knew very well how to bestow his favours on all, but he never forgave the wicked, although he might be his son or minister or friend; it was thus that he served his people's weal. After having destroyed his prosperous and powerful enemies and having placed the royal umbrella over his head, Rinchana went to Achchhoda[61] lake.

Now Timi, brother of Tukka[62], feeling weary in the way, took some milk from a milkwoman in a village by force, and drank it. The milkwoman instantly informed the king of it; and when questioned by the king, Timi was struck with fear and denied what he had done. The milkwoman, who was suspected of falsehood, did not lose her presence of mind. The king then caused Timi's stomach to be cut open in order to ascertain the truth, and from the severed stomach milk issued in a stream. The face of the milkwoman was gladdened at this act of the king. There were two men living at Vanabala,[63] they had two mares which gave birth to two foals, similar in appearance, in a wood. One of the mares lost its young which was seized by a lion, but owing to the similarity in appearance, behaved towards the other as if it were its own offspring. Both the owners of the mares claimed the foal as their property and, unable to settle the dispute, went to the king. The king listened to their contention, and caused his own men to bring the two mares and the foal to him. The foal jumped about playfully owing to its young age, and went to some distance, while its mother and its nurse both signified their affection for it and neighed. The courtiers were unable to give any opinion and the two owners accused each other. The king took the two mares and the young one in a boat to the middle of the Vitasta. Then the wise king threw the foal into the river from the boat; whereupon its mother instantly jumped into the river after it, while the other only neighed. Thus when the difficult suit was settled, the people thought that the golden age had returned.

## Devasvami's rigidity

The king asked Shri Devaswami to initiate him in the *mantra*s of Shiva, but as he was a Bhotta, Davasvami feared that the king was unworthy of such initiation, and did not favour him. Vyalaraja[64], in his regard for truth, became to the king as his younger brother, his son, kinsman, minister, companion and friend. Vyala was not influenced by the king's acts, but the king was influenced by those of Vyala. The mind is not influenced by the actions of the body, but the body is influenced by the workings of the mind. The inclinations of the king, who was like the sun to the world, were reflected in Vyala who was well-versed in the Sastras and was possessed of good taste, and destroyed the impenetrable darkness of the world; even as do the rays of the sun when reflected on the watery moon.

At this time Shri Udyanadeva[65] of Gandhara, impelled by fear, and also intending to take advantage of the king's weakness, thus directed Tukka and others:

> "While the king is yet alive, you should enter the city which he is ruling with prudence with a view to acquire fame. Vyala is enjoying there the prosperity which you have earned even at the risk of your lives, even as the tongue enjoys what the hands acquire by their industry. As Mahadeva besmearing his body with ashes, and discarding golden ornaments, induced snakes to coil round him, even so the king, who possesses plenty of riches, is raising Vyala to power, and neglects you though belonging to a high caste. Afraid of your valour, he killed Timi, simply for taking some milk, as one kills a Timi (whale)".

## Rinchana wounded

This message alienated Tukka and other Shukkalankitas from the king, and they conjointly attacked him at Vimshaprastha.[66] Vyala struck them with his sword and expelled out of them their pride begotten of wealth. The king fainted, his enemies believed that he had been killed and that they had obtained victory. Their wrath was assuaged and, ambitious of seizing the kingdom, they entered the capital. The king afraid of receiving another blow had, for a short time, remained like one dead; but when he saw that the enemies had proceeded to some distance, he got up. By the time that these men of little sense had reached the capital, they saw the king who had recovered from his swoon and was approaching them. Then these impudent and poor-witted men became afflicted with sorrow, and asked one another whether the king had not been killed by one of them, and they quarrelled among themselves. They robbed the palace and became angry with one another, and they accomplished their own destruction, a work which the king should have done. The haughty king then impaled the survivors, thus he lifted them high but down they went. The angry king ripped open by the sword the wombs of his enemies' wives in the fort who were with child, as one tears open beans by the finger nail. The violence of the king's mind inflamed by the treason of his enemies was thus pacified by the destruction of their descendants; but the wound caused by their sword on his head was not healed. As one who has dreamt an evil dream is relieved of his fear on awaking, so was the world relieved of fear and obtained peace after witnessing for a while the deeds of Tukka.

The king was pleased with Shahamera who was not implicated in the treason, and he placed in his hands his son Haidera, together with the child's mother Kota, for the purpose of bringing up the prince. Nourished by queen Kota and brought up under the care of Shahamera, the child grew in beauty, even as a tree brings forth new leaves when nourished by rains and protected by shade.

The king caused a town[67] to be built after his own name, and it was surrounded by a moat, as if by the disgrace of his late mishap. As the sun shines for a time on the world on a cloudy day in the month of Pausha, so did the king shine again for a few months. In the dewy season, the wound on the king's head became worse in consequence of nervous disorder brought on by the inclemency of the cold. The king had relieved many people of their heads, but alas! his head became worse. On the eleventh lunar day of the month of Pausha, in the year 99, the physician death relieved the king of his death pangs. King Rinchana went to heaven after having ruled the country for three years, one month and nineteen days.

His son Haidara being young was not coronated by Shahmera, and as Shahmera had not the necessary strength, he did not himself rule the kingdom. The Lavanyas, though they had risen against Rinchana, did not oppose the wise Shahmera, as he was the chief of his tribe; and Shahmera bestowed on Udayanadeva the country of Kashmira, together with queen Shri Kota who was like the goddess of victory incarnate. The exalted but fickle goddess of Royal Fortune, who is sought by men of worth, left Rinchana and went to the present king, as if she descended from a high station to a low one. The king then gratified Jyamshara[68] and Allesha, two sons of Shahmera, by bestowing on them the lordship of Kramarajya[69] and other places. At this time queen Kota was all powerful; she was, as it were, the mind, and the king the body who carried out her orders. The Lavanyas, who had like stars been hidden by the rays of the sun-like Rinchana, now shone out during the reign of the present king, as at nightfall. Why should it cause any regret that the Lavanyas attacked the possessions of the feeble king whose very house was in the power of Kota? The king did not molest the country of the Lavanyas or the abode of the *chandalas*, but like one versed in the Vedas, he spent his time in bathing, in penance, and in prayer. How shall I describe his faith in God who dressed himself like a hermit, and who tied bells in the neck of his horses through fear lest worms should be crushed to death. To God Vishnu he gave all the golden ornaments in his treasury, making them into a crown and necklace for the deity.

## Achala's discomfiture

At this time the proud Achala[70], whom the lord of Mugdhapura had supplied with soldiers, forcibly entered Kashmira, like another Dalacha. Achala attacked the country and filled all sides with his partisans, but the king did not deal with him as Indra dealt with the mountain (achala) which harassed the world with its wings. When the army of Achala reached Bhimanaka[71], the king was humbled and speedily fled to the country of the Bhottas.

Then Shri Kota sent a letter to Achala through the ministers stating that, as the country was without a king, he might govern the kingdom as if he were the head of the dynasty and asking him to send away the soldiers who were not his own, and not to harass the country needlessly. Achala was deceived and he sent away the army of his ally. The foolish Achala who had sent away his army was then detained by the ministers on pretence of celebration of festivities in the way. In the meantime queen Shri Kota set up one Rinchana[72], a Bhotta, as king with a view to protect her subjects in the capital. All the friends of Achala sorrowed for a long time over his want of sense, as a widow sorrows over the death of her child born after her husband's death. The fear of king Udayanadeva now abated, he spent a day in the worship of Tusharalinga[73] and returned to his own country from the country of the Bhottas. The king destroyed Rinchana in the capital; and Kota respectfully received him with her head bent down, even as the eastern hill receives the gloom-dispelling full moon on its head.

Shahmera had brought up the son of Rinchana, and owing to his affection for the boy he was an eyesore to the king. But the queen was equally disposed towards both her sons,[74] and the king, through fear of the queen, did not harm Shahmera though he was an object of animosity to him. During the dreadful time of the troubles caused by Achala, the people in fear had taken shelter of Shahmera, and Shahmera did not deem the king even as grass. He frightened the king day and night by holding up Haidara before him, even as one frightens a bird by holding up his hawk.

## Shahmir's growing power

Strange that this believer in Alla became the saviour of the people. As a dried up river allows men to cross it, and gives them shelter on its banks, even so this believer in Alla, calm and active, protected the terrified subjects. Shahmera had two grandsons of great merit, named Shirhshataka[75] and Himda, and they beautified all the sides like the sun and the moon. Proud on account of his connection with the lord of Dvara[76], and prepared even to disobey the orders of the king, Shahmera was like the gate of danger to those who served the king. He had bestowed the daughter of Alleshvara[77] on Lusta the lord of Dvara, and had conquered Shri Shankarapura and thus magnified the fear of the king. His son Jymsara was a man of business, and Bashailakashura married Jymsara's daughter and obtained the lordship of Bhangila[78]. Shahmera[79], who was as a lion among men, and who had achieved many victories and won the goddess of fortune, kept the turbulent province of Shamala under control, even as Nrisimha, who could assume many forms, the lord of Lakshmi, controlled the Daityas. Deep as the sea wherein abides the goddess of Victory, and terrific in his power, Shahmera taxed the people of Karala.[80] His fame smiled on him, and he thought of the conflagration of Vijayeshapura of king Kalasa.[81] In order to secure his possessions, Shahmera fortified the Chakradhara[82] hill and showed to the people that his works were imperishable. Shahmera marked out the lord[83] of Kampana, and gave him a large fortune, and obtained a spotless fame even as one obtains a marriage present. Then Shahmera accepted the daughter of the lord of Kota whom he welcomed. The lord[84] of Kota was as the first actor on the stage of kings. The irreligious Lavanyas were brought under his subjection, some by conciliation and others through disunion caused among themselves, some by gifts and others through fear. The Lavanya people bore his daughters like garlands, but they knew not that his daughters were like life-destroying serpents of deadly poison. The Lavanyas were brought under the control of Rajavji[85], and they were all brought under the power of the king, as elephants submit to the power of the lion.

As a tree in a marsh is overcome by lotus-covered water, so was the king overcome by Shahmera. And as if overpowered by loss of authority everywhere outside his palace, the king relinquished his life along with his fame. On the Shivaratri night, on the thirteenth lunar day, in the year[86]14, that forbearing king left the world polluted with the touch of Shahmera.

## Kota's fears

Then Shri Kota, out of fear of Shahmera, kept the death of the king a secret for four days, suppressing her own feelings. She discarded her eldest[87] son lest Shahmera should rule the kingdom through him, and she discarded the other son also because he was only a boy. Grieved for her sons, bewildered by the infirmity of old age, and annoyed at being kept shut up, the queen Shri Kota, supported by the Lavanyas, comforted (ruled) the country as if it was her co-widow. All the ministers—Shahmera and others—remembered the benefits they had previously received, and bowed to her as to the crescent of the moon. As the summer rain allays dust and heat, and nourishes plants, even so she brought back prosperity to the subjects.

The queen feared that Shahmera would destroy her prosperity, and with a view to check his rise she bestowed honours on Bhatta Bhikshana.[88] It was through his intelligence that the queen managed to perform her duties, as one crosses by a boat the dreadful ocean which is difficult to traverse. Shahmera could not in his heart tolerate the ascendency of Bhikshana who was helped by Kota, for the proud can scarcely bear equality even of his shadow. Fire manifests itself by heat and smoke, but no sign of anger manifested itself in that wise man. The wise Shahmera pretended illness and caused it to be known that his end was near. Queen Kota then sent Bhatta Bhikshana with Avatara and others to see him. They found people at the door discussing whether perspiration was good for one who suffered from biliousness; and these people prevented the Bhatta's party from entering. Bhikshana and Avatara, however, went in to Shahmera, but their protecting deities did not enter with them, as if on account of the difficulty in getting admission. Shahmera at first complained to them in detail of his illness, and when the proper time arrived, he buried their own weapon in their bodies, and thus allayed the illness of his mind. Blood issued from their heads, and water came out of their eyes; their lives left their bodies, and the rancour which Shahmera had felt, left his mind. Shahmera was bathed in their blood as one bathes after recovery from illness; their two heads were like the two halves of a vessel, and their wounds were like the marks of the lamp.

Queen Kota was determined to besiege Shahmera, and she was capable of doing so; but her evil-minded ministers deterred her from doing so, and reminded her that Shahmera and Bhikshana had brought up her boys, and that it was Fate that had killed the one by making the other an instrument. That in order to assuage the grief which had arisen from the death of a Brahmana, the senseless Shahmera would sacrifice the lives of others in the blazing fire of his anger.

## Kota slips out

As the canal nourishes cultivated fields with water, so did the queen nourish the people by bestowing much wealth on them.

She was to the kingdom what the moon is to the blue lotus; and to the enemy she was what that luminary is to the white lotus. On one occasion she marched against the lord of Kampana, with the intention to fight, because he had disobeyed her orders. But the lord of Kampana captured her in a mountain defile and put her in prison, even as one catches a bird in its nest and puts it in a cage. Her best minister named Kumarabhatta pretended to quarrel with her other ministers with a view to release her. He took with him a young student who carried in his hand a water vessel and who resembled the queen in his appearance except that he was a man. The wise Kumarabhatta went over to the lord of Kampana, praised his intelligence, and admired his magnanimity and beautiful appearance. "O Lord!" he said "by obeying the orders of a female we live with our heads humbled, but you have this day made our manhood triumph. With your permission I, your servant, will go to the prison, and by reproving and consoling her by turns, I will take out her money and give it to my lord. She has accumulated money, being a woman, and being unable to part with it of her own inclination." The lord of Kampana was thus deceived and suffered Kumarabhatta to go to the prison. The evening which paints the world so skillfully now approached as if to see queen Kota come out of her prison. Accompanied by the boy who carried water for his evening prayer, Kumarbhatta entered the prison, and the grief of the queen left it. He left the boy dressed in the queen's garments, and made Kota[89] to follow him wearing the dress of the boy, and thus issued from the prison.

## Shahmir

Shahmera, who had thus risen by art, was not devoid of circumspection; the wise when they are in enmity with the powerful never remain indifferent. Kota was neither favourable to, nor angry with the powerful Shahmera. Enmity attended with want of circumspection is the first germ of destruction. Once upon a time when the queen had gone to Jayapidapura[90] on some business, the powerful Shahmera possessed himself of the capital. And when the Lavanya people were subdued by the strong Shahmera, the queen closed the gate of Kotta[91], in the hope of thwarting her enemy. The strong and the wise Shahmera, a lion among men, closed the front of the cavern-like fort and Kota, like a she-jackal, was struck with fear. The fascinating Shahmera sent word to the queen through his messengers, stating that she might sit with him on the throne, and on his breast, with the goddess of Royalty, and that she might live in his heart with the virtue of forbearance. The queen was won by the assiduity and he took possession of the Kotta country and of queen Kota. He spent one night with her in the same bed, and when he rose in the morning, he caused her to be captured by the Tikashnas.[92] Then on the tenth bright lunar day in the month of Shravana in the year 15, the queen dropped from her kingdom like a star from the sky. Shahmera who was as the *kalpa* tree to his kinsmen and relatives, and wise in his actions, and chief among the warriors, imprisoned the two sons of the queen. The results of our acts manifest themselves in every direction, and generate wisdom or ignorance. The influence of *karma* is surging with the influences of time and of local circumstances and leads to results. I bow to the god of *Karma*[93], be it soul or Shiva or Hari or Brahma or Buddha or Jaina.

## Sultan Shamas-ud-Din

Shahmera then overawed the Lavanya people and spread his fame on all sides. He took the country into his hand, placed the goddess of fortune on his breast, and put Kota in prison. The king then assuaged the troubles of Kashmira and changed its condition, and called himself Shri Shamsadena. The scar of the bow string on his mighty arm was like the smoke, issuing from the flame of his power, which could have burnt all sides like a forest. The king removed the suspicions of his ministers, but the ministers could not remove his circumspection; as the diamond pierces jewels, but the jewel pierces not the diamond. The king who had won fame worthy of praise, caused the Rajputs[94] who were at Kashthavata to flee through fear. His fame increased, and he wisely placed on his two sons, who were not inferior to him, the burden of the kingdom. He reigned for five[95] years and three days and died on the full moon day of Ashadha, in the year 18.

## Jamshed

Then Jamsara[96] protected the country at Satisara, undiminished in prosperity and obeyed by the principal feudatory princes. Like the two pillars that support a gate, the strength and the intellect of the king's younger brother supported the kingdom and they became objects of apprehension. He was not inferior to the king in making gifts or in receiving presents, in awarding punishments or favours on the people, in undertaking pleasure trips or in the luxuries of the table. The king ceased to trust him as he had trusted before, and the mind of the young prince was inflamed by the people around him. When the Rajputs heard that the king's mind was alienated from his brother, they instantly communicated the fact to the young prince. And when hostility was inevitable, the rash young prince left the protection of the Rajputs and went excited to their chief town Avantinagara.[97] The king accompanied by his soldiers efficient in war, took shelter in Napalapura[98] and sent the following message to his brother: "If you have not underestimated my affection by the instigation of wicked men, why do you not tremble in fear of the censure of the people? The wishes of the king who has gone to heaven, our father, to protect each other should be obeyed. Think of this and turn your affection again towards me."

After the king had sent a messenger with this intimation to his brother, he sent his son to kill the lord of Kampana. The king's messenger was detained on the pretence that the young prince had gone to hunt, while the prince, whose treason had by this time become known, went to kill his brother's son. Lakshma[99] Bhatta became anxious as the messenger did not return for a long time. He went to the king and said that since the messenger was delaying he feared that the king's brother was bent on rebellion and had gone to kill the king's son. He also said that in order to frustrate the king's design, the messenger was no doubt detained on some pretence or other, such as that the young prince was bathing or eating or sleeping. He proposed that as soon as the king's brother repaired to Shri Devasarasa[100], they should destroy Avantipura which would then be left without any protector, and the king's victory would then be complete. The powerful king agreed to the proposal. He went to Avantipura with his efficient soldiers, and besieged the town; so that the river Vitasta, the current of which was blocked up by dead bodies, flowed backward as if to inform Alieshvara of the slaughter of his men.

Meanwhile Alleshvara defeated his brother's son and returned. Jamsara, who was resting from the toils of battle, fled. The wise Alleshvara came to an agreement with the king that hostilities should cease between the brothers for two months. Allesha left his soldiers and Avantipura behind, and went to Ikshika[101] by the Kshiri road. Jamsara, beaming in splendour, left the protection of the capital in the hands of his own minister Sayyaraja[102], and went to Kramarajya. But the young prince alienated Sayyaraja from the king by promises of gifts and honours, and got possession of the city by artifice. The king, now king only in name, died after having suffered troubles for one year and ten months in the kingdom of Kashmira. Then Alavadena (Allesha) knowing that the time was unsuited for further disputes, immediately bestowed the lordship of Dvara on his (third) brother, in order to smooth all difficulties. Jamsara had caused a bridge to be built to cross the river at Sujjapura[103], but did not devise means to cross over his dangers. He had excavated a tank and raised buildings by its side, close to the mountains, as resting places for travellers. For this beautiful act of improving his own country, Shri Shivasvamika[104] had obtained from him the lordship of Dvara.

## Allau-ud-Din

Once upon a time the prince was wandering for amusement in the forest of Vakpushta[105] when he saw a circle[106] of the *yoginis* in the cavern of a mountain. His friends Udayashri[107] and Chandradamara also saw them; for what is not visible to those who follow great men? Small things like bells tremble and make a noise, but great things like the minds of valiant heroes remain unmoved. They wished that the *yoginis* might not disappear, as they were anxious to see them and to speak to them. The heroes then alighted from their horses and were not afraid of the *yoginis*. Shining in their formidable strength, these valiant men proceeded slowly and silently, and approached the *yoginis*, The leader of the *yoginis* recognised the prince from a distance and sent him a cup of liquor with incantation and blessing. The king drank his fill; Chandra partook of what remained and, though pleased with it, he left a portion for the sake of Udayashri. Udayashri was much gratified with the drink and, owing to some fatality, forgot the groom of the horses and left nothing. They were pleased with the strange sights they saw. The *yogini*, who understood omens, thus said to the prince with clasped hands: "Your kingdom will remain entire, and Chandra will enjoy a part of your wealth and Udayashri, as long he lives, will be blessed with undying prosperity; but the groom bereft of our favour will be soon left bereft of life." Thus she foretold the future, and vanished with the other *yoginis*, and then the life of the keeper of horses departed.

It is owing to the merit of the subjects that such kings are born, who raise the prosperity of the kingdom and deliver the people sunk in the gloom of injustice. The king abolished the evil custom under which a childless widow, though unchaste[108], obtained a share of her husband's property from her father-in-law. The great and wise king made Jayapidapura his capital, and built at Sri Rinchanapura an edifice named Budhagira.[109] In the year 19, a famine of unprecedented severity, the effect of the sins of men, harassed the suffering people. Having ruled the kingdom for twelve years, eight months and thirteen days, the king died in the month of Chaitra, in the year 30.

## Shahab-ud-Din (1355-73)

The halting description of the reigns of bad kings now gives place to an account of the very powerful Shahvadina (Shahab-ud-Din), When he became king, the country creased to remember the prosperity and dangers, the pleasures and afflictions of the time of Lalitaditya.[110] As the sky, after the departure of the different seasons, obtains the bright sun in summer, so the earth passed under the rule of many kings, and obtained this sovereign at last. The king did not repair to the city of sinful Jayapida. Adorned with pearls and necklace, this king was the most prominent among all kings, past and future. Though he obtained victory at every step, yet the fire of his valour was not satiated, even as the ocean receives rivers from all directions and is not satiated. He counted as lost those brief periods of time in which he obtained no victory. The march with his army was as dear to him as a young wife is to an old man. Deer-eyed women attracted not his mind, nor the pleasures of drinking nor the light of moon. Only the march with his army occupied the king's attention. Neither heat nor cold, nor evening nor night, neither hunger nor thirst obstructed his march. When this proud king was on his march, he found no difficulty in crossing unfordable rivers, inaccessible mountains and barren deserts.

In his conquering expeditions the king first went to the north which had never been conquered by previous kings and which was peopled by the Parasikas.[111] He took Chandra, Laulaka, and Shura with him for help, even as the world-conquering Kama takes the spring, wine and woman as his auxiliaries. This destroyer of the proud filled his soldiers with strength, his enemies with grief, and all sides with dust. Udabhandapura[112] ruled by Govindakhana, was first entered by his arrows and then by his soldiers. When the army of the king reached the top of the mountain, his opponents descended from the high peak in fear. The ruler of Sindhu, unable to make presents befitting the king, presented his own daughter to him. The weight of the country of the Gandharas was added to the king's glory, but strange! that the weight of the fear lowered the hearts of those people. The powerful king destroyed the pride of the country of the Shingas but did not destroy their swords. On hearing the lion-roar raised by the army of the lion-like king, Gajnipuri[113] (the elephant city) fell bereft of pride, and struck with fear. At Ashtanagara[114] the Veda-readers and the Kshatriyas wept through fear, as if the smoke from the fire of their youth and valour, which was extinguished, affected their eyes. When the king had robbed the wealth and the fame of Purushavira[115], the name of that country lost its meaning. The women in the villages[116] assigned to the Brahmanas shed tears, as if they offered water to the dead and food to the living. When the leaders of the cavalry had gone away on the pretext of repairing to the banks of the Ghoshadhatu[117] river, the king administered a severe chastisement to Udakpati.

Returning thence, he marched southward, and assuaged the toil of the journey in the waters of the Shatadru.[118] He harassed Udakpati who had arrived after plundering Dhilli, and blocked his way. He then bestowed horses and clothes on petty kings and sent them to their countries, and they looked as if they were the embodiment of the king's fame. The king of Susharmapura[119] apprehended danger from the king of Kashmira, and he forsook the pride of his fort and sought the protection of the queen. It was owing to the humility, not to the pride of the Bhauttas, that the king's horses eager to ascend the mountains, were checked. The king arrived at the banks of the Sindhu which he found difficult to cross, but the gods smoothed the waves of the river. This strange fact has been heard from elderly men. Thus in his unceasing endeavour to conquer other countries, his own became to him as a foreign land, and foreign countries became his own. Thus, having filled all sides with his valour, he entered Kashmira and instituted festivities to delight the eyes of the citizens.

In the course of our narration, we are describing the superhuman abilities of this king, and shall perhaps be considered by future generations to be flatterers. Once, when the king was marching to a distant country, he heard of a woman beautiful like an Apsara, with eyes like those of the deer, and became eager to enjoy her. He deceived his followers by some device, and alone entered the country where she lived, and like a second Kandarpa[120] fascinated her by his wit. He drank the nectar from her lips and quenched the desire of his heart. When his soldiers missed him, they feared that he was killed by some enemy, and lost their reason in their anger. They searched for him and when they saw his horse tethered in the courtyard of a house, they thought that he had been overcome by his enemies. Without any armour, the soldiers blockaded the house with a view to fight with Shauryyasvami[121] and Anuga. But on hearing a voice like the roar of a lion from within the house, Iheir hearts that knew no fear were softened with gladness, their faces were subdued with awe, and their heads were bent with good sense. The king caused many columns of victory to be raised, proclaiming his great deeds, in places where his enemies had been destroyed like sacrificial beasts in the flame of his prowess. In the management of the affairs of his own country be depended on his two ministers Kotabhatta and Udayashri, and in battle he depended on Chandradamara and Laula. Kotasharma was like the moon in the sea-like dynasty of Devasharma.[122] Indifferent to worldly concerns, he left the wealth repeatedly bestowed on him by the king and retired to a forest.

## Inundation

Surely it was to display the prowess of the king that on a certain occasion a calamity befell troubling his subjects grievously. In the year[123] 36, a cruel inundation distressed the subjects. What the sun is to the kumuda flower, or a hero to his enemies, so was the inundation to the city and the trees. The city was under water, but the mighty inundation still increased and reached the hills which shed tears in the shape of waterfalls. There was not a tree, not a boundary mark, not a bridge, not a house, that stood in the way of the inundation, which it did not destroy. The king who never took shelter in a hill fort through fear of an enemy, now frequently resorted to such forts through fear of the inundation. It subsided within a few days, as if dried up by the prowess of the king; but the king wished to build a town on a hill in fear of another inundation.

He consulted his queen named Lakshmi and built a celebrated town which equalled his own greatness; and the people saw before them, at the base of the Himalaya, the town of Sharika[124], inhabited by virtuous men, even like Alaka, at the base of the Sumeru. At the junction[125] of the Vitasta and the Sindhu, he built a town after his own name, and the town was reflected in the waters, as if it had hid itself in the river through modesty. Loladamara[126], on whom fortune shone steadily, built a town after his own name, and the high edifices were like glory amassed. The ever restless world soared upwards (in the shape of hills) as if to reach the heavens, and thus (casting its shadows on the town) deprived it of the rays of the sun.

## Infatuation for Lasa

Lasa was the daughter of queen Lakshmi's sister and was brought up by the queen. Her image was now reflected on the mirror of the king's heart. He was for a long time held by ties of respect to Lakshmi, but those ties were snapped by the passion inflamed by the beauty of Lasa. The goddess of Fortune[127] had, with the beautiful image as of Krishna, taken her seat in the bosom of the king, and the fortunate Lasa was now allowed a place by her side. The shadow is not cast in the direction of the sun, for the sun enjoys the glory of the day, and the shadow brings darkness and destroys the beauty of the sun. It has been well-said that women have four times the intellect of men, and none can frame crooked and penetrating devices better than they. The chaste Lakshmi, though she was the daughter of a common Bhatta named Avatara, became displeased with the king who had become attached to Lasa; and she went in anger to the king of Sindhu who was her countryman. But the king of Kashmira, out of shame, though not out of deep affection, brought her back. The she-elephant of the wilderness, when her agony caused by heat is relieved by the water of a lotus-tank, nevertheless troubles the water, and rudely shakes the mosses and the lotus in the tank. Even so Lasa, the beloved of the king, behaved ungratefully towards Lakshmi, the sister of her mother, and who had nourished her like a mother, as the full moon which is nourished by the bright fortnight terminates and destroys that fortnight. The *kumuda* flower is destined to bloom by night; otherwise the night, like a wicked woman, could have destroyed it by the help of the moon which destroys the wakefulness of the world.

## Liberal outlook

Once upon a time Lasa, in the enjoyment of her prosperity, thus spoke to the king with the wile of a serpent; and the king listened with anxiety, and his breath dulled the splendor of his lips: "If the sun had not by its rays expanded the lotus, who would have cared to destroy it through jealousy? Who cares to destroy the moss? Unable to bear the favours bestowed on me, your queen is devising for my destruction. The queen watches me through her spies, and out of her enmity has directed Udayashri, who has become her favourite by his services, to employ magic[128] against me." But the wise king replied to her that Udayashri was inimical to the gods, and could not therefore perform magic. Lasa repeated the charge; and in order to convince her of her mistake, the king thus addressed Udayashri: "O! Udayashri! The treasury has become empty by excessive expenditure, but the people ask the king for everything, as if he was the *kalpa* tree. There is one way which is apparent to me for making money. By cutting up the huge brass image of Shri Jayeshvari[129] and turning it into coins marked with my name, we may meet the required expenses, and deeds of deathless fame may be done." The mean-minded minister thus replied to the king: "The idea is a good one but the image is light, how much can we obtain from it? Rather let the image of the great Buddha[130] be coined into money." On another day, after the necessary preparations had been made, and Lasa had been convinced (that Udayashri was not a believer in the gods), the king thus said privately to that minister: "Past generations have set up images to obtain fame and earn merit, and you propose to demolish them! Some have obtained renown by setting up images of gods, others by worshipping them, some by duly maintaining them. And some, by demolishing them! How great is the enormity of such a deed! Sagara became famous by creating the sea and the rivers, and grieving for Sagara's sons Bhagiratha obtained fame by bringing down the Ganges. Jealous of Indra's fame, Dushyanta acquired renown by conquering the world; and Rama by killing Ravana when the latter had purloined Sita. King Shahvadina, it will be said, plundered the image of a god; and this fact, dreadful as Yama, will make the men in future tremble." When the king had spoken thus, Udayashri held down his head, as if seeking for a hole in the ground, wishing to go down into the interior of the earth.

When the sun rises in the sky he causes harm to his sons, the Saturn and other planets. So when Lasa reported against the sons of the king, the king, at her instigation and out of his affection for her, exiled the princes from their own country as if they were his enemies. They went to the assistance of the lord of Yoginipura[131], and displayed their prowess by superhuman acts.

As advised, the king killed the rebellious Hindukas[132], and the rebellious Shekandhara and other *mlechhas*, to whom he had assigned salaries out of his generosity. Alarmed by wicked men, the hero Madanalavika prepared to rise against the king, but was prevented by his soldiers. Accustomed to hunting, the king made a quick march with his soldiers, and removed the beautiful bridge of boats over the Sindhu which was like a moat.

The heroic king, with the steady courage of a lion, wandered at Khadganagari[133] in pursuit of game, and he ran after a lion. Riding a horse, the king ran past the den, followed only by Maḍana who was much devoted to him. The lion, with its mane erect, threw down the brave and lion king, who was alone and who struggled for a long time. The hero Madanalavika soon alighted from his horse and killed the lion with his sword. The grateful king whose life was thus saved rewarded him with wealth but, apprehending the death of Madanalavika at the hands of wicked men, he wisely sent him forthwith to the king of Dilli on pretence of marriage.

Once upon a time a man named Sharkarasuha saw in a dream a great city of gold which shone like *champaka* flowers blown in the sky. He dreamt that he entered into house after house, but he found them all empty. In a palace, however, he found a woman of radiant beauty. He asked her why she was living alone but fearless in that great city, like the crescent of the moon in the sky; and he enquired whose city it was, why it was tenantless, and whose body was lying before her. She replied that like a beauteous woman whose husband was dead, or like the night without moon, that city belonged to the king of the Gandharbhas; and the king, in order to govern the country of Kashmira, had left his body there, and with all his ministers had descended on the earth. He was known in the three worlds by the name of Shahavadina, and that she alone was staying there to keep watch over the body. She said that after completing his work on the earth, the king would return within three months to protect his own city. When Sharkarasuha awoke, he was sunk in excessive wonder and grief and meditation, and he narrated his dream to the king. The king thought to himself that there was no cause for fear if the dream turned out to be false, and if it proved true he would attain superhuman power; and so the king was not troubled with grief. The king then sent letters to his sons, who were at a distance, to come to him, but they did not come. This wise sovereign then placed the Hindukas[134] in their own posts, and on the fourteenth day of the bright moon of the month of Jaishtha, in the year 49, he cheered celestial beauties by his embraces.

## Qutub-ud-Din

King Kumbhadina[135] succeeded; his orders were placed on the heads of kings, his bounty delighted their hearts, and his praise was on their lips. He captivated the hearts of all, even like the sun when he is in the equinox, and is neither too powerful nor too weak.

Those whom the late king had sent to reconnoitre Lohara[136] had run away in fear of the lord of that country. All the luminous plants become dull when the moon sets, and the sun-jewel loses its brilliancy at the setting of the sun. With a view to attack Lohara, king Kumbhadina sent the powerful Damara Lolaka from the city, and Lolaka surrounded the hill of Lohara on all sides. The lives of the great men who devote themselves to their master's work are like grass. The lord of the fort, unable to defend it, sent Brahmana messengers to the Damara chief, in order to deliver it up. But the Damara, who had kept his temper even in the heat of battle, believed the messengers to be spies in the garb of Brahmanas, and he chastised them. Brahmanas were as gods to the lord of Lohara, and when he heard that punishment had been inflicted on Brahmanas, he took courage, held out the fort, and did not despair of his life. And when he and his people found that death awaited them whether they fought or fled, they resolved on battle which is the avocation of Kshatriyas. Terrible in battle, they discharged their arrows and stones, and as they descended from the hill of Lohara, their fame ascended to the skies. Lola the Damara chief was struck by stones and perished with his deeds, for who can escape the decrees of fate? The stone discharged by the enemy covered the Damara Lolaka, so that he was not deprived of burial, the last rite of the *yavanas*.

King Shahavadina had exiled his own sons, but just before his death he had invited them to return by letters written with his own hand. The eldest and the most meritorious among them, the prince named Hassana, came to Mahendramandala[137], and met with no opposition. Here he heard of the death of his father and shed floods of tears as the pearl-oyster sheds pearls, and as if he thereby offered water to the dead. The following letter of his father's brother, the king Kumbhadina of Kashmir a, made this pure-minded prince continue his march, and prevented him from retracing his steps: "King Shahavadina has left us his servants out of his friendship for Indra, and has departed to heaven. He has left us to seek the company of the celestial Apsaras, and we have performed the funeral rites which you should have done; and we have held that kingdom on our head according to the orders of the departed king, the wisest of men, in order to protect these realms strung together, like a garland, by his policy.

## Invites nephews

"By going to exile under the orders of your father, and now returning by his desire, you have filled your country with fame, like Rama. By your own merit you have obtained honour, and will earn yet more. Accept the post of the heir-apparent and lighten the weight that is on me. Your fortitude, the company of courtiers and friends, and the duty of protecting the people will soon assuage your grief. As the dead derive no pleasure from fame, even so great men who live in foreign lands derive no pleasure from wealth. You are the image of him who has gone to heaven; show yourself to us, and relieve us of the sorrow we feel for him. Let the people of a foreign country no more point you out their finger, as they do an ordinary person, and say 'this is the son of Shahavadina'. Do not look up for favour to princes who are dependent on me and who receive my favours; do not slight the wealth of Kashmira. As the serpent which, supports the world places its weight on the Meru mountain, even so shall I place the weight of the kingdom on you and enjoy repose and wealth. So long as I rule the subjects, you will live in the same dignity which king Shahavadina bestowed on me. Do not therefore decline our request and thereby disappoint (your mother) Lakshmi who acts according to the advice of Udayashri and other ministers,"

The prince did not know that kings are guided by other men as elephants are guided by their ears. He read the letter and descended along the road to Kashmira. He was, as it were, forbidden to enter that country by the clouds which gathered before him and thundered. He shed a lustre on the road to Kashmira as he entered it, but the instigations of the wicked poisoned the ears of the king. Wicked ministers are to the world what the fire is to the forest. Some of them, in their ambition to rise, agitate the mind of the king, as crocodiles agitate the sea. Some, in their pride, shake the king as the wind shakes the tops of plants.

## The seeds of discord

When prince Hassana had entered Kashmira, the wicked thus said to king Kumbhadina: "The wisdom of the king is superior to that of others; the ministers may, nevertheless, be permitted to speak to enable him to decide what is beneficial and what is harmful. Even sovereigns, who comprised in them a portion of Indra and of the rulers of the four directions of the sky and the four corners of the universe, were injured by the members of their own family. A brother is like a black serpent which is known to live on air and whose course is tortuous; such a brother's touch is destruction. Who can then be safe from danger? The prince will not be satisfied with wealth or submit to you; the fire does not become cool by coming in contact with cold objects. Do not think that he being alone can do no harm to thee who art a king. What is the king of elephants with his herd in the presence of a lion? But it would not be wise by our advice to destroy his power, for the sensible Udayashri, out of regard for his late master, guards the prince. O! Chief of Kings! Hassana is not a fit object of your favour nor is he to be cast off; he will become proud if you favour him, and will cause you harm if you cast him off; as a man of spirit he will never forgive a wrong. Does not the submarine-fire always heat the sea? Imprison him therefore and remove the anxiety of the people, those who are anxious for the king and also those who are not." As water becomes unsuitable for drink if it flows into a lake from a dirty pool, even so the king became estranged from Hassana by the words of the wicked.

The king noticed the strange and haughty conduct of the prince, he marked it, he heard of it, and he felt it; but as the prince was his brother's son, the king did not imprison him out of affection. Udayashri noticed that the king was vexed with the prince, and thus said to the prince's nurse, the widow of Loladamara: "Damara Lolaka died out of his affection for his late master, and he did not tarnish his honour by serving a new and wicked master. There is no hope of obtaining wealth from the present evil-minded king, and the life of Hassana who was brought up by you is in danger. Ask the king therefore to accept the wealth which you possess, so that this avaricious man may come to your house. When he is once in your house, we will kill him or seize him by force, and then the prince will prosper."

## Udayashri slain

It so happened that this plan was revealed to the king; Udayashri became alarmed, and caused Hassana to flee. Men like him are precious like the philosopher's stone, and are worthy of praise in this world, for he remained fixed in his resolution, and he caused another to flee. He was engaged in an undertaking than which nothing could be more desperate; and he was detected in it, but the forgiving king did not behead him. Udayashri's faults were concealed in his worth, and he passed his days, pure in appearance, like a lotus in the mud. Though the moon-jewel be at a distance from the moon, and concealed in water, does it not even then emit moisture when embraced by the rays of the moon?' Thus thought Udayashri to himself, and he felt a desire to go to the prince, but the king, who had heard of his treason, placed him in prison; and, as if instigated by the gods who seemed to know his purpose and that of his instructor, slew him in anger. The elephant which crushes the lotus, the wind that breaks the sandal tree, and the king who destroys good men deserve censure in the three worlds. This world is like a garden, and men are the flowers, and it is in their words that praise, which is like perfume, is sought. As the blind man who has lost his hands and feet becomes excessively timid, even so prince Hassana became timid at the death of Udayashri. The evil-minded Khasha chiefs were glad at the reward bestowed on them by their master, and even attempted to kill prince Hassana.

When the enemies were confounded and dis-spirited, and they melted away, the wisdom of the king became like a light to the people, Then on the banks of the Vitasta he built a town[138] marked with his name, and the lofty golden umbrella placed upon it seemed, by its beauty, to mock the skies. The king saw that the people died of famine every year and he performed a *jajna*[139] in the month of Bhadra, and distributed large gifts.

## Sikandar born

In the old age of this king the hair about his ears became white as if by listening to the nectar-like words of good men. But the king was not yet blessed with a boy who would have been an ornament to the family, a rock of support to the world and a destroyer of the enemy's prosperity. At last there came a *yogi* named Brahmanatha to Kashmira and, through his favour, the king obtained a son after a time. The queen gave birth to a son who was the ornament of the family and the delight of his father, who was like a feast after a fast, a subverter of darkness, and a destroyer of the eyes of enemies. The king of the world saw the child who was like the abode of love and he named it Shringara.[140] In the festivities which were held on the occasion, the king, out of gladness of his heart, ordered the imprisoned to be released, and it is strange that the boats in the bridge of boats were still kept chained. The queen gave birth to another boy, named Haivata, whose beauty rebuked the moon. It was a spot in the character of the king, as there is a spot in the moon, that he took unto him as his wife the dame world, although she was of his family. On the second day of the dark moon in the month of Bhadra in the year 65, king Kumbhadina, the chief among kings, died. The queen was sunk in sorrow and the two princes were infants; the subjects were therefore without a master and were struck with fear. The profuse tears of the queen were like the rains in the rainy season, and the ministers were like fish therein.

Uddaka[142] and Sahaka consoled the heroic[141] queen. They said that it was useless to indulge in grief, that one must have patience under such a misfortune, and that the evil-minded people were rising in the kingdom which was without a strong ruler and without a king. They then crowned the elder Shekandhara (Sikandar) as king of this great kingdom. By the order of the new king, Uddaka treacherously burnt Mahammada, son of Saha, and his own daughter and son-in-law to death. The huge whale unwittingly devours its spawn, and the bee which is destined to perish when its hive will be robbed of honey, destroys its own mother. What wicked deed will not foolish men do under temptations, their sense perplexed, and knowing that at the end they will be consumed by fire? The prosperity of the great queen Shri Shobha[143] was worthy of admiration. She beautified the world with a golden linga, and the heaven with the mark of her own virtue.

## Intrigues

Uddaka apprehended that as he had destroyed the king's friend, he would be killed and he removed the king's brother by poison. He had sworn to Sahaka that he would by his own sword cut his own throat before rising against Sahaka. By such assurance he obtained the confidence of Sahaka and killed him. To the evil-minded, whose destruction is near, their evil deed becomes the harbinger of their death. The king was apprehensive that he would be killed like his brother, but he had now grown up and he made his party strong. But the proud Uddaka who had returned after conquering the Bhauttas was unable to brook the advancement of others, and he killed Khunjyaraja, brother of Shri Shobha. Uddaka then ordered Mammaka[144], a dependent of his, to create a disturbance at Dvara and, discarding the king's affection for him, he went in pride to Helara. He heard that Labdharaja and others were following the king, bow in hand, and were prepared for battle in some deserted[145] place. They whose destruction is nigh think themselves to be sensible men and generally mistake their own shadow for ghosts. The soldiers of Uddaka had come prepared for fight, but when they saw some she-buffaloes at Vallamatha on the other side of the Vitasta, they mistook them for horses, and fled. The king pursued them and at night captured Uddaka at Vitastapura[146], but was afraid of a disturbance in the city and returned. Though Uddaka deserved to be killed, the king cast him into prison out of pity. But Uddaka was stained with the sin of treachery against those who had confided in him, he feared death from the king who was mild on account of his kindness, and he cut his throat by his own sword. As the king of birds kills serpents and the lion kills jackals, so the king of the world killed the guards placed on him. His kingdom and the safety of his body and mind and his personal freedom were preserved to the king even like the fruits of penance performed in the midst of five fires.

The king dispelled the gathering gloom of the pride of other kings and commenced his march which, alas! terrified Indra. His great prowess coloured the world red, but made colourless the nails of the sorrowing wives of hostile kings. At this time the king[147] of the *mlechhas* had plundered Dilli and made it like a widow deprived of ornaments and without a protector. When the king of the *mlechhas* returned, he was afraid of the king of Kashmira, and gave him two large elephants as presents. The elephants exuded moisture as they passed and the line marked by the moisture was the boundary of the kingdom of Kashmira which the king of the *mlechhas* himself seemed to demarcate. The two big elephants looked like peaks of the Himalaya, and Agastya became angry, apprehending that the Vindhya mountain was rising in dimension. When they crossed the Vitasta, they saw their own reflection in the water, and became angry, mistaking the shadows for rival elephants. They were proud of their rounded foreheads which mocked the beauty of the bosoms of the king's wives. They were stabled in the elephant-stable which was like a prison to them.

The beautiful king not only satisfied those who asked with gifts of gold, but even distributed it of his own accord. When he made gifts, his hands hung down and were contracted, for he felt abashed at the praises of those who asked and obtained what they asked. Who can describe his gifts? He dipped his hand in water[148] before making a gift, and his hand looked like a lotus under the water. The lines on his thumb were like barley grains, but they did not sprout by being constantly drenched in water; because, I imagine, of their constant contact with the handle of the sword.

## Foreign immigrants

It was perhaps owing to the sins of the subjects that the king had a fondness for the *yavanas*, even as a boy has a fondness for flies. Many *yavanas* left other sovereigns and took shelter under this king who was renowned for charity, even as bees leave the flowers and settle on elephants. As the bright moon is among the stars, so was Mahammada of Mera country among these *yavanas*; and although he was a boy[149], he became their chief by learning. The king waited on him daily, humble as a servant, and like a student he daily took his lessons from him. He placed Mahammada before him and was attentive to him like a slave. As the wind destroys the trees and the locusts the shali crop, so did the *yavanas destroy the usages* of Kashmira. Attracted[150] by the gifts and honours which the king bestowed, and by his kindness, the *yavanas* entered Kashmira, even as locusts enter a good field of corn.

On a certain occasion the king subdued the king of Udabhandapura, and being pleased with his daughter Shri Mera, obtained her as the goddess of victory incarnate. She was surely a goddess, born in the family of Shahi[151], and her son was destined, on a future day, to consolidate Kashmira destroyed by the *mlechhas*. That boy named Shri Jainollabhadina was like virtue incarnate in the Kaliyuga and like the king of hermits, he became the king's favourite.

A certain wily alchemist named Mahadeva gave some drug to the king and spoke to him of alchemy, and said that the golden Meru was indebted to the king for having constantly borne the weight of the world and had, through Mahadeva, bestowed much gold on him. But his alchemy did not remove Mahadeva's poverty. He deluded the sight by deception, and exhibited gold in the crucible, and the delusion lasted for a long time. But the king by his strong sense detected the trick and told Mahadeva of it. Alarmed at this discovery Mahadeva committed suicide.

Ladharaja, the physician Shankara, and Bhatta Suha were the councillors of the king and were intimate with him. Three sons were born to queen Mera, beautiful as Cupid, and like Virtue, Wealth and Desire personified; and they were adorned with the names of Merakhana, Shahikhana and Mahmadakhana, as the worlds are beautiful by the waves of the Ganges. The sons of queen Shobha were adopted children and were therefore banished. One of them, Piruja, was, however, not banished from the city by the king. On the side of Pradyumna[152] hill, the king built a town, even like the town of Alaka reflected on the Manasa lake, and inhabited by virtuous people.

The *yavanas*, who had accumulated wealth, were indifferent as to the king's treasure, whether it was large or small. The kingdom of Kashmira was polluted by the evil practices of *mlechhas*, and the Brahmanas, the mantras, and the gods relinquished their power. The gods who used to make the glory of their prowess manifest, even as fireflies manifest their light, now hid their glory on account of the country's sin. When the gods withdrew their glory, their images became mere stone and the mantras mere letters. Owing to the sin of the *kaliyuga*, the merits of those who did virtuous acts were lost, and the gods deserted the images, even as serpents cast off their skins.

## The iconoclast

As a crystal becomes red or white or black by the reflection of the object that is near it, even so the king became changed. Suhabhatta[153] who disregarded the acts enjoined by the Vedas and was instructed by the *mlechhas*, instigated the king to break down the images of gods. The good fortune of the subjects left them and so the king forgot his kingly duties and took a delight, day and night, in breaking images. Of the tree of misgovernment (which was now planted) Harshadeva[154] the Turushka was the seedling, sinfulness was the root and the terrible devastation caused by the Lavanyas were the leaves. Its flower was Dalacha, the king of the *mlechhas*; and its fruits were the daily troubles of the king who broke images at the instigations of the *mlechhas*. He broke the images of Martanda[155], Vijaya Ishana, Chakrabhrit and Tripureshvra[156]; but what can be said of the evil that came on him by the breaking of the Shesha[157]? When Sureshvari, Varaha and others were broken, the world trembled as if through fear, but not so the mind of the wicked. There was no city, no town, no village, no wood, where Suha the Turushka left the temples of gods unbroken. Of the images which once had existed, the name alone was left and Suhabhatta then felt the satisfaction which one feels on recovering from illness.[158]

Suhabhatta with the leaders of the army tried to destroy the caste[159] of the people; it was like a boy eating the unwholesome food. The Brahmanas declared that they would die if they lost their caste and Suhabhatta subjected them to a heavy fine[160] because they held to their caste. At the time when his dependants who belonged to the Brahmana and other castes forsook their caste, ambitious to obtain the favour of the king, Shri Simha and Bhattakasthuta, two merchants, became worthy of praise and Shri Nirmalacharyya deserved praise in the three worlds. Nirmalacharyya gave up all his property, as if it was worthless as grass, but did not by accepting the king's favour pollute his own caste. It is an established rule that the master is responsible for the fault of his servant and, therefore, for the fault of Suhabhatta Death became angry with the king. Having coronated his eldest son, King Shekandhara died on the eighth lunar day of Jaishtha, in the year[89].

## Alishah

Alishaha, then, like the moon when his *sun-like* father was set, dispelled the world's darkness which came at nightfall. He was a boy and unfit for the joys of love, but the goddess of fortune, born in the family, bent herself down and embraced him again and again. The other kings bowed to this boy as they had done to the late king. He who is bitten by a serpent does not venture to assail a rope. Suhabhatta had devoted all his energies to doing mischief to the gods and he therefore became chief among the king's ministers. Ladha[161] the Margapati had, suspecting nothing, left aside his arms but he was seized with all his sons except Mahammada. When the powerful Mahammada, who knew well about the roads of the country, heard about the capture of Ladha, he fled by the hill road of Bhangila. Shankara, the physician, was besieged but he remained fearless and the intellect of the armed men though sharp was fruitless against him and did not afflict him. The lion which proudly overlooks danger may set his foot in a trap, but it is strange that the bird which can see from a distance should also be entrapped.

## Mohammad imprisoned

When Mahammad heard of these events, he was anxious and wished that he could come to Kashmira in a day, and day and night he felt ill at ease as a poor man feels for his daughter. In order to give himself a little rest, Mahammada entered the house of Govinda, whom he trusted, in the country of Durddanda.[162] The cloud which is born of smoke quenches the fire, the fire which is born of the friction of trees destroys the forest, the poison tree dries up the land on which it grows and thus the people overpowered with covetousness behave with enmity even towards those who do them good. When Mahammada the Margapati arrived at the house of Govinda the Khasha, suspecting nothing, the latter thus communed within himself for a time: The minister Suhabhatta, with a view to prevent a tumult in the kingdom, had opposed the evil-minded Mahammada who was getting up a faction in the country, and this sinful and powerless man who was trying to create a disturbance in the kingdom had that day, out of fear, entered his place.' It did not appear therefore to the Khasha that Mahammada deserved protection. In the meantime, the shrewed men who had been sent by Suhabhatta in search for Mahammada came to the house of Govinda, the chief of the Khashas; and that wicked-minded man violated the ties of friendship and the duty of protection to one who seeks shelter and betrayed his friend Mahammada. As a hunter binds a sleeping lion, so did the Khasha bind him, as if he had been an animal, and left him and those who had come in search of him soon took him to Kashmira.

## Escape

As the monkey strikes the serpent rendered powerless by incantations and as the hunter scatters the mane of a lion that is dead, even so a strong man may insult one who is tied down, but what does he gain by it but censure? Fearing that the captive should run away, they placed the honourable, but insulted, Mahammada in the great fort at Bahurupa.[163] The new cloud at night raises the hopes of travellers bound for a distant country by the light of its lightning but finally overpowers them; the lion inspires confidence in his victims by looking backward before he springs on them. The Saturn moves in a curve when it overthrows the Ram and other constellations, so does Fate by a propitious look inspire confidence in the sinful, but overwhelms them in the end. Mahammada was consoled by Shaha, a female servant and was removed from his place of confinement by the sons of his nurse. Mahammada, when he was covered with perspiration, deceived his sentinels by pretending to go to bathe. He entered the bath and thence he escaped. He then reached the place where an opening had been cut by the sons of his nurse and he went out, as a swan does from one great island of this earth to another. There was a waterfall at Jampa[164] deafening the ear as if in anger and Mahammada left the fort which looked like a precipice. The stones and the guard could not prevent his departure, while the noise of the waterfall drowned the clanking of the chain in his feet. The sons of his nurse then broke his chain and they thought that they broke thereby the friendship between Suhabhatta and his friends.

Suhabhatta feared that the old Margapati would escape as Mahammada had done and though he had robbed the old man of his money, he killed him on the way. When the Margapati was killed by the evil-minded Suhabhatta, all the people blamed the latter and wept as at the death of their father. Suhabhatta, for fear of the people, went about every night under the guidance of skilful men, like a bird fallen from his nest. To this helpless man the day was as night and the night as day. Surely when fate becomes unpropitious everything turns out wrong. As a fisherman becomes sorry when a large fish leaps out of his boat and escapes, so was Suhabhatta at the escape of Mahammada from the prison; and he often thought of Mahammada.

## Feroze repulsed

The people had nursed and protected Piruja and when they beheld him, they thought that he was Shikandhara who had gone to heaven. Though Piruja was the son of Shikandhara by his wife Shobhadevi, Shikandhara had exiled him from his own country, in order to prevent a commotion. He was a prince and was welcomed by the king of the north; and he now came back bringing with him Mahammada, in order to conquer the people of Kashmira. When Suha heard that Piruja had come with the Turushka soldiers he sent Shri Ladda and Gauraka to oppose him. The Turushka army was destroyed by the wisdom of Shri Laddaraja[165] and by the valour of Gauraka, even as disease is destroyed by gift and prayer. Relieved of fear, the minister Suha made Laddaraja, lord of Kampana and Gaurabhatta, lord of Kramarajya. As in the evening which darkens the mountains, neither the sun nor the moon is visible, so when Suhabhatta, who had made himself felt by the king, became powerful, neither the king nor the heir-apparent could raise his head.

## Brahmin-bashing

The hawk kills other birds,, the lion destroys other animals, the *vajra*-jewel pierces other jewels and the brilliant sun throws about the planets like flowers, and thus destruction seems ever to be caused in this world by one's own people. Though the king Shri Shikandhara was often instigated by Suha to persecute the twice-born, he, whose purpose was tempered by kindness, fixed, with some difficulty, a limit to the advance of the great sea of the *yavanas*.

But Suha passed the limit by levying fines on the twice-born. As the night prevents the people from seeing anything but darkness, so this evil-minded man forbade ceremonies and processions[166] during the new moon. He became envious and apprehended that the twice-born who had become fearless would keep up their caste by going over to foreign countries; he therefore ordered all the guards on the roads not to allow passage to any one without a written passport.[167] Then as the fisherman torments fish in an enclosed river, so this low-born man tormented the twice-born in the country.

## Self-immolation

The Brahmanas burnt themselves in the flaming fire through fear of committing sin and through fear of him who was like the heat of the fire; and thus they escaped. Struck by fear some Brahmanas killed themselves by means of poison, some by the rope, others by drowning themselves in water, others again by falling from a precipice and others burnt themselves. The country was contaminated by hatred and the king's favourite (Suha) could not prevent one man in a thousand from committing suiqide. This wicked man disliked the weight of the kingdom which was hard to be borne, but he delighted in the cries of the twice-born, which gave him pleasure. A multitude of Brahmanas who prided on their caste fled from the country through by-roads as the main roads were dosed, even as men flee underground when the doors of their houses are closed. Even as men depart from this world, so did the Brahmanas flee to foreign countries, the son leaving his father behind and the father leaving his son, to the Death like Suha who sorrowed at the escape of the Brahmans. The difficult country through which they passed, the scanty food, painful illness and the torments of hell during life-time removed from the minds of the Brahmans the fear of hell.

Oppressed by various calamities, such as encounter with the enemy, fear of snakes, fierce heat and scanty[167a] food, many Brahmanas perished on the way and thus obtained relief. Where was then their bath, their meditation, their austerity, and where was then their prayer? The Brahmanas wandered about in villages, begging and thus spent their time. The wrong which was done to the Brahmanas proved beneficial to them, since exiled by Suha, the twice-born removed their sins by visiting holy places. Some twice-born men who were anxious to save their wives, emaciated by want of food, did not depart to foreign countries, but wandered about in Kashmira wearing the dress of the *mlechhas*. Suha withheld the allowances of the twice-born with a view to extinguish learning and they, in expectation of a mouthful of food, went from house to house, putting out their tongues like dogs. It was out of his devotion to the religion of the Turushkas, not out of antipathy towards the twice-born, that he oppressed the Brahmanas; and hence his victims did not much complain. This was what Suhabhatta told them in order to remove the impression which his action created that he had antipathy towards the Brahmanas.

The Brahmanas, the supporters of the world, had taken refuge of Ratnakara[168] in order to preserve their party and this little Brahmana became the favourite of Suhabhatta. But Malanoddina[169], the great guru of the *yavanas*, feared that Ratnakara would rise in rebellion and caused him to be arrested. From the time that Malanoddina arrived in the kingdom which was then without *chamara* and umbrella, the desire of enjoyment did not leave Suhabhatta even in dream. But enjoyments are the fruits of austerities, and the vain desire of enjoyments was painful to Suhabhatta like the disease of the eye. The ministers attained or lost rank and honour according to the will of the powerful Suhabhatta, even as the duration of the seasons laden with fruits is under the control of the sun. When Shahikhana saw that wisdom and power were centered in one person, he became alarmed and anxious, and did not sleep. When he saw the serpent-like Suha with his poisonous appearance, he was surrounded by darkness which he could not illumine. Suhabhatta spent three or four years oppressing the twice-born, reviling the *Sastras*, thinking of rebellion and undergoing medical treatment for his disease. As if sent by the virtues of the people, and gathering strength from the sins of Suhabhatta, his consumption[169a], which defied treatment, withered him up. What could not the sun-jewel have effected if its fire had not been quenched at the rising of the moon when the moisture of the moon-jewel allays the heat of the earth? Why did he not live for another three or four years and witness in this world the effect of his own sins at the time when Shahikhana[170] rose to power.

## Shahikhan's rise

When Suhabhatta was living, Ladharaja had fled through fear, and Hamsa[171] and Gaura captured him after allowing him a little respite. But when Suha died they were incited by the lust of royal power to fight against each other, even as two bulls are attracted by a cow and engage themselves in breaking each other's horns. At the time when Ladharaja was released from prison by Hamsa, Gaurabhatta died in battle and gladdened the hearts of the celestial females. Fortune, ever moving as the elephant's ear, now abandoned her fickleness, and settled on Hamsa in the absence of a more deserving object, even as an unchaste woman clings to an old husband. But Shahikhana, though a boy, did not brook the pride of Hamsa, as the new moon does not brook the darkness increasing during the dark fortnight. The wise heir-apparent (Shahikhana) held a council of the Thakkuras[172], and killed in battle Hamsabhatta who had killed Ladharaja. The love of the people flowed towards Shahikhana as the water flows downwards. As black bees disregard the *kunda* flower and go to mango blossom, so the Royal Fortune felt a desire to embrace the heir-apparent, now flushed with victory. But the time had not yet come for the prince to be a king and Royal Fortune remained therefore in a state of suspense. Owing to the excessive love of the subjects which the prince enjoyed and owing also to his cleverness, the king bestowed on him the management of the kingdom out of affection. Then Merakamsara[173], the evil-minded Turushka, guided the powers of the prince as the iron rod guides an elephant blinded by madness. Men could not for a long time pollute the king's mind by dark and evil counsel, as the dark clouds cannot pollute the Manasa lake. The king was affectionate towards his devoted and able younger brother (the heir-apparent); and was also affectionate towards those who sought shelter with him; but urged by evil-minded men he became uneasy.

## The King's pilgrimage

The king at last wished to go on pilgrimage, and for the protection of the people he thus addressed the heir-apparent and his servants; "Wealth cannot be had because those who ask for it will be glad to have it; our mind becomes corrupt without meditation and without offerings to the dead, and our body becomes polluted without pilgrimages to holy places. I have placed the weight of the kingdom on you as on the world-supporting elephants, and am, like a second Ananta Naga, anxious to serve Narayana." Agitated with affection, as the sea with the Mandara[174] hill, Shahikhana replied to the king with this speech, sweet as the new moon, "Let thy untimely desire to go to pilgrimage, which is of doubtful good, abandon thee; rule thy subjects and thus win the sure gate to fame and virtue. If you, a warrior, cruelly leave this hereditary kingdom after having ruled it for a long time, it will be thought that you leave it for want of ability to rule. If you are anxious to go on pilgrimage, then what work shall be left to us, whose duty it is to serve you?" When the heir-apparent had thus expressed himself, the king of men made the following speech graced by his smile: "The little virtue that is earned by merely ruling the subject people is like a chemical compound composed of many components. You are like my arm though not joined to me in person; wherefore then should the people think of my incapacity when they behold your prowess? And if you do not carry out my order, my hopes which are placed on you will be at an end." The king said thus, and was resolved to go on pilgrimage, and after a long time made the heir-apparent accept the weight of the kingdom, and blessed him saying, 'Long may you reign under the name of Shri Jainollabhadina!'

## Alishah returns

In the hope of visiting holy places, the king went out of his own country, but not from the prince's heart which was blessed with love which like a bolt held fast the king. The prince gave out valuable jewels from the treasury, and beautiful horses, and for two nights he followed his brother. Wicked people spoke to the king on the way, about the troubles of the journey, the difficulty of attaining virtue, and the small merit of visiting shrines, and thus removed from the king's mind his respect for holy places. The proud king of Madra[175] (Jammu) thought of the reproach which his son-in-law (the king of Kashmira) would incur, (by going on pilgrimage), and caused him to return from the holy places of Hara.[175] When the autumn season, like a season of good luck arrived, the king of Madra took the king with him and returned to Kashmira. Glad at the return of his brother, but angry at the approach of the army of the ally[176], the king of Madra, Shahikhana became sunk in joy and displeasure at the same time. But the noble-minded prince cast aside his anger and, out[177] of his affection for his brother, gave up the kingdom. When the day expires, the sun gives up his radiance to the fire, and in the morning the fire returns it to the sun and becomes an object of praise, and worshippers pour on it the offering of new ghee during the day and thus increase its power. As the breeze carries with it the scent of flowers, even so the prince was accompanied by all the Thakkuras who were the lords of the country, and he went out of Kashmira. Left by the Thakkuras the army of Madra descended into Kashmira in peace, like a river without alligators.

The king Alishaha now ascended his wide ancestral throne, but did not win the hearts of good men. If the bright sun does not set, how can the moon with its visible spots ascend? When a powerless and feeble man is thoughtlessly raised to power by a warrior, he thinks the victory due to his own valour, and considers the universe as a blade of straw. As monkeys disturb a shady garden by breaking the branches of trees, so did the Turushkas[178], the servants of the king, disturb the kingdom. The *yavana* Merakamsara caused a commotion in the kingdom, unmindful of any discipline.

As the black bees pollute the closing lotus, so did this barbarian pollute the wives of the citizens, who were taken to him for his enjoyment. As mountain-elephants, with their long trunks, and blinded by madness, agitate and pollute a tank, so did the Turushkhas agitate the country and spread alarm. The people of Kashmira became possessed of Rakshasas who could not be prevented by the council of the ministers from doing evil, and who did not cease to oppress even in the day time. It is better for a kingdom to be without a king than with such a king. It is better for the ear to be without an ornament than with an iron pendant. Lofty houses, excellent horses, fine dresses, large gems,—all that adorned the king were now wrested by the *yavanas*. This inert king reigned for five or six months more, not through his merit, but through the fullness of the sins of the subjects. The smoke continues to cause injury and annoyance until the fire glows brighter and spreads its flame; the smoke withers flowers, obscures all sides, weakens the eyes, and intercepts the rays of the sun.

The king did not wish to repay the debt for the kingdom bestowed on him by Shri Shikandhara, but was anxious to increase his fortune, and urged by envy towards Mahendra, the lord of the Khuhkhuras[179] sent messengers to Shahikhana and asked him to come away to his own country. If the alligator[180] did not come out of the water, and the crow did not leave the lofty tree, and the rat did not quit his hole in the forest, how could these be killed? The king, in his anger, marched against Jasratha for giving shelter to the heir-apparent who was hostile to the king. The king was eager to overcome Jasrath, the chief among the strong, and his eagerness was not checked by his ministers whose influence was overshadowed by that of the *mlechhas*. The envoys and those who profited by dissensions informed the king by letters of the rising prosperity of the heir-apparent, and increased by their advice his eagerness for battle. The monarch was flattered by the *yavanas* who hoped to obtain his favour, but his soldiers lost courage at the triumph of the heir-apparent and they became alarmed and blamed the king's attempt.

## Ali Shah's exit

As the king of Kashmira marched, the sun shone against him, and the chiefs who were friendly to him did not join him. The *mlechhas'* army, maddened with pride, saw darkness personified in the dust that was raised by them. The king became furious and caused Rajapuri and other countries, which he should have taken under his protection, to be harassed by plunder, as if they had been his enemy's territories. When the king arrived at a place named Mudgaravyala[181], the king of Madra, who was very powerful, sent him the following message: "Though in your camp there be infantry possessed of wealth, and swift horses, and warriors skilled in fight, yet be not confident in your war against the world-renowned artifices of the Khuhkhuras. We know their artifices in battle, for serpents, not others, know the ways of serpents. So long as we do not come to your help, you should remain stationary in the mountains." But blinded by pride, the wicked chief of the *yavanas* believed that the king of Madra had sent the message in order to gain renown for himself. The foolish king then descended from the hill, as from his high dignity, and his banners waved in the air as if they trembled in fear of the army of the king of Khuhkhuras. By the charge of the cavalry, the earth was filled with dust, and Vasuki[182] was overwhelmed with fear. The sandy ground was dug up by the hoofs of the horses and drenched in blood; and the warriors sacrificed their lives in battle in their valour. As the waves in the sea break the force of the air, so in this sea of battle the king was overpowered[183] by misfortune.

## Zain-ul-Abdin assumes power (1420 A.D.)

Brahma displays his mercy by bidding the sun rise when the world is merged in darkness, by causing the advent of the spring when the joys of the earth are destroyed by the cold wind of winter, and by sending a perfect and blameless king when the world is disturbed with fear by a wicked king. The sinless Shri Jainollabhadina, flushed with success, entered Kashmira like propitious Fate. This king called forth words of praise from the lips of good people, and filled all sides with the sound of the kettledrum, and entered the capital, but not before he had entered into the hearts of the people. When the king bathed during his coronation, the minds of his subjects were washed clean; and when he displayed his royal umbrella, the power of his enemies became still. His wise policy was like the sugar in the juice of the sugarcane, and it removed the people's thirst for the good kings of old. The king revived the disregarded laws of previous kings, as the spring revives the plants destroyed by the winter. His prowess and his wise policy vied with each other in overcoming his enemies who were hard to subdue; and sometimes his prowess and sometimes his policy prevailed. Beauty dwelt in his person, and the goddess of learning on his lips. Fortune rested in his breast, and patience in his mind; and when Fame saw this, she spread his reputation afar. The king's virtuous mode of government in the *kaliyuga* became glorious like the very middle of the *satyayuga*. The younger brother of the king of Kashmira named Shri Mahat[184] Madakhana became his partner in royalty, his councillor in matters of policy and a judge in the investigation of the *shastras*. What more need be said of Shri Mahat Madakhana than that through the king's influence he became like the king, save only that he had not the royal umbrella[185] and *chamara*. What the spring is to Cupid, what the master's favourite is to other servants, that was the king of the Khuhkhuras to the monarch, the most beloved of all who served him.

## The King's virtues

As the fruit of his obtaining the kingdom, the king thought it proper to abolish evil practices from the country ruined by the *mlechhas*;

whereupon his favourite officers awarded to the oppressors the punishment that was due to them fearlessly, openly, and without asking for the king's orders. The king sowed the seeds of fame on all sides, planted prosperity in good men and happiness in the people, and then uprooted his enemies. In this way he reversed the usual agricultural process (of uprooting wild plants first, and sowing and planting afterwards). The sun is always powerful, and the moon is always mild, and as if to surpass them at once, the king combined both these qualifications in himself. How shall I describe all his innumerable virtues in this condensed narrative? Can the king of the elephants find room in the hole of the jackal? I therefore paint his virtues in a picture, or as the sun is reflected in a mirror. As the cold and the heat are of equal power in the early parts of summer, or as the days and nights are equal when the sun is in the equinox so the king looked with equal eyes on his own as on others. As the traders do not allow any inequality in their deals, so the king did not brook inequality (in his administration). As the lion does not attack other animals in the peaceful hermitage of saints, so the Turushkas who were much alarmed, did not now oppress the Brahmanas as they had done before. Brilliant as the sun, the king bestowed his favours on men of merit (Brahmanas) whose very existence had been endangered by the moonlike Suha, the very source of evil. Possessed of merit and appreciating merit in others, the king encouraged learning; and the stream of learning which had run downward, like a canal which breaks through a gap, now began to flow smoothly once more. He was the destroyer of evils, and he preserved by various means the good usages of Kashmira, even as a physician helps our digestive functions by medicines. As if to purify the earth polluted by the touch of Suhabhatta, the king kindled the fire of his prowess which lighted up the great firmament. He pursued his policy in five different ways, and his enemies, as if to defeat his purpose, dissolved themselves into the five elements (died). To praise him for having conquered his external foes, would be to reproach a monarch who had conquered the ever present internal foes (the passions).

Though great in his strength, the king of the world undertook expeditions only when there was an enemy to overcome. The sun marches through the sky only to overcome the moon and stars. Powerful as he was, he did not wish to conquer others for the thirst of wealth; the lion does not kill elephants for the sake of meat. His enemies in the hilly regions were subjected, as if for their purification, to five fires, *viz.* - the sun, the forest fire, the king's prowess, the fire of grief, and the fire of fatigue. Although a dweller of this earth the king never went astray, even as the moon when full never rises but when the night begins. The politic king levied taxes[186] from his poor subjects that they might not perish through their pride. The fame of his enemies along with their Royal Fortune, sacrificed herself in the fire of the king's prowess at the extinction of their own.

Once upon a time Jasratha, oppressed by the king of Dhilli[187], took shelter under the king, and he protected him as the mountain protects darkness in its caves from the sun.

## Dispenses justice

During the time when this restrainer of the wicked ruled the country, there lived a Brahmana at Jayapidapura. He had a cow which was the very embodiment of the hope of the gods. The cow once broke away from him and fled, either in quest of corn in villages, or by the will of fate. The Brahmana went to Madavarajya to bathe at the shrine, and there recognised his cow, the marks of which animal he knew. He knew that the cow was his and he followed the animal in the evening and quarreled with the master of the house to which it went. The master of the house was urged by cupidity, and the Brahmana was certain that the animal was his, so their quarrel did not cease, and they took their dispute before the king's court. There they were unable to meet each other's arguments, and the king threw some water-nuts before the cow in order to test their claims. The cow had been accustomed to eat the nuts in its younger days, it smelled them and ate them with alacrity like fruits; but its calves did not eat them for a long time. The people who had not been able to determine the case, praised the skill of the king, and the king caused the pretender to be punished by the twice-born, even as one deserving of punishment is punished.

## Judges restrained

Though the king was kind-hearted, yet for the sake of his people he would not forgive even his son, or a minister, or a friend if he were guilty. Mereshya[188] the *yavana* was once drunk and killed his wife without any fault, and though he was the king's favourite, yet the king caused him to be executed. He who was like Indra on earth humiliated his enemies and honoured those who were saintly and wise. He was graced with power, kindness and wisdom in a greater degree than any other king that had reigned before. Cupid causes *apachita* (suffering) to parted lovers, but the king who was graceful as Cupid paid *apachita* (honours) to the wise. Beauty and fierceness were blended in the king. Where except in these can be seen both poison and nectar, both water and fire together? Judges used to take money from the plaintiffs and the defendants since a long time, but the practice was disallowed by the good and virtuous king.

## Forgery uncovered

There was a Brahmana named Laularaja who for some reason sold a plot of level land out of ten pieces which he possessed, and the sale was effected in writing. Laularaja died in the year of sale after telling his young son Nonaraja and others of the transaction. Nonaraja and the others were weak, and consequently the powerful purchasers took possession of the other nine plots though they were not sold. They were powerful and for a long time kept possession of the ten plots, but in order to secure them legally they forged entries in the document. Before the time of this king who was a careful judge, they had caused the words 'ten pieces of level land have been sold' to be written by Nonaraja's son. I was in the court, and was grieved that the land was thus forcibly taken possession of. Then by the king's orders the litigants brought the document written on *bhurja* and the judicious king read it and threw it in water. The newly written letters were effaced and the old ones remained showing that 'one piece of level land had been sold'. The king then caused it to be read by his courtiers. Thus the king's fame spread on all sides. I obtained some lands, the forgerer received severe punishment, the subjects were happy and the wicked remained in fear.

## Boil heals

The moon, when full, is sometimes afraid of Rahu; the cloud which gives rain sometimes strikes us with terror and hurls thunderbolts on trees; and even so the Creator, who creates good men for the delight of the world, sometimes causes apprehension by sending disease. At one time a poisonous boil gave much pain to the king in his forearm, and to his subjects in their hearts. As flowers are not obtainable in the month Magha on account of the mischief caused by snow, even so physicians who knew about poisons could not, at that time, be found in the country owing to the oppression of the *mlechhas*. The servants of the king at last found out Shivabhatta[189] who knew the antidotes of poisons, and who performed religious sacrifices, even as travellers discover a well in a desert. He was well-versed in the art of healing, but out of fear of the *mlechhas* he, for a long time, delayed to come. When he arrived, the king gave him encouragement and he completely cured the king of the poisonous boil, even as an elephant uproots a poisonous tree. When that boil was healed, the fame of the physician increased with the comfort of the king, and the gladness of the people. The king was pleased and gave him much wealth. But Shivabhatta did not look at wealth, even as a man who has conquered his passions does not look at beautiful women. He spent the gold and silver in payment of fines by which the twice-born preserved the purity of their caste.

The king caused rest houses for travellers to be built at the outskirts of villages, and they were supported by the villages; and he caused shelters to be built within forests. The buildings raised for the goddess of death at every place appeared to laugh at Suhabhatta. Thus the king, with unabated kindness, saved the world oppressed by the *mlechhas*, even as Narayana saved the world oppressed by the Danavas.[190] The king humbled those who were high and raised up the lowly, and he thus levelled the world in order to sow the seed of his fame. The king had vowed not to touch the wives of others, but he broke the vow when he embraced the goddess of Fortune who had belonged to others before.

## Patronises non-Muslims

Then the king, who had gone through all the circumstances of life, and who knew all things, placed Tilakacharyya, the Buddhist, in the highest position. Shivabhatta, Tilaka and Simha the astrologer became the steps by which Brahmanas rose to appointments. As the *kokila* increases his passion by tasting the juice of fruits, even so the king developed his finer sentiments by serving the principal Brahmanas. Shrimana Karpurabhatta, the preserver of lives (physician), drew men of worth into the celebrated court of the king by his merit. Ruyyabhatta could, without the labour of calculation, but merely observing the course of the planets in the past year, know their position in the year to come. At times Shri Ramananda's[191] explanation of steam in the country of Darada....

## Overlord

The kings[192] of Gandhara, Sindhu, Madra and Adri of this king. At this time the king of Khukhuras defeated and captured Maladeva the king of Madra, but the king caused him to be released. The king, the king of Rajapuri*** soon opposed the march of Ranasuha and caused him to roll on the ground.

The king of Udabhandapura, though supported by the king of Sindhu, was repeatedly overthrown by the king like a pebble, and was then cast down. Once upon a time the king dyed his arrows in the hot blood of the people in the Gogga country[193] in the land of the Bhauttas; and he pleased his own people by his virtues. Having won the battle in the country of Shaya[194], the king saved the golden image of Buddha from the *yavanas* by issuing severe orders. The power of the king was like a test-stone for the power of the Bhauttas. The king destroyed the beauty of the city of Luta.[195] The hearts of the Bhauttas which were empty, were filled with the fear of the king, but their treasury where wealth had been accumulated since a long time remained empty. The kind hearted king, though engaged in endless wars, made due enquiries after his subjects, even as a cultivator does after the *shali* crop. His bow was unable to brook equality with the bow of Narayana or of Mahadeva, but it was not much used, as his work was accomplished from a distance.

## Punishes the guilty

Nosrata, son of Laddaraja, had been favoured by the king but was now sent into exile, though his wealth was not confiscated, as the king considered him to be a rebel. A *yavana* named Sadaula[196] came from the country of Makka (Mecca) and arrived before the king bringing with him many books. The king loved men of merit and he appeared before him, but the man was boasting of his own qualifications. * * * The judicious sovereign soon perceived that the man was as void of qualifications as a drum is empty within. But that sea of mercy, that lord of the life of the world, did not withdraw his favour from the vain Sadaula, although void of merit, even as the father does not withdraw his affection from his son. Like the darkness of the night, and like nocturnal lightning, the many vices of this wicked man frightened the people.

At this time, a great hermit who had conquered his passions seated himself on a high pillar in order to obtain emancipation by the practice of *yoga*. For nine days he sat on the pillar with closed eyes and without food, and by his blessing the queen gave birth to a son. Thus he sat there at *yoga*, and on the ninth day, the great festivity on account of the birth of the prince took place. Sadaula became jealous at seeing the hermit constantly favoured and, having lost his senses by intoxication from wine, he killed the hermit by arrows with the help of *mlechhas*. At the sight of the deed, the warm and sorrowful tears of the people fell on the ground, and their censure fell on the king. When the king heard of the act, he drowned himself, as if for purifying his person, in the sea of fear, shame, anger, and surprise, and in the thought of what he should do. On that day, when his first son was born, the king did not bathe, nor eat, nor speak, nor do anything. On the next day the king consulted his religious guide and learned men versed in law, and he learnt that Sadaula deserved to be killed. Sadaula was not killed, owing to king's kindness, but the king ordered him to ride on an ass with his face towards the tail, and to be led about every market place, his beard unkempt and drenched, his head shaved, every one booing at him, and his hands tied with the entrails of the dead man. The punishment was like death to him though he was alive; and pure flowers from heaven which perfumed all sides fell on the king as well as the blessings of the citizens, for this act of justice.

Like Dashratha, the king had four[197] sons given unto him, and they were the delight of the people, and were born of the two daughters of the king of Madra. The eldest was named Adamakhana, the second Hajyakhana, the younger ones were named Jassarathakhana and Baheramakhana.

## Public works

The Mandara hill churned the sea of cream, and recovered the nectar and the precious stones, which were lying useless before, and brought them to use by bestowing them on proper persons. That Mandara hill, worthy of praise, is the king of the mountains. Even like him the king obtained wonderful fame by joining a waterfall to a stream, and the rivers which had been dry became filled with water. The king caused the canal which ran along the field to be extended to the lands at Utpalpura[198] and he thus made both the canal and the lands useful. He caused a canal to be carried down to the desert of Nandashaila[199], and thus made the people think of the Chakradhara in the midst of the sea. This beneficent king held high his unsullied fame and made the country of Karala a theme of praise by means of a canal. In Karala[200], the king built Jainapuri where the Brahmanas had their rent-free villages, and where women had necklaces. The king, whose history is pleasant, caused a canal to be constructed in the lands of Avantipura, and the canal was rich in shali crop. When the water of the Ganges was made to unite by a mountain channel with the Manasa lake[201], was the water of the Ganges[202] purified by that of Manasa lake, or the Manasa lake purified by the water of the Ganges? The king embellished the Manasa lake by building a town[203] on its side, and its image was reflected on the lake and looked as if it were another town. This prosperous king connected Suyyapura[204] with the bank of the Vitasta, and thus removed the great trouble which the land had experienced from heat. He built Jainanagari[205], rich with *mathas*, provided with rent-free lands for Brahmanas, and with market places, extending from Pradyumma hill to Amareshapura. That town with its high stone-built houses of the Nagas, was reflected on the Jainaganga[206], as if it rose from the water to conquer the heaven. The pious king of unsullied fame, forgot the joys of worshipping the feet of Hari in the favour of the god Ranasvami and Jainaganga. On the other side of Suyyapura, he built a town named Snanagiri[207] and adorned with houses, it became equal to Kailasa hill. The king whose fame had extended on all sides and was widely known, and who had subdued his enemies, built a royal city named Siddhipuri at Siddhakshetra[208], in Sureshvari; and above the palace he built the two temples of Martanda and Amaranatha which illumined the distant sky. In former times, Suyyaraja[209] had sought to increase the prosperity of the country. Since then several kings had passed away, but owing to the poverty of the people's virtue, there was not the least increase; nor did plenty put forth twigs, or flowers or fruits by the strength of religious penance. But owing to the purity of the religious penance of Shri Jainollabhadina, prosperity was soon attained; or how else could the prosperity be accounted for? When the virtues of the previous kings had worn off, they fell, but this king (so multiplied his acts of merit) by obtaining this kingdom, as to secure another in the next life. The land was previously dependent on the rain (for its crops), but the king made it dependent on the river; and he granted rent free lands to Brahmanas, At *Barahakshetra*, Vijaya[210] (Kshetra) and Ishanaka[211] the great king opened houses of charity and thereby caused even Indra to tremble. In places where lands were sold the king opened offices in order to note the sale on *bhurja* bark, so that the sale might not be subsequently denied.

## Precious minerals

King Jayapida had, by the favour of the Nagas, discovered a hill of copper[212], and the hill yielded him that metal as a tribute. During this reign, the earth gave out from its mines jewels such as are difficult to be found, and such as humble the pride of the ruby. These jewels are known by the name of Jainamani[213]. During this reign the people collected from the sandy banks of rivers gold which humbled the pride of talc and which resembled turmeric in color. Pressed by the people the king caused an order to be inscribed on a copper plate to the effect that future kings should take only a sixth part of the gold obtained from rivers. The Damara Kacha, superintendent of the capital, built in the city a stone bridge one *krosha*[214] in length, on the road which was difficult to traverse. Thus the virtuous king not only raised himself from mire, but delivered all men within the city from mud by the construction of the bridge. Shivabhatta[215] built large mathas in various localities, and the other ministers of the king also built many religious houses. As two powerful elephants, elated with pride, are ever ready to agitate the water in a tank, and in their madness fight with their trunks and perish within a short time, even so Sayedha[216] and Shura, born of the same family, sons of the king's nurse, were unable to brook each other's prosperity, and endeavoured to do harm to each other. The king, however, assuaged their anger, and they felt affection and kindness towards each other; but they killed a man (as described below), and prepared themselves for a commotion. Masoda Thakkura was pierced, in presence of the king, by the taunts of Shura, which were sharp as arrows, and casting away his weapons went unarmed at night, attended by a limited number of followers; Shura finding him in a defenceless condition killed him. His brother, Vinna Thakkura, celebrated for his valour, demanded permission from the kind-hearted king to kill Shura. The Thakkura then killed Shura with his followers, and thus increased his fame and relieved his mind.

## Respect for saints

The king honoured the saints to such an extent that even the king of Madra and others attended on them like dogs. The king took his instructions about religious penances and about the pleasures of life from both superior and inferior hermits, and gave them ear-pendants, vessels of gold, and clothes, Indra, the conqueror of the three worlds, is not satisfied with the fame he acquired by cutting off the wings of mountains, by obscuring the sun in clouds, and by performing a hundred religious sacrifices, but he also displays in unsubstantial clouds, composed of smoke, air, and water the lustre of his person in varied tints-yellow, white, black, red and green. Likewise, the king who appreciated courage desired, for the sake of obtaining fame, to perform what was beyond the power of the past sovereigns, and what will be beyond the ability of future kings. Time is endless, and great is the expanse of the world, so that some future kings in some distant country may believe it possible for them to perform such worthy and enterprising acts, and accomplish deeds which may almost rival his. The king was not pleased to hear of the deeds of enterprise achieved by past kings in inaccessible mountains or lakes. And as the poet arranges words according to the sound, so did the king act according to the advice of merchants in pursuit of wealth. The king was anxious to make oblations to the fire, and leaving all other thoughts aside, he heard Nilapurana[217] and other *Sastras* read by the *panditas*.

## The Wular lake

For a long time the king had conceived that this world was to the universe what the face is to the body, that Kashmira was the principal portion of this world as the eyes are of the face, and that the line of mountains around were like eyelashes. Inside, like the eyeball, was located the Mahapadma[218] lake where large lotuses grew, and like the * * * if the lake could be filled up and gradually built upon by any means, the kingdom * * * This prince of lakes whose fathom less waters extended over twenty eight kroshas, like the great purpose of great men * * * In order to accomplish his purpose the king went by a boat to the middle of the lake, even as a *yogi* attains the Supreme Soul by means of his own * * * Previous kings did not go to the great Mahapadma lake constantly agitated by waves through fear that the boat might be demolished. It was either by the power of penance, or by his patience, or on account of the greatness of his aim, that the king moved in the waters of the lake as easily as he would on land. What the mind can conceive can be worked out after a time; but what the ordinary mind cannot conceive is possible to genius alone. The good king could not at first settle what to do, but he at last devised means to convert the lake into land. He thought of filling up that lake, by conveying stones in carts and throwing them into it one above another, even as a sea is filled up by peaks of mountains. The wagons if built of pine planks with iron clasp, would not, he thought, break or wear off.

The eager king then returned and sought the help of old men, and they came to him. As the Sudarshana *chakra* encircles Dvarika[219], even so was the peaceful capital of this king encircled by these men. The presiding god of his city, the serpent lord, Mahapadmanaga protected the people of the four castes as if they were his sons * * * It was owing to the influence of the *kaliyuga* that the people of the country followed evil practices day by day and yet prospered. * * * Then as the fruit of their evil practices, and owing to adverse fortune, the lord of the Nagas[220] became angry, even as a good man does on receiving an offence. In a dream he said to a potter who had not left off his good usages that he would drown the citizens who had adopted evil practices. When the potter told the people in the morning that the Naga would drown them for their evil practices, he was laughed at by all the citizens, as if he was an irrational beast. Then the Naga agitated the lake by his hundred hoods and the roar of the water seemed like that of an enemy who had surrounded the city. Then the Brahmanas chanted their incantations and bowed to the Nagas, and boys began to cry; but like the king of death the king of the Nagas neither felt fear nor pity. The boys clasped the necks of their mothers in fear and the mothers shed tears as if they worshipped the lord of the Nagas with pearls. (As the water rose), the children got up from the feet of their mothers to the lap, then to their shoulders, and then to their head, and finally departed from them even as life departs from the body; and the agitated water of the inundation clasped the trembling limbs of the women like a lover. It covered everything, small and large, thin and thick, little and great, and spread itself over all like darkness. The lord of the Nagas, unable to brook the touch of the wicked who were drowned in that fathomless water, stayed like a good man in the woods. Kaliya was the name of the lord of the Nagas, and his head when pressed by the feet of Narayana received the impression of the feet, and hence he obtained the name of Mahapadma.

## An artificial island

The king heard some one telling him in a dream that he was an incarnation of Narayana and that his purpose to reconstruct Kashmira which lay in ruin would be fulfilled. For a short time he revolved in his mind as to how he could accomplish the work. The Naga did not refrain from punishing the city for the evil practices of the people; why should a great being like him put with a wrong when even an inferior being does not. Thus informed by the lord of the Nagas (in a dream) the king thought to himself that he would raise the land like an umbrella and make it beautiful as a jewelled cup * * * *

In that great land which would be raised in the midst of the billowy lake, in that holy and lonely spot, the hermits would attain emancipation. With stones carried in strong wagons the king filled up the centre of the billowy lake which was fathomless before. When the middle of the lake became land the king built on it * * Jainalanka * * * It was on the extremity of this very lake that king Jayapida[221] had raised land by the help of the king of the Rakshasas. If in the dewy season the lotus plants, the water nuts, and the *kavuka* plants be uprooted, the foundation of Shri Jayapidakota can be seen in the bottomless gulf. On the margin of the billowy lake were Suyyakundalaka and many other villages with traces of large houses.

## Township built

The king now built the rich town of Jainalanka in a deep part of the lake where even hills would be drowned, and he appointed a superintendent of the town * * * Ruyyabhanda, a man of beaming intelligence, decorated the palace gates * * * At Kramarajya he built Suratranapura[222] graced with houses that humbled the pride of the peaks of the Himalaya. The king, who had subdued his enemies, built Jainakotta[223] with houses all around and adorned with silk banners above the buildings. It was through the king's orders and by the intelligence of Ruyyabhanda that dilapidated buildings were repaired and new ones constructed. On the margin of the Mahapadma lake the king, whose epithet was Jaina, built two towns named Jainakundala[224] and Jainapattana; and there were planted the creeping fennel which bore tender leaves and beautiful roots, and by which the towns were adorned. O! how mild were even the punishments which he inflicted, tempered as they were with mercy; for without killing the Domba thieves, or fastening their hands in chains, and subjecting them to constant beating * * * The king forbade the killing of birds and fish in several tanks and spread his fame on all sides.

Once upon a time the king came to know that thieves had stolen a cow, and the owner lamented its loss. The king after questioning the man caused the thieves to be brought in; but the truthful Brahmana could not state the age of the animal or describe the marks on it, and he thus caused regret to the court. He only stated that the cow had bent horns. The thief addressed the king and said that as it was natural for the human body to have moles, so it was natural for a cow's horns to be bent. The king asked (the verdict of the court), but the court remained silent. The king then, with a view to examine (the animal), applied some contrivance on the horns by which he exposed the artifice of the thief and refuted his plea about the crookedness of the horns. The ministers who composed the court of justice were elated with joy by this fine judgement of the king. The chief judge Gauraka the Gnanapati pleased the people by his forgiveness, his good sense and the dispensation of equitable punishment, and imposed upon himself the king's duty of ruling the subjects. Some men had bribed Malvana Mallanasaka[226] and had received favours from him; but after a lapse of time they became ungrateful and disclosed in court the amount of gold they had paid as bribe. Upon this the king became angry and caused Malvana Mallanasaka to restore the amount to them.

Daryyavakhana had first seated himself at the feet of the king, then went hand in hand with him, then placed himself before his eyes, and finally reached his head. The grateful king had purchased this man (as slave), and bore him even as Mahadeva bears on his forehead the crescent of the moon which sheds soft light. The sun does not dispel the darkness which settles on the world under the cover of the cloud-like night; but it is dispelled by the moon which reflects the sun. Wearied[227] with the weight of the kingdom and ever exposed to danger from the sword, the king felt a relief at the sight of the riches which he had himself bestowed. The talented[228] Mahmadakhana now died. Where do we see length of life in those who are agreeable to others? This truthful and prosperous Thakkura who every year ministered through the Pratihara[229] and others to the wants of those who came to beg, now went to heaven. He was openly murdered by one of his own family whom the king had exiled from his own country and who came on the pretence of delivering a message. Enfeebled by journeys to places of pilgrimage, Vinna[230] returned to the town of Sou (dha?) where the king's tolls were collected on articles brought from the Sindhu country, and there he died. At this time, the great Shri Shivabhatta[231] who superintended the king's courts of justice, also went to heaven (died). Though these men died, the king's acts of virtue did riot decrease. The elephants who prop the four sides are but as pageants to the serpent who really supports the world. In one day, the king distributed one koti of dinaras[232] to the boys through Jayyabhatta.

A collection of wonderful things was made in the kingdom during the reign of this king, otherwise how could he be the incarnation of Narayana? He planted the country round Marttanda with sugarcane, compared to the juice of which the nectar that flows from the moon is poor as a beggar. On account of the greatness of his *yoga*, Shri Jainallabhadina escaped wrinkles and white hair incident to old age, and displayed the faculties of a god. He made *** the river[233] which flows into Bharosa, and which injured his power and wealth.

Here ends the second *Rajatarangini* by Jonaraja.

## References

1. Gonanda: Yudhistra, the Pandava king, is assumed to have ascended the throne in the year 653 of the Kali era. On the basis of an earlier version of the *Nilamatapurana* (now lost) which was available to him, Kalhana believes Gonanda I, the first king of Kashmir mentioned by him, to have been a contemporary of the Kaurvas and the Pandavas.
2. Kali Yuga : the iron age regarded to have commenced in 3012 B.C. for 432,000 years.
3. Jayasimha: Kalhana's contemporary, ruled Kashmir during 1128-55 A.D. Sempore village near Zevan owes its name to him.
4. Jainollabhadena: Zain-ul-Abdin, Sultan of Kashmir 1420-70 A.D.
5. Shri Shiryyabhatta (S.K.) ... Sanskrit was regarded as 'elaborated, refined, cultured and civilised'.

6. An essential ingredient in the cookery of Kashmiris.
7. Sussala, Jayasimha's father, ruled Kashmir during 1112-28 A.D. with the exception of the year 1120-21 when Bhikshachara was on the throne.
8. Trigarta: a part of the territory of Punjab watered by the three rivers Ravi, Beas and Satluj. Cunningham identified it with the Jullundar *doab* and Kangra with its fort at Nagarkot.
9. The term *yavana* is used frequently by Jonaraja and his successors for foreigners. According to PH many princes of upper Panjab, including Jaisimha of Kashmir, joined hands to oppose the advance of a general of Chengez Khan who invaded India in A.H. 545.
10. *Malla* (also as Malchander or Mulchander) built a castle at Gaganger in the Sindh valley, about 60 km from Srinagar.
11. Use of incantations, charms and black magic has been frequently mentioned by Kalhana and his successors.
12. Year 30: *i.e.*, year 4230 of the Saptrishi era. Christian era started when the Saptarishi (or Laukika) era was 3075 years, 8 months and 19 days old.
13. Bhishayaka/Bhishyakapura: identity with Bachhapore has been suggested.
14. Vartideva: Vantideva (SK).
15. Kalhana mentions several instances of election of kings in Kashmir, including Sandhimat and Yasashkara (A.D. 938-48).
16. Vopyadeva: Vopadeva (SK).
17. Sureshvari: a shrine on a crag above the village Ishabar where goddess Durga was worshipped. Several nobles including the king Patvagupta (949-50 A.D.) retired to the shrine in anticipation of death.
18. Lavanyas: a powerful clan of king-makers. Jona refers to the 'terrible devastation' caused by Lavanyas, later known as Lones.
19. Madhava: Vishnu or his incarnation Krishna.
20. Gunarahula: Gunakarahula (SK); Krahala (PH).
21. umbrella, etc.: insignia of sovereignty.
22. Rajjupura: several villages bear the name Rajpur or Rajapur and it is not possible to identify the site of Jagadev's temple.
23. Dvara: a mountain pass leading into Kashmir. These 'gates' or entrances were kept under strict watch and the high officers charged with guarding these passes were designated as *dvarpati* or *dvaresha*, *i.e.*, lord of the gate. The most important stations were at Baramulla, village Drang at the foot of the Tosamaidan pass and the Pir Pantsal pass beyond Herapur. Padma had been raised to the office of the lord of the gate.
24. Kashthavata: Kishtwar in Doda dt.
25. Salhana: the fort existed at the village Seer in Khovurpur in Anantnag Tehsil (PH). Its identification with Solina, near Haftchinar, is doubtful.

26. Baladhyachandra: grandson of Mulchandra. Baladhyamatha later known as Balandimar was near Maharajganj. Also known as Malechhmar or Malchimar later. Bates places it at the north-west end of the town.
27. Khasha tribe: inhabitants of the hilly areas outside the Vy of Kashmir to the S. and W. of the Pir Panchal range.
28. The cry 'I am not a Bhatta...' was again raised during the reign of Haidershah (A.D. 1470-2). Kashmiri Pandits are referred to as 'Bhattas' locally.
29. Vimalacharya: Jumalacharya (PH) was granted an estate in Jamalnagar in Arvani (PH). The year 950 Saka appears doubtful; Saka 1913 corresponds to A.D. 1991.
30. Rajoloka: Ruzul v. to the S. of Panzath in Ver Pargana.
31. Shamala: Hamal, in Kupwara Dist. It was a stronghold of Damaras who frequently revolted against the central authority. Now renamed Rafiabad. PH regards Tunga as lord of Skardu.
32. Rajapuri: Rajauri.
33. Damaras: class of feudal landowners who played an effective role in political
34. Domvas: Doombs were originally engaged as watchmen for villages but became unruly later, and sometimes anti-social.
35. Vijaycshvara: Bijbehara, where a temple of great sanctity dedicated to Vijayeshvara, the lord of Victory, existed from ancient times, takes its name from the shrine. According to Stein, Ks. *bror*, 'god' is derived from Skrt. Bhattarka, corresponding to Ishvara. The town was built around the shrine by Vijaya who succeeded Tunjina to the throne. According to the *Nil-n.* (v. 1353) 'one attains the world of Rudra and saves one's family by taking bath in the Vitasta in front of the Vijayeshvara shrine'. The present temple was built by Maharaja Ranbir Singh (1857-1885 A.D.).
36. Year 28: year 4328 of the Saptarishi era, *i.e.*, A.D. 1252.
37. Salara: in Dachinpur on the way from Bijbehara to Pahalgam. The fort was built by Sangramdeva (PH).
38. Ledari: river Ledar.
39. Utpalpora: at the site of the present Kakapur on the left bank of the Jhelum founded by Utpala, grandfather of Avantivarman (855-83 A.D.). Sangramdeva overcame Tunga in Hamal pargana.... Bhishyakapora: See n. 13 above.
40. Samudramatha: later known as Sadramar (from Samudramar), near Habakadal on the right side of the Jhelum.
41. Six branches of learning/schools of philosophy: *Nyaya, Vaisheshika, Sankkya, Yoga, Purvamimansa* and *Vedanta*... Mahila: Ahala (SK). Obviously the present Ahlamar is meant.
42. Khajjala: Kuchhal, a sorcerer from outside took his residence at the foot of the Shankaracharya hill, beguiled many among the

simple-minded Kashmiris and created serious disturbance till Sangramchander, son of Balladhyachander, mobilised his troops to crush him (PH). Some others identify him with Khajlak, the Mongol, who invaded Delhi in A.D. 1287 (SK).

43. Dhyanoddara: presumed to be in the eastern part of the Valley. Probably an *udar* known locally as *karewa* or upland.
44. Iddagali: Kularaja, the city prefect during the reign of Jayasimha (1128-55 A.D.) abolished the fine which was levied on householders when a married woman of the family was found guilty of immoral conduct (RT. viii-3336). But he punished people for 'carnal intercourse' with dancing girls who had become wedded wives. PH states that the king felt extremely gratified at the enchanting display of the art of dancing by Iddagali and revoked the order as a boon to her.
45. Panchgahvara: valley in Poonch dt. – upper catchment area of the Ans. Garbharpura is identified with Gabbar in the same area.
46. Noble family "should read: ... Kurushaha was bom of the noble family of Babravahana".
47. Enamukhi: Shamsdenamukhi (SK): 'foremost among them, Shams-ud-Din, would rule'.
48. Taharaja: Tahralo (SK): Tahir Shah.
49. Shahmir came to Kashmir from the Panchagahvara area. Some later historians have tried to trace his descent from the Pandva hero Arjuna. Sahadeva bestowed on him an estate in Daraver in Kruhin pga. (PH) which stretches from Gulmarg to the Wular in Baramula dt. and is drained by Ningalnala. Probably one of his ancestors was named Pandav.
50. Year 89 (*i.e.* Saptarishi era 4389) *i.e.* 1313 A.D.
51. Dalacha: the name has been spelt as Zuluchu, Julju, Zulqadr Khan, Dalchu, Dalcha etc., by later historians. He appears to have been a Mongol leader.
52. Fasting: Kalhana mentions numerous instances when Brahmins resorted to collective fasting to exert pressure on kings. Brahmin leaders were occasionally bribed to scuttle such fasts.
53. Kalamanya Bhottas: pb. the ruling family of Ladakh at the time. Some writers identify the Kalamanyas with the Khurmang tribe of the Baltis. (PH).
54. Vyala, Tukka...: Bhautea supporters of Rinchana, son of Bakatanya (Vakatanya) of Ladakh. Rinchana descended upon the Valley via Sonamarg.
55. A good military road: Tarabala route (SK)—a pass through the mts. of Devasar pga. which led to Vishalata identified by Stein with the vy. of the Bichlari r., south of Devasar (ref. pp. 39, 147 & 178). Should read '...having destroyed the country and its gods and afraid of .... went out by the Tarabala route ....'
56. Mountain that touched the sky: Gaganger, which is also the fort of Lahara or Lar. The trslr. has paraphrased the name.

57. Ramachandra, son of Sangramchandra, a descendant of Mulchandra, had his ancestral castle at Gaganger. Rinchana and Shahmir carried out his orders and overcame the Khasas who had overrun Maraz, or the southern districts. Rinchana killed Ramchandra treacherously inside the castle and seized power. PH names the castle Andrakot.
58. Breast: Some historians state that having married Kotadevi, daughter of Ramachandra, Rinchana conferred a very high office on her brother Ravanchandra.
59. Mandala: Paramandal in Khovurpur, Lidar vy.
60. Surtrana: Sultan, King. He permitted traditional festivities to win over people.
61. Achchhoda lake: lake with clear water. Identity uncertain
62. Takka/Tukka: Durgappa in Tibetan (PH). He was the leader of the Tibetians of Shukalankita dynasty who conspired to kill Rinchana.
63. Vanabal: Vanavale (SK): a v. of this name exists near Sgr. but the identity cannot be certain. RNS suggests Baravul in Sindh vy. as the place, but it is far from the Vitasta.
64. Vyalaraja: Vyala. Playing with names thus often creates confusion.
65. Udyandeva, brother of Suhadeva, had taken refuge in the Kabul kingdom of Gandhara when Dalacha seized Kashmir (SK).
66. Vimshaprastha: the present Idgah (SK).
67. town: Rinchanapora, below Alikadal, right, later identified with Bodhager where Alaudin built an edifice (PH).
68. Jyamshara and Allesha: Jamshed and Alishah or Alisher. The former ascended the throne on the death of his father Shahmir or Shams-ud-Din in 1342 A.D. till overthrown, shortly after, by Allesha who assumed the name Allau-ud-Din.
69. Kramrajya: Kamraz, the part of the Vy. below Srinagar on both sides of the river. In *Aini Akbari* the pgs. of Lolab, Hama, Uttar and Machhipora are mentioned as belonging to Kamraz.
70. Achala: according to some historians he was the son of Ravana, Kota's brother. PH names him Urdun. Mughdapura: pb. in the hills to the S. of Kashmir.
71. Bhimanaka: identity unknown; could be Bimnoh near Verinag. Achala, however, entered via Herapur (PH).
72. Rinchana : Khe Rinchana (SK).
73. Tusharalinga: a *linga* of ice, pb. the one in the cave of Sri Amamath.
74. Both sons: Haider born to Rinchana and another, reportedly named Jat, to Udayandeva.
75. Shirashataka: assumed the name of Shahab-ud-Din on ascending the throne while his younger brother Himda became known as Sultan Qutub-ud-Din (1373-89 A.D.).
76. Lord of Dvara: pb. the commandant of the gateway at Baramulla is meant. Shahmir was granted an estate at v. Daraver in Kruhin, Baramula (PH).

77. Alleshvara: Alisher or Allau-ud-Din. Shankarapura stands for Patan. Jymsara: Jamshed.
78. Bhangila: pargana or sub-division to the south-west of Paraspor right upto the hills.
79. Some missing stanzas regarding the matrimonial alliances contracted by Shahmira have been retrieved in SK. They state "The daughter of Alisher, Shahmir's son, was married to the chief of Shankarpura (Patan). Lusta, the daughter of Jamshed was given in marriage to Tilakshura, the chief of Bhangila. Alisher in turn married the daughter of Lakshmaka, the commander-in-chief (Kampaneshvara) and Guhar, Shahmir's daughter, married the Kotaraja of Bhringi."
80. Karala: Ardhvani or Advani to the north-east of Devasar.
81. In the family feud between king Ananta (1028-63 A.D.) and his son Kalasha, the latter set fire to the sacred township of Vijeyshwara where the king had retired for some time. Somadeva composed *Kathasaritasagara* to console Ananta's queen Suryamati.
82. Chakradhara hill: a magnificent temple dedicated to Vishnu stood on the present Tsakdar Udar, one mile below Bijbehara on the Jhelum, left. The temple premises provided refuge to men and women in a civil war during the reign of Sussala (1112-28) when a *damara* set fire to it to destroy one of his personal enemies who was inside.
83. Lord of Kampana: Kampaneshvar: commander-in-chief (Stein). Here Lakshmaka, the father of Alisher's wife is meant. Kampana is not a place name.
84. Lord of Kota: Kotaraja of Bhringi.
85. Rajavji: *rajbij*: diplomacy (SK). Not a proper noun.
86. year 14: Saptrishi year 4414 or 1338 A.D. There appears to be some confusion as Shivaratri is celebrated on the dark thirteenth night of Phalgun.
87. Eldest son: obviously Haider
88. Bhatta Bhikshana: Pechabhat of Kakapore, a Brahmin (PH).
89. A similar strategy was employed by Devasarma to secure the release of Jayapida — R.T. (iv-546 *et seq*).
90. Jayapidapora: the town founded by Jayapida, grandson of Lalitaditya, near Sumbal, with the castle at Andrakot.
91. Kotta: Andrakot... year 15 (*i.e.* 4415): 1339 A.D.
92. *tikashnas*: sharp shooters. According to another version Kota killed herself with a dagger thrust in her belly before going to bed at night. [W-K.] [PH..]
93. Karma: clearly reminiscent of Lalleshvari's *vaakh*:

*Shiv va Keshav va Zan va Ka'ma'laz*
  *Natha' naam darinai yo'so,*
*Me'y abli kaa'si'tanam bhava' ruz*
  *So va so va so va so.*

94. Rajputs: Rajasthaniyas according to the original, a class of officials (Stein).
95. Five years: less than three years, from Shravana 4415 to Ashad 4418 (1339- 1342 A.D.).
96. Jamsara: Jamshed... Satisara: Kashmir, known as Satisar from the remote past.
97. Avantinagara: Avantipore, 30 km. from Sgr. on the national highway. PH regards the site of confrontation to be higher up at Zainapore.
98. Napalpora: Utpalpora (SK), the present-day Kakapore.
99. Lakshmabhatta: obviously Lakshmaka referred to as c-in-c.
100. Shri Devasaras: Devasar sub-division through which routes led to other hill states and the plains. Ref. n. 55 above.
101. Ikshika: sub-division or pargana of Ichh to the S.W. of Sgr. in the vicinity of the airport... Kshiri road: Ichh is drained by the Dood Ganga which bears other names as Sangisafed, Chhatskol and Kshirinadi. The prince, pb. crossed the Vitasta and marched along the Kshirinadi to reach Ichh.
102. Sayyaraja: Sathyaraj (SK), Siraj-ud-Din. (PH).
103. Sujjapura: Suyapura (SK), Sopore.
104. Shri Shivasvamika: Shri Shirashataka (SK), Shamak (PH) who ruled later as Shahab-ud-Din. He is the 'prince' referred to in the next line.
105. Lordship of Dvara: the exalted office of the commandant of the gate which entailed control over mtn. passes. Pb. *Baramulla* region is meant here.
105. Vakpushta forest: According to local tradition it was in the vicinity of Jaivan or Zevan. Vakpushta, queen of Tunjina, followed her husband to death at this place (R.T. ii-57).
106. Circle of the *yoginis*: *yogimchakra*—prb. the mystic diagram of Shrichakra. PH states that Lalleshvari was the chief among them.
107. Udaishree etc.: Raisherdil and Jhanda (PH) Odsheh Rawal and Chandra (*B.S*). Liquor: milk (PH).
108. Unchaste: see also n. 44 above.
109. Now a quarter of the city near Ali Kadal, right. An ancient Buddhist shrine already existed there.
110. Lalitaditya is believed to have ascended the throne in S.E. 3776 Jayapida, his grandson ruled during 746-781 A.D.
111. Parasikas: Tribes that inhabited the area between the Indus and Afghanistan.
112. Udabhandapura: or Und, a v. in the Kabul vy., 15 miles above Attock. According to Stein, Und was the capital of Gandhara bordered on the south by the Indus. Marble slabs with Sanskrit inscriptions in Sharadha characters were removed from Und by Alexander Bumes in 1837 and deposited in the Calcutta Museum (Elphinston). The kingdom was ruled for a long time by the Shahis. Bhima Shahi was the grandfather of Queen Didda (980-1003 A.D.) of Kashmir.

Me built a temple at Bumuzu in the Lidar vy. Sindhu: Nilab or the upper Indus region (SK). Shingas: pb. Chingas across the Pirpanchal range.

113. Hajnipur: Ghazni.
114. Ashtanagara: Hashtnagar in Peshawar distt.... Veda readers: Shrotriya and Kshatriya are probably tribes. (SK.)
115. Purushavira: literally the hero among men; Peshawar is meant.
116. Villages assigned... : the name of Nagaragarhara (present Nangarhar), identifted with the dt. of Jalalabad, has been misinterpreted because of its resemblance to *agrahara*, w. given to Brahmins.
117. The Ghoshadatu river: the Hindughosha or Hindukush mtn 'Udakpati: the 'Lord of the North', pb. a Mongol chieftain (SK). The verse should read: 'He appreciated the act of his cavalry in severely chastising Udakpati on the slope of the Hindukush.'
118. Shatadru: The Satluj river.
119. Susharampura: Nagarkot in Kangra. queen: *devi* in the original Sanskrit refers to the temple of Matadevi, or Vajreshvaridevi in Jullundhar (Kangra).
120. Kandarpa: Hindu god of love.
121. Shauryasvami:... pb. not persons; the verse could be taken to read as: '..to fight out of heroism and affection for their lord' (SK).
122. A person named Devasharma was the minister of Jayapida. He immortalised his name by his sacrifice for the king.
123. The year 36: the year 4436 of the S. era or A.D. 1360.
124. Town of Sharika: referred to as Lakshmipura by Srv.
125. Junction: Shahab-ud-dinpur or Shadipur.
126. Loladamara: Laula/Lauladamara. Probably the town is Lalpur, near Beeru.
127. Fortune: pun on the queen's name.
128. Magic: references to sorcery and magic are not uncommon.
129. Shri Jayeshvari: identity uncertain. Jayadevi, mother of Chipita Jayapida (RT. iv-681) built the shrine of Jayeshvara.
130. Great Buddha: Brahat Buddha...a lofty brass statue of Buddha existed in the shrine Jayendravihara, built near Nauhatta by Jayendra, maternal uncle of Pravarasena II, the founder of Pravarapura, *i.e.* Srinagar. (RT. iii-355). Kshemagupta, husband of Didda had the *vihara* burnt down as a rebel had taken shelter there.

    *B.S.* states that the king destroyed idols. PH also makes a similar charge. Jona. who belonged to the generation almost next to Shahab-ud-Din's clears him of these allegations.
131. Yoginipura: Delhi, named so after the Jogmaya temple.
132. Hindukas.. *mlechhas* : Hindukhan (SK) and Sikandar were pb. some outsiders in the employ of Shahab-ud-Din.
133. Khadagnagri: identity uncertain. Cunningham identifies Khagipura with Kakapur. Gandharbhas: celestial beings.

134. Hinduka: Himda (sing). *i.e.* Qutub-ud-Din (... in his own post).
135. Kumbhadina: Qutub-ud-Din.
136. Lohara: Loharkot in the Loharin valley across the P-P pass. Also ref. p. 95.
137. Mahendramandala: central Panjab, between the Beas and the Jhelum. PH states that the place the prince reached was Jammu.
138. town: Qutub-ud-Dinpura, Alikadal left.
139. *Jajna*: the king appears to have been liberal-minded.
140. Shringara: Shrangar (SK) ruled later as Sikandar.
141. heroic queen: Subhatta (SK), Sikandar's mother.
142. Uddaka: Uda Bandi (PH names him Rai Madri) was the son of the maternal uncle of Sikandar's mother and his wife Diwath was the chief wet-nurse of Sikandar.
143. Shri Shobha: Sikandar's senior queen.
144. Mammaka: Nimmaka (SK) ... Helara: Holda (SK)-Volar-Tral-Avantipora
145. Deserted place: Padmapora-Pampore (SK), plateau of Vallamatha : identity not certain.
146. Vitastapora: Vethavatur; pb. Uda wanted to cross the hills five fires: refer p. 65.
147. King of the *mlechhas*: Timur's massacre of Delhi took place in Dec. 1398 A.D.
148. Water, gifts given to Brahmins are moistened with water.
149. boy: Mir Syed Mohammad Hamdani, son of the illustrious Mir Syed Ali Hamdani, was only 22 at the time. The latter visited Kashmir in 1372, 1379 and 1383 A.D.
150. Attracted...a second party of foreign immigrants entered Kashmir with Syed Jalal-ud-Din Bukhari as their leader.
151. Shahi—see n. 112 above. May be Shahi Khan, later Zainul-Abdin, was named after his mother's dynasty.
152. Pradyumana hill: Hariparbat...town: Sikandarpora - Nauhatta.
153. Suhabhatta: mentioned earlier as Bhatta Suha.
154. Jonaraja calls Harshdeva (A.D. 1089-1101) a Turushaka as he broke many idols and turned them into coins. Jona. attempts a rationalisation.
155. *Martanda*, the well-known temple, dedicated to the sun-god, built by Lalitaditya on Matan plateau. Vijayaishana : Vijayeshvara temple at Bijbehara. Chakrabhrit: Vishnu temple at Tsakdar Udar.
156. Tripureshvara temple near Harwan, Sureshvari at Ishabar, Varaha: temple at Baramula
157. Shesha: not a name, it means: 'of the rest'.
158. Illness: Suhabhatta is said to have been suffering from consumption.
159. Suhabhatta. it is said, sought conversion to Islam when the Brahmins outcaste him for eating food they considered polluted.
160. Fine: poll tax.

161. Ladda the Margapati: mentioned also as Lada Magrc or Ladaraja in Persian chronicles. Ladi was a non-Brahmin Hindu who had embraced Islam (SK). Margapati/Margcsha of the Hindu times meaning 'lord of the route' turned into 'Ma'gre'.
162. Durddanda: in the territory of Khasa tribes on the outer hills (Stein).
163. Bahurupa: Becru. Bahurupa is named as an important Naga in the *Nil-n.*
164. Jampa: waterfall
165. Ladda: a person other than the former Margapati
166. Processions : religious sacrifices and Naga festivities.
167. A similar restriction was placed on the people of J&K state for some time after the invaders were driven out of the Valley in November, 1947.
167a. History repeats itself.
168. Ratnakara: 'The abode of gems, the ocean'; pb. a leading Brahmin.
169. Malanoddina: some people seek to identify him with Sheikh Noor-ud-Din of Tsrari Sharif who is held in great reverence by all Kashmiris. This opinion is not shared by many scholars. According to *BS.* the Maulana appears to have been sympathetic to the establishment.
169. Refer also n 158 above.
170. Shahikhan: assumed the name Zain-ul-Abdin on ascending the throne.
171. Hamsa: pb. a brother of Suhabhatta Gaura: mentioned earlier as Gauraka and Gaurabhatta.
172. Thakkuras: Kashmiri Muslim noblemen. The appellation was given also to the sons of Zain-ul-Abdin's nurse.
173. Merakamsara: Merakessara (SK).
174. Mandara hill: the gods used the hill to churn the ocean,
175. King of Madra: Maldev of Jammu...Hara : *hatha* (SK): compelled him to. Maldev ruled during 1360-1399 A.D. Alishah was pb. joined by Hamirdev (1400-23)
176. Ally: the chroniclers had no good opinion about the Madra (Jammu) troops. In later chapters the adjective *khyudra* has been frequently applied to them.
177. Out of ...: PH states that Zain-ul-Abdin was defeated in a battle by his brother and he fled to Sialkote.
178. Turushkas.: mercenary retainers from outside Kashmir.
179. 'The lord of the Khuhkhuras: Jasratl Khukhar/Gakkhar was inimical towards the Raja of Jammu (Mahendra) but closer to the heir apparent. 'Gakkhar was a descendant of Khokkhar, vazir of Dharam Chand Chib of Bhimbcr. Khokhars were the caretakers of the '*mazar*' of Dharam Chand.
180. Alligator: reference to the well-known *Panchtantra* talc... *Mlechhas;* since she king and his ministers were also Muslims, this term

obviously refers to foreign retainers for whom the term *yavanas* is also used off and on.

181. Mudgaravyala: obviously in the vicinity of Rajauri. Some identify it with Thana.
182. Vasuki: king of the serpents represented as supporting the world.
183. overpowered: Srv. says that Alishah was killed by the son of Jasrath (Ref. p. 112).
184. Mahatmadkhana: Mohammad Khan.
185. umbrella and *chamara*: insignia of royalty.
186. should read: the politic king levied taxes on well-to-do subjects that they may not perish through their pride or oppress poor citizens.. Jasrath: pb. Jasrath Gakkhar.
187. King of Dilli: one of the Syed kings... Jayapidapura: close to the Wular lake where water-nuts abound.
188. Mereshaya: Mereshkaro (SK) Mir Shikaro. *bhurja*: documents were recorded in ink prepared specially from burnt almond shells.
189. Shivabhatta: Shiryyabhatta (SK). A locality in Z.'s capital even now bears the physician's name. 'Shiryyabhatta Day' is celebrated on the dark 15th of Chaitra.
190. Danvas: demons who warred against gods.
191. Text defective. Should read: Learned men frequently consulted Shri Ramanand's commentary on *Mahabhashya*... (SK)
192. Text defective. Should read :The kings of Gandhara, Sindhu, Madra and others accepted, like docile subjects, the overlordship of the king who had conquered all his enemies'.
     Maldeva was the chief of Jammu in 1359-99 A.D. Prob. some confusion makes him a contemporary of Z. Ref. also nn. 175 and 179 above.
193. Gogga country: pb. a place-name in Ladakh.
194. Shaya: a village with a palace-fort near Leh. Spelt 'Shel' in Tibetan, meaning a crystal. A well-known folk song, 'Song of the Girl of Shel' mentions the castle, a lake with turquoise-blue water and a *chorten* of white crystal.
195. Luta: Suluta town (SK). Udhbhandapura: Zain-ul-Abdin's mother Mera was the daughter of the erstwhile king of Udhbhandapura.
196. Sadaula: Saidal or Saidullah.
197. four sons: Jassarathakhana has not been mentioned again. The eldest is Aadamakhana according to original orthography.
198. Utpalpora: Kakapora.
199. Nandashaila: Z. extended irrigation facilities in the command area of Nandi canal (excavated first by Nandi, a danseuse), including the *karewa* of Zainapore. Probably dry land near Tsakdar Udar was also thus irrigated. Kalhana states that Lalitaditya used water-wheels to irrigate dry lands at Chakradara (RT. iv. 191) Chakradhara is one of the names of Vishnu resting afloat on water.

200. Karala: the sub-division from Khur Narvav, west, to the lower course of the Vishav. Also Ardhvani, leading to the present name Advani.... Jainapuri: Zainapore near Bijbehara.... Avantipura: a short distance above Pampur.
201. Manasa lake: Manasbal with the subtle suggestion that the Kashmir lake has the same sanctity as the Mansarovar lake.
202. Ganges: According to the *Nilamatapurana* the river Sindh of Kashmir has the same sanctity as the Ganga, and the Vitasta that of the Yamuna. Canals fed by the Sindh were led to Manasbal, Safapur and Srinagar.
203. Town: Safapore
204. Suyyapur: Sopore founded by Suyya, the engineering genius of Avantivarman. It should read: The prosperous king connected Suyyapur on the other side of the Vitasta with the Pohru' [The king had a barrage of stones raised on the bed of the Pohru river to draw a canal to irrigate Zainager, 10th mile on Sopore-Kupwara road].
205. Jainanagri: identified with Naushahra, 3 km. below Nauhala. Pradyumana hill: Hari Parbat. Pradyumna has been named in the *Nil-n* as one of the important Nagas in Kashmir. In a tale of the *Kathasaritasagara*, Somadeva states that Pradyumna, son of Lord Krishna, opened for his own son Anirudha a passage to the underground abode of the Danvas with the help of a peak of the hill and goddess Durga, under the name of Sharika, guarded the funnel door thus created. Hence the name ..... Amreshapura: Amberher, 16 km. from Sgr, on the highway to Leh.
206. Jainaganga: the stream which carried water from the Sindh to feed Z.'s capital city. Later it was extended to Ranaswami temple and to Jama Masjid. Ranaswami: temple of Vishnu-Ranaswami was founded by Ranaditya. Stein has suggested its identity with the structure at the *ziarat* of Pir Haji Mohammad near Malaratta.
207. Snangiri: Jainagiri (SK)... Sureshvari: Sarishor near Ishabar (Nishat).
208. Siddhakshetra is not a place-name. The poet eulogises Sureshvari as a place where the aspirations of devotees attained fulfilment.
209. Suyyaraja: Suyya the founder of Suyyapur or Sopore Barahakhetra: Baramulla.
210. Vijayeshanaka: Bijbehara. Writing on birch bark with ink made of burnt almond shells was reported to be indelible, (ref. p. 67 and 71.)
211. 'At Ishanaka the great king made grants for comfort and rest of people coming from outside' should read: 'At Vijay and Surpura the king opened houses of charity'. Ishanaka has no separate identity.
212. See RT. iv. 615 for 'hill of copper'.
213. Jainamani: Jain (Zain-ui-Abdin) plus mani : jewel.
214. *Krosha* : about 3 km.
215. Shivabhatta: Shirryabhatta (SK).
216. Syedha and Shura: Masodha and Shura (SK). sons of Z's nurse.

217. Nilapurana: *Nilamatpurana* which gives valuable information on the geography of Kashmir, customs of the people etc.
218. Mahapadma lake: the Wular. The verse should read: '...lotuses grew, and shown bright as the stars in the sky.' The next line: '...by any means, it would bring prosperity to my kingdom. '
219. '...Dvarika, even so was the township of Sandhimat encircled by wise men and good.'
220. for the legend referred to here see *Nil-n*, w. 1004-24.
Ullol: lake with waves rising high, the Wular.
221. Jayapida : grandson of Lalitaditya Muktapida (RT iv/506) *kavuka*: plant with long thin stalk and large disc-like leaf; water-lily .... Suyya Kundalaka: dyked v. founded by Suyya.
222. Suratranapura: two villages bearing this name exist in Bla. Distt. (*i*) Sultanpore Khai, near Nayidkhai in Sonawari teh. and (*ii*) Sultanpore Kandi, near Shrakawara. Exact identity is uncertain.
223. Jainakotta: nowzainakot, near Shalteng, the site of HMT factory.
224. Jainakundal, Jainapattan: identity uncertain. *Kundala* was originally suffixed to names of villages protected with dykes. The lake is about 25 sq. km. in area.
225. Gauraka: the chief judge Gauraka who considered all cases in minute detail.
226. Malvana Mallanasaka: Maulana Malla Ishaq (S.K.)
227. Wearied with...'the king felt a relief...bestowed'.
228. 'The talented Mohammadkhan now died and the endearing traits of his personality died with him...'
229. Pratihara: a high ranking officer, the chief of the palace-guards. Literally one who maintains strict control and discipline.
230. Vinna: brother of Masud and murderer of Sura.... Soudha: Songhya; Songhya/Sangoi is situated between the Salt Range and the right bank of the Jehlum S.W. of Jhelum town (Pakistan). Sindhu country: the region of the Indus. (SK).
231. Shivabhatta: Shiryyabhatta.
232. Dinaras; a copper coin estimated by Abul I Fazal to be equal to the 4000th part of a rupee.
233. 'The Sindh river which caused damage to ripe paddy fields near Tulamula was diverted through village Bharosa'. Bharosa is a village nearby.

**Shrivara's**

*Jainarajatarangini*

## BOOK 1

# Sultan Zain-ul-Abdin

### Prologue

I BOW to Shiva who is the sole lord of the three worlds, and who has attained eternal godhood and freedom from endless pain. May Shiva, one half of whom is female[1], give us faith in the unity of godhood! Witnessing one half of Shiva's person united with one half of Parvati's, the moon also cut off one half of his body and united himself with night, sable as the locks of Parvati.

The court-poets of celebrity who make their compositions elegant by the proper arrangement of words and who distinguish milk from water, (*i.e.* good from bad), are entitled to respect. In this world, which is without a master, and covered by the darkness of uncertainty, what is it that can make the things of the past known except the works of poets[2] which are like lamps? Kings were perishing in this world, but the poet Jonaraja enabled them to live in their fame to the end of time. Fate, however, removed the poet Jonaraja from the world, as if in anger. The learned Jonaraja became merged in Shiva (*i.e.* died) in the year[3] 35, while writing the *Rajatarangini*. I am a pupil of this Jonaraja, my name is Shrivara Pandita, and I have undertaken to finish the remainder of the Book of Kings. What a difference between the production of my master and that of mine, I who am possessed of little sense! How can chalk do the work of camphor merely because it resembles it in colour? The good hear me read[4] for the sake of the annals of kings and not for the merits of my work, and they understand my composition by their intelligence. Let other poets compose works of beauty, my work has been undertaken to commemorate the accounts of kings.[5]

## Gratitude

I have received various benefits, gifts of wealth and of villages, and the privilege of performing the homa[6] sacrifice; and I have been brought up by the king like his son. I will narrate his history, therefore, partly to free myself from my endless obligations to him, and partly because I am attracted by his merits. How much of his merits can be described by one tongue? My words could have described them if I had as many tongues as there are hair on the body. Truly, my words are not able to enumerate the merits of the king which are like the stars in the clear and boundless sky. Yet as the three worlds are represented within the limits of a picture, even so shall I delineate the merits of Shri Jainollabhadina. I will describe according to my understanding what has not been described by my *guru*. One can free himself from obligations for houses, gifts, and honours received by describing the reign of this king and of his son[7]. The *Jainarajataringini* will recall to mind the prosperity and the adversity of men who are now dead, but whom many have seen; and in whose mind will it not raise a feeling of indifference to worldly desires?

## Zain-ul-Ahdin

Shri Jainollabhadina having destroyed his enemies in distant lands returned to his paternal kingdom, and obtained it even as Rama had done. The treasuries were drained, but he collected what remained in order to carry out his designs, even as a poet collects from the vocabulary his words and meanings suited for his work. The reign of this king, after that of Alishaha who was ignorant of the art of ruling, was like the cooling sandal paste after the heat of summer in a desert had departed. The punishments which his enemies received from his hand were like those received from Yama after death, each getting it according to his merit. Though the king possessed great merits and executed good works yet, strangely enough, he was always possessed of riches of various kinds. The goddess of Fortune certainly lived on his face graced with his bright eyes, and dwelt in his house bright with silk, rich with virtue, and adorned with women of lotus like beauty, while his fame, like the notes of music, spread over Bangala, Malava, Abheri[8], Gauda and Karnata. Radiant as the sun but soft as the moon, learned as Buddha, and wise as Vrihaspati, the king obtained the names of the planets, and all the planets were in his favour. The king was like the jewel that fulfils every desire, and his merits attained great luster, even as the *kumuda* flowers do at night on seeing the moon. The six schools of philosophy which gladden the learned, delighted his heart, as the six seasons, which gladden men by flowers, adorn the garden of Indra. The three faculties (majesty, perseverance and wisdom) found in the king the three amiable attributes (virtue, wealth and desire), and like lovers they lived in harmony in the king. Like Partha[9], the king satisfied every day those who came for alms, and his fame spread on all sides, as if to invite the poor. Artists considered him as Vishvakarma descended on earth, *yogis* considered him as Goraksha[10], and chemists looked on him as Nagarjuna.

## Overall impression

The king favoured those who showed their skill in arts or in letters, and they were thus encouraged to persevere in their callings. He spent his life in listening to poems and songs, in dance and in the music of the harp, and in shows, and was not overburdened with work. He directed those who knew the *Shastras* to persevere in their duties, for they work justly who know the *Shastras*. Driven by the irresistible force of his arrows, his enemies always lived like insects in woods and remote places. His spies made daily enquiries about his enemies' affairs as well as about his own, and the king knew all about his subjects except their dreams. No one could exact even five gandas of cowries from a pious householder engaged in prayer. The king caused the feet of the *chandala* thieves, who ought to have lived by agriculture, to be chained, and he compelled them to work on land. Knowing that low caste men take themselves to thieving when in want of means of livelihood, the king gave them provisions. He knew Chakras[11] and others of Kramarajya to be wicked men, and he therefore confiscated their land, made provision for their livelihood, and kept them in the Madava[12] country. The annoyance from thieves being thus repressed by the prudence of the king, travellers slept at ease in the woods as in a house. The king lived in a simple way and in doing good works; his actions were free, all his state officials were prosperous and he gave himself up to enjoyments in various towns. Who does not praise the eternal sun who rises on the eastern mountain and drives away the mischievous darkness, the lover of the lotus, who sheds his beams on it and is adored by it, and who withers the *kumuda* flowers, and displays his power to men?

The Thakkuras, sons of the king's nurse, were elated with pride, made ill use of their wealth and fortune, and like unchecked elephants, became the destroyers of the king's joys. The eldest of them, Merathakkura, though conspicuous on account of his position as judge, and an aged Mausula (Musalman), became illustrious by his literary work. It was with difficulty that he reached Kashthavata[13] from Vatapatha; there he found himself in the midst of snow with which his feet were affected. He stayed for some time before the shrine of god Manikya[14] on the shores of the lake, and having obtained a few attendants, he arrived at Chiba[15] country after a long time. He reached there, worried by hundreds of difficulties, and his feet were washed by a Saida as by a servant, and in order to allay the pain of the sore, physicians bandaged one of his feet with thongs for life. In this place he lived five years with difficulty, and made various attempts to reach his own country and to take possession of his wealth.

The king, after he had conquered Sindhu, Hinduvat[16], and other countries outside his dominion, went with his army to conquer the Bhutta country. As soon as the army had entered a forest, they saw with wonder a black skeleton of a man by the light of a lamp placed on a wall. The wise men who had appreciated the king's worth used to assert that, by performing penances extending over a long period, the king had attained emancipation, and had cast off his (former) body as a serpent casts off his skin. Their words were now proved, or how could the king know of hidden things if he had not been a saint?

## References

1. Female: Shiva in the form of *Ardhanareshvara*.
2. Poets: Shrivara's predecessors Kalhana and Jonaraja have expressed similar sentiments.
3. Year 35: *i.e.* Saptrishi or Laukika year 4535 corresponding to A.D. 1459.

4. Read: these chronicles, and other works, were obviously read in gatherings of the elite.
5. Kings: of the dynasty of Zain-ul-Abdin.
6. *Homa*: restrictions placed on many religious practices by earlier rulers were withdrawn by Z.
7. Son: he portrays the reigns of the grandson and the great-grandson also.
8. Abheri: Different portions of India carried this name. Pb. a state in Rajasthan is meant here.... Gauda: south of Malda-Murshidabad area in Bengal....six schools of philosophy: ref. 79/41.
9. Partha: a title given to the Pandva hero Arjuna.... Vishvakarma: the great architect of the Universe.
10. Goraksha: Gorakhnatha, the founder of a system of *yoga* known after his name.... Nagarjuna: a well-known chemist of the 9th/10th century, the best chemist of old according to the late Dr. P.C. Ray.
11. Chakra: the clan of Chaks who are believed to have come to the Vy. from Dardistan in the reign of Sahadeva and settled in the Trehgam area of the Kupawara dt. Alamkarchakra, a powerful Damra of Karnaha, helped the pretender Bhoja against the king, Jayasimha, in 1143-44.
12. Madava: Madvarajaya (Ksm. Maraaz), the region to the south of Srinagar as against Kramarajya (Kamraz) to the north of Srgr.
13. Kashthavata: (*i*) Kishtwar (Doda dt.), (*ii*) Kathavar near Baramula. Sussala came from Loharkot by this route (Kathavar) in advanced season in 1112 A.D. In the present context Kashthvata in presumed to be in the hills to the west. Vatapatha : *avatapatha* or rock-infested tracks, overshadowed with rocks (RNS).
14. God Manikya: enjoyed the hospitality of Raja Manikyadeva of Bhimber, Jammu.
15. Chitra country: where Chib Rajputs had their stronghold....Chibyal, Bhimber. Chib Chand, son of Narayan Chand, came from Kangra to Thakiyal estate, Bhimber, and married the lone princess. Chib founded Kangra, near Bhimber. His descendents came to be known as Chib Rajputs [(*i*) Dr. M.L. Kapur (*ii*) Narsingdas Nargis.]
16. Hinduvat: Hinduvada from Hindubag (RNS) could not be Handwara which was already under Z. and has been referred to either as Kramarajya or Uttar. The place is presumed to be outside the main valley of Kashmir, either to the west or near the Kishen Ganga basin. Bhutta country: Ladakh and Tibet, Ref. also pp. 277 and 298.

**Shrivara's**

*Jainarajatarangini*

## CHAPTER I

# The Battle of Mallashila

### The King's sons

The king begat three[1] sons, the eldest Adamakhana, the second Hajyakhana and the youngest Vahramakhana. The eldest was handsome and he pleased his father by the natural grace of his person and by his appearance, even as the moon pleases the sea. Hajyakhana displayed his greatness in his daily boyish pastimes, even as camphor indicates its nature by its sweet scent. The two boys were beloved of their parents, and the happy king left them in charge of two Thakkuras, the sons of his nurse, in order to be brought up. The two Thakkuras, sons of the nurse, knew how to serve their own interests and to damage their opponents; and they became to each other like the two disputants in logic. They cut the stem of the tree of brotherly affection and, owing to their mutual envy, became envious of the princes; and the three worthy sons of the king grew up in mutual enmity caused by the Thakkuras. The country was like a body of which the king was the soul: when the king felt happy all others felt happy, and when he felt miserable, all others felt miserable. It was owing to the wicked policy of the ministers that the princes felt angry with each other, and the elder and the younger did not perform their mutual duties.

Once upon a time the king heard of the enmity which his sons bore against one another, and he ordered Adamakhana to prepare himself for departure without delay to a foreign country. "O bad son," he said "if you do not act according to my reasonable command, difficulties will arise which will destroy your dignity, life and wealth." When he had heard these words of his father, the prince said to his servants that he would go to Parnotsa[1] where they always live in happiness. They replied that his brother was of magnanimous mind, and liberal, and could bestow wealth on his servants; and they asked him if he could do so. "We would rather die in his service and before his eyes", they said, "than serve you who are so weak and devoid of powers." As an arbitrator stands between the two who are engaged in making a partition, so Fate stood between the elder and the younger brother in order to equalise their happiness and misery by reversing the scales. The king was afraid that the life of Adamakhana was in danger, and he sent him out of the country within a few days on the pretence of sending him to Bhutta.

## Cannon

Mechanics showed to the king different kinds of thunder weapons (cannon) which make men tremble with the deep sound they make. The king brought out these weapons made of different metals, new and hard; and at his command I composed the following lines in praise of the weapons: "In the year 41[2], in the Saka year 1386, the king, Shri Jainollabhadina, renowned like the lord of heaven (Indra), the victorious, the ruler of Kashmira, constructed this weapon which is well known to the world and is spoken of in the Mausula language. It destroys forts, pierces the hearts of men, strikes horses with terror, throws arrows (balls) of stone from a distance, and remains unseen by the soldiers, from encampments, strong, well-regulated, of deep sound, and of great value – such was the engine constructed by the mechanics. The engine will be useful to the king like a new town. May it be useful by the large quantity of the different metals of which it is composed, and by its frame, by its sound, and by its power of expansion." The engines, vying with the thunder in their roar and their fire, were inscribed with these lines, and they looked graceful.

In a short time Adamakhana returned after the conquest of Bhutta and Hajyakhana went to the mountains of Lohara[3] under the orders of the king. The king knew that two swords do not find room in the same scabbard, and so he caused one of his two sons to go out and the other to come into the country. Adamakhana bathed and drank and played and engaged himself in amusements every day before his father. The swan that lives at ease in the Sati lake does not leave it in the rainy season till he is struck dead by the fowler.

## Factionalism

In the year 28 Hajyakhana wished to return to Kashmira when Ravatralavala[4] and others thus spoke to him: "O Master! the friends of your elder brother are enjoying the delights of Kashmira, we alone have left our home and are pining in a foreign land. The powerful Rajanaka[5] the Prathihara, Kulaja[6] the Margapati[7], and others who are proud of their prowess are awaiting us in Kashmira. Even if you be disobedient to your father, will the merciful king kill us all in his anger? Should Adamakhana come out with his forces to fight, he will have to fly before you, even like young birds before a hawk. The people of Rajapuri[8] wish us good, let us therefore go by the way of Rajapuri. What can we not win through courage? Now that Riga the Pratihara is dead, there lives no hero in the country; you should therefore proceed and snatch the throne of your father. We warriors, your subordinates and followers, will fight with your father's men and you should see what heroism is."

"Be it so" said the Khana, and he asked the opinion of two ministers, Sphiryya Damara[9] and Tajatantresha, and they thus replied: "O Master! Your servants are anxious for their homes, and are speaking without due consideration of circumstances, and their advice will lead to mischief. How can we get into the country so long as the powerful king is alive? Who can with a coconut shell cover the radiant sun in the sky? No one will be able to oppose the king so long as he lives, hence for the present you should do what is pleasing to him. What prosperity may we not attain if your father be favourably inclined towards you? The virtuous have reverence for their king and senior; and even when angry he is more propitious to you than others, even when they are favourably inclined. The light which emanates from the sun even on a cloudy day, is more than what emanates from a burning lamp. The king always renders justice, and the purity of his mirror-like heart is not destroyed by the foul breath of the wicked. He is attached to the doctrine of *nirvana*, and is equally versed in all the *Shastras*; he is kind and does not inflict any pain. Though he had risen against his father's party, he did not discard his affection for his father, and his father's last moments were hallowed like those of king Jaina. His officers are wise, friendly, humane, and worthy of him, and it is on account of this happy circumstance that his sons are prospering. He is your father and you his son, and we all are your servants. If you go and fight against him, how can we gain a victory? The king has many servants, and if some of them perish, his loss will be little: if the Garuda bird loses a plume, is his speed impeded? There is no auspicious omen in our favour, the country of Kashmira is mountainous and difficult of access; and the king is your father; for these reasons we should avoid a war now. Let the king rule over the interior of the country, and let us rule over the other country; what blessings have you not got here by his favour except the royal umbrella? If they come to fight us here, they will not be able to conquer[10] us, and if we go into the interior we shall never be able to overcome them."

## Hajikhan marches against his father

The Khana, however, instigated by the wicked, and in his own pride, set out by the Surpura[11] road in spite of this advice, and keeping Rajapuri before him, came to Kashmira. The king in the meantime had heard of the sudden arrival of his son and had taken his army with him, and he soon issued out of the capital. While marching with the army, the king felt certain that he would die and caused this verse to be read: "The thought of war and peace always creates alarm; and when such alarm is caused by one's own son, his happiness is at an end." As the king marched, he heard blessings of men in villages, and people said that the son was under the control of the ignorant and had caused pain to his father, not to speak of the sin committed in rising against his father. While the king was yet reigning, his son, forgetting the affection due to his father, had come to bring affliction to the country; that the prince might with his army speedily fall like an insect in the fire of the king's valour, and the virtuous king might reign without opposition, and his enemies, defeated in battle, turn back. The king heard this and more, and arrived with his army at a place named Suprashamana.[12]

## The messenger

Then when the armies of the father and son met at Mallashila[13], the king sent a Brahmana[14] as messenger to his son. But the messenger was in no time surrounded by the angry people who were anxious to know his message, and they shouted and asked what the Bhahmana had to say. The messenger thus fearlessly delivered the message of the king, "O prince! O mighty armed! O Sea of Amrita! Attend to what your father orders which I speak unto you: The son is to the family as the fruit is to the tree; he is the benefactor in this as well as in the next world, and always delights the eyes of the parents; by whom can such a son be discarded? All people endeavour to provide for their sons, since in old age an obedient son brings comfort and ease. You, who are born my son, are my stay in this world and in the next; but now all my hopes of ease have fled, and my anxiety has increased. The protection which you are giving to the wicked men obscures my reign, even as a breath obscures a mirror. The unruly Khashas, ever ready to destroy, will not remain long with you, even as swans do not remain long in tanks. Why have you of your own accord, and without my orders, come into the country? Who can obtain the kingdom by force except when propitious fortune favours him? You were ruling over all the outer countries, wherefore were you not satisfied with them, and wherefore have you come to take away the rest of my kingdom by force? O son! cease to entertain vain and vicious thoughts; the sin of the destruction of the two armies will rest on thee. This have I told you in the words of your father; but I tell you truly that, like a sparrow before a hawk, your warriors will fly away from the king." When the soldiers heard these unpleasant words of the Brahmana, they *cut off* his ears and with the blood they marked the foreheads of their friends.

When Hajyakhana saw this he felt ashamed and came to Abhimanyu the Pratihara, and asked permission to leave his soldiers and to bow at the feet of his father. "Be the king pleased or angry", said he, "he will deal with me as he likes. I shall always serve the feet of the king and he surely will protect us. In my judgement this battle should not be begun. I do not even in dream think of mischief to the king; he who bestows on me happiness both in this world and in the next is greater to me than a god. My elder brother is approaching in the front and my father is preparing for battle; I have not come prepared to kill my father." When Tajatantripati[15] and other ministers heard this, they held the bridle of the prince's horse keeping it in front and told him these cruel words: "When we told you that it was not the time for battle, and advised you to return, you slighted our words. You must now, therefore, complete[16] the work you have begun. If you two, father and son, be reconciled with each other, the enemy will be pleased with your conduct, but we, who have suffered in the hope of serving you shall be ruined. Heated oil remains on the pan, but whatever is thrown between them is instantly burnt. You are our master, we your servants, witness our heroism now. If we win, you gain the kingdom, and if we lose, you return as you came. Wait as long as we fight; when we are killed, do whatever be your duty. If deceived by your father you reject our advice, we will do violence to your person, and then go away hence." The prince felt frightened at these words of reproach, sank into a sea of anxiety and was induced to give battle.

In the meantime when the king saw the Brahmana in that plight, he became angry like Krishna and prepared himself for battle. The king, who could observe the stars, and whose name[17] was derived from the position of the planet Venus in a lunar mansion, placed himself in a position so as to have the sun behind him, and made arrangements for the protection of his men. The sun shone on his sword from behind as if to assure him of victory, and then descended from the sky. While the king was trying to guess the number of the troops led by his son, those troops appeared before him glittering in the rays of the sun, and illumining the earth with their splendour. And he saw his own troops also, and the armoured and spirited horses moving swiftly in companies. Whom could not the king or his eldest son with the help of his army overthrow, were he Hajyakhana or any other hero?

## Battle at Mallashila

There at Mallashila the soldiers met and displayed their various quick manoeuvres, even as dancers show off their steps on a stage. The army of the king was like a cloud, furnished with weapons like lightnings, and it showered forth arrows with deep and prolonged roar. The men who met one another got mixed; they produced sounds like those of brazen gongs, and they bore mutual blows making a loud noise. The drums of Hajyakhana sounded loudly as if to say "the soldiers are compelling me to battle, do not press me hard." I[18] (the author) saw the Prathihara and others, men of great and of little prowess, but all powerless in this battle, as clouds are powerless to arrest the course of the sun.

Then the two Thakkuras, Hassana and Hossana, sons of the nurse and well-wishers of the king, came out in their wrath from among the king's forces. The Rajputs Suvarna[19] and Sihanagra were struck with many weapons, and they sacrificed their handsome persons even as *shri* fruits are sacrificed in the smoke of a *yajna*. Warriors moved to and fro in the presence of their master in that field of battle, ambitious of obtaining fame, even as black-bees roam about in a garden in the presence of spring, seeking for flowers. Soldiers whose heads were lopped off lay in the battle field, like morsels of food in a vessel for the hungry *yama*. What with the sound of the war trumpet, what with the uproar of men, and what with the lion-like shouts of heroes, there was a noise the like of which was never heard. The king's servants, who had received the king's favours as a debt, now repaid it by casting aside all hopes of their life; and they earned merit and praise by saving many bewildered people. The sharp arrows of the royal troops fell on the party of the Khana as if in fear and seemed to convey to him a friendly hint to save himself. His banner also trembled in the breeze and fiew backward, as if seeking shelter behind in fear of the battle.

## Hajikhan defeated

The field of the battle where slaughter took place was like a lotus plant, the severed hearts of warriors beaming like lotuses, and the chariots moving like leaves on the water. The king beheld the extraordinary heroism of his son and his army, and when at last the battle was over, he thought that he had obtained a new life. All through the day while the battle lasted, Hajyakhana was held by force by his servants, and now he turned back from the combat, surrounded by the guards. When the timid elder brother saw his younger yield, he pursued him and killed the soldiers who were overcome by their fear and felt ashamed at their defeat. What need be said of the cruelty of the elder brother who in his folly even killed some travellers who were going to a marriage party in Surapura? The king marched in the midst of all his troops to that distant part of the country in the south where the sun shines mildly. They who entrust the duty of ruling the earth to wicked warriors, who depend on their heavy lances and are fond of horses, who listen to the advice that leads to the mischief of others, and who are not anxious to preserve their religion and caste, like the sons of Kuru, do not win in the battle.

On the following day Hajyakhana collected the remnant of his force, repented of what he had done, and decided to live in the Chitra[20] country. He consoled some of the men who were in distress, supported others who were broken down, nourished those who were hungry, and spent the night on the summit of a hill. The kind-hearted king returned from battle after passing orders that none of his men should harass his son. He had thought to himself that by placing the burden of the kingdom on his son he would obtain rest, and with this view he had entrusted the administration of the country to his kindred, to the lords of the kingdom who had surrounded themselves with horsemen, and to his principal servants whom he had favoured. But they had all sided with his son and had come to fight with him to usurp his kingdom. He blamed himself for having cast aside prudence[21] in his kindness, and accused himself as the cause of the mischief. Thus he reflected and blamed the servants who by the work of Fate had become his enemies, and he returned to his own city in grief. The king caused the heads of the great warriors who had fallen in battle to be brought, and over them he built a beautiful edifice in the town. In this way many warriors lost their lives in battle that year in the quarrel between the father and the son, owing to the wickedness of the servants. Dissensions among kindred are like a curse, and are as little conducive to the king's happiness as the fall of snow is to the full blown lotuses, or as the dreadful comet, the destroyer of wicked men, is to an ill-fated kingdom.

Here ends the first chapter named 'the account of the battle of Mallashila' of *Jainarajatarangini* composed by Pandit Shrivara.

## References

1. Three sons: ref. also p. 61....Parnotsa: Poonch (Ksm. Proontsh')... The events recorded are not strictly in chronological order.
2. Year 41: L.E. 4541 corresponding to 1386 Saka and 1465 A.D. The event is of later occurrence chronologically.
3. Lohara: the principality of Lohara in the Rajauri-Poonch sector with its impregnable castle played an important role in the politics of Kashmir during 9th-16th centuries. Queen Didda of the house of Lohara, whose grandfather was Bhimashahi of Gandhara, was married to Kshemagupta of Kashmir. Many of her successors also came from the same house. The chiefs of Lohara and other hill states accepted the overlordship of strong kings of Kashmir but held their independence otherwise even under the Sultans. The garrison in the castle of Lohara offered stiff resistance to Mahmuo of Ghazni

and he had to call off the attempted invasion of Kashmir. Lohara is, however, to be distinguished from Lahara, Lar pga. in the vy. of the Sindh river.

4. Ravatralavala: an officer of high rank appears to be meant. RNS states that on the basis of Kshemendra's *Lokaprakasha* Ravatra was a sub-caste of the Brahmins of Kashmir.
5. Rajanaka: 'almost a king'. The title was conferred for service rendered to the king. According to Stein the title has survived in the family name Razdan among Kashmiri Pandits and Muslims. Didda conferred this title on her faithful minister Naravahana. This tradition continued under the Sultans and the title Rajanaka was conferred upon Muslim nobles. This came to be modified to 'Raina' in course of time.
6. Kulaja: Kulajada Margapati (SK).
7. Margapati: Lord of the routes (across mountains), also known as *margesha, margadipati*, etc., was a high ranking officer who made arrangements for guarding a route and checking infiltration.
8. Rajapuri: Rajauri is to the s. of Lohara. In the medieval age it lay on the highway leading from Kashmir to Panjab. Among others, Hieun Tsiang trod this highway.
9. Sphiryyadamara: Phirya Damara (SK). Tajatantresha : pb. Tazibhatt (see also p. 208 n. 7).
10. Conquer us: Loharkotta was practically impregnable.
11. Surapura: watch-station at Surapore or Herapore founded by Sura, minister of Avantivarman (A.D. 855-83). Herapore is about 80 km. from Rajauri and 10 km. beyond Shupayan. For 'before' read 'behind'.
12. Suprashaman: medieval administrative sub-division to the w. and n.w. of Shupayan.
13. Mailashila: 'rock of the warriors': a place near Suprashaman where soldiers practised various feats. Another v. with the same name is in Beeru t.
14. Brahmana: When Bahram Khan was overcome by Hassan Shah's soldiers, it was again a Brahmin who saved his life by sheltering him within his arms.
15. Tajatantripati: Kalhana modified the names of persons, *e.g.* Garga, Gagga, Gargachandra. The present chronicler also resorts to the trick in such names as Tantripati: Lord or leader of the Tantry clan. Mentioned earlier as Tajatantresha and later as Tajabhatta (Tazi Bhat).
16. Complete: Harsha (1089-1101) was similarly accosted by his bravos when placed in a similar situation (RT. vii. 655 *et seq.*).
17. Zain-ul-Abdin: literally means 'captivating' (alluring) 'notable' among the pious.

18. Shrivara appears to be a gentleman of considerable versatility: a scholar, poet, soldier, courtier, historian and a fine musician.
19. Suvarna etc.: Suvarnasiha, Ganga and others (SK).
20. Chitra country: Chib country (SK), Bhimber where Chib Rajputs lived.
21. In this observation the chronicler veils his own comments on the conduct of the Sultan.

Shrivara's

*Jainarajatarangini*

## CHAPTER II

# Famine of the Year '36

Owing to the wickedness of the younger son, the strong and pure stream of the king's affection now flowed towards the elder. He now won the affection of the king, enjoyed good fortune, had his councillors and shone owing to the absence of the heroic prince from whom much was expected. After a long time the king returned to the capital and made over to Adamakhana a few of the adherents of his younger brother who were at Kramarajya. Adamakhana appropriated all the wealth of Hajyeaodharakhana[1] which was in the house, or in villages, or in the temples of gods, even as the submarine fire consumes the water. From that time the elder brother remained at ease in Kashmira in the presence of the king as heir-apparent, and spent five years enjoying the dignity of kings.

### Untimely snow

Fate augments the happiness of men by increasing the crops, and Fate also brings calamity to them in the shape of famine. The clouds that make the grass grow by rain also destroy it by the weight of snow. The country was rich in crops when, in the year 36 in the month of Chaitra, the sky suddenly rained dust. It is well known from the *Mahabharata* that the year 36 (of a preceding century) had become terrible to all on account of the destruction of the race of Yadu. The leaves and the flowers hung down, grey with dust, as if sorrowing for the people threatened with famine.

The chief of the soothsayers was consulted by the king and he said that owing to the[2] dust-rain there would be a famine in such a year. The year 36 of the last century was the harbinger of a severe famine and men feared that the present year 36 would become like the one that was past. The country was beautified with the *Shali* rice when snow fell in the month of Agrahayana and caused distress. The earth covered her face with snow, as with a white mantle, as if unable to bear the sight of the people's distress.

## Famine

The ripe *shali* crop which had gladdened the hearts of men was covered with snow, even as men of learning and merit are covered with sandal paste in an assembly of the wicked and the ignorant. The monster famine soon stamped its mark on the country; there were emaciated men distressed for want of food, oppressed with hunger, and with eyes inflamed. A hungry man distressed with the thought of what he should eat, entered a house at night and leaving aside gold and other riches, stole rice from a pot. All day, and even at night, the beggars entered the house where there was rice, one after another, even as arrows enter a body. Some took shells[3] (coweries) with them, went to houses where there was grain, and obtained dry cakes with which they sustained their lives; and some died after eating after too long or too short an interval. Feeble, emaciated men in villages longed to obtain rice which was like nectar to them, but lived on edible leaves, roots and fruits, as if they had taken some religious vow. Some again supported themselves by cooking rice after a long interval, and by edible leaves.

The high price of ghee, salt, and oil was reduced on account of the dearness of rice, as the greatness of good men is detracted by the pride of the low. Those citizens who had been garrulous before about many things now began to talk a great deal about rice only. The *bhandhujiva*[4] flower, which is like the life of a friend, was neglected even like the *akanda*[5], for without rice the people were blind with hunger, and the sight of a flower inflicted pain. Formerly one *khara*[6] of paddy could be had for 300 dinnaras, but owing to the famine, the same khara of paddy could not then be obtained even for 1500. What more need be said? In some parts of the kingdom the poor people were denied even the gruel of rice. Before this the people had thought little of the luscious *vrihi*[7] and the coarse grain, and it was for this, I think, that they new suffered from this calamity.

## Debt relief

Being of a kind disposition, the king became anxious for his people, and after he had fed his distressed subjects for a few months, like his children, with his own rice, a plentiful crop grew, as if on account of the greatness of his heart. A truthful king has not to grieve for a long time. It was the sea, I think (by not supplying the clouds with water) that troubled the earth with the calamity of the famine, in order that the king's humanity might be displayed. Thieves delight at the time of anarchy, unchaste women in the hours of darkness, and those who sell grain delight in the time of famine. As the people were oppressed by hunger, precious things were received in exchange for grain; but after the famine the king caused them to be paid for at their proper price. During famine men had eaten up walnuts[8]; so the intelligent king observing the condition of the people caused oil to be extracted from the pine. Out of humanity he cancelled the deeds on *bhurja* leaves drawn up between the creditors and the debtors. The sixty-four branches of learning, arts and science and progress, all remained dormant in the distress caused by the famine. For new books exhibiting the play of words and sentences, the arts of singing, music, and dance, and women skilful in the arts of love delight not the hungry.

Here ends the second chapter named 'the account of the famine of the year 36' of *Jainarajatarangini* composed by Pandit Shrivara.

## References

1. Hajyeaodharakhana: Hajya Khan later ruled as Sultan Haider Shah. Year 36: year 4536 or 1460 A.D. Events of 1465 A.D. and 1452 A.D. have been narrated in the previous chapter.
2. The translator witnessed a dust rain at Jammu during the winter of 1885-86. For the year 36 of the earlier century, *i.e.*, 1360, ref. p. 42
3. Shells: coweries were used as a medium of exchange even in the earlier decades of the twentieth century.
4. *bhandhujiva* flower: also known as *guli dopahar* (RNS).
5. *akanda*: destitute of stem or stalk.
6. *khara*: a measure of weight equivalent to 77 Kgs.
7. *vrihi*: *brihi* (SK) barley. Before World War II rice sold in the Vy. at Rs. 3/4 for one *khara* (77 kgs.) and people thought little of it. At intervals

during the last thirty years the price shot up far beyond expectation. The price continues to soar.

8. It appears that oil extracted from walnuts was used on a pretty large scale during the age.

**Shrivara's**

***Jainarajatarangini***

# CHAPTER III
# Floods and Festivals

Fate, like a mad sovereign, can in a moment bestow unusual favour on his subjects when propitious, and inflict untold miseries when unpropitious. Who can understand the caprices of Fate? While the people had not yet forgotten the miseries of the famine of the year 36, they witnessed in the year 38 a dust-rain descending on the earth from the sky, and indicating a famine in the future from the failure of *shali*. Not long after, heavy clouds with the rainbow and peals of loud thunder terrified the people, even like enemies with their arrows. Flood bubbles[1] appeared on the water, beaten by the rain, and seemed like the hearts of snakes intent on destroying the crops; and the clouds which raised the bubbles threatened to destroy all that would grow. Everywhere the rain fell on the leaves of trees, and the sound seemed like the wailing of the trees at the calamity which was about to overtake the people.

The Vitasta, the Ledari, the Sindhu, the Kshipitika[2] and other rivers, seemed to vie with one another, and drowned the villages on their banks in their fury. The waves of those rivers ran like coursers, swift and tumultuous, and the roar of the whirlpools rose above the waves. The waters then became ungovernable and caused mischief, lowering objects which were high, and lifting up things that were low. Who taught them then to lift the earth from the foot of the hills and to fell trees? They swept away beasts and kine and living beings, as well as houses, grain and other things, and became terrible as a host of the *mlechchas*[3]. The river Vishoka[3a] caused misery in Madavarajya, and entered Vijayeshvara as if seeking to walk round the shrine, and a line of houses soon fell into the water as if to bathe in the river which flowed eastward, to have their sins removed. The river Vishoka is celebrated in the Purana as the destroyer of afflictions, but owing to the misfortunes of the people it belied its name. The buildings in the city drowned themselves in the water, as if to avoid the sight of the distress of those who had raised them. The king had built a flag-house on the Vitasta made of stone and wood, and consisting of four towers, and it served as a bridge to the people who came to visit him from the villages[4] of Darad, even as the four steps of virtue serve to ferry men over hell. But owing to the rush of water over the bank of the river, the portion of the building which was on the side of the town was destroyed, and only the columns remained and the two towers like two legs, as if to call on future kings to complete the other two.

## Zainakadal partially destroyed

In Kramarajya, the Mahapadam lake caused suffering to people by its waves, and its water rushed within Durgapura.[5] The edifices in the town witnessed this from a distance and apprehended that some other lake had come on a joyous visit to the Padmanaga lake; and they threw themselves into the water, fearing to be beaten down like trees by the waves. The Vitasta, far away from her lord the ocean, was alarmed at this intrusion, turned in her course, and flowed in an opposite direction.[6] Landmarks were submerged, roads were destroyed, and the land was full of water and polluted with mud, even as *Kaliyuga* is polluted with apprehensions. At the time when Indra thus poured torrents of rain, the king was filled with anxiety on account of excessive water, and set out in a boat. His soul was full of kindness towards men; and he wandered about and saw the cultivated fields submerged under water and his sorrow made him weak. Embarked on a boat, he saw the place where the milkmen had their quarters, and which was not visible before, so densely was it wooded. Within a few days the ruthless flood subsided, and was dried up as if by the fire of the king's prowess. The people were then soon delighted with the sight of the wealth of ripe *shali* crop that grew that year, as if through the virtue of their king's charity. And the kind heart of the king of Kashmira became full at the prosperity of the people, even as the sea becomes full at the increase of the moon's crescent. The virtuous king is like the soul, and the subjects are dear to him as the body. By the increase of the king's happiness the subjects become happy, and by his afflictions they become afflicted.

## New townships

The king apprehended the recurrence of a similar calamity and wandered about with a view to build a city on the high banks of the Vitasta near Jayapidapura. On an elevated side on the banks of the river he built a town called Jainatilaka, which was like an ornament to the earth, and humbled the pride of Alaka. The moonlight rested on the walls of this white-washed[7] city, as if the goddess of the *capital*! lingered there to see the king. The houses in the city looked like Kailasa, as if it had come there in sorrow, for the favour shown by Mahadeva towards Ravana who had uprooted that mountain. The city with its white-washed houses seemed to laugh at Jayapidapura where the houses and fields were mouldering in decay. The wise who saw the new city remarked that the king in his search for the way into the nether world must have come across the city of Asura[8], the Asura.

The beautiful water from the river surrounded the city and flowed by its gate, white as lime, and seemed to laugh at the city of Dvarika[9] in the pride of its beauty. It was here that the king, on the anniversary of his birth day, marked Jayasimha of Rajapuri with the symbol[10] of royalty. The king who loved the Brahmanas was pleased with the services rendered by Jayasimha, and as he sat here, he gave Jayasimha the charge of the beautiful kingdom of Rajapuri. In this same year the king showered gold in the courtyard of the palace where all the songs of Kashmira and of the Khasha[11] countries were chanted. In the neighbourhood of this city, a servant of the king named Helala killed a mad elephant, and the king built a small town called Helalpura[12], in order to commemorate the deed. Within Jayapidapura, the king erected a high seat of stone, and he built a beautiful palace by the side of a tank, and having drained off water from the tank which had been submerged by the inundation, the wise king built rows of houses for royal offices, befitting his palace.

## Festivities

Every year, on the day of *nagayatra'*[13], and during the festivity of *ganachakra*, the king fed the devotees here for five days. He made tanks here which were filled with wine, cream, and curries, and fed every body. Here was also heard frequently the sound of horns of a thousand devotees, which made even the serpents of the Manasa[14] lake shut their eyes. There was no kind of rice or meat or vegetables or fruit or food with which the king did not feed the people at the time of this feast. Out of his reverence for the devotees the king put up with their indecorous behaviour arising from intoxication which even ordinary men would not have borne. He dressed Mera, the chief of the devotees, in valuable robes and gave him presents, and marks of honour, and made him like himself in splendour. On the twelfth[15] day of the moon the king dismissed the devotees after having laden them with quilts, attendants, money and walking staves.

## Birth anniversary of the Vitasta

On the thirteenth[16] day of the moon the king wished to see the display of lamps made on the occasion of the worship held on account of the birth of the Vitasta; and he embarked on a boat and went to the capital. While on the water he listened to well-composed songs, and at the time of embarking and disembarking he accepted the blessings of the citizens. The display of lamps offered by the citizens to the river looked graceful as if the spirits of numberless holy places had come to the Vitasta for adoration. The rows of lamps placed at the ferry on both banks looked beautiful, as if the gods had scattered golden flowers for worship of the Vitasta. The moon was reflected on the river, but trembled on the water as if overcome by superior beauty, and humbled by the lovely faces of the citizens' wives who came to make offerings to the Vitasta and to worship. The king who had curbed the pride of his enemies spent the whole night in the pleasure of listening to songs[17], even as Garuda spent in feasting on the Gandharbhas.

## The King's authority weakened

Where is the place where the rising of the sun is not seen? All men are pleased at the sight of the adorable sun who dwells in the zodiac and is the friend of the virtuous. But his two sons Yama and Shani, unlike their father, bring trouble to men and are cursed by the people; they have obtained the title of death and are wicked planets. At this time the wicked Adamakhana impelled by envy towards his younger brother, caused much trouble to the whole country. The wicked ministers and leaders of men had become independent of the king and indifferent about the welfare of the kingdom; and Adamakhana who was hard-hearted like a stone was puffed up by pride but was afraid of his brother. He was fond of women and not of learning; he was addicted to hunting, and amused himself with dogs; and the night was like day to him. What need be said of the meanness of him whose servants, like pedlars, sold in towns the plumes of birds killed by hawks.

## Adamakhan's oppression

The prince was vain, as being the heir-apparent, and once upon a time went to Kramarajya attended by a numerous retinue, in order to secure possession of the country. The oppressed country resounded with the cries of villagers, wherever that sinful man passed through like a dire calamity. Like the course of a dreadful planet his course was marked by the confiscation of lands which had been previously given away as marks of favour, although the title deeds were clear. The covetous Adamakhana plundered the people of their riches in some places by the usual methods, in other places by threat or craft or by deceiving them with false hopes, and in some places by force. Like a common man he pretended friendship with the several Lavanyas, came to their houses and out of covetousness robbed them of their wealth. His servants oppressed timid women, made insulting proposals to them and as the women refused compliance, they cruelly treated the villagers and took care to avoid courts of justice. Adamakhana was invincible to the people of the kingdom even like a clever logician, and his shameless servants forcibly entered into houses where there were handsome women: wives, daughters, or daughters-in-law of citizens, and ravished them. In wine shops, these servants drank in *fishpots*[18], and when they became intoxicated, they began to blow the earthen pots like jesters. In their violence, they consumed rice from the barns, got drunk with wine from the casks, and exacted enhanced rents. What more need I tell of their unlawful acts? At night these wicked men besmeared the villagers with ghee, and made lamps of them at the junctions of roads by placing them in vessels full of oil and setting fire to them, and the flame rose as if in laughter.

The king became distressed on being informed of these heinous acts, and could not leave his house in his sorrow. When the king's messengers asked the servants of Adamakhana not to oppress the people, they replied,—"Let the king cry in his illness."

## Adamakhan revolts

When a man oppresses the good and nourishes the wicked, when he hoards riches instead of spending them in gifts and on his own comforts, and when he tyrannises over defenceless villagers without cause, then surely his end is near and his wealth becomes a curse and a misfortune. Adamakhana collected his army at Kuddadenapura[19] and came to Jainanagara against the king. On that day the king had heard evil reports and collected his army in fear of his son. The king had constructed a bridge on the Vitasta, named Jainakadli, with four towers made of stone and wood, and it was the tenth bridge on the way from the Darad[20] villages to the city. This same bridge, constructed by himself, now caused alarm to the king and he apprehended that his foes might take advantage of it and thus cause him harm. The king also apprehended commotion within the town and was struck down with fear. With great difficulty and through the council of his advisers, he succeeded in dislodging his son from the city.

The sun's passage towards the north brings heat to the world and the sun, as if conscious of this, retreats southwards and thus causes cold. I bow to the sun who thus brings relief to men, and who again moves northward to remove their sufferings caused by cold. Adamakhana reached Kramarajya and the king, fearing that his state would be divided into factions, wrote a letter with his own hand thus, and sent it to Hajyakhana: "O son! Calamities have befallen me which I find it difficult to surmount; my life is in danger and I have no other help but in you. As soon as you read my letter, sit up at once if you were sleeping, stand up if you were seated, run if you were standing. What more need be said in this matter? If you come without delay, and without minding the trouble which this bad news may cause, truly your desire will be realized in full. But if you do not arrive here speedily while I am yet alive though distracted, there will be no use in your coming to me after I am dead." Now Prince Adamakhana had crossed over to Svayyapura, and engaged his force in a fierce encounter with the royal army. Along with Nathabhatta, the king's officer, the whole army was crushed and the contest between the two armies soon became a general confused battle, marked by great ferocity. The battle in this year 35, like that in the year 28, was caused by wicked people; they created enmity between father and son, and caused harm to them both. The people of Darad and others drowned themselves in the water of the river through fear of Adamakhana, and the lake became full of corpses. The three hundred men of Adamakhana, fierce as death, slaughtered men in the field that day and then tore up the bridge of boats, and crossed the river.

As the king went out of the city he saw citizens in the streets with their feet burnt and suffering from the agony; and he heard them crying and lamenting thus: "Fie to the cruel man who instead of subduing foreign countries oppressed his father's dominion which he should have protected. The vicious Shikhajada and others who accepted pay from both father and son, and harassed the king, are now suffering the punishment of their treachery. The wicked planet Saturn believed himself to be as great a benefactor to men as the matchless Sun, and aspired to equal him; but then the precise Sun arose, brightening everything, and by his greatness destroyed those whose ways were tortuous. Adamakhana has been deserted by his wicked followers who have brought misery on their country and destruction on the people, and he has also been deserted by fortune and prosperity. The people survive other calamities like excessive rain or drought, or the destruction of crops by mice, locusts or birds; or even a foreign invasion; but let not the king have sons bent on destruction or divided by mutual enmity; or if he has only one son, let it not be a wicked son who causes misery. The two sons of the king, cruel destroyers of the people, were to him even as the rising of the saturn and *yama* is to the sun. Where can such another king be found, lenient even to those who caused trouble, forgiving to fallen enemy and liberal in the appreciation of merit? It is owing to our misfortune that the king was put to trouble by his wicked son."

## Villagers censure Adamakhan

When the king went to Svayyapura he heard villagers on the road censuring his son for the slaughter of men, saying: "When the king saw the birth of his son, he felt happy, for he thought that his son would bear the burden of the kingdom; and the king raised him to prosperity out of his affection, even against the dictates of policy. But the king now knows his son to be as powerful as himself, and fears him, and though surrounded by joys he can never sleep on account of his anxiety. There was a great slaughter of men owing to the animosity between brothers, and king Alishah was bound and killed by the son of Mallika.[21] Similarly, what calamity has not befallen king Jaina, out of the jealously of his sons? Let not many sons, the destroyers of the country, be born therefore in a king's house."

The armies of the father and son were now encamped on either bank of the Vitasta; they were now near each other and each was eager to overcome the other. In the meantime Hajyakhana who had reached Parnotsa without delay, approached, like Garuda, the neighbourhood of the Sadvarna[22] country. When the king heard of the arrival of the prince with his army at the outskirts of Varahamula, he sent Vahramakhan to greet him. Hajyakhana, who was expecting him, greeted and embraced his youngest brother, who was gratified with his conduct and agreed to what he was told. The next day Adamakhana who found his younger brother won by his father, was overcome with fear, felt forlorn and fled the country. He went to Shahibhanga[23], courageously crossed the Indus and braving many difficulties, reached the principality of the chief of Sindhu (or Nilab). In the year 35 (*i.e.* 4535) the eldest son having been driven away and the second son won over, the king as well as Hajyakhan felt pleased as they entered the city. (The eldest son) fell on evil times, was separated from his kith and kin, suffered from cold and icy winds and had to seek shelter in caves and ravines. For the second son the spring returned at the end of dire cold, butterflies enjoyed the juice of flowers and the world was bright, gay and full of comfort.

## Hajikhan the heir-apparent

At this time Hajyakhan was appointed the heir-apparent by his exalted father and king. He retained this love-jewel (devoted attachment to his father) and never parted from it even as Vishnu never lets go the *Kustabha* jewel. He kneeled before his father and exercised utmost humility. As an embodiment of devotion and humility he attained great fame. There was no festival, no shrine, no rally, no durbar which the king visited without Hajyakhan. The king was daily attended upon by his two sons and hosts of devoted courtiers and subjects. Doing good and beneficent deeds for his subjects, he also delighted assemblies of musicians and actors. He was the very embodiment of splendour. How can we find words to portray his glory?

Here ends the third chapter entitled the 'account of floods and festivals', of *Jainarajatarangini* composed by Pandit Shrivara.

## References

1. bubbles: bubbles are believed locally to harbinger incessant rain. Kshipitika: a diversion canal in Srinagar known locally as Ka'ta' Kol, from Kshiptikakulya.
2. *mlechhas*: barbarians
3. Vishoka: the Vishav which flows through Kulgam and joining the Ranbiara merges into the Jhelum at Sangam, 5 km. below Bijbehara. 'Vishoka' literally' means 'griefless'. *Nil-n* regards the Vishoka as the incarnation of goddess Lakshmi. The Vishoka countered the flow of the Jhelum.
4. vv. of Darad: text incorrect. Should read; '...built a flag house and bridge of stone and wood with four piers to enable the people to cross the river even as the four...' Obviously Zainakadal is meant here.
5. Durgapura: the place has not been mentioned anywhere else.
6. direction: owing to excessive flow of water in the Pohru-Mavar basin the Jhelum is often found obstructed at their confluence at Doabgah and the water is seen flowing in the opposite direction towards the Wular. In the language of the people it means that Pohruraja approaches Wularraja to seek the hand of his daughter... Jayapidapura was founded by Jayapida (746-781 A.D.).
7. White-washed city: limestone is quarried in the vicinity.
8. Maya the Asura: Mayasura demon creating a false illusion.
9. Dvarika: identity with v. Tarazu has been suggested on the basis of the Vitasta Mahatamya. Srv. probably refers to the city of Sri Krishna.
10. *symbol* of royalty: *tilaka*, hence the name Jainatilaka.
11. Khasha: songs of Kashmir and the countries around (*Kashmir aadi deshe*-RNS).
12. Helalpora: not identifiable now.
13. nagayatra: the fifth of the dark half of Shravana (August) is known as *nagapanchmi* and a festival is held at Panzathnag, Vessu. *Ganachakra*: virtuous people were fed during the festival. Some interpret it as the public aspect of the secret *chakrapuja*. From the details it appears the king had arranged large-scale feeding for monks and others on a mass *shradha* ceremony for departed *sanyasis*. Ref. also pp. 122-23
14. Manasa lake : Manasbal lake, near Safapore, appears to be meant.
15. Twelfth day: of the moonlit Shravana (August). A fair is held at Shupyan and gifts are given even now.
16. thirteenth day of the moon in Bahadun (September) is celebrated even now at Vethavatr as *Vitasta triyodashi*, the birth anniversary of the Vitasta river or Veth. Lighted lamps are floated on the river in Srgr. and other places. Akbar also witnessed such a festival.

17. According to some the festivities took place in the bright half of Bhadun: *ganachakra* on the fourth (*Vinayaka Choturthi* sacred to Annapurna), Ganga Ashtami on the eighth, the birth anniversay of the Vitasta on the thirteenth, *nagyatra* on the fourteenth (festival at Anantnag) and *Indradvadashi* at Baramula on the twelfth.
18. fishpots: it appears liquor was consumed by the common people on a much larger scale at the time than is the case now.
19. Kuddadenapura: Qutub-ud-Dinpora, on the left bank of the river, was linked to the main city, on the right, by Zainakadal.
20. Darad: text defective. Should read: 'The king had constructed Zainakadal, a bridge of stone and timber, with four towers and wide enough for ten riders, for the benefit of those who wanted to cross the river. Ref. n. 4 above.
21. Mallika: Malik Jasrath, the Gakkhar chief. Jonaraja is silent over the death of Alishah... Alishah was buried at Tsodur....: year 35: 1459 A.D.
22. Sadvarna: small vy. in the Pooneh-Rajauri area from where passes at lower attitudes lead into Bla. dt.
23. Shahibhanga: pb. Bangash, towards the northern border of the Vy. Babar complained that Bangash was infested by Afghanrobbers.

**Shrivara's**

***Jainarajatarangini***

## CHAPTER IV

# The Festivity of Flowers

In due course the friend of Cupid, the Spring, returned. As the moon is the lord of Rohini constellation and makes the *kumuda* flowers to bloom, even so spring perfects the beauty and make-up of nature. It was like the sun to the darkness of vanity and showered radiance on creeper-like beautiful maidens palpitating with life. During the spring festival the king, in order to see the play of flowers (*pushapalila*) embarked a boat and went towards Maraz. The waves in the Vitasta shone as brightly as the celestial vehicle (*viman*) of Indra fitted with sun-shades. Reaching Avantipura he proceeded to Vijesvara to find enjoyment in the demonstrations of actors, dancers, etc. In that bright assembly the king was unconquerable, as though born of Mahadeva, and his courtiers who waited on his pleasure were like Cupid multiplied into many parts as though to overcome him (with their displays). Scholars with reputation in *alankara, siddhanta, yoga,* etc., were assembled there as also those who had mastered music and the science of sounds. From different villages had come men and women who could present felicitous songs in bewitching tunes. People assembled there knew different arts and branches of knowledge and enjoyed peace and harmony without a feeling of doubt. Songs in *ektal* and a variety of *talas* were being displayed by adepts in music and dancing.

## Dance and acting

The spectators and the singers knew literature, rhetoric, and philosophy, and appreciated merit. Young women, proficient in music, possessed of sweet voice and with a genuine ardour for song, graced the place. The men were learned and dignified, and fond of enjoyment; and they displayed their taste and their intelligence on the stage. And the songstress Utsava who was even like Cupid's arrow, charming to the eye and proficient in dance, both swift and slow, entranced everybody. The actresses, who displayed the fortynine different emotions seemed even like the ascending and descending notes of music personified. As they danced and sang, the eye and the ear of the audience seemed to contend for the enjoyment. The scene was indeed beautiful, the songs of the actresses were like the voice of the *kokila*, the stage was like a garden where the lamps on it looked like rows of the *champaka* flower, and around them were men intoxicated with wine, like bees around flowers. Rows of lamps surrounded the king, as if the gods pleased with his government had come to witness the dance, and had thrown a garland of golden lotuses round him. In some places the rows of lamps were reflected on the water, as if Varuna had, out of favour towards the king, illumined his court with lights from the Naga world; and the lines of lamps shone like jewels on the heads of the Nagas who had come to witness the dance. Those who were at a distance doubted if the lights were really lamps, or the spirits of former kings assembled to view the present sovereign, or stars and the moon descended from the sky to attend on the king, or the spirits of holy men who had attained emancipation, or if they were the great gods assembled there in their grace and beauty. The spectators seemed to view Indra himself in the king; the poets and *panditas* beside the king were like demigods, his servants were like the attendant gods, and the *yogis* around him were like holy men who had obtained salvation; the actresses were like *apsaras* whose charms were heightened by their emotions, the singers were the *gandharvas*[1] and the stage was heaven itself.

## Fireworks

Fireworks of various colours made by the mixture of charcoal powder, sulphur and saltpetre pleased the men. Tubes were filled with saltpetre and the thick sparks of fire which issued out of them looked like a creeper of gold; and the spectators were filled with fear and wonder on beholding a flame issuing out of water like a serpent. From the tubes rose balls of fire to the sky, beautiful as silver, and looked like the planets Jupiter and Venus. A tube filled with saltpetre was tied to a string; it went off to a distance like a flame, and when pulled, it returned in flames. Such flames shot from the king and returned to him like bright shooting stars; and the spectators fixed their eyes on them in wonder and joy. These flaming tubes of saltpetre were held by the actresses in their hands, and they shone like golden stars of beautiful colours, falling from heaven.

The king was skilful in manufacturing fireworks, and he instructed Habhebha[2] to display them. It was difficult to obtain powder before, but the king showed how it could be manufactured, and so it became easily procurable. He gave his instructions to Habhebha in the Parasi (Persian) language, in the form of questions and answers, and many others began to write books after this example. Where can now be found one like king Jaina in the greatness of intellect or in the art of invention, in fondness for song and music, or in capacity for rhetorical discussion, in writing books, in listening to holy *shastras*, or in composing new works?

## Song, music and letters

Sujya[3], the pupil of Abdolkadara, was possessed of all accomplishments and he pleased the heart of the king by his proficiency in music. One Mallajadaka[4] came from Khurasana and received inestimable favours from the king by playing on a lute made of tortoise shell. Another named Mallajyamala,[5] a singer in the *mlechhas'* language, pleased the king as Narada pleases Indra. I, who am versed in all kinds of song, and who hold a lute made of gourd, displayed my skill in exhibiting a part of a new song of infinite variety; and Japharana and others sang with me the difficult Turushka metres before the king. We sang songs in twelve different modes, in the court, and as the sound arose from the string, the voices accorded with it harmoniously, as if in joy. Pandita Utthasoma[6], versed in vernacular and Sanskrit literature, composed a life of Jaina in the vernacular, and approached the king. Yodhabhatta, a poet in the vernacular language, composed a drama, pure like a mirror, called the '*Jainaprakasha*', in which he gave an account of the king. Bhattavatara, who had perused the

*Shahnama*, vast as the sea, composed a work named '*Jainavilasa*', as the counterpart of the king's "Instructions". The king was pleased, and caused the lute, the gourd instrument, the ravava[7], and all other instruments of music to be set with gold, silver, and jewels, and they looked very handsome. When the people saw the stage effulgent with decorations and beheld the play distinguished by the excellence of sense, gestures, and feelings, they called the stage a four-faced god. Thus it was that the king who was possessed of the three cardinal virtues, whose fame was spread over the three worlds, and who like the gods was subject only to three stages of life (not to old age), spent the three watches of the night in witnessing the three kinds of dance.

The king repaired to a house bedecked with jasmine flowers, and full of merriment and laughter, even as a foil moon appears in the sky bedecked with stars; and he began to drink from stainless vessels, attended by his son and friends. The respectful Hajyakhana, filled with the love of his father as with *amrita*, extolled him thus under the pretence of describing the spring: "Like an expert actor Spring, the king of the seasons, teaches the humming black bee the art to sing, and instructs the breeze in the art to make the creepers dance. O King, who appreciates songs, has the Spring come to serve thee? The beauty of the stars is destroyed by clouds covering the sky, and during the day they are invisible; and even the moon waxes and wanes. Humbled by such mishaps, the stars have come to serve thee, O Lord of men! in the shape of flowers in the garden. May the flood which fills the country with mud, annoys the people in the midst of their ease, and destroys roads, remain confined to the basins of the lakes and beautify the country! The floods are disappearing through thy power at this pleasant time of spring, this season of pleasure, even like a city of snow at the rising of the sun." When the king heard this he was glad, and gave Hajyakhana a matchless dagger of gold. The king bestowed lands in the Ghosa[8] country on those who served the prince. These servants had once been reprimanded, but now they received silken clothes, the emblem of favour, even as men who falling into the waves of the Sindhu are ferried across in a boat. The king shed tears of joy for having got back his son; and showered gold on the learned, the singers, and the servants. He paid the travelling expenses[9] of his subjects who came to witness the performance, and they were made happy, being honoured and clothed in silk. King Jaina saw the houses and gardens, beheld his boat filled with flowers, and after praising the inhabitants of Madavarajya, reached his own capital.

Here ends the fourth chapter entitled the 'account of the festivity of flowers', of *Jainarajatarangini*.

## References

1. *gandharvas*: celestial singers.
2. Habhebha: Habib. PH uses, the name Jeyo.
3. Sujya : Khujya (SK & RNS).
4. Mallajadaka: Mulla Oodi (PH). On page 157 Abdul Qadir is mentioned as a pupil of Mulladaudaka. 'Oodikhwaja was the pupil of Abdul Qadir' (*Ain-i-Akbari*).
5. Mallajyemala: Mulla Jamil.
6. Uttasoma: Nathasoma (SK). The works in the vernacular language mentioned here have not been discovered so far.
7. *ravava*: *rabhabha* in the original (SK).
8. Pb. Gushuddar in Pulwama t.
9. A rare instance of patronising the common man.

Shrivara's

*Jainarajatarangini*

## CHAPTER V

# The King Promotes Learning

The king had his son by him and was at ease and, being disposed to do good work, engaged himself in excavating new canals and consecrating them. I have not described those works of which the poet Shri Jonaraja has written in his book through fear of enlarging my work. Surely there is but one city about the construction of which nothing is known. That city is Amaravati, but the gods live not there, but wander about in aerial chariots. This king has built hundreds of new cities where the Brahmanas live with dignity, and are like Indra on earth. In Shri Jainanagara, a new lofty palace was built in the year 15 on the Devagaha[1] (hill); the king built a new palace near it of bricks[2] and wood, in the year 40; and the top of the palace was adorned by a bright and beauteous golden dome, like a lotus thrown down by the renowned Indra. Men were employed at the gate of the palace, serving in various ways according to the directions of the king. The king left his capital and lived here till the end of his life. The swans in the lakes of this place drew near the singers as they sang, attracted by the sweetness of their voice, and seemed to praise their song by their twitter. It was here that the king, now that his foes had been quelled, enjoyed, like Indra, the pleasant songs of the singers all day long. Within this palace was the audience hall adorned with the three cornered throne and wide spacious walls lined with glass; and here were many columns of victory in the palace, and here the breezes blew pleasantly in the morning.

Once when he had gone to visit the fort of Lahara[3], he repaired a dilapidated palace and made it new. He built many villages shaded by trees along the margin of the Mahapadma lake, from Samudrakota[4] to Shri Dvaraka, and marked with the name of Jaina, and there were many houses, beautiful like the palace of Indra. At Tripureshvara[5], the king fed the beggars with rice, until their stomachs were full, and it was thus that the king who was abstemious became like Ganesha. At Varahakhetra the king held his feast of rice, and the head of Ananta was bent with the weight of rice, and Indra's head was also bent down in shame. At the confluence of the Vitasta and the Sindhu, he daily fed small fishes with rice, and afforded them protection. It was at the request of the mendicants whom he fed that the king planted trees at Shri Shankarapura[7] which gave shade but bore no fruits. At Ashrama[8], the king held the feast of rice, until flavour of the curries overcame the scent of the saffron. The inhabitants of Vijayeshvara were continuously fed with rice, and they became fall, until it became difficult for them to bow to the king. After the king had fed the people with rice, he loaded the wayfarer with food at the toll bar on the road to Surapura. There was no man in Kashmira who was not fed with the king's rice, be he learned or dunce, wicked or good, a *yavana* or a twice-born.

## Excavates canals

Mahadeva, Narayana, Brahma, Jahnumuni and Bhagiratha of the solar line had laboured before and by their united efforts the Ganges descended on the earth, and their selfish object was fulfilled. But this king, guided by his own intelligence, excavated many rivers (canals) in the country for the benefit of others, and led them by diverse courses. Everywhere were seen houses high as hills, and full of rice lately grown on extensive fields. These granaries were indeed like the breasts of the earth from which the people derived their nourishment and throve day by day. Like Suyya, the king grew crops in places where lands could be obtained with difficulty, or where they seldom yielded crops before on account of calamities. There was not a piece of land, not a lawn, not a region, and not a forest where the king did not excavate a canal, and where he did not build houses marked with his name. There was not a river, not a field, not a village, not a town, not a piece of land which the king did not mark with the name of Jaina. Wherever the ground was low, the king caused a tank to be formed by means of canals, and it was adorned with birds, lotuses and water-nuts. Praise is due to the cloud which benefits the earth with water which it lifts from the sea where the water lies useless, and showers it upon fields; such showers make the grains grow and men, whose wealth is grain, are made happy.

## The Dal Lake

In this country there is an unfathomable lake known as the Dala, a brief account of which will be given. There the large lake of Sureshvari (another name of Dala) extends to the capital, and the king went over it every day in a boat, even as the moon travels over the clear sky. The king's boat adorned with fluttering banners, floated on the water like a young bird, with its oars which were like wings, and was manned by a crew who understood the weather. The river Tilaprastha[9] issuing from Tripureshvara, joins the Satanka[10] at this place, as if anxious to visit Lanka[11] where the hill of Shri, extending over six *kroshas*, meets the river and bathes in its water day and night, as if wishing to obtain the merit of bathing in a shrine. There, reflected in the water, trees look like mosses, hills like tortoises, and towns see like the realms of the Nagas. There the waving *shali* crop stands on the ground, and bends down as if to smell the perfume of the lotus. There Lanka is situated and the sun courses north and south to view this town and the other Lanka in the south.

## Hermitages

On the side of this lake stands the shrine of Sureshvari[12], adorned with many holy spots, affording both enjoyment and salvation and outshining Varanasi. The king made this place seem like heaven by adorning it with *viharas*, and villages given to Brahmanas, with monasteries which help in the performance of pious acts, and with hermitages where the inmates have not to labour. There the people saw from a distance well-nourished and agreeable *siddhas* with long four-stringed beads in their hands. The palace of the king was named Siddhapuri,[13] and was constructed like rows of chariots of the *siddhas*, so as to be true to its name. Within the palace, the king repaired the delapidated temples by props, or built them. He made floating islands fruitful by depositing grass and earth on them. When the hermits of the

Shri Jaina[14] monastery celebrated the worship of vessels, the king forgot his high rank and helped[15] them in their worship. There the moon was reflected in the Yogichakra[16] in the middle tank, as if he came there to drink its sweet water. The king fed thousands of hermits, until they closed their eyes in peace and joy and perfect repose. The renowned queen[17] Shri gratified the people there with food and feasted them. The rice prepared and heaped for the feast looked like a white elephant or the white cloud of autumn which is mistaken for talc. There was heard the sound of horn and hunting, mixed with the cries of the cranes, and the sound[18] indicated the death of the forest deer, like the destruction of sins. The king rejoiced to see the sinless hermits feasting on savoury cakes until they were satiated, and the curd which they quaffed with their busy fingers was strewn on their seats, and looked like the crescent of the moon melted by the power of their *yoga*.

## Cremation tax abolished

The river Mari[19] flowed from this place into the Vitasta and was used by the citizens for the purposes of drinking and bathing; and the king joined it at Hastikarna[20] with Shali canal which was extended to the confluence of the Vitasta and the Sindhu. This junction of the Mari with the Vitasta is known in the city as the Mari-Vitasta confluence, and is used for the cremation of the dead, and it is the way to heaven. Previously, the owners of the land, the servants of the king, and the Panchavarikas used to levy a rate at this place every day from the citizens for the cremation of the dead. When my father died, I informed the king of the tax, and the king punished the Kiratas[21] and abolished the rate on the cremation of the dead. From that time the common people on their death are cremated on that spot, to the grief of the uncultured who are averse to witness cremation. The bhurjja makers (who burn the dead) danced with their umbrellas and played on musical instruments on this exemption from the tax. Here, according to the custom of distant countries, females immolated themselves in the pyres of their beloveds; and were not forbidden by the king.

It was for the benefit of the poor of the city that the virtuous king built an extensive Vihara[22] on the bank of the river, near the Mari confluence. This Vihara and the one on the opposite side of the river at Hajya[23] were like the centre jewels amidst the jewel-like houses of the two cities. The king was then at peace with others, and he built other buildings. (A line appears to be wanting here in the text).

## Promotes learning

When Shri Harsha[24] became king in the realm of poetry, every one became a poet. What more need be said? Even women, cooks, and porters were poets; and the books composed by them exist to this day in every house. If the king be a sea of learning, and partial to merit, the people too become so. The meritorious king, for the purpose of earning merit, built extensive lodging houses for students, and the voice of the students studying logic and grammar arose from these houses. The king helped the students by providing teachers, books, houses, food and money; and he extended the limits of learning in all its branches. He was a shelter for all, and belied the saying of Munis that learning and pleasure, like light and darkness, cannot exist together. He made the country happy by his good government, favoured learning, and desired to promote the prosperity of the country as of his own son. He esteemed learned men, and valued them for their merits above all the various productions of his country. Even the families, which never dreamt of learning, produced men who, through the favour of the king, became known for their erudition. Learning, like the *kalpa* plant, shot into many branches, thrived by means of scholarships, and bore heavenly fruits. There was not a branch of learning or arts or literature or fine arts which did not become celebrated in the world during the reign of king Shri Jaina. Feudatory kings saw that the king befriended merit and respected learning, and they diligently applied themselves to it.

The heat of the earth consumes much of the grass and shrubs in the summer season, but the pleasant rainy season revives them. Thus in times past, king Shekandhara had, through the influence of the *yavanas*, burnt all books of learning, even as fire burns grass. At that time all learned men had fled precipitately to distant countries, owing to the oppression of the Mausulas, taking their books with them. What more need be said? There were the Brahmanas in the country, but all their excellent books were known only in name, as lotuses are at the advent of winter. But the king who now graces the land and is dear to the learned restored the books, even as the spring revives the black bees. He caused the Puranas, books on logic, the Mimmamsa[25], and other books to be brought from distant lands, and distributed them to the learned. The king heard me recite the *Vashishta Brahmadarshana* composed by Valmiki which is known as the 'way[26] to salvation'; and when he heard the annotations, pervaded by a feeling of tranquility he remembered them even in his dreams, even as a lover remembers the gestures of his beloved.

## Translations

Holding that a man can receive instruction only in the language which he knows, and not in other language, the king caused translations[27] of the various *Shastras* to be made by those who knew Sanskrit, vernaculars, and Persian. Even the *yavanas* can comprehend minerology, chemistry, and *kalpa* if studied in their own language. The king caused *Dashavatara*[28] and *Rajatarangini*, the books of Kings in the Sanskrita language, to be rendered into Persian. In the same way the mlechhas read the *Vrihatkathasara*[29], the *Hatakeshvara Samhita*, the *Puranas*, and other books in their own language.

## Pilgrimage

One hears after a long time the pure and beautiful Dharammashastra recited, and holds it to his heart, even as a white cloth holds the impression of colours, and acts according to its injunctions. Others again hear it every day, but receive no impression, as the leaf of a lotus plant, though growing in the current and held fast to the water by the stalk, never becomes wet by water. The king heard of the advantages of going on pilgrimage to Naubandhana[30] hill from the Adipurana, and felt a desire to undertake a journey some time to a shrine. The king was bent on going to a pilgrimage, and he went to Vijayeshvara in the year 39, on the last day of the fortnight fixed for giving offerings to deceased ancestors. He saw the ground full of spectators, clad in clothes of many colours, even like a garden full of flowers. Vandarapala[31] and other chiefs with their armies were glad to see the king. The sky was beautified by Venus and Mercury, and was full of other stars by night, and the ground was graced by poets and learned men, and shone with rows of lamps, so that the sky and the earth vied with each other. The pleasant earth was lighted on the day of the dark moon by the moon-like faces of the hundreds of citizens who had assembled. There a tree of lamps was borne by a man and it looked like the Pleiades risen in the midst of the stars.

The king accompanied by his two sons left Vijayesha, and reached Durmarga[32] on foot in three days. Wearing a noble appearance in his piety, he saw Vishnu's[33] foot mark at the Krama lake, and felt the joy of bowing at the feet of Vishnu. The waters from the hills of Brahma, Vishnu, and Mahadeva[34] seemed by their sound to enquire after the welfare of the king, who was a part of Mahadeva. The great king saw the hill and the land darkened by the flowers of the *kasturi*, and was rejoiced like anchorites when they view the longed for person of Narayana. He then embarked on a boat surrounded by five or six boatmen, and went about in the lake supporting himself on me and Simhabhatta. From me he heard the songs of Gita[35] Govinda, and then arose in his mind a feeling of piety towards Govinda. The sweet sound of our songs was echoed from the groves, as if celestial musicians sang after us from the groves[36] in honour of the king. After he had wandered about on the lake for some time, snow[37] began to fall, as if the gods, pleased with his piety, showered flowers on him. The encircling snow on the lake might well be mistaken for a portion of the peak of the Kailasa hill which one attains by bathing at the holy shrine. Truly, the king was an incarnation of Vishnu, and he thrice walked[38] round the lake out of piety, and also to test his power of walking. Then when the boat was fastened to the Naubandhana hill, the hill became what its name implies, and the king saw the hill and went to it. When journeying to the Sukumara[39] lake, the king drank of the water of that lake and meditated on the god Sukumara, and he felt a delight as if he had obtained the purity of his soul. The king heard the names of holy places, touched the auspicious waters from the shrines, tasted the cool water, saw the beauty of the forest trees, and scented the perfumes of plants and flowers, and thus performed the pilgrimage that gives pleasure to the five senses, and then returned to his capital.

Here ends the fifth chapter, named 'the account of the pilgrimage to Krama lake', of *Jainarajatarangini*.

## References

1. Devagaha: Devgreh (SK), a plateau. Year 15: 1439 A.D.
2. bricks: mentioned as building material for the first time.
3. Lahara: Lar, with the fort at Gaganger.
4. Samudrakota: v. Sadrakot on Sgr.-Bandipur road. Dvaraka: Pb. Tarazu v. (*Vit. Maham*) RNS identifies it with Andrakot.

5. Tirpureshvara: The shrine at Triphar, near Harvan. Avantivarman who made a pedestal and silver conduit for bathing at the shrine repaired here on the eve of his death.
6. Varahakhetra: Baramulla: Kotitirtha... confluence: Shadipur.
7. Shankarapura: Patan. The shady tree is pb. the chinar.
8. Ashrama: pb. Asham near Safapore is meant. A lofty Khanagah was built there by Z. for Syed Mohd. Amin Owesi (PH). The text should read: At Ashrama...rice until the flavour... superseded the scent of flowers. At Padmapora the flavour of curries overcame the scent of saffron. The name as recorded by Srv., has two short 'a's, at the beginning and the middle. With the elision of 'r' its pronunciation is the same as at present.
9. Tilaparastha: Stein identifies it with the Telbal *nala*.
10. Satanka: The text should read: 'The river Tilaparastha coming from Tripureshvara and flowing along alluring foothills appears to be eager to proceed to Lanka where the image of Shriparvat (or Hariparbat)....meets the river and ...shrine".
11. Lanka: the two islands in the Dal are meant.
12. Sureshvari: the area adjoining Ishabari with holy shrines, springs and temples.
13. *siddhapuri*: where boons are granted.
14. Jaina monastery: Jainavatika, the grove of Z. said to be located in Jainanagar, was 2 sq. miles in area. The mention of the Mari river suggests the location of the monastery close to Sureshvari.... worship of vessels : *paatra puja* in the original meaning, pb., large scale feeding.
15. 'participated' is closer to the original then 'helped': the king unmindful of the inconvenience involved, performed the *patra puja* of the hermits at Jainavatika, *i.e.* fed them in large numbers in plates *ceremonially cleaned*.
16. Yogichakra: Kashmir has been known from times immemorial for the worship of the Divine Mother represented by the mystic diagram.
17. queen: two daughters of the king of Madra were married to Z. In another interpretation credit is given to the meritorious king himself. Talc: pb. soapstone found in the area.
18. sound of horn: the hills and forests skirting the Dal invited hunters. (Dachigam higher up in the hills is still a game preserve). Should read: There was heard...cranes, and the sound indicated that the activities of the king promoted righteousness and brought about the death of the forest deer of sinfulness.'
19. Mari (or the Mar canal): Verse 1371 of the *Nilamatapurana* states "One is honoured in the world of Rudra by seeing the mountain Mahadeva after having a plunge in the Mahuri in front of Tripureshvara". Mahuri is obviously the stream flowing from the

Marsar lake. One channel takes a southern turn towards Tral and the other flows towards Harvan and, finally, into the Dal Lake. Mari or Mar is a modification of 'Mahuri' or 'Mahasarit'.

20. Stein places Hastikarna at Vagahom in Dachunpur. *Nil-n.* mentions two nagas with the same name Hastikarna. In the past the water of the Dal flowed into the Veth or Jhelum near Haba Kadal. Z. had an embankment raised and diverted the water through the then newly constructed Mar canal to irrigate the Achhan pga. (PH). By Shali canal is meant, pb., the watercourse passing through Shalabugh in Anchar area and Hastikarna of the present verse should be sought somewhere in that direction. Another rivulet of this name rises in the Pir Panchal hills and joins the Doodganga near Wahathore in Chadura t. Stein observes that the Hastikarna mentioned by Srv. must be in the vicinity of Srgr. Kalhana refers to it as the place near which Harsha was betrayed.

(R.T. Vii-1640)

21. Kiratas: underlings, woodsmen, who benefitted from the tax. Mari-Vitasta confluence: now called Maisuma. Panchvarikas: a class of underlings.

**22. (Jaina) vihara, it is surmised, was built a short distance above Ahlamar, pb. near Basantbagh.

23. Hajya: in another context this structure is named Hajyavihara, pb. in the name of Prince Haji Khan. Refer also p. 293/25.

**24. Shri Harsha (1088-1101) patronised poets, musicians and actors on an extravagant scale. 'Even women, cooks...': the compliment in these words was first paid to his country by Bilhana.

25. Among others a copy of the *Atharva Veda* was got from Pune,

26. way to salvation: 'Mokshopaya'.

27. translations: No Kashmiri work of the period, either original or in translation, has come to light so far.

28. *Dashavatara: Dasavataracharitra* by Kshemendra in which Buddha is recognised as one of the incarnations of Vishnu.

29. *Brahatkatkasara*: *Brahatkatha* written in Paisachi by Gunadiya is not extant. Translations in Sanskrit of parts of it have enabled scholars to assess its merit. Somadeva based his *Kathasaritasagara* on Gunadiya's work. Probably reference here is to Somadeva's 'Ocean of Stories'. Kshemendra also presented a number of G's tales in *Brihatkathamanjiri*. Out of modesty Shrivara omits a reference to his own Sanskrit work *Katha Kautakam* which is a translation of Jami's *Yusuf va Zulaikha*.

30. Naubandhana hill: the central of the three lofty hill peaks above Kramsaras (Konsarnag) lake owned by Shankara (*Nil-n*). The hill crowned with the three peaks is meant here...Adipurana: interpreted as *Nilamatpurana* also.

31. Vandarpala: Bandaipala (SK) The names of many Rajauri chiefs ended with '-Pal'.
32. Durmarga: a stiff route/ascent. Not a place name.
33. Vishnu's foot: Kramsaras or Kansarnag lake, a short distance from Shupayan, resembles a titanic foot in shape and has been known as Vishnupadtirtha from ancient times. According to *Nil-n* Rudra, Hari and Brahma were perched on three peaks of the mtn. adjacent for their encounter with the demon Jalodbhava.
34. Mahadeva: *Nil-n* mentions Rudra, Hari (Vishnu) and Brahma.
35. *Gitagovinda*: the famous composition of Jaideva.
36. At 13500 feet the lake is above the tree line. Pb. shrubs are meant.
37. Weather frequently changes at the lake. Snowfall regarded auspicious for the king.
38. Walked round: *pradikshana*: went round (in the boat).
39. Sukumara lake: *Nil-n* states that gods, sages, *gandharvas*, etc. took their abode here. Precise location uncertain. 'Kramsaras' instead of Sukumara has been suggested. Sukumara could be interpreted as a part of the bigger lake.

**Shrivara's**

***Jainarajatarangini***

## CHAPTER VI
# The Sultan's Friends

In order to satisfy his longing for the Krama[1] lake, the king caused a new lake, like the Krama lake, to be excavated within Padmapura[2] and called it the Jaina lake. It was the time of autumn when the land was darkened by the full blown flower of saffron, and it seemed as if the dark water of the Yamuna had come to join this lake in gladness. The king who was rich as the god of wealth, built a beautiful palace on its bank and called it Kuloddharana[3] Naga. Like the moon placed on high, he was pure and full of grace. His kingdom lacked nothing, his learning was without any deficiency, and he removed all sorrow from the minds of his people. Where is the man, even if he were a foreigner from a distant land, who could see such a king and not wish to serve him?

### Relations with other princes

Kings of distant countries heard of his great attainments and showered presents on him. The king of Panchanada[4] sent him, on account of his friendship, his own horse named Tajika, great in size and surpassing the wind in swiftness. The horse-faced[5] singer of heaven is celebrated for his voice, but does not know how to dance, and the king's horse remembering this, proudly danced on the road when the king rode him. The horse's mane was like the coral hands of the king, and the bit of the bridle was to the horse even as enjoyment was to the king. Possessed of auspicious signs, the horse considered himself as great as the king and needed no chastisement. Its four legs were adorned with gold as well as its mouth, and so it was known by the name of the five good[6] omens. Khalashya[7], the king of Mandavyagauda[8], gratified the monarch with presents of clothes named *darandama*; and the monarch, saintly as Yudhisthira, sent to Khalashya, among other things, a beautiful poem composed by himself in his own language. Khalashya was not so gratified with the invaluable presents sent to him as with the poem, ornate and beautiful in its arrangement of words and meanings. The king of Kumbha[9] presented to the monarch a cloth named *nan kunjara* and gratified the heart of his excellent queen. Tugaraseha, the beloved king of Gopalapura, presented to the monarch, for the festival of music, a book named *Sangitachudamani*, comprising rules of singing, of fine arts and acting and also containing the best songs. When that king Tugaraseha died, his fame was as widely extended as the sea, and his son retained, like his father, the goodwill of the monarch by sending him presents. The lord of *Mandalika*[11], who was the superintendent of the capital, was pleased with the monarch and sent him a handsome horse, and also *muchukunda* birds beautiful in the variety of their colours and charming in their eyes. *Balluka*[12], the king of Dilli, though blood-thirsty and restless in his work of destruction, was nevertheless bound to the monarch like a tame deer on account of his virtue.

## Distant countries

Someone[13] presented this great monarch with a pair of swans, and other swans were born of them, and the mighty monarch was pleased. They floated in a line on the lake without fear, and looked like white lotuses agitated by the waves. The king of Khurasana was the lord of horses; his order was held on the head by the kings of the countries around like a garland of *mandara* flowers. His servants were armed with fearful weapons, and they shook hands with the god of death, and roamed about in the world. This king of the north, named Merjjabhosaida[14], sent an accomplished messenger to the monarch with high horses and mules. Mahammada Suratrana, king of Gurjara[15], gratified the monarch with presents of textile fabrics celebrated by the names of *kateha, sohasa* and *glata*. The kings of Gilana, Mesra (Egypt),

Makka, and other places sought to benefit themselves by sending various rare presents to the monarch.

## Arts and handicrafts

Who did not seek to please the monarch, and what artists, possessed of great designs in art, did not come from distant countries, like bees, to the monarch who was almost like the *kalpa* tree? It was then that the people of Kashmira learnt the use of the weaver's brush and loom, and today they are weaving valuable cloth of silk. The woollen fabrics called soha[16] (shawl) and others, manufactured in foreign countries and those made in Kashmira today, are both beautiful, but the latter are strong and fit for kings. Other clothes were made, on which variegated plants[17] were produced by various methods of weaving, which painters saw and remained dumb with wonder. The monarch's kingdom, known by the name of Kausheyaka[18], and his dress of silk, alike became famous, the former on account of the various tribes of people that inhabited it, and the latter for the various coloured threads that it contained. By his own intelligence, the king invested his country and his dress with a peculiar beauty; the country graced by its people of various tribes, its capital town by its decorations, and by its learning and its dignity; and the dress was beautified by many circular designs, and by designs of Durga[19] and of men. The country was excellent and unconquerable, the dress was celebrated for its silk and gracefulness, both delighted him and both were of incomparable worth. The silk was glittering, and the country was brightened by festivities; in the silk there were a good collection of threads, in the kingdom there were good laws and riches.

Here ends the sixth chapter named the 'account of the development of the art of colour and of the description of art', of *Jainarajatarangini*.

## References

1. Krama take: Kramsaras or Konsamag lake.
2. Padampura: Pampore.., Jaina take: Jainasar or Zainasar,
3. Kuloddharana naga: According to *Haricharitchintamani* it was located 14 miles to the n.w. of Vijeshvara or Bijbehara....dark Yamuna: according to *Nil-n* the Sindh has the sanctity of the Ganga and the Vitasta that of the Yamuna.

4. Panchnada: Panjab, the land of five rivers Shatdru, Vipasha, Iravati, chandrabhaga and Vitasta (Satluj, Beas, Ravi, Chenab, and Jhelum)....Tajika: pb. Tuzuk (sharp, swift).
5. horse-faced: *kimnara*, celestial Choristers and musicians.
6. five good omens: Panchkalyan or five auspicious marks. A horse with four white leg and a white patch on the forehead is considered highly auspicious.
7. Khalshya: Khalacha (SK) pb. Khalji.
8. Mandavyagauda: pb. Mandu in Malva. The ruling dynasty descended from a Ghori noble. In 1436, Mahmud, a Khalji, murdered the Ghori descendant and usurped the throne. The poem remains untraced.
9. Rana Kumbha: the chief of Mewar, Chittor (1438-83). *nari kunjara*: cloth fine as a lady's hair (cf. Subandhu: Swapna Vusvadata-204).
10. Tugarseha: Dugarsiha (SK). His son was named Kirtisinha (not Kirtisindh), the ocean of fame....Gopalpur: pb. Gwalior. In a different context Stein places a locality of this name in Rajauri area.
11. should read: The chief of Saurashtra, out of love of the monarch, sent him a handsome horse and also a pair of beautiful *muchakunda* birds (birds with beautiful eyes) ..'
12. Balluka: Bahlol Lodhi (1451-38).
13. Someone: the present is attributed to the king of Lhasa by Persian chroniclers.
14. Mirza Abusaid of Khorasan, grandfather of Babur. Ponies from Yarkand and other places in the region were popular in Kashmir till recent times.
15. *Gurjara*: Gujrat. Sultan Mahmud I ascended the throne in 1458 A.D.
16. Soha: Soph (RNS) Woollen fabric associated with Sof (Iraq).
17. plants: tapestry designs.
18. Kausheyaka: the kingdom is of course Kashmir where the king encouraged weaving of silken cloth. According to another interpretation, *Kausheya* stands for silken cloth and not for the monarch's kingdom: 'the use of new tools in weaving elegant silken cloth brought fame and riches to Kashmiri people.... (RNS).
19. Durga and men: *Tantrasampati*: 'the country was enriched with handicrafts and textile industry'.

## Shrivara's
## *Jainarajatarangini*

# CHAPTER VII
# The Last Days

If the king be liberal, the people display their song and dance; if the clouds pour water in the rainy season, the *chataka* birds dance with joy and become pleasing to men. At this time there came to the king, who was renowned for his gifts, a *yavana* from Uttarapatha.[1] He knew the art of walking over a rope, and the king, accompanied by his family, came one occasion to Vimshaprastha[2] to see this feat. The man made himself ready to display his art, and stretched a long rope on two high pillars that stood at an interval of one hundred bows.[3] Then by a rope fixed to the ground the fearless man ascended like a bird into the air. This master of his art did not fall, but moved with wonderful steps on the rope, and the mind of men was pleased even as by a poem. Like a planet he moved on high and successfully walked over the rope to the wonder of the people.

### Ominous portents

Fate had for a long time showered blessings on the people; he now inflicted an insupportable calamity on the country; even as clouds rain for the benefit of agriculture and then rob its fruits by hail. At a time when there was no cause left to disturb the king, the people suddenly saw signs of a severe calamity to the country which had hitherto been happy under good government. A comet was seen at night in the north; it is the cause of the destruction of men, even as excessive rain is of embankments. Its long tail was of resplendent beauty, and surely *Yama* hurled down his axes in the form of the comet for the destruction of kings. For a period of two months the comet was visible in the clear sky, and the kind heart of the king remained anxious through fear of mischief that might happen. The elephants which were at Rajjupura[3] remained pensive as if apprehensive of the mischief that would fall their beloved king. The dogs were always heard to bark in the city during day time as if they foresaw a calamity and howled in grief. An eclipse of the moon and of the sun took place within a fortnight, as if meant to upset the king and thereby to destroy the kingdom in which there had hitherto seen no division. The passage of the sun from one sign of the zodiac to another occurred on inauspicious days, and men were alarmed, and apprehended some disaster in agriculture. The hooting of the owl was heard under "the umbrellas", as if the metropolis of the kingdom bemoaned and enquired if its builder was about to perish. On the second day of the moon that luminary was seen with its face upwards in the sky, as if it prognosticated the advent of another king.

## Famine

In the meantime there happened a terrible drought in another country such as brings on a famine; and the beggars of that country came like embodied sprites into Kashmira. The king saw them and made enquiries of them, whereupon they informed him thus: "In many countries, and in all directions, the time of distress has come, like the all destroying *Yama* on account of drought. Precious stones have lost their value on account of this famine, even as good men, who could be of service to all, lose their usefulness through the influence of evil men. Oppressed by hunger, the dogs have devoured the dead in their tenantless houses, and are now preying on one another; and good Brahmanas, majesty! who used to perform penances for taking food touched or eaten by others, are now eating everything owing to hunger. Brahmana women, who could judge as to what food is acceptable and what is not, have in some places killed themselves and others by means of poisoned rice. Some people have left their homes and some have died on account of the drought, so that a tenantless town or village can be seen at every step. Merjabhosaida the Suratrana, king of Khurasana, your friend, marched out of his country for want of food, surrounded by one *koti* of soldiers, and forcibly entered the country of his enemy; but the king of Iraka captured him and killed him.[4] At the time of his capture, and even when bound, he displayed valour like Duryyodhana, and innumerable Turushkas died. The time of distress has come in other countries, and owing to the destruction of the weak in mutual conflict among kings, there are dangers, O King! at every step. We have heard, O King! of thy country happy in wealth, in its store of food and other things, and we have come sorely oppressed with hunger, now save us". When the king heard this pitiable news, he felt as if the calamity had befallen his own subjects, and moved by kindness, he gave them many things.

## Sopore burnt and rebuilt

In the meantime, the great Svayyapura, built by hermits[5], spontaneously took fire, and became like a deserted forest. The great records of Kramarajya that were kept in this place on *bhurja* leaves were all reduced to ashes together with the cases that contained them. At this place the king had caused an edict to be inscribed on a copper plate to the effect that at this shrine[6] of Jainagiri, future kings should take one seventh of the crop that grew as tribute. It ran thus: "Shri Jainalavadina begs future kings to take one seventh of the produce of the land which he by his money has cleared and brought under cultivation at Jainagiri. He has descended into water and ascended hills in order to build this high place which is like the banner of virtue, and which they by their goodwill should enlarge." These happy sentences were inscribed by Srivakashisha[7] on a copper plate which was not destroyed by the fire, neither did the fire destroy the palace though it was in the midst of the flame that rose high even like the virtue of the king.

When the wise king heard that the town was burnt, his heart was burnt with sorrow, but he built it without delay, new and beautiful, with houses made of wood. The king had previously built a palace at Varahamula, but he caused the materials to be brought from that place and built a new large one here. There was in it a room for keeping the records of the kingdom. A swinging bridge was also newly constructed, and it looked like the necklace of the goddess of fortune which presided over Kramarajaya. Thus was the beauteous Svayyapura built. There was the swinging bridge with the rows of houses like jewels, and in the midst of them the palace displayed its umbrella and looked beautiful like the jewel that hangs in the centre of a necklace. The multitude of men lived happily here, as creepers do at the advent of the pleasant season of spring in a new forest; and their friends, like so many flowers, stayed with them for a few days and then retired well pleased. What new-fledged birds are to other birds, so are kindred to men; they live with them for a time, but when they can depart with ease they go away, to the regret of their friends.

## Death of the Queen

Meanwhile the king's beloved queen named Vodhakhatona[8] died. She was to the family of the Saidas what the moonlight is to the sea. It was by union with her that the king had thought his life happy, and now by her separation his body became burnt with sorrow and all things appeared to him as nothing. The moon-like king, the defender of the kingdom, had placed his sister's son Kramadena in the post of Suratrana in the country of Sindhu. He was graced with every virtue and was loved by the king as his own son, and was dearer to him than his own life. The king heard that this chief of Sindhu was killed in a battle by Evvarahima.[9] He was to the king a joy in times of pleasure and a solace in those of affliction, and by his death the king felt as if his own right hand had been cut off. On account of the death of Daryavakhana and others, a new body of ministers was formed, but they, with their boon companions, were ministers only in name. At this time died also the proud and liberal Merakhushahmada who had obtained the king's friendship by working for him. The king received some bad news every day and saw his subjects harassed by the mutual enmity among his sons, and he became sunk in anxiety. He thought of his relatives and servants and friends who had passed away, and believed himself as it were like an elephant that had strayed from the herd.

## Evils of drinking

In the meantime Hajyakhana suffered from a disease brought on by excessive drinking. He was heroic and noble; and as the king was excessively fond of him, his illness nearly dried up in the king's heart all the pleasures that he derived from his kingdom, even as a plant is dried up in a garden by fire. He caused his son to be brought before him, and saw him ill and much reduced, and out of affection thus addressed him in the presence of his ministers: "O son! You, who are addicted to an evil habit, have reaped the fruit of drinking. Even like the moon, you have got the disease which wastes you. Have you no friendly servant who looks to your interest as your protector, who gives good advice to you who are addicted to the sin of drinking? What wonderful enjoyments are there within your reach even to this day? But why should you then, like an insect, be attached to one pleasure only when life affords to you others which are not accessible to other men? If you think that there is nothing better than wine, then you are a very vicious man indeed, and it will be of no use telling you of the ancient heretic kings. Mighty kings, who were to their powerful enemies even as the wind is to cotton, are known to have been destroyed by wine. Think of this. Maliek Jasratha[10] who took possession of a kingdom knew of the sin of drinking wine, but he was wise and kept himself aloof from it. His son Shahimasoda[11] began to drink at sports and pastimes after his father's death and lost everything. The great city of the Malleka, rich with the seven[12] requisites of royal power, has now become a thing of the past, owing to the evil habits of the wicked son, and is even like a corpse with seven members. Wine is red in the cup, and by its colour I take it to be the heart's blood of him who drinks it. There is no enemy to the living like wine which is taken as beneficial; for when taken in excess it kills. Men drunk with the *maireya* (wine) will commit deeds which even a madman will not do, for even he shrinks from such acts. The spirit in the shape of wine enters the body of the man who drinks and in a moment destroys his life while he is weeping or laughing. O son! You have come to your present condition by taking wine which is poison; now save your life, and give up this hateful wine from today. You are foolish and addicted to evil habits, but if you do not give up wine without delay, you will be deserted by your good fortune, and your life will be short."

## Family feuds

When the prince heard these very commendable words of his father, he replied that he would drink wine no more without the king's orders. The king saw his son lusterless, weak, emaciated, and devoid of affection even like a lamp with a thin wick and without oil, and he was surrounded by the darkness of despair. The word of advice is dear to those who are fortunate, but those whose adversity is high repent because they did not follow the advice in time. The prince began to drink the poison as soon as he went home, though he was bound by promise to abstain from it. Advice is useless to those who become blind by addiction to a vice. The ministers feared that the king doted on him, and sent secret letters to bring Adamakhana from a distant country. Alarmed at the approach of the younger brother, the elder had on one occasion set out to meet him, but now alarmed at the approach of the elder brother the younger started from the country. When Adamakhana arrived, the king remained indifferent, determining as before, not to be troubled by the quarrels between his two sons. When the uncle arrived in Kashmir a, a terrible battle took place between him and his nephew for the capture of the fort of Androta.[13] At this time the people witnessed the patience of the powerful Hasankhana; for though anxious for the country, he did not march out without the orders of his grandfather.

When the eldest brother entered the house of his father he saw Hajyakhana at the door joined by the youngest brother, and out of policy made peace with him. But though they had sworn peace by the god of the Mausulas, their hearts were not freed from enmity, even as silk[14] cloth does not give up its colour. When people saw that they had met in peace before the king, the country, the nobles, and their own family, they looked upon them with misgivings, as on four lions met in a cavern; and apprehended that ruin arising from their mutual enmity was at hand.

In the meantime the king considered Vahramakhana as the best of his sons; he was the youngest, and the object of jealousy of the other two brothers. The king caused him to be brought before him, and when alone, he thus spoke; "O Vahrama! Your eldest brother has been made your enemy by your unfriendly deed. He will remember the harm you have done to him, and will never be your friend, and it is with vain expectation that you are serving the other brother. How can he leave his own son and attend to your interest? Therefore do not commit such wicked acts as will bring misery in future. Leave him without delay, rely on me alone, and employ your time accordingly. Adhere to the path of rectitude, and prosperity will then come unto you. Otherwise, O foolish man! you will be burnt in the fire of their enmity, even like a thing placed in an iron pan full of heated oil." When he heard these words of his father, he thus replied in his folly: "It appears to me, O King! that Hajyakhana loves me exceedingly like a father. I will never forsake him, but serve him. He will protect me in time of need, and who is at present more powerful than he ?" When the king heard this he was angry, and he thus spoke to the son who had made up his mind: "Fie to thee, that thou hast discarded me and acknowledged another thy father! Ah, foolish man! On what hast thou fixed thy mind after having disregarded my words? There is no doubt that thy expectation will soon be disappointed." He said this and left him.

Then at a time when the king was alone and was not afraid of any mischief from his son, he thus thought in his own mind: "Alas! From me, bright as a house on fire, have sprung these three sons, and they are like the ashes of a wood fire; unlike me, useless, and without luster and he said aloud: 'What should I do at present?' The wise men who were around him said in reply that his kingdom was being ruined by his sons who were aspiring to the throne, and they asked the king why he did not bestow the kingdom on the one who was most friendly to him, so that neither he nor his subjects might be troubled thereafter. Even then, they said, Manikyadeva[15] powerful on account of his wealth, would hear of the newly appointed king, and might turn an enemy and soon cause destruction in the kingdom.

## The King's apprehensions

The king who knew the characters of his sons replied: "The eldest has superior qualifications, but he is a miser, and has therefore no worthy servants who can consolidate a kingdom. The second is very liberal, but his expenses are so great that if he had gold as high as the Pradyumna[16] hill, there would not be one *karsha* of it left. The youngest is wickedly inclined and addicted to vice, he would soon ruin the court. I do not consider any of them to be a good and worthy son. I will not bestow the kingdom on any; he who is the strongest will get it when I am dead; this is my purpose. Who will appreciate my worth unless many perish in the conflict after I am gone? Men will then appreciate my peaceful reign. One does not know that the sun has set if darkness does not cover all sides, and men's sight is not blinded, if robbers do not rob, and good people are not alarmed. I have obtained the kingdom by my own power, and have governed it by my intelligence, but by quarrelling among themselves my wicked sons are destroying everything. The royal power with its seven constituents, and with its mineral wealth is like a body with seven limbs and blood; but it is being wasted by the three wicked sons, as by three diseases. There does not exist a good minister today who, like a physician, can restore it to health by nourishment and treatment. I have long enjoyed this kingdom, and have tasted the joys of religion, song, literature, and my life is satiated. I have no other work to do. I have, owing to my love for my subjects, increased all the new productions of the country threefold by means of canals, cultivation, and by other ways. I have always conversed with learned persons for the preservation of the six schools of philosophy, have invited such persons from all places, and granted lands for holy purposes. But as there are gaps between the teeth in the mouth, so there are defects in the government of the country, and they are causing me pain every day. I shall therefore secure happiness by leaving the kingdom. As a lamp is hateful[17] to the eye of thieves, so have I become hateful to many; but they will soon have to pine for in the country. Even my sons have not been able to remain quiet all this time while I am alive; they will not die in a hurry; and I wish to depart from this life so that all my sons may obtain what they desire."

When they heard this speech of the sorrowful king, they again said: "If this be thy intention, O King! why have you then kept great treasures accumulated? Spend them while you are alive and make it pay your way to the next world."

When the king heard this he replied, "That is well said, but listen to the reason why the treasury is kept full. When I am dead, any of my sons who may gain the kingdom will be satisfied with the savings left, and will not covet for the wealth of my subjects who are dearer to me than my sons, and I think it my duty to protect them. I will thus prevent the future oppression of the subjects with the savings I have made. He enjoys whose treasury is full, and when it is drained, he oppresses the subjects. If the lion's hunger is satisfied, he plays within the cavern: but if hungry, he devours the beasts of the forest. One will call me a foresighted man, and will not speak ill of me when the subjects will be free from oppression in future on account of my savings. When the palace is full of riches, men outside it will become rich and will be friendly to their king. If the clouds did not take water from the sea, how could they shower it on the ground? It is always by the means of riches that all the beautiful objects which the king possesses are obtained; the fruits, the leaves, and the flowers that grow on the trees are produced by one cause: the sap within the ground."

When those who had questioned the king heard this reply of the experienced sovereign, they were silenced. The king's palace attended by soldiers is like the sea attended by rivers; it is full with various objects, and people come there in quest of those objects. The abundance in all things is the beauty of the palace as of the sea. When afterwards the people found that all that the king had said was verified, they all were afflicted with sorrow, and recalled his sayings to their mind, and praised his experience.

## Withdrawal of desire'

There was none among the ministers, servants, sons, friends, relatives and kindred who could console the king. He heard of the affairs of his sons who were enemies to one another, but were now united in hollow friendship; and he remained in the central room of the palace and was afraid to come out. I knew how to explain to the king the way to remove worldly afflictions, and for nights together he heard from me the Samhita[18] which is the way to salvation. The king was for a time consoled by listening to my explanations, the modulations of my voice and well-turned beautiful passages. "This appears to me most strange that this waking illusion of good men like the color of the sky (vacuum) sinks into oblivion in which there is no memory of the past. O son of Raghu! Be it long or be it pleasant, know this mundane existence to be a long dream as unsubstantial as a large imaginary kingdom. If there had been no birth, old age, or death, no fear of separation from the beloved object, and if all had not been fleeing, who would not have wished to have been born in this world? Men will be freed from objects from which they withdraw their desire; a man cannot know of greater happiness than by withdrawing his desire from all earthly things."

## Bitterness

The king learnt *shlokas* like those mentioned above by listening to my explanations, and also many others which indicated his own condition, and he himself read[19] them. The king heard me read the "Way to Salvation", and pondered over the meaning of many verses, and on one occasion he told the learned who were about him that some one seemed to whisper to his ear enquiring why he loved his sons none of whom was friendly to him. He thought to himself: "By eating meat with our teeth, flesh is served with flesh, and in such meals, which enriches our blood and gives us strength, I see no harm. I am mild in my temper, and I promote the happiness of all, but alas! my sons are attempting my destruction as insects destroy woollen cloth by making holes.

"None of those with whom I have spent my former years are left behind; the affliction which I feel for their absence will last to the end of my life. O Muni! My body is like a cottage which is worn out, and is covered with hair as with grass; it is full of rents, and my mind dislikes it in this evil day. The districts of my kingdom have been ruined by my sons, even as the members of the body are bitten by serpents. The only means left to me is to part with them, otherwise there is no peace." After he had thus thought he composed a book in the Parasi language named *Shikayat*[20] treating of the vanity of all objects.

## Dissensions and defections

The sons of the king's nurse and others of proved and honourable character left the party of the king and went over to Hajyakhana. What else need be said? Those shameless men who were seen with the king during daytime, were at night found seated at ease before the Khana. The king remained indifferent to the affairs of the kingdom, and his servants reviled one another, and consequently there was a tumult in the country. When the king was in danger who would not go over to his sons, as if hoping to obtain thereby one half of the kingdom? Thus thought the king and he was ignorant of the true movements of his servants, and became disgusted with all the members of his family. He who was seen today to be with the king, was heard of as attending the Khana the next morning. Like the Sarasa birds the servants nowhere remained steady. The king did not find a single servant devoted to him, who could give him consolation, and to whom he could describe the troubles of his heart. The people came to the palace unopposed and uttered words such as had never been uttered before and spoke of things such as had never been seen or heard of before. Bahramakhana, by his various acts of duplicity and by his eagerness to foment quarrel between his brothers, became like Karna, the source of evil. A stick of wood, if it contains oil, will give light, but does that light last long? Does it not spread darkness on all sides with its smoke?

## The war of succession

It was to protect the king that Adamakhana had come, and protection was expected from him, but he was incapable of protecting himself. He informed the king one day that Bahran had joined his brother Hajyakhana, and had sought by cruel stratagem to destroy him, and that he (Adamakhana) had no other course left but to seek the king's protection. From Bahram he had no hope of life, and he therefore asked the king to save him. If the king reigned in the kingdom, Adamakhana feared nothing. But the people eager to engage in a battle between the brothers were on that day coming to attack him, and he was overcome with fear at the news. Thus informed, the king replied that he had no attachment for his own kingdom or for his own life, and he called Adamakhana a coward, and advised him to go and save himself, and told him that he need not have come to him. Thus rebuked by the king, Adamakhana went to Kudmadinapuri and kept himself on the watch, afraid of an attack from his younger brother. The king had thought that this ambitious man Adamakhana was worthy of his protection, hoping to find comfort in him and expecting that he would remove the king's fear of his enemies. But Adamakhana was himself assailed by his enemies, he was like a horse afraid of the harness, and became a cause of trouble; and the king was surprised to hear that his other two sons thought that he had taken their elder brother, the object of their hatred, near him out of his fear of them. Neither the king, nor the king's son nor the ministers could sleep owing to mutual fear.

## Dotage

The servants did not serve in accordance with orders but tried to please their masters by words only, and when the servants did perform the duties by the king, he would declare that he did not remember what he had ordered. He left off the old practice of signing his orders, and knowing the unsettled state of his mind, he left the administration to his ministers. "The wicked men have set the fire of enmity to my house, and have received pay *from both sides*. But they do not care to quench the fire. Let my ministers and my sons perish: I helped them to prosper and they now wish to obtain my kingdom and will rejoice in my ruin." Thus sighing and unsettled in mind, sorrowful and devoted to religious meditation, the king wished that they might all perish. The citizens exclaimed that the king was indifferent to everything, that his sons were engaged in mutual enmity, and that a great calamity had befallen them.

## The King's sorrow

When the month of fasting for the *yavanas* arrived the king left off taking meat, and reflected thus: "Those who brought this wicked son from a distant country, are, alas! for their own interest destroying my whole kingdom. On one side of the city are the two sons with their combined army, and on the other side is one son alone attended by wicked men and wicked ministers. A great calamity has come! The sons will fight, but I am sorry for this city which should, like a good wife, be guarded. What would be the use of my living if the city be destroyed while I am alive? The servants who were devoted to me, and strong, are ail gone, whom shall I ask for advice and what shall I do? The king's mind was afflicted by these anxious thoughts and by sorrow caused thereby. Stricken by such grief, the king, who was solicitous for the welfare of his kingdom, became like one inanimate.

The city, with its population, old and young, was agitated with alarm on account of many evil news; and it was like a boisterous sea which the king could not calm. On the next day when Shivabhatta brought the king his meals, the king became angry and said that he had eaten what he could eat, and told him to take the food away. In the excess of his anxiety the king became distrustful even of a shadow. He heard that the ministers intended to rise against him, but he took no care of his own life. For a few days he remained like one whose intellect was gone, and when questioned by his friends, he made reply to none. On one occasion when the ministers asked him some questions about the affairs of the state, he uttered some words without meaning, and as if oppressed with illness he laid himself exhausted on the bed. The physicians did not know the cause nor the symptoms of his illness, but I think he took the vow of fasting in order to get himself rid of his affliction. High as lofty trees, yielding food with extended arms, of high renown, and beloved of Brahmanas as the trees are beloved of birds, the good kings are struck down by evil fate as by a gale.

## Bahram's plans

In the meantime the three sons disorganized all the seven constituents of the kingdom, as terrible diseases destroy the humours of the body. The Rajputs[21] were alarmed, and came every day, with many soldiers, and found the king in his miserable plight and almost dumb. The king was afraid of his sons, but in order to give an audience to all, he was placed in his wretched condition before the gate of the palace, with his elephants and horses. Men belonging to the palace and those outside thronged to see the king; they heard the sound of religious festivities and beheld the king with gladness, as one beholds the moon on the second day after the new moon. Bahramakhana became alarmed when he heard of this and came near to the palace, but he knew by the symptoms that the king was on the point of death. He then went to a distance and thus said to his brother: "Our father will not live; he fell on the ground before the gate, and was almost dumb and unconscious. Vainly is he being raised up by the cunning people. Therefore arise, and let us go to the rear of the king's palace clad in iron mail, and bind the wicked ministers, and take possession of the horses and of other things. We will cut down the bridge of boats, and that will prove the ruin of your elder brother." When Hajyakhana heard this, he said: "This should not be spoken before me. I do not even in dream wish any harm to my father and king." He then spent one night in grief with his father.

When Adamakhana heard the report that his father was dead, he moved with his army towards Shri Jainanagara with a view to usurp his father's kingdom. In the way he caused his soldiers to be clad in armour for his own defence. He then passed one night secretly in a house at the outskirts of the capital. In the meantime, Hassana, the treasurer, blinded by self-interest and deceiving others, took oath to Shri Hajyakhana and sought his shelter. On the next day the eldest brother, driven by the minister, reached Kudmadinapuri with his army; but there his good fortune left him. Though he was the eldest and possessed of a strong intellect, though himself a hero endowed with unusual energy and patience, and attended by followers, he was still unable to perform any signal deed in the time of action; for men devoid of virtue cannot achieve success. Had Adamakhana killed a guard that night and captured the horses, he would have got the kingdom. But the intelligence of a man is according to his merit.

In the meantime Hajyakhana sent by the treasurer and his youngest brother, went into the yard of the palace, and took possession of his father's horses. When those servants of the prince who had been impatient for fight, heard of the news of the capture of the .animals, they suited their action to the time, clad themselves in armour and entered the palace. Abhimanyu the Pratihara[22], and others reviled them, but they were soon punished by the confusion that followed. Hajyakhana with his army remained that day outside the palace, afraid of a rising, and though he was anxious to see the king he could not do so.

## Adamakhan's flight

While Adamakhana heard of this news, he became alarmed. He was in a defenceless condition, and despairing of success, he went with his followers by the road leading to Vipulata.[23]

Surrounded by his own men, Adamakhana marched by the way of Tarabala. His younger brother pursued him and killed many of his soldiers. When Abhimanyu the Pratihara and others beheld the superhuman prowess of Adamakhana, they found that he fulfilled what his name implied.* He killed many men in his anger and their corpses were heaped in the caverns of the mountain. In the meantime prince Hassankhana, resplendent with many virtues, soon passed over Parnotsa and came within Kashmira. The tree growing on barren soil is dried up by the heat of summer, and becomes sapless, and casts no shadow, and is forsaken by travellers; but when nourished by the copious waters of the rainy season it is decked with flowers, it shelters men from the heat, and becomes enjoyable. As a river is equally accessible from both its banks, even so the kingdom was hitherto accessible to the two belligerents, but now it became favourable to one party. Thus by the conduct of the two brothers, victories and defeats were brought about by fate in a way which the people had not anticipated. Who does not wish for a son? And when a son is born, who does not feel both happiness and anxiety on his account, and does not strive by various means to bring up the child? But Alas! when the child is grown up, he seeks through his avarice to obtain his father's wealth, and is even anxious for the time when the father would die, and considers him as a hindrance in his way.

* It is difficult to unravel this pun. It seems that the pun lies in the similarity of the sound of Adamakhana and *Admi-khun*, the latter is a Hindi word. (Trns-r)

## Death of Zain-ul-Abdin

At this time the king, surrounded by a few servants, remained without as if he had not heard of the reports which had reached him. He gave out that owing to illness his voice had failed and he had lost the power of deglutition. His beauty was gone, and he became like the moon when near its end. It was owing to the misfortune of his subjects and for the affliction of all, that the king, shorn of his beauty and suffering from malady, appeared like the sun about to set at the end of the *kalpa*. By the quivermg of his life it was known that he was praying, and he expired at noon on Friday, on the twelfth[24] day of the moon in the month of Jaishtha. At the time of his death Fortune seemed to abandon all his limbs and appeared on his face, and I saw him in that state. His face, methought, was the dwelling place of the goddess of Fortune, and perspiration issued from it, even like a stream of good luck. His breath left him, taking his life with it, and as if afraid of having stolen that jewel. After life had departed, tears still issued from his eyes, as if his eyes which were like the sun and the moon melted away and his affection for his subjects trickled down.

King Shri Jaina reigned happily for fifty-two years, and went to heaven in the year[25] 46. The corpse was placed in a litter and was borne on men's shoulders, and on it were placed the umbrella and the chamara, and they looked like the sun and the moon dropped from the sky in their sorrow. At that time the ministers, servants, slaves and citizens offered oblation to the dead in tears of lamentation. The king had obtained the kingdom in the month of Jaishtha in the year 96; and the period of the sun's course towards the north[26] ended with him. He had counted sixty-nine years, and the beauty of the flowing black beard was still seen on his face. After death his body became a corpse and he became a Shiva.

## Funeral

Such was the king that was borne on a litter and, adorned with umbrella and *chamara*, was brought by the weeping ministers to the burial ground, where the previous kings looked beautiful as in sleep, and the earth, as if out of affection for her lords, had received them in her bosom. All sides resounded with the loud lamentation of the sorrowing citizens as if with the noise of sounding brass. Within the city no other voice was heard than the cry of "O King. O life of the people! Where art thou going, leaving thy subjects behind." The ears of the men were incessantly filled with these cries, so that they sometimes seemed to hear the cries in the air. The king was then lifted from the litter which was being borne on men's shoulders, and was covered with doth, and laid within the bowels of the earth beside his father[27]. The people looked on the face of the king with tearful eyes, and, as required by their rites, they threw a handful of earth on him, as if to indicate that there would be no other king like him and that the world was ruined by his death. Monarchs who had conquered powerful enemies in battle, had covered the earth with riches, and had given wealth to all; who had built cities named after them, and were well-known in other countries; who had long reigned in the country possessed of the seven component parts of royalty, leave all behind in the end, and receive only the winding sheet for their portion. Scorched by a hostile country, as by a forest fire, the deceased king enjoyed the sleep of ease in the cool interior of the grave-yard.

Hajyakhana saw the face of his father graced by fortune, and appearing as if in sleep, and for seven nights he performed the rite of *mastakam.*[28] He exclaimed: "O father! Bent on wickedness I have many a time transgressed against thee, and methinks you have left me in your anger, and have gone to heaven alone. Admirable is king Shekandhara who is in heaven and now beholds thee. Fie to me, O King! that I am deprived of the sight of thee. Nowhere, O Father! at the time of festivity did you enjoy yourself without me; how then do you now enjoy the pleasures of heaven alone? You could not obtain sleep on a soft bed and surrounded by men, how can you now sleep on the gravel in the midst of those buried in the earth? When I left you and returned to my house who did not curse me in anger saying that we two might not speak to each other again? We wicked sons always kept you sleepless, and art thou now having thy long sleep? O King! your person was consumed with ever present anxiety; has that anxiety of yours been now transferred to another? O father! I see thy face in the portrait[29] and in my imagination, but where shall I, who have so much sinned against thee, hear thy voice? Without thee, O master! my kingdom is a thing of danger to me, the day is night, the good garden is a cemetry and life is death. Come, O father! and show thyself to me, be thou angry or propitious. I am unable to bear this death-like pain of separation. O father! where hast thou gone leaving me, thy servant, behind; the lotus bud does not expand without the sun. Art thou angry O king? I am thy servant bent on serving thee; and in consideration of my excessive solicitude speak but one word to me, for without thee I shall not live."

Thus the prince lamented, and performed the rites of the *bhuja* night; he gazed on the face of the king for a long time and wept around. Thus loudly lamenting, Hajyakhama was our come with grief and when the day declined the ministers forcibly took him to the palace. For the benefit of his deceased father, the son, while yet he was on the burial ground, gave away his own village of Salora[30] for the supply of drinking water to the people in the hot season; and for the services of those who provided the water, he permanently endowed lands in that village and allotted them for a religious purpose. At this time the sun, as if unable to look upon the earth without a king, set in the sea; and the earth casting away her garment of evening cloud, spread the gloom of the evening which was even like her dishevelled hair to weep in sorrow for the king. A darkness prevailed in the kingdom at the death of the king. He had raised high hopes in men, he was of princely appearance, and a friend of the men of merit. No one cooked[31] his food that day, no smoke arose from the houses, all were dumb with grief and breathless. Such was the state of the capital which seemed to be without life.

## Reflections

A long crystal stone was placed in the grave-yard, it was the highest among those that were there, and was like the figure of the king in a recumbent position, and it was illumined with verses. Men came to see the place out of curiosity and they lamented and shed tears on the king, which looked like offerings of pearls. It was Friday when the citizens went to the grave-yard, and their images were beautifully reflected on the stone, as if the king out of curiosity had drawn them near to him. The people remembered the king's breast broad as a door panel, his face beautiful as the full moon, the tip of his long nose like the beak of the Suka bird, the eyes tender as the lotus, his hairy eye-brow and forehead bright with auspicious signs, and his intellect and his qualifications, and his attention to kingly duties. All these came to their mind as if they were standing before the king himself; and they spoke lightly of the world, as devoid of worth and substance.

If the moon beams of the full moon, the beauty of the flowers of spring, the purity of the autumnal sky, the budding youth of women, and the rule of a wise king, all these that afford happiness to men, were made lasting by fate, men would not long for heaven. In his boyhood, the king lost his father, and apprehended mischief from the principal[32] minister, and was involved in a quarrel with his brothers and servants. He was living in foreign countries when he got the kingdom; then there was a distressing war with his elder brother; his nurse's sons then caused him anxiety; and afterwards the opposition of his sons lasted till his death. Fie to the life of living beings on this earth, ever attended with sorrow, and ever evil eye towards his sons, it was no doubt owing to the position of the stars at his nativity that he suffered so much affliction from the hands of his children.

All the king's learned men and even the poets who were ever so eloquent, became silent when the king was gone, even as *kokilas* are found mute in the month of Pausha. The books of the learned, which, even like the eyes of the goddess of learning, had ever remained open (during the king's reign) were now tied up and became shrunk. There were men who in order to win the king's favour had worked in logic, in grammar, and in other branches of learning for the benefit of the vernacular[33] of the country, and who had been honoured by the king and had enjoyed ease and prosperity in their homes. They had exerted themselves, day and night, to obtain books, and had learnt the *shastras*, and when questioned on the subject of their study, could make recitations from their books. But where was grammar, where were the discussions of logic, and where was the labour in the cause of literature after king Shri Jaina died? That king who was the master of all learning, who was benevolent to men, accessible, meritorious and natural, the king who knew the literature of many languages, who was favourable to the men of merit, and untiring in work of kindness and of virtue, that king, alas! is now laid on the ground. Fie to us, sinful and depraved in our hearts! Overcome by the love of the world, we still live therein, and do not fly to the wilderness in sorrow.

## Consolidated Kashmir

As the bosom of a woman does not look graceful without a necklace, nor the intellect without learning, nor the expanded lotus flowers without the sun, nor the human body without youth, nor the night without the moon, nor a wife without her husband, even so the kingdom of Kashmira did not look graceful without its king. Good men felt sorrowful at heart, and found no rest; and they always lamented and said that king Shri Jainollabhadena was the greatest among all sovereigns, that he was versed in all learning and loved the study of logic and other branches of knowledge, and that he consequently shone in the glory of the learned. He was distinguished by his desire to see learned men collected around him, and by his wish to bestow gifts and honours on them, as well as by his well-deserved fame. They said that he had consolidated Kashmira, and had gone as if to consolidate heaven which was in a state of confusion.

The royal family, like a bamboo group in a garden, decked by variegated grass and a profusion of leaves, was an object of beauty for a long time; but alas! domestic broils, like a fire caused by friction, burnt all the things in the garden from one end to the other. The office of Shri Jaina, owing to his curse, melted away within one year, even like a dream; and in the kingdom which was disturbed at his death, only one in a hundred of his servants remained, even like jewels in the ocean after it is agitated by a gale. Servants remain with the master and honour him as long as he who supports them remains in power. The bee, the *kokila*, and the frog hail the spring with their voice as long as spring lasts on earth. Even those few servants of the king who remained, withered like grass under innumerable scorching suns.

Here ends the first book named 'the account Jainashahi' of *Jainarajatarangini* composed by Pandita Shrivara.

## References

1. Uttarpatha: northern route....*yavana*: an outsider, pb. a Muslim foreigner.
2. Vimsaparastha: *maidani* Idgah (S.K.).
3. Rajjupura: see also p. 23. Identity with Rathapora in downtown Srinagar has also been suggested. A bow is equivalent to two yards.
4. killed him: this happened in 1469 A.D.
5. hermits: should read 'built by Suyya who accomplished what he aimed at.'
6. shrine: does it refer to the shrine at the place now known as Zinpore (from Jainapur)?
7. Srivakashisha: Shri Baka (SK).

8. Vodhakhatona: daughter of Syed Mohammad Baihaqi, died in 890 h. (1465 A.D.). The king had also two daughters of the Madra (Jammu) chief as his wives. Suratrana: Suitan....Kramadina: Oayama-ud-Din.
9. Evvarahima: Ibrahim.... Merakhushamada. Mir Khush Ahmad.
10. Mallik Jasrath was a Gakhar leader of the Murree hills who headed rebellion at Sirhind and Jallandhar (Lane Poole.) Z. overcame Alishash with his help.
11. Shahimasodha: Masud Shah.
12. seven...: the king, ministers, citizens, the capital city, the treasury, the armed forces, and the friendly states (the *Arthasastra*).
13. Androta; Androtakotta (SK), the citadel of Jayapida (746-81 A.D.) Another v. named Androth is in Rajauri t. Since Hassan Shah came from Poonch to Rajauri, a confrontation at Androth could not be far-fetched.
14. Silk: another interpretation makes it 'woollen'.
15. Manikyadeva: the chief of Madra or Jammu and the maternal uncle of Adama Khan. Dewan Kripa Ram's *Gulabnama* refers to him as the son of Maldev who died in 1399 A.D. But Manikyadev should be two generations distant in the present context.
16. Pradyumna hill; Sharikaparvat close to the capital.
17. hateful...: it indicates that some people were not happy with him. These included the sons of his nurse.
18. Samhita: 'Mokshapaya Samhita' from *Yogavasishtha*.
19. read himself.: Z. could obviously read and understand writing in Sanskrit. The *sloka* is: yedi janma jara mamam na bhavet/yedi veysht viyog bhayam na bhavet/yedi sarvam nityam idam na bhavet/dih janmani ratir na bhavet.
20. *Shikayat*: 'Complaint'.... Parasi: Persian.
21. Rajputs: Rajputras (SK); could also mean princes (as of Rajauri) who had accepted Z.'s overlordship. See also 212/86.
22. Pratihara: later became a clan-name in the form of 'Padar.'
23. Vipulata: Vishulata (SK). PH states that Adamakhana departed from the Baramula route. Stein identifies Vishalata with the valley of the Bichlari river to the s. of Devasar and the hill dt. of Banihal. Tarabal: see 78/55.
24. twelfth day: should be of the dark fortnight as Z.'s successor Haidershah took possession of the kingdom on the first of lunar Jeth, four days later.
25. Year 46: there appears to be some discrepancy in the length of Z.'s reign as given by Shrivara. From Jeth '96 to Jeth' 46 the total is only 50 years,
26. north: pb.Z. passed away on June 22.
27. father: at the royal cemetry below Zainakadal.
28. *mastakam*: pb. bowed respectfully; *bhuja* night: Waved arms in reverence.

29. Portrait: appears to have been lost.
30. Salora: v. on river Sindh opp. to Ganderbal.
31. Cooked: till recent times, people in Kashmir, out of respect for the deceased in their neighbourhood, did not eat or even cook food till the cremation was over.
32. Principle minister: pb. Suhabhatta *alias* Sadr-ud-Din.
33. Vernacular: no trace of the works in Kashmiri composed during the reign of Zain-ul-Abdin has been found.

**Shrivara's**

***Jainarajatarangini***

## BOOK II

# Sultan Haider Shah

I bow to the god (Mahadeva) who is the master of the hidden significance of all words, and who pervades all the universe. Who does not, by prayer in the form of a partial description of his person, attain the fruit of worship? His right foot is fixed in the ground, and his left foot, though oft in motion, seeks to rest, and describes a circle on a straight line. The god not unoften performs a dance while walking in the evening. Let that deity, a god and a goddess in one, ever bestow happiness on us.

## Coronation

By an order under his seal, Hajyakhana now declared his name to be Haidarashaha, and took possession of the kingdom on the first[1] day of the moon in the month of Jaishtha. A festivity was held on the occasion of his taking over the kingdom in which the performance of religious acts predominated, and joy was promoted by gifts, and many auspicious acts were done, and many who sought happiness found it. Shekandharapuri[2] was full of happy men, the favourites of the king were clad in clean garments and the city looked as beautiful as the sky when full of stars. The new powerful monarch sat on a golden throne in the yard of the palace, even as the sun sits on the peak of the Meru mountain. In his front sat his son[3] and his handsome youngest brother, who looked like the planets Venus and Jupiter before the moon. The treasurer Hassana distributed money, as ordered, and put the mark of royalty on the forehead of the king with offerings of gold and flowers, As in the rainy season the clouds rule the world with lightnings, even so did the king Hajyahaidhara govern the country. The king's youngest brother Bahramakhana was even like himself and, through affection, the king made him lord of Sukshiti[4] in the Nagrama[5] country[6]. It was after a long time that the king met his son, and overwhelmed as he then was with sorrow for his father, he found even greater comfort than what he had felt when he was appointed heir-apparent of the kingdom. Avatara[7] Lavaka and others found great favour with the king, and were invested with authority in the kingdom. Other servants also obtained favours from the new king and obtained the gifts of villages, good or indifferent, according to their previous services. The king then parted with the kings of Rajapuri[8] and Sindhu who had come to see him, after decking them with ornaments befitting kings. In the king's palace, ministers, feudatory kings, captains of armies, and others, adorned with daggers of gold, mingled in the rejoicings, and with them moved the servants to whom were given valuable garments of silk. The king, free from all vices, protected his people, even like the waxing moon[9] in her fortnightly career.

## Alliance with Syeds

There lived one Merja Hassana[10], son of Saida Nasira, and he was the chief of Bahurupa and other provinces. He was of an affectionate nature and fond of nursing children; his mind was devoid of avarice and anger; he dispelled the darkness of ignorance and he was honored in the kingdom as his father was. In festivities and on all joyous occasions, Merja Hassana and his party were honoured as the foremost. The king therefore thought that by attaching him to his son he would make his son as powerful as himself, and he accordingly caused his son to marry the daughter of Merja Hassana. The king had killed Jehangira, son of Jyamsara the Margapati, and attracted by the merit of Merja Hassana he now bestowed Bhangila[11] on him. The king favoured even those who did him harm; the lion first stoops before elephants and then kills them.

## Traits of conduct

The king kept his purposes concealed, and through his spies informed himself of the acts of Hassana the Treasurer,[12,] and he bestowed honours on Hassana and brought him under his power. The prowess of the king made his enemies grieve; he concealed his anger, and was like the fire which lies concealed in ashes and is the cause of death to many. He affected friendship with some, and they did not apprehend any danger until he found his opportunity to act against them. Others he honoured out of policy, and thus he acted from various motives. He was like Kuvera[13] to his servants when he bestowed his favours, but he was like death to them when they were at fault. Phiryya Damara and other ministers knew of the fierce anger of the king, and bore their sorrow in secret. Thieves, immoral men, and the enemies and oppressive servants of the king were like jackals in the kingdom, they wandered about during day time in fear.

## Oppression by Purna

After the death of king Shri Jaina the king's officers again harassed the people, even like serpents deprived of their head jewel. Even the full moon, which illumines all sides and becomes worthy of the enjoyment of the gods, has its stain, and the king likewise had one stain in his character. The courtiers of the king combined among themselves, and urged by the fear that the king would kill all of them when he would hear of their faults, they plotted to bring in a stranger. A barber by the name of Riktetara[14] became the favourite of the king; he advised wicked deeds, was full of vices, and accepted unfair bribes. Men addicted to enjoyments cannot leave off evil habits, and thus the present sovereign, though daily reproached by the late king, could not cast off this barber who had become his favourite. This wily barber, who had accumulated riches through the toil of the people and who was skilled in devices for accomplishing his purpose, now became widely known by his gifts of money. The cunning man kept concealed by the sweetness of his tongue the hardness of his heart which led him to oppress the people. Having thus attained the power he wickedly harassed the subjects who had been protected by the king, as if they had been his sons. The wise and renowned Merabhokhara[15], who was devoid of all angry feelings, became the minister of the king, and through the king's favour Machuryya[16] was made the accountant, but the latter appropriated money, which belonged to the king, from all the offices.

The cloud which produces water and is the delight of the pea-fowl, which causes a plentiful crop to grow in cultivated fields and drives away heat, also afflicts the people by discharging the thunderbolt. The king remained in a state of insensibility through wine, and instigated by wicked ministers, did unwise acts, and caused the misfortune of the subjects. He wished to build an edifice by the side of Shekandharapuri, and ordered the lofty trees in the Amrita[17] Park to be cut down. The bees saw the trees with the flowers cut down and left them, and raised a hum as if in lamentation. The people did not sympathize with the king's attempt to build the edifice; it was like the desire to light a lamp under the sun. He was surely drunk when he did this. We say this because he did many things that were harmful to him. The barber obtained the orders of the king when he was drunk, and mutilated many men. The relentless and sinful barber cut off the Thakkuras[18] and courtiers of the king's father by the saw. Five or six persons were going to their elder brother for the purpose of performing the rites of *svavana*[19], but the barber arrested them in the way, impaled them, and thus caused them to be killed. They lived for a few nights, their sufferings were narrated by their relatives, and they were seen by the citizens fixed to the pales with tears in their eyes. The barber knew Vaiduryya the physician to be a calumniator, and a partisan of the enemy, and he released the physician from arrest after cutting off his arms, his nose, and his lips. Similarly, Nonadeva, Shikhajada[20], and others, five or six persons in all, had their tongues, noses, and a hand cut off. By such outrageous acts as mutilation and impaling, the barber Purna became the butcher of men. Jayya the son of an Acharyya, as also a Brahmana named Bhima were maimed, and they struggled and threw themselves into the Vitasta.

## Patronizes musicians

In this reign, owing to the prevalence of drunkenness, wine came to be prepared from molasses as from grapes, and this wine became as common here as the wine prepared from sugar is in other countries. When the king became addicted to wine and averse to all other kinds of enjoyment, molasses and candies and other things prepared from the juice of sugarcane became scarce. Malladaudaka[21] was a great master of music, and his pupil Khujyabdolkadira taught the king to play on the lute. He acquired proficiencies in the music of the lute and other instruments from us and he devoted all his life to the music of the lute, without a moment's intermission. The king understood the art of playing on the lute and was well-skilled in it, so that he gave lessons even to the professors. Vahlola and others played on the *ravava*, and what did they not earn thereby through the favour of the king who showered gold on them. Every man was afraid of the king who was always under the influence of the wicked even when he was in his private apartments or among his women, and the wicked were like demons well-skilled in dissimulation.

## Revolt brewing

Once upon a time the ministers sent the barber Purna to the king, and when the king was alone, the barber asked him what he intended to do with the former ministers. "These your father's ministers", he said, "destroyed your party, and yet you have made them powerful now that you have obtained the kingdom. These men, Hassana the treasurer and others, are loved by your youngest brother, and cunning as he is, he is trying to win them over by his wiles. Your body is frail and you have always confided in your brother, so that it will not be long before the destruction of yourself, your sons, and your servants is effected." When the king heard this he said, "It is true that my youngest brother dislikes my son, but I will tell you the reason why, nevertheless, I give protection to this wily man. My youngest brother is violent in temper and my eldest, who is active in his preparations to usurp my place, is cunning. I intend to quell my eldest brother by means of my youngest, even as a thorn is extracted by a thorn. It is for the sake of this service that I am giving him shelter, not out of respect for him." When the barber heard this he made two or three great men acquainted with the intention of the king.

In the meantime the king's haughty elder brother arrived at Parnotsa with his army from the Madra country, with the intention of usurping his brother's kingdom. When the king heard of this, he became angry; he caused his father's officers to be brought before him and asked them what should be done. They replied, "Your elder brother has come, but we will go and cut the bridge over the narrow river otherwise, should he arrive here, he would be irresistible. O master! order us to do," When the king heard their request, he misunderstood their motive, and suspected that they were deserting him to go over to the side of his brother; and he replied, "So will it be."

The king then left them, and at night called before him his ministers Phiryyadara and others, who had become cruel in the prosecution of their work. They informed the king that it was owing to the conspiracy of Hassana, the treasurer, that his elder brother had come, and that if Hassana were destroyed his brother would retire, otherwise he would enter the capital. They advised that Hassana should be brought by some artifice and killed in the morning. Accordingly the king concealed his anger and gave orders to his servants. On the morning Hassana the treasurer and others, being summoned by the king, left their attendants behind and came out of their homes. The affrighted horse, as if it knew the purpose of the summons, remained motionless and began to tremble, and it was after much urging that, with tears in its eyes, it came to the yard of the palace. Hassana, the treasurer, Merakaka[22], and others, five or six in all, then seated themselves on a valuable carpet, and were anxious to learn what the work of the king was which had to be performed. As ordered by the king, Jamsara[23] and other servants first won the confidence of the party by dissimulation and then killed them within the room in the palace. The treasurer rose and acclaimed against the treachery, but with one stroke of a hatchet he was deprived of his life. Struck by the weapon, and on the point of death, Merakaka blessed the king and then expired. Ahmadamera, a man of merit, a lover of learning and the delight of the people, was murdered while engaged in writing, and every one was grieved for him. While alive these men had lived united, and when cut off by the hatchet their blood mingled: just before their death they had been seated on a coloured blanket, and when dead, they were seen on it as if in sleep. The death by the hatchet which they met, all in a moment, inside the palace, was such as is unattainable by others, and it was a glory to them. Thus were they killed and at their last moment neither riches, nor wife, no servants, nor tombs were of use to them.

## Debtors punished

The fear of the king was more distressing than the fear of death; the people were chastised or imprisoned for debts, and the friends of a debtor deserted him through fear lest the debt might devolve on them. Even one's own wife deserts a man on such an occasion, not to speak of servants. It was more dangerous to serve the king than to embrace fire, to go before an angry cobra, or to fall into the ocean. The *chandalas* at night took the bodies as of men who had no friends, and buried them in a hole in the ground at the foot of the Pradyumna hill, and covered the place with bricks. The Mausulas always take care about the structure over their graves and pay money to the architects. We often forget that no one can know, except God, when or how one may die. He alone is fit to build a tomb who knows the period of his life, and to whom Death is obedient as a friend. This is my view. Vaishravanabhatta and others had built their tombs, but when in the end they died in a village, they were laid there on the ground. An ordinary man carefully encloses a hundred cubits of land and prevents others from entering it; should he not stop short of this? It is said in the (Mohammadan) *shastra* that if a small stone be laid on the grave that stone becomes a source of joy to the man who has gone to the other world. Some great men seem to enjoy their life in taking pains over building tombs.

## Property confiscated

Those who acquire wealth, even if as great as a king, by oppression and do not spend any portion of it in charity or in enjoyment, they by their sinfulness earn misery which is the fruit of sin. All objects belonging to such men depart from their houses and become the property of the king, and their indigent relatives do not get even a shell. The treasurer had amassed vessels of silver filled with gold, and when the king saw them he spat on the ground exclaiming, "Fie to the miser"! Everything which Vahmarga[24] and other partisans of the treasurer had hoarded, was taken away, and with the exception of Saida Hossana, they were all thrown into prison. Others received the punishment of death from the king, for the guilt of their father even as the Kshatriyas did of old from Parashurama.[25] The king remembered the injury he had formerly received from the worthy and able councillors of his father and got himself rid of them. He remembered too the affection which Habhebha and his five or six friends had borne towards him and towards his father, as well as their services rendered to him, and he maintained them in great dignity.

## Adamakhana killed

When Adamakhana at Partnotsa[26] heard the news of the death of the treasurer, a message that bore the true import of his name, he was struck with fright, and returned in the same manner as he had come. Bahramakhana was also very much alarmed at the death of the treasurer, but on coming home he received assurance from the king who understood business. In the meantime the fine army under Manikyadeva[27] was destroyed in a battle with the Turushkas, in the Madra country. In this battle Adamakhana went out to fight, along with his maternal uncle, and he was killed, his face being pierced by an arrow. Some said that he was there killed by men of his own party who were afraid of him; while others said that he died of a wound in a vital part by a lance. When the king heard of his death from the messenger he was very much grieved, and caused his body to be brought[28] from Madra country and placed before his mother. Though he was the eldest of the brothers and a hero, and though he had an army under him, and possessed wealth and the part of the country where he was born, yet he did not in spite of endeavours, obtain the kingdom which was his due. An object wished for is not attained unless it is so decreed by destiny; or was it in him that his father's curse came to be realised? For though he returned to his own country he died in a foreign land.

## Ominous portents

Signs of great calamities and of alarm appeared in the sky, in the air, and on the earth, each striving to come foremost. First, when the king went to Madavaraja to indulge in the festivity[29] of flowers, there occurred a great earthquake. The buildings, as if perceiving the misery of their builders, began to tremble like men. Then there appeared a comet, a sign of calamity, extending over the sky with its tail towards the east. It was first seen by Vahramakhana. Its tail was like the bearded lance of death, and its wide extending form was seen even in the day time, towards the west. A mare in the king's stable gave birth to twins, and the king, in order to remove the animal from the country, gave it away to the *yavanas*. Lions and other animals of the forest wandered about during the day in Shrinagara town, and a bitch gave birth to kittens. The *sadanandi* tree, which had been barren, bore fruits, and flowers grew on the roots of pomegranate trees near the palace. A rain of blood fell on the clothes that were in the garden[30], and when men saw this, they felt as if salt had been sprinkled on a wound. In the meantime the Hindus, excited to anger by Purna the barber, were guilty of severities[31] on Saidakhana Agaha and others who were residing in the town. When the yavanas heard of this, they became angry, and went to the king and lamented aloud, and the king ordered a persecution of the Brahmanas.

## Brahmins persecuted

In his fury the king cut off the arms and noses of Ajara[32], Amara, Buddha and others, and even of those Brahmanas who were his servants. During this time of the pillage of the property of the Brahmanas, they gave up their caste and their dress and exclaimed "I am[33] not a Bhatta, I am not a Bhatta". There were in the city many rich and principal[34] gods, and the king ordered the plunder of their images at the instigation of the mlechhas.[35] King Jaina had given them lands after he was satisfied as to their excellence, but the officers of the present king robbed them of their estates without any reason. The month of Samahisphara[36] is celebrated in the religion of the *yavanas*, that month now came for the destruction of religion; to whom did it not appear terrific?

## Misrule

When the king was seen in an intoxicated state day after day, when the ministers became subservient to the king, and the king's friends took bribes, were fickle-minded, and oppressed the weak, then the people thought of the many virtues of the king Jaina. All the old men in the country, who had held high posts for a long time, were now in danger, as the king had ordered them to be disgraced, and they gave vent to their grief in cries and lamentations. The curse pronounced for the sins of men, as described in the Persian poem, was verified in the country of king Shri Jaina. Wicked men had wished for the death of the wise old king expecting to obtain money from the son; but even these servants who were dissemblers and had so long lived in joy now came to be greatly oppressed as if through the curse of the late king; and they lamented with tears in their eyes and with loud cries, saying, "Why has Fate destroyed our protector, the old king?"

This short reign became intolerable and appeared long even as an evil dream that is dreamt in a summer night. The king's servants felt happy in amassing wealth by plunder, in purloining household articles, and in oppressing the people, even as owls are happy in darkness. The king lay drunk with wine and did not perform his duties towards his subjects, but spent his time rolling on his bed within the palace. He listened day and night to songs sung by a potter, and did not give audience even to men of merit who were worthy of a king. The beautiful palace in Lakshmipura[37] which was completed in the reign of Shahabhadena, was burnt down by fire. The great row of buildings in the neighbourhood of Baladhyamatha[38] was also consumed together with the wealth of many citizens. When men saw the destruction of houses and witnessed other calamities in the country, they said that the disasters would cease only with the death of the king. The king ascended the palace and saw his own five chambered house in flames; he felt happy[39] and sank into the pleasures of drink.

## Exploits of Prince Hassan

In the meantime Neyadhishana[40] sent the king's son on an expedition into foreign countries. At the sight of the army the kings of the foreign countries disappeared, even as stars fade away in the day when they see the rays of the sun. First, Jayasimha, king of Rajapuri, gave handsome presents to the prince, and his sister pleased (married) the prince. When the prince approached the river Kalidhara[41], which looked like the blade of his sword, every one there trembled in his house out of the fear of him. The troops, the dispellers of fear, that were at Dinnarakotta[42] came to that river and made offerings to it, even as offerings are made to the goddess Mangala enshried on a high ground. The kings of Madra, Gakkhra, and Chibba[43] came to him with attendants dressed in shining white, even as swans come to a clear lake. Even his maternal uncles the Muhlanas[44] brought presents; they were assiduous in their duties towards the sovereign, and behaved like cranes. The Mohilas[45], when they saw the destruction of Kaumara[46] town, lost their firmness, though still possessing an army, even as women lose their composure at sight of the man on whom they have bestowed their favours. As the prince's army crossed the river Kalidhara in a line and proceeded to[47] Jyalami, it looked like the bridge which Rama had built over the sea. The army, still unwearied, then arrived at Kutipatishvari[48] and looked as if issuing out of the navel of Narayana. The houses in the city of Bhogapala[49], which had long been peopled by the Madras, were burnt and the hearts of the men were afflicted. The prince's army, with his prancing horses, reached the Unnada[50] lake, and arrived at the foot of Balyeshvara hill. The gallant army with its prancing horses, seemed to shake the roads on which they passed. As the army marched, the ground became shorn of grass, the pools were drained of water, and the forests bereft of wood. At this time I was honoured by the king and was sent to the prince. I explained the *Brihatkatha*[51] to him and became his reader. The prince who had reduced kings to the state of tributary chiefs had stayed for six months out of the country, but at the end of Chaitra became anxious to return to Kashmira.

In the meantime Bahramakhana. who knew that the king was addicted to vices, attacked the ministers and the leaders of the army and moved unchecked and unopposed. The king's constitution became weak by constant drinking, his strength and beauty faded, and he was attacked with gout and the spitting of blood. The king received Hassankhana who had arrived, and as the full moon dries up the lotuses, so did he reduce the ministers. But instigated by the wicked, the king became angry with his son because he had not brought Ruja[52] the Gakhvara bound. When Bahramakhana heard of the coming of the prince, whose arrival he had as little expected as the coming of the eastern hill to the west, his exertions became lax. The king did not show his affection towards his son even when he had attained greatness; the intellect of those whose end is nigh departs from them as if in fear. Entreated by the ministers and the leaders of the army, the king merely gave an audience to the prince who had returned from the expedition. Surely the king was then afraid of his youngest brother, or why should he make only gifts of robes to his son? Surely he thought that Vahrama would oppose his son, and like the *shami*[53] tree, he kept the fire of his resentment hid within himself.

## Haider's fatal fall

Meanwhile, as if urged by death, the king, with his servants, ascended the top of the palace in order to indulge in drink; and there within the apartment named Pushkara, in the glass room, the king fell down while running about in sport, and bled from his nose. The servants stretched their arms and carried him to the bed room of the apartment, but he fainted away and lay on his bed, and was like a mirror that did not reflect any image on it. The trusted physicians of the king were neglected, and a certain *yogi* tried on the king his medicine which was strong on account of its poison, and caused him pain. The king's body became excessively heated through the administration of the medicine, and day and night he longed for death, nor wished to live for a moment. The prince, accompanied by the minister[54] Ahmad, remained for three days within the palace near his father. When the prince learnt that the nobles had come to see his dying father, he placed soldiers at the gate in order to prevent their going out.

## Ahmada's proposal

The king's youngest brother was agitated both by fear and delight, and remained in his own house, but sent his spies around even as the sun sends out his powerful rays. Royal Fortune now favoured both the uncle and the nephew, as if in doubt which of them to select. At this time the minister Ahmada held a consultation with the other ministers, and went to Bahramakhana, and spoke to him these words of reason: 'Today your brother king Haidharashaha, whose name is auspicious, having wished you a long life, has come to the end of his career. Now you are the eldest of the family; do you, therefore, ascend the throne, and give Hassankhana the post of the heir-apparent. This city was protected by your father with great care, and today this alarmed town should be protected by you, even like a chaste woman of good family. What more need I say? Let the plunderers of the city, who are like greedy crows, turn back as they came, with their dark features and their cries of evil."

## Struggle for succession

When Bahramakhana heard these words he replied in language harsh on account of his anger, "Did I, in disregard of my self-interest and of the future world, separate myself from my father, mild and bounteous as the *kalpa* tree, and did I oppose Adamakhana by various devices, in order to serve this brother who was never himself? Who does not know how I obtained the kingdom for him? Who is my brother's son today, and what is his worth? Who beside me is worthy of my father's kingdom? He is younger, I am older in age and better in qualification. Where is the place now for conciliation in this world which the powerful is always destined to enjoy?" When he had said these unworthy words, they left him. Bahramakhana did not, after this, expect to get the services of those with whom he used to consult before, and to co-operate in the administration of the country, and he therefore fell in despair.

When destruction is nigh men's intellect wanders the wrong way, even as the water in a tank does when the embankment gives way. If he had wisely distinguished reasonable advice from unreasonable, if he had gone out and secured the horses which belonged to him, if he had killed his confiding nephew, and had taken possession of the treasury in his father's palace, or if he had gone out of the country and then returning to Kramarajya had leisurely attached the kingdom, then he would not have sustained the loss which ensued on account of his vacillation and the unreasonable advice of his childish and foolish servants. He might have secured everything in good time but owing to inexperience, alas! what did he not lose?

## Bahram's vacillation

Now the minister Ahmadamalla thought to himself that no one possessing intelligence should hold the kingdom from him for any length of time. He would rather give the kingdom to the ignorant son of the king and be at ease. Accordingly he applied to a powerful favourite of the king, and held a council with other ministers, and he proposed to bestow the kingdom on the king's son. Abhimanyu the Pratihara, in his pride, proposed to attack Bahrama, and determined to march out with his troops. When Bahramakhana heard of this, he immediately joined his son, but being without support, he went out of the city. He alone who is ambitious can dive into the sea and can fearlessly quell the monsters of the sea, in order to find invaluable gems and pearls and corals. Bahramakhana, who had his son with him, heard strange accounts of his brother's son; his army was greatly alarmed, and he went by the road leading to Dvara.[55] The same circumstance under which he had caused Adamakhana to flee from the city, now befell him at night. Sin does not take long to bring forth its fruit.

## Death of Haider - April, 1472

On the fifth day of the bright moon, in the month of Vaishakha, in the year 48, the king went to heaven; having reigned for one year and ten months. Some said that a sprite had taken its abode in the room adorned with pillars and high poles, and enraged by the wicked actions of the king, tore him to pieces. Others said that the *yogi* administered a strong medicine with an unskillful hand, and the king said that his wicked brother urged the physicians to adopt a bad treatment in order to remove the king, as the king's son was not then attending on his father. Some said that the king died because he had killed the chiefs of Saujala[56] and other places after swearing good faith towards them on the Veda of the Mausalas, and inspired their confidence, and also because he had killed those ministers of his father who had placed the mark of royalty on his forehead at his coronation. Surely within a short time he melted away like a mass of snow in the heat, on account of the curse of his father and because of his many crimes.

## Haider as poet

The prince believed that there was no enemy within the city, and entertaining no apprehensions, he carried his father's body on a litter to the graveyard. There he took out the corpse from the coffin, and covered it with a single piece of cloth, and placed it within the womb of the earth at the feet of the deceased's father. All the people considered the body as a handful of dust, looked at its face, and threw a handful of dust on it. When the hollow of the grave was filled, they placed over it a stone of moderate height; and it seemed to proclaim to all men that the late king had a heart of stone in his battles. His servants remembered the favours they had received from their master, and they smote their breast, gave vent to loud lamentations and wept. His servants who had received favours from him thought his short reign to be happy and glorious, as if they obtained the heaven in dream. The king had composed a book of songs[57] in the Persian language and in the dialect of Hindusthana, and who does not praise him for it. The king used to keep up nights in listening to the Puranas, the Dharamashastras, and the Samhitas which lead to salvation.

Owls and other birds are anxious for the approach of the night, and work mischief in the houses of men. They hate the rising sun, and live in caverns or wander in the woods in sorrow when the sun rises in glory. The wise but sorrowful prince knew that Mereptakara[58] and others who were living in the city were wicked men, and he threw them into prison the next day. He performed expensive ceremonies for his deceased father, and in sixteen days made preparation for assuming the government of the kingdom. Owls and other birds that bring harm to people, and fly about at night without difficulty, frequent the sky as long as the powerful sun does not rise and illumine all sides by its bright rays.

Here ends the second book, named 'the account of the reign of Hajyahaiderashaha,' of *Jainarajatarangini* composed by Pandita Shrivara.

## References

1. First day: four days after the death of Z, probably Tuesday. Refer also 153/24.
2. Shekandhrapuri: Haider ruled from the township of his grandfather near the Jama Masjid.
3. Son: Hassan, the heir-apparent.
4. Sukshiti: pb. not a place-name. Should read 'It gave him great satisfaction to bestow the estate of Nagrama on...'
5. Nagrama; a sub-division to the s-w. of Sgr. 16 km. away. A fort was constructed there by Baladitya of the Karkota house.
6. a line is missing: 'He conferred on his son the lordship of Kamraj and of Ichh (pga. to the w. of Nagrama or Nagam).
7. Avtara Lavaka: Ravatra Laulaka (SK). Pb. a group of partisan officials. See also p. 95,
8. *King* of Rajapuri: Jaisimha. Z's sister's son Qayam-un-Din was installed as the king of Sindhu but he died while Z. was alive. Refer p. 137.
9. Missing lines read: 'Out of sorrow for his father he had given gifts in charity to many servants and they waited upon him in right earnest. As the moon wipes out all darkness at dusk, so did the king root out all evils in the country.'
10. Merja Hassan: Meya Hassan (SK).... Bahurupa: Beeru.
11. Bhangila: a pargana, adjacent to Beeru, extended from Paraspur on the Jhelum to the hills on the west. The verse should read 'He took away Bhangila from Jamsher Margesha and attracted by the merit of Merza Hassan bestowed it on him.'
12. The treasurer: Hassan Kuchhai (Skt. Koshesha) of the Persian chroniclers.
13. Kuvera: treasurer of the gods.
14. Riktetra: lit. 'full', Also named '*Purna*' and 'Luli'.
15. Merabhokhara: Mir Iftikhar (SK).
16. Machuryya: 'Chut' (SK and RNS). Chutagnanapati.
17. Amrita Park: A'anta Bhavan near Vicharnag (from Amrita Vihara or Bhavan), a lofty Vihara constructed by Amritprabha, queen of Meghvahana, for the benefit of foreign monks.
18. Thakkuras: On the return of Alishan his younger brother Z. left the Valley accompanied by Thakkuras who are believed to have been Kashmiri Muslim nobles. Purna pb. punished some Rajputs also.
19. *Svavna*: purificatory ablutions. RNS renders it as :....for the purpose of security but the barber...

20. Shikhajada: a partisan of Adamakhan.
21. Malladaudka: Mulla Daud, pb. the same as mentioned in 120/4 under the name of Mulla Oodi, a contemporary of Z .... Vahlola: Bahlol.
22. Merakaka: pb. Mir Iftikhar. Omens are referred to to prepare the reader.
23. Jamsara: Sanjermer (SK).
24. Vahmarga: Bahaduraga (SK).
25. Parashurama: the sixth incarnation of Vishnu wielded an axe and cleared the earth of the Kshatryes 'thrice seven times' for killing his father. He was a champion of the Brahmins, the caste he was born in.
26. Parnotsa: Jammu (PH) name: refer p. 147.
27. Manikyadeva: Raja of Madra or Jammu, maternal uncle of Adama. PH mentions Malikdeva Turushukas: Mongols or Mughals.
28. Brought: his body was buried at Sehayar, near Nawa Kadal, Srgr.
29. Festivity of flowers: See p. 116 *et. seq*.
30. garden: Sumanvata, (pb. Sonavar) in the original.
31. Severities: out of indignation against oppression, especially of Purna, the Hindus burnt some mosques built with temple material (PH) Saidakhanaqaha is pb. Khanaqahi Maula.
32. Ajara, Amara, Budha,: pb. images of gods in temples.
33. 'I am not a Bhatta': See also p. 24.
34. principal: Bahukhatka (*bhairava*) and other principal gods (SK).
35. mlechhas: vulgar, unruly elements. Shrivara generally uses the term for outsiders or people of low conduct.
36. Mahisaphara: the month in the Hijri calendar following Muharam. Persian poem: identity uncertain.
37. Lakshmipora: township built near Hariparbat in the name of Lakshmi, queen of Shahab-ud-din (see also 43/124).
38. Baladhyamatha: on the Jhelum river in downtown Srinagar.
39. Reminiscent of Nero of ancient Rome.
40. Neyidhishana: not a proper name. Interpreted as : '...at the instigation of evil-minded people the king, well-versed in diplomacy, sent his son....'
41. Kalidhara range of hills lies on the Jammu-Srgr. route *via* Akhnur and Budhil pass, between Chauki Chaura, 31m. from Jammu and the next stage Paoni 14 m. beyond. (*K.M.*). From the suffix *dhara* the translator has mentioned only the river, but the expression 'the blade of his sword, used by Shrivara is sufficiently indicative. Referred to as a river again on p. 227. Pb. a stream close to the hills also bore the name.
42. Dinnarkotta: pb. one of the several forts in the area. Mangaldevi: is the name of a v. and castle in Bhimber tehsil with pb. a shrine of the goddess named here. Like the other forts it is located on a

conspicuous crag several hundred feet above the bed of the river. Another castle, not far from it, was at Traj or Trunj.

43. Chibba: Chib Rajputs were settled between the Chenab and the Jhelum around Bhimber (28 m. from Gujrat, Pakistan) their headquarters founded by Chib Dev, son of Narayan Chand of Kangra who married a Thakiyal princess and inherited her father's estate. He founded a village Kangra near Bhimber.
44. Muhlanas/Malhanas: descendants of Malhana Hamsa, a prominent leader of Manhas Rajputs of Akhnur-Bhimber area. The patriarch was also known as Man Haras. Manhas Rajputs are believed to be a branch of the Jamwals who took to agriculture and flourished in vv. Purgowal, Chaprar and Thub below Akhnur...
45. Mohilas: Mohyal Rajputs.
46. Kaumara town: misinterpreted. Should be '...destruction caused by the youthful prince'.
47. Jyalami: the Jhelum river or Jhelum town.
48. Identity uncertain; literally 'cloth worn round the hip'.
49. Bhogpala: some landed baron.
50. Unnada lake: another interpretation suggests: 'army with its prancing horses raised noise and clamour and arrived at the foot of Balyeshvara hill...'
51. *Brihatkatha*: pb. the Sanskrit version is meant. Earlier the *Brihatkathasara* is mentioned.
52. Ruja: Feroze Gakkhar (SK).
53. *shami*: it is said that friction between two pieces of *shami* wood produces a flame.
54. Minister Ahmada: Malik Ahmed Yatu (Ayukta).... Greedy crows: breakdown of law and order is complete.
55. Dvara: pb. Baramulla pass is meant.
56. Saujala: Shyavtala (SK), pb. the lake at Shaya (Shel) in Ladakh.
57. Book of songs: neither appears to have survived.
58. Meraptakara: Mir Iftikhar.

**Shrivara's**

***Jainarajatarangini***

## BOOK III
# Sultan Hassan Shah

(1472-1484 A.D.)

I bow to Shiva who is the sole lord of the three worlds, and who has attained the rank of an immortal god and freedom from endless pain. That poet, the lord of the *yogis*, who has given an account of the past in his work, is worthy at the present time to receive our reverence.

I, Shrivara Pandita, received the king's gift, which was the means of my subsistence, and I will now narrate the history of that king, and thus free myself of the debt I owe him. I have witnessed the prosperity, the misfortunes, and the death of the kings with my own eyes, and remembered the events; and this *Rajatarangini* will create in all a feeling of indifference for this world. Let good people attend to my account, not for the sake of any merit in my poem, but for history of the kingdom which it narrates, and let them by their own intellect assimilate what they hear. This has been composed, like the records of the Kayasthas, for the information of those who will come in the future, so that other learned men, when they read this, may compose elegant works.

### Coronation

King Hassana, whose mind was free from evil intention, left Shekandharapuri[1], the town of his father, and went to the superior and finer city of Jainanagara built by his grandfather. Seated on the throne, clad in elegant robes and ornaments, he gladdened the earth and looked beautiful even like the rising moon on the eastern hill. The chief *malla*, the minister Ahmada, himself marked his forehead with the mark of sovereignty[2], and adorned the new king with flowers of gold. Royal Fortune, as if recognizing him as the sole remnant of his dynasty and the ornament of the family, protected him by placing him on the silver throne[3], as in a casket, and covering him with the royal umbrella. Looking at the moon-like face of the new king, the face of the city, which was like the lotus, expanded!

The smoke of *homa*[4] ceremony, performed at the king's coronation, rose high in the air, as if the earth sent her breath upwards in gladness and looked bright. In the echoes of the music which played, the surrounding space seemed to express its gladness, and the air from all directions poured forth blessings. The long lines of blood-red banners which were displayed seemed like crests of the fire of the new king's prowess. In the decorations of lovely white flowers, Royal Fortune seemed to smile after a long period at the ascendency of the young king. All the servants of the new king wore clothes of bright silk which looked graceful like waves, and displayed their changeful prosperity. Large expenses were incurred on account of silk in those parts of the kingdom where the people used to wear cotton clothes. Those who used to rob the people disappeared when the king obtained the kingdom, even as clouds disappear when the sun attains the season of spring. When the sun grows bright, all sides become clear, the sun-jewel sparkles, and the fire that issues from the jewel dispels darkness; for what cannot fire accomplish? The father and the uncle of the king had laboured in vain to obtain the kingdom which the grandson got with ease, and without an enemy. All the wealth of his father, his grandfather, and his uncle flowed to this fortunate king, even as rivers flow to the sea. The king freed himself of envy, and learnt the six schools of philosophy[5]; and the different works of these six schools became one in him.

## The new team

The minister Ahmada, with his son, was employed in all the work of the king; he was mindful of virtuous acts, and he always acted as the king's counsellor. The king then made this minister Mallika Ahmada the undisputed master of Nagrama[6] and the villages attached to it. Nauruja, the minister's son, did the work of Dvarapala and became powerful on account of his possession of villages and wealth. He enjoyed the lordship of the country of Ikshika. There amidst the pleasures of drinking he showered on all the nectar of his favour, and in a moment quenched the fire of the people's poverty. Tajibhatta had served the king when the king was a boy and in a foreign country; and he was loved by the Mallas[7], and was greatly beloved of the king. The king was prompt in dispensing punishments and favours; he bestowed on Tajibhatta the post of an envoy and Tajibhatta was to the king like the tongue of his kingdom. Formerly the stream of power had flowed by hundred channels, but now it rested in Tajibhatta without flowing through a second channel. Jonarajanaka and others soon obtained favour according to the services they had rendered previously.

In all things the king acted as Ahmada, the chief of the Mallas, advised and he did not disregard this minister, even as the sea, though agitated, does not overflow its shore. It was by the advice of this minister that the king liberated those who had been hostile to his father and grandfather and had been imprisoned[8] in Bhutta country. The king, who knew all schools of philosophy and who placed his intelligence under the guidance of his minister, re-established in the kingdom the practices of the time of his grandfather. The king was of a forgiving nature and grateful, and the minister was devoted to the king and devoid of vanity; it was after a long time, and owing to the virtue of the subjects, that such a combination was seen. When the Margapati, the Thakkuras, and other officials had been seated on high seats, by the side of the minister, the minister inclined himself before king as If he had been their envoy. He performed the work of the king even at the risk of his life, and his devotion to the king, as to Mahadeva, was unmoved. He made a good use of his wealth by building *mathas* and endowing villages in favour of Brahmanas, by the exercise of hospitality and by serving the king.

## Bahram returns

As a mad, dark elephant, when it sees a lotus, pure and beautiful, and adorned with its cup, comes proudly and flapping its ears, to destroy the flower, but gets entangled in the plant and sinks in the mud of the tank, and dies along with the bees, even so

Bahramakhana gave up his attempts to conquer foreign countries, and puffed with arrogance, came to make war in Kashmira. The king's officers had written to him promising to join his army at the time of battle, and this made him hope for success. Formidable at the head of his army he came from the interior of Karnaha[9], scaled the mountains and, with a view to usurp the kingdom, arrived at Kramarajyapura.[10] At that time the king with his ministers was staying at Avantipura; but on hearing of Vahramakhana's arrival he soon retraced his steps and came to Svayyapura. Here, filled with anxiety at the return of his uncle, he called together all his ministers, and thus spoke in the midst of the assembly:

> "The kingdom descends from father to son; I am the son and ought to get it. Who is this uncle of mine who is attempting to obtain the kingdom? He is senior to me in years, but junior in claim. Or, leaving alone the law of inheritance, the kingdom should belong to a hero; and let him be the sovereign of the kingdom who becomes victorious in this battle between us."

When the chief minister heard these words of the king, he replied that it was for his benefit that Adamakhana and others had been destroyed by Fate: and how could Bahramakhana fight, who had only a small force, and depose the king from his seat? But there was no time for action that day. In the court, he added, there were some who received pay from both the parties[11], and he did not know what to do, should they join Bahramakhana. The minister, therefore, advised that the contents of the treasury should be brought and the army should then march out into the country, and then it would be able to accomplish the work. When Mallika heard this in the assembly, he addressed the king advising him to remain quiet with his ministers, and promising to send the king's troops which had served under Adamakhana, to subdue Bahramakhana. Should these troops be overpowered then they would march with the whole army. There was no fear from Bahramakhana, he had no support and he could do nothing. When the king heard these various and uncertain views, he settled the plan of action according to the advice of Ahmada, chief of the mallas. He kept with him the troops of his father and grandfather, and sent Tajibhatta and others accompanied by Phiryadamara, with the troops of his uncle (Adamakhana) and with his own troops, in order to fight Bahramakhana who was in the Mavari[12] country.

## Bahram captured

Bahramakhana hoped to overcome this small army, and hastened to Dulapura.[13] But though the nobles of the king had held out hopes to Bahramakhana they did not come to him, and he considered himself betrayed by them, and became despondent. On that day Royal Fortune remained as if in doubt between the two, the uncle and the nephew. As thieves like darkness, even so Chakrabhava[13] and others who were born in Kramarajya liked the confusion of a civil war, and were glad to hear the latest news. But when the king arrived at Jainagiri bent on prosecuting the war, messengers came to him and said:- "O King! Bahramakhana did not act wisely in rushing to war, together with his son, like a mad elephant he has been captured in battle. Bahramakhana who fought against your force, was thrown down in the field of battle, and was deserted by his servants, even as a tree in a garden is forsaken by leaves in the month of Pausha. Then Sanjaramera and other leaders of the army raised a shout and came upon him like a black cloud and showered their arrows. Worthy of praise are those who die in the presence of their master, and the memory of their death is worthy of being cherished. Such men remember the favours they had received from their master, and sacrifice their lives like grass. They consider the favours of their master as a debt, in payment of which they yield their precious lives, when the time comes, welcoming the weapons of the enemy even as flowers. Such men are few among the servants of a master, and they are worthy of praise.

"It was owing to thy greatness O king! that Shirala, Margapa, and other servants and warriors of Bahramakhana perished. It is strange that none of our army died, but the arrows discharged by our men pierced the scabbard of the Khana and he was unable to draw his sword, so that his weapon became useless, his condition pitiable, and he was surrounded by our soldiers. The Khana's ardour abated, even like that of the funeral fire alter a shower of rain. The soldiers came up to him and attempted to kill him, but Phiryadamara in his mercy promptly saved him by sheltering him within his arms. The earth was full of mud, and there was an excess of rain, a Brahamana[14] was before him, and in his helplessness and fear of death what miseries did he not feel. Oppressed by the cold wind and by fear, sunk in the mud of the field, naked and deserted by his craven troops, spoilt of his property by the low, and witnessing his poor and afflicted son crying aloud, Bahramakhana thought at that moment of his brother, his attendants, and his home! He found himself and his son captured by the enemy and did not know to whom he could address himself or what he could do. Better were it, he thought, if death had come and his life were extinct. He remembered that what his father had said had come to pass that day, and he blamed himself that he had rejected jewels for glass! Thus accusing himself, and disconsolate in his grief, the Khana is living like one dead, like a tall bare tree, devoid of leaf and fruit, in the month of Pausha! Enjoy O king! the kingdom that has descended to thee in succession, and has been given to thee by God. Virtue, owing to good fortune, has borne fruit unto thee. What more need be said? Order speedily what should be done to Bahramakhana". When the king heard this he was glad and gave rewards to the messengers.

## Bahram's misery

All the army were the next day pleased with the music of victory, and they brought Bahramakhana, and his son, surrounded by troops, before the king. The king went to the top of his palace in order to welcome his soldiers proud of their victory, and for a while beheld from a distance his uncle in the midst of the garrulous citizens talking in high or low voice, his head bent down in shame and fear, as if he sought for a hole in the ground to conceal himself. He was bereft of ornaments which had been robbed by the soldiers at the time of battle, and was covered with a worn-out garment which had been given to him by some humble and kind-hearted man. His turban was soiled with blood from the wound caused by an arrow in his face, and he was favoured by the goddess of misfortune. The citizens saw Bahramakhana with his son bound before the king who was favoured by good fortune, and Bahramakhana's heart was sore. Whose prosperity can be permanent? Those whose intellect is wrapped by covetousness are deceived by prosperity, they lose the sense of right and wrong and are unable to rid themselves of the lust of prosperity which they have once enjoyed, until it is forced from them by others. If prosperity thus becomes a source of incessant grief, then may it, fickle as a prostitute, never exist in this world.

When the people saw the Khana brought forward bound, they remarked that he had, for his own interest, neglected his father in his last illness, and had by various means opposed his elder brother Adamakhana; and that when his another brother suffered from an incurable disease, he with a wicked intention had gone over to that brother; and avaricious of obtaining the kingdom from his nephew, he had risen in rebellion against him. It was for these sins, they said, that he received his punishment that day.

Some again remarked that it was owing to his father's curse that Bahramakhana had lost his sense. On one occasion when Bahramakhana was opposed to his father's faction, his father had privately told him that his two elder brothers were ruining his kingdom by their mutual enmity, that they had caused him annoyance and harm, and he accordingly proposed to discard them and to take Bahramakhana into his favour, and asked Bahrama to trust in him. When Bahramakhana heard this, he replied that he would not desert[15] his elder brother who had always sought his welfare, and that the eldest of the three could effect nothing against the other two brothers combined. When the king heard this, he said that the second brother had been intending to kill his elder through Bahramakhana, and though the second brother had now given protection to Bahrama, it would be the killing of a servant of the house by means of a guest. For if the second brother succeeded in his purpose, he and his son would turn Bahrama's enemies, and what then would Bahrama do? Bahramakhana knew the Sanskrita language and when he had heard this, he replied in the following *shloka*:

> "Those who know the *shastras* wash off their sins at the shrine of learning; the virtuous wash off their sins at the shrine of truth; the *munis*, at the shrine of the Ganga; the *yogis*, at the shrine of self-knowledge; young women of good families at the shrine of modesty, the munificent at the shrine of charity, and kings wash off their sins at the shrine of the sword."

When the king heard this, he replied to his evil-minded son in these angry words: "I have witnessed many of your battles, O miserable man! and you were proud in wielding your sword in war, in which I could not cope[16] with you! What shall I say to you, O evil-minded man? I see your eyes which are worthy to be plucked out! You will soon be ruined and will then repent." What the father had then said came to pass this day. Thus the people said in sorrow to one another when they saw him.

Here ends the account of the defeat of Vahramakhana.

The king distributed befitting gifts and honours which pleased his army, and was himself happy in mind; and he came to his capital the same day. He took with him his enemy bound, and embarked on a boat with his son. He ordered Bahrama to be confined in Bahrama's own palace. The king's mother was glad to see her son back again from battle, as if he was born again. The king was afraid of relations of Avatarasiha[17] and others, and within a few days, sent them to prison in his anger. That wicked Mallikataja[18], born in Panchgahvar, secured royal favour by flattery and became a source of misery to men. The whole country was deceived into bribing him, and he robbed the country in order to amass fortune.

## Bahram blinded

Abhimanyu[19] the Pratihara obtained the lordship of Devasara; he was of an independent character among the ministers and was proud of his strength. This covetous man caused trouble in every house and field with a view to plunder, and became the object of the people's curse. He instilled fear into the king's mind for his father's brother who was imprisoned near the palace, suggesting that some one might bring him out of the prison and set up a civil war. Incited by these words, the king, whose intellect was yet immature, became angry with Bahramakhana, and ordered his eyes to be put out. Bahrama's eyes were accordingly covered with cotton, and this unworthy descendant of Jainaraja caused a hot iron rod to be applied on them for their destruction. The sin[20] of him who destroyed the eyes, and the pain of him whose eyes were destroyed, cannot be described in our words. Some said it was an unwise act, some said it was the work of God, others remarked that it was the fruit of acts done in a previous birth, while there were others again who observed that it was the punishment for keeping low company. Some said that it was an inhuman act committed for the sake of wealth, and others remarked that it was done owing to the king's timidity. When the people heard that the Khana was blinded, they made remarks which are not fit to be repeated. Let none be born as man, they exclaimed, or if so born, let him be born rather as an ordinary individual; let no one take his birth in the house of a king.

The king's time passed quickly in the enjoyment of new delights of prosperity, and in various pleasures and recreations.

But even a dream appears like a *kalpa* to one in the afflictions of misfortune, who broods over his past prosperity and his present danger. Bahrama's feet were bound in iron chains, and he remained imprisoned and blind, and passed the remainder of his life in thinking of the pleasures he had enjoyed in the days of his prosperity. He who had always been served by his servants, shampoing him in every limb in his bed room had now sparrows and insects for his attendants. He who had lived under canopies such as even the gods did not possess, had now to live under rows of spiders' nets spread over him as a canopy. His tender limbs which had once adorned a bed of silk and cotton, now lay on the ground without a bed. He had been bounteous before, and used to say 'Give it to others', now he raised the same voice with difficulty, and said 'Give something to me'. His authority was gone, his servants were killed, he had lately been defeated and bound in chains, and was suffering agony on account of his eyes being put out. The blind son of a king meditated on all this, and he could not call to mind any one who had suffered like him even in a tale. The bee sees the lotus, bright with its cup, and seeks to feast on it as he roams at pleasure, but the moon thwarts him, the night approaches, and the bee is enclosed in the lotus and dies. The palace which had been built by him for his enjoyment now became his prison! Who can foresee what may befall him. Thus he suffered agonies for three years, his body became a skeleton, and he died. He who treats his enemies with bitterness, and takes no account of time and place, perishes in spite of his strength and wealth.

## Intrigues: Abhimanyu blinded

The cruel Abhimanyu, the Pratihara, was puffed up with vanity for having performed some acts of prowess and could not bear the powerful faction[21] of the ministers. He was inflated with a spirit of independence and his harsh words preceding from pride were like needles in the eyes of the ministerial party. The Pratihara went on devising plans to get rid of the minister Mallika Ahmada, and the Mallika also secretly entertained hostile feelings against the Pratihara but found no opportunity to bring him under his power. At last, on one occasion when the king was proceeding to his palace at Viyaeshvara, the minister induced him to cause the Pratihara, who did not mistrust the king, to be arrested within the palace. Abhimanyu himself was known to fame, but his sons Pandava and others were unworthy as jackals. Fie to the uncertainties of fate! If the lion did not in his madness enter into a trap, who could ever overcome that strong animal, at whose sight even large and powerful elephants flee afar, followed by bees.

Then the Pratihara, with his sons, was brought in a boat by Tajibhatta, bound and bereft of his wealth, and thrown into prison. Within a year his eyes were put out, even as he had induced the king to put out the eyes of Bahramakhana and as Bahramakhana had suffered intolerable pain, even so did he suffer pain which others cannot describe. On the same day and in the same month of the year in which the Pratihara had done injury to the Khana, did he himself suffer injury. He too, with this sons, suffered like Bahramakhana for two years the tortures of hell, and died in prison and in misery. The wicked Pratihara had once remarked that his eyes were gratified[22] at the sight of the death of Jainaraja, the foe of his family, and of the plunder of his property; for these cruel words he was now punished with the destruction of his own eyes; so the people observed. The grandson of Jainaraja accomplished with ease what that king had meditated but could[23] not do. The very means which a man adopts for the injury of others lead to his own destruction. The deer uses his antlers for the death of others, but is killed by arrows discharged from bows made of the self-same horn.

## Malik punished

Thus the people had for a long time beheld, with pleasure, as it were, the graceful chumps of bamboo in a grove beautified by various coloured grass and thick foliage. But a fire rose from friction, and all was destroyed in the grove from one end to another; the offices founded by ancient kings passed away in a short time, and were only remembered as a dream. Some one falsely reported to the king that Mallika[24] Jada intended to bring forward the son of the blind Khana and usurp the kingdom. When the king heard this, he ordered the Mallika to be imprisoned after confiscating all his property. All those who had envied the Mallika were pleased with this. Mallika Jada had obtained wealth by violence and by violence did the officers of the king take away his riches. No one pitied him in his misfortune, for he had oppressed the people by exacting bribes and money. It was with much difficulty that his wealth was taken away from him, for his vile hand, and the vile wealth he had acquired by force, had become fast friends. It was with difficulty and by means of coercion that the officers of the king extracted from him what he had stored, even as a serpent is pulled out with difficulty from its hole. The barber Purna and Mallika Jada and others spoilt of their riches, died after long imprisonment. Thus Jainaraja's fatal curse reached all those who had wronged the realm. O ye ministers! endeavour to improve the country by your advice. Verily I say, if you wish the destruction of the king, you will not obtain happiness either in this world or in the next. Those of the sons and attendants of king Jaina who had injured him did not attain happiness. Others among his servants, great and low, who had done him harm now perished.

## Syeds exiled

As long as the spring lasts the bees enjoy themselves, but when the spring departs, they wander about listless and unhappy. Knowing that Saida Nasira and his people were born of the family of Paigamvara[25] and that they were men of great accomplishments, and had come to adorn his kingdom, and were deserving of honour, the king Jaina had given them very high seats in his court, had shaken hands with them, and assigned to them estates in the kingdom. But now, Saida[25] Jyamala and others of that family were known to the present king as turbulent chiefs. He accordingly exiled them from the country, and confiscated their hoarded treasure. Saida Nasira was admired by the wise, and famed[26] in battle; he foresaw the future, and left the country during the lifetime of king Jaina. The Saidas enjoyed many large[27] estates, and by their marriages with the king's daughters had lived like kings for a long time. They now wandered about hither and thither; some of them went to Dillipura, and others, owing to their avarice, did not leave the country though exiled, but remained like bees in the month Magha. These foreigners, who used formerly to live on the refuse of grains, had become rich after coming to this country and had forgotten their previous history, even as men forget their previous life on coming out of the womb. They oppressed the people, and owing to the weight of that sin, they were despoiled of their wealth and were exiled by the king; and they lived in fear of their life like fish taken out of a lake.

## Alliances among leaders

The Mallika (Ahmada) formed alliances by marriage with the Rajanaka people, and with the Thakkuras, and the Margapatis;

and for the sake of Tajibhatta retained in his hand the possession of all the offices of the great kingdom. He thought to himself that Tajibhatta belonged to his family and was adopted as his son, and noticed that he began to prosper speedily. Ahmada therefore forgave all his shortcomings. Jyahamgira[28] the Margapati found that his sister was slighted by the Saida, and he drew up a deed for her divorce. At the request of the wise Mallika the king caused the elder sister of the Margapati to be given to Tajibhatta. Jyahamgira the Margapati understood the wisdom of the act, and forgave the marriage of his elder sister to Tajibhatta. Wife and wealth come to the fortunate even as bees come to the garden or as rivers flow into the sea. She had lived in the family of the Margapati as a *kalpa* creeper in a garden and possessed many excellent qualifications; and the Bhatta obtained her as one obtains the goddess[29] of fortune. The people remarked that while king Jaina could not banish the Saidas, his grandson had done it with ease.

## Erection of buildings

When the country was rid of these thorns, the king, with the approval of the Mallika, engaged himself in erecting buildings; and his courtiers were also similarly engaged. The people were happy under the good administration, and they occupied themselves in marriages and festivities, in building good houses, in dancing and processions, and they thought of nothing else. The king built in the year '50 a beautiful palace at Diddamatha[30], on the banks of the river, unmindful of expense. The new palace with its (four turrets in the) four corners which were like hands upraised, was reflected on the water, and looked as if it danced there day and night, conscious of the people's admiration, while the old palace remained tenantless. The golden umbrella over the palace looked as if the sun in semblance of an umbrella had descended from the sky to see the building, as none of his (solar) dynasty had erected any building equalling it. The architects made wooden figures of Garuda[31] and placed them on the corners of the building, so that the birds in the sky were afraid of them and did not fly over the palace. The queen mother Golkhatona[32] was like the former queen Didda, and she also built a large religious edifice called the *madrasa*. Accompanied by his mother's father, the king entered the building and felt happy, and he ordered festivities to be held at great expense for a fortnight.

Even then the king thought that the ceremony of consecration was but half done, and was not equal to the occasion. He built a *khanagaha* within the town for the benefit of his father's soul. The king renewed the palace that had been burnt by fire on the banks of the river at Kuloddharananaga[33] and made it beautiful. The old palace on the banks of the river at Vijyaesha was renewed, and owing to its excessive brightness, it looked like the central jewel of a necklace. The dome of the building looked beautiful, and the umbrella over it was reflected on the waters of the Vitasta, and it seemed as if the gods in their gladness had thrown down a golden lotus. The palace built by the king at Suyyapura looked graceful, and being white-washed, seemed to laugh at the old palace. There also he built in his own garden[34] a royal palace which was unique in the kingdom and at the sight of which surely Indra acknowledged his inferiority! I do not describe the other buildings which the king erected in his kingdom through fear of lengthening this narrative.

## Stone causeway

The minister Ahmada built at Diddamatha rows of buildings unmatched in beauty; and near the great stone wall which surrounded the courty-yard of *masodaha*[35], and beautifying it, he raised a religious edifice, the celebrated *khanagaha*, where many travellers come from various countries. To such an extent were new buildings erected at Diddamathapura, that the whole town became pleasing to the eye. The minister invited the king on the occasion of the first entry into the building, and spent sixty lakhs. He assigned the village of Satipusha[36] for the supply of food (for travellers). Even his wife Shaha built a *matha* for religious purpose, on the road leading to Kheri[37], and gave alms when it was completed. His son too, the minister Nauruja, built a new religious *matha*, and constructed a stone causeway from the town to the Kshipitika[38]; and when it was completed as far as the island in the river, the people of the town ceased to wonder at the sight of a long causeway supported on pillars. The two other brothers named Richaka[39] and Nuthaka, who were worthy of praise, built two *mathas* in Kramarajya, beautiful as palaces. Tajibhatta, who had become rich and great on account of the king's affection for him, built a *matha* at Jainapuri in Karala[40] country, and erected a new edifice of stone at Kudmadinapuri. Indra himself, on viewing these structures, would become desirous of erecting edifices!

## Constructions by the nobles

Edarajanaka[41], master of the royal wardrobe, built a *khanagaha* at Baladyamatha, and a new *matha* in his native land. The *matha* was built by the side of the funeral ground and was adorned with apartments for the accommodation of wearied travellers. He constructed rows of buildings—*matha, agrahara, masjeda, vihara,* - and altogether erected twenty or thirty buildings in the kingdom. Phiryyadamara built at Jainapura a well-proportioned *khanagaha*, and a *mosodaha* beautiful on account of its extensive yard, and he spent one koti on the occasion of the first entry into these edifices, distributing gifts according to all *shastras*. Hayatakhatona[42], the beloved of the king, and radiant with wealth, repaired the *matha* at Mrigavata which had been burnt down; and queen Bhomarakhatona built a new *matha*, at Jainanagara with her own money near the palace. The princess Jayarala[43], born of the royal family, built a new *khanagaha* by the side of Shekandharapura. The barber, Pherathakkura, was an officer of the king, and the works of piety which he built, like the yard of *mosodaha*, adorned Jainapura. He was bent on doing good deeds, and built a beautiful *matha* on the banks of the river at Vijayesha. Sayyabhandapati[44] built a *vihar* at Vijayeshvara, which was to the cause of religion as a spacious *road* by which an army can march. His brothers Lakshmamera and others, chiefs among merchants, built a new stone temple of Bhimasvami Ganesha. The faces of the *mlechchas* became dark and were bent down, as if at the sight of that high white-washed temple of Ganesha. Others also erected various buildings high and low. and the country was covered with them, and looked like heaven. A virtuous man thinks to himself that many rich people have lived before and spent years in hoarding, but only a few cowries were placed on their bodies when they died, and even these they left behind. And thus if he who had become rich, fails to perform acts of piety by consecrating buildings, he too will have to depart alone when he dies. It is considerations like these which incline virtuous men towards pious works. When the king became angry with wicked men, he destroyed[45] them but not their buildings. In former times, the houses of those who rose against the king were demolished. The fear of such punishment, however, left the minds of the wealthy in this reign. What more need be said? Trees were cut down for building houses, so that woods were laid bare even like an enemy's country.

## New coin

The king found that the *dinnaras* of Shri Toramana[46] had ceased to be current, and he gave currency to the new coin, *Dvitinnari*, which was impressed with the figure of a *naga*. The old copper coin was twenty-five (dinnars in value), but owing to the dearness of articles its value had become somewhat reduced.

The mother of pearl, which rears pearls out of water from the clouds, is worthy of being placed on the head of kings. But when men take out the pearls, the objects of her affection, it, like a good woman, does not survive long. Golkhatona, the king's mother, died suddenly; she had, during his infancy, reared him with her milk. She had opposed the king when he began to form irregular habits, and restrained his wavering heart even as the sea shore always restrains the sea. She favoured the customs of the Hindus[47] as the light of the sun favours the lotus; and all men thought of her, lamented and wept for her. When his mother left him, the king appeared covered in a black dress, and looked like a lotus shrunk with sorrow when forsaken by day-light.

When seven days had past, Mallika (Ahmada) made the king wear a white dress, and money was spent on the occasion, and he caused the king's sorrow to abate. The king ordered a large new bridge of boats to be built at the extremity of Shahabhadinapuri with his mother's money so that her righteousness might increase in merit.

## Birth of heir-apparent

The queen Hayatakhatona, born in the family of the Saidas, was beloved of the king, and was the object of his love, his joy, and his consolation. The king was not attached to any one[48] else, and he gave all things to her, utensils, ornaments, and household furniture. The moon-like king derived pleasure from that highly accomplished queen alone, as the bee does from the *malati* plant. There is prosperity in this world, but only a few can attain that desired object; few are the peasants who chance to find pearls when the clouds rain! A prince was born to the king by this great queen and he was named Mahmadakhana, a name worthy of the Mausulas. The king, happier than before, entrusted his boy to Tajibhatta for being brought up, even as the sea entrusts the moon to Mahadeva.

## Festivities

In the month of Vaishakha, in the year '54 the king held a festival on account of the birh of his son and a large sum of money was spent to make the ceremony an imposing one. All spent money, as liberally as Kuvera, on men of wit and the promoters of festive sports, on dancers and singers. In the reign of Shri Jaina, the king had bestowed silk dresses on feudatory chiefs and ministers in order to do them honour; but in the present reign when the festivities were carried on at a great expense, the promoters of the festival and dancers obtained silk clothes even from ordianry men. The youthful king, on whom Royal Fortune was propitious, brought in men expert in singing and enjoyed music. Jyahangera the Margesha and other courtiers, versed in music and accustomed to a life of pleasure, looked like stars before the moon in the presence of the king. Great actors[49], skilled in acting, and graceful like so many moons placed in a row, excited in the king a desire to see their performance. Jesters were like fun personified, with their hanging breasts and artificial beards, with the movements of their teeth and brows, with their jests and antics, their laughter, and the laughter of their eyes, expressive of various emotions, and with their cries mimicking the cries of animals.

Malla Hassana, more skilful than his father, first invented the delightful lute with ten strings, and I held up the gourd-lute, by the order of the king, and showed my skill in vernacular and in Persian songs. The king who was fond of vernacular songs was well-versed in Sanskrita and he repeated the following *shloka*[50] in praise of music, setting it to music: "The power of music renovates withered trees, subdues the lower animals, and makes the gods descend to woods and speak unseen; in sorrow and pleasure it gives joy to the ignorant and the learned, to the young and the old alike; may such music abide with me"! With a sweet voice he sang many high-tuned songs of unparalleled music and in many tunes, and surprised us. Then the great king ordered me, who am the head of a section of the music department, to introduce the singers to his presence. I brought in Vahavadena[51] and others, who were superior to all, and the leaders among[52] singers, and I named each of them and placed them before the king: Shikshakara and four other singers seemed to spread the influence of the god of love under the pretence of singing five tunes. Their charming voice issued from their faultless throat and pleased all men; they had studied the art of singing and were well-skilled in instruments, and they laboured to dispaly their skill. The singers from Karnata sat gracefully before the king as if they represented the six tunes[53], *viz.* Kedara, Gauda, Gandhara, Desha, Bhangala and Malava.

## Display by actresses

The female dancers of the king shone beauteously and bright like the lamps at night. They were inflamed by the god of love and were young and full of emotion, even as the lamps were fed by wax, and were new and supplied with wick. The female dancers Ratnamala, Dipamala and Nripamala danced charmingly displaying emotions and gestures. The king praised the beautiful actress Ratnamala, her forehead marked with *tilaka*, and he praised her dancing and owned that she had melted the hearts of all by her steps and her movements, by her tremour and her action. How she commenced the expected dance! And how her gestures, her movements, the expression of her passions, and the swelling song which flowed incessantly from her throat, inflamed all men! The vaunt of the skilful is worthless as straw in comparison with her. Possessed of loveliness and famed for her beauty, she was the renovator of men! Her song was without a fault, her person was decorated with jewels, her beauty was great, and she was possessed of merit. The Creator made her face like the full moon, and out of a portion of the nectar (of which the moon was made). The beauty of her face was nectar, and a drop of nectar hung from her nose in the form of a pearl pendant. The pearls which hung interwoven in the locks of hair which fell on the cheeks of the women were looked upon by the king as drops of nectar metling away from their moon-like faces! Thus the youthful king praised the women in presence of his boon companions, and took cups of wine from them. Admirable are the kings who devote themselves everyday to learning and to the compositions of poets, who encourage beautiful women skilled in music and overpowering as the five arrows of the god of love, and who devote themselves to the affairs of the world and of men.

## Duet songs

Pavarakadana was celebrated for his song, his poetry, and his music. He had heard of the king's fame which was gratifying to his ear, and he came to Kashmira from his distant country. He sang songs composed by himself in the assembly, and the king was pleased with him, and showered gold on him. He was skilled in singing duet songs, and once he sang a duet song named *lila* in the vernacular before the king. The king did not understand it, and I was asked to explain, and I at once explained it to him from *Bharatashastra*[54] and others. When the king had heard the six verses sung in a beautiful voice, songs which were delightful to the ear on account of their music, he became anxious to hear more. Pavarakadana hesitated while I sang aloud, and the king remarked to me that Pavarakadana was vain on account of his abilities, and he directed me to discuss the subject of music with that musician. I agreed, and the king initiated the discussion between us. And when the discussion in the assembly had been closed by a reference to books on music, and when Pavarakadana heard me speak about duet song, he expressed his wonder, and exclaimed that the Kashmirians were wonderfully skilful people, knowing all the *shastras*. He said so, and embraced me and freely acknowledged me his preceptor.

## Shrivara honoured

When the king found me thus victorious in the discussion, he was pleased, and favoured me by bestowing on me silk robes which made me happy. What has not king Shri Hassana given to me, Shrivara, far beyond my worth? He has issued a proclamation about me, which, as it emanates from the king, is a source of pleasure to me. He has given me strong and swift horses, and thick holy thread, and other beautiful articles beset with gold and jewels; and he has also given me beautiful boats with sails, and robes from his own person, and wealth. Shamsadena was gracious, Alabhadena[55] was politic, Shahabhadena was a hero and Kudvadena was wise. Shri Shekandhara was the favourite of the *Yavana* nobles, Alishaha was a liberal, king Shri Jaina loved all branches of learning and was versed in the literature of all languages and king Haidharashaha was an expert in performance on lute. But the present king is a master of music. People observed that every one of the former kings of this country was famous for some special qualification, but it is said of the present king that even Shri Jyahangira the Margesha, and others bowed at his feet when they heard his melodious and delightful songs.

Whenever the people of this country forsook their old customs owing to religious changes, or amassed money by practising deception, they were generally punished by calamities such as storm and conflagration, excessive cold and snowfall, hostilities and diseases. Once upon a time some merchants of the city, who were the favourites of the Mausulas but who had followed the customs of the Hindus from their birth, killed cows within the city. But when these wicked men had eaten the flesh of the kine, the part of the city where the animals had been slaughtered caught fire as if to purify itself, and the *vihara* there also was in flames. Then the terrible south-west wind began to blow, and became unbearable on account of the troubles that it brought. When these calamities overtook the people a *pandita's* son meditated for some nights on the strange and baneful wind and composed this *shloka*: "Afflicted by clouds that bear the tint of fire, by the sun that has the hue of the moon, and by the powerful south west wind, whither, O people! will ye flee?"

## Fire engulfs Jama Masjid

In the year '55 a fire suddenly broke out at one end of the cow[56] market at Pravareshapura[57] and extended its devastations to the side of the Gulikavadhika.[58] In a moment the city was consumed and looked like a burnt forest. From the great *masjeda*[59] the flaming barks of the *bhurja* tree, carried by the wind, came rushing, like messengers of calamities, to the place where the Brahamanas and mendicants are fed. The *masjeda* was a spacious building, extending on all sides, and was always white-washed. It was like the embodiment of the fame of king Shri Shekandhara. It was within this building that crowds of worshippers used to fall down and rise at prayers, imitating the high waves of Sangaravara.[60] It was here that the *yavanas* chanted mantras and looked graceful, like thousand lotuses with humming bees. It was here that on Friday[61], worshippers issued from the four doors on the four sides, so that it seemed as if the countrymen who had been buried were coming out! It was here that the four high minarets looked graceful like the supports of virtue, as if virtue had left his own place and descended to this spot to witness if the people observed the rules of religion. It was here that the sun shone like an umbrella of gold, as if he came hither to listen to the vanities uf the world. Such was the great building which towered to the sky and was decorated with wonderful sculptures, and which appeared like a fortress for the preservation of the faith of the kings.

In a moment the fire, all-destroying like the fire at the end of a cycle, left nothing of that building but its walls. It was here that in times of *Eedha* and other festivities, the Mausula people used to gather in crowds and observe the rites of religion with devotion.

There were houses built by Vahramakhana called the Panchavasas, and the fire flamed widely over them with a great noise, even like the Khandava[62] forest. The flaming barks of the bhurja tree fell on the waters of the Vitasta, and the boats in the river could not be saved from catching fire. What thousands of houses were burnt on the same day in the herdsmen's quarter at Surapattana[63] on account of the destructive wind! One hundred fowlers perished that day in the waves of the Mahapadma lake, agitated by the boisterous wind. The planet Mars predominated that year, and caste rules were not strictly observed, and the presiding goddess of the city was exiled from her house. Or was it that the righteousness of the righteous builders having wasted away, Fate gave an opportunity to new builders to rise to fame? The area of the great building which was burnt down was filled by the king with new buildings and it looked graceful again, as if the king's righteousness manifested itself. The town that had been burnt down was renewed within a short time, and the new town was like a young wife to the youthful king.

If the king's addiction to evil habits can cause ruin to this land of snow, the iniquity arising from mutual jealousies of the great ministers is also capable of destroying the whole kingdom in a moment. A kingdom where the seven[64] conditions are favourable, expands in strength and becomes prosperous. But if in such a kingdom mutual jealousies exist among the principal ministers, then, it melts away within a short time, even as the body withers when attacked by three diseases. The authorities should guard against such mutual jealousies, and then they need not fear foreign foe, even as an atheist fears no God, Ministers who violate the above maxim of king Lalitaditya, excite mutual jealousies and perish. It was on account of the quarrel amongst Malesa[65], Kadaryyavakhana and others, that Shri Jaina's kingdom went to pieces through mutual disagreement; and from that time when Shri Jaina found his kingdom ruined, no minister had ceased from being jealous of others. Alas! that in the king's court no minister repressed the monster envy, the destroyer of all things! Neither the disease which defies treatment, nor the serpent which possesses powerful poison, nor even fire is so dreadful as the disunion among the ministers.

## Jealousy among ministers

The minister Ahmada, though well versed in the science of government, became fickle-minded, like one not possessed of self-command. Once Nauruja and other sons of Ahmada unable to brook the prosperity of Tajibhatta, privately accused him before their father. They said that among all the ministers Tajibhatta had monopolized the power to confer favours or award punishments to men; that he was haughty on account of the support he received from the people, and that he had risen to prosperity for the ruin of the country. They also alleged that the guardianship[65] of the prince in the palace had also been given to him; and that these circumstances have concurred for their ruin. They further said that the queen, like the king, was favourably inclined towards him, that he was the commander-in-chief of the forces, and that if he were not destroyed, he would soon oppose them.

When his sons said these things, the Mallika regarded Tajibhatta with jealousy, and was angry with him, though he had been adopted as his son. The minister had administered the kingdom suitably to the requirements of the times, and had personally looked into the affairs of state, but as the merit earned in his previous birth was exhausted, he too gradually lost his sense. Those who serve their master by being attentive to his work and sacrificing their own interest, suddenly follow a different line of conduct when the time of their destruction comes nigh. Mallika devised various plans intending to do mischief to Tajibhatta. At one time, he spoke thus in anger, in the king's court:

"What avails it, O King! that you have obtained this kingdom while the surrounding countries are overspread with enemies? No one takes heed of that. Allow me to march out against the enemies according to my discretion as long as they remain undestroyed. Give me this order O master?" Tajibhatta was eager to undertake some bold adventure; so when he heard this, he also asked the king to place a general of the army under him, so that he might march out. When the king heard this, he, by the advice of the Mallika, furnished Tajibhatta with an army, and sent him out of

Kashmira. Tajibhatta's servants followed him with great din and noise, in fear and in gladness, even as black bees follow their chief.

## Tajibhatta's campaign

When the king of Rajapuri and Jyabhadeva and the men of the Madra country saw the costly and well-equipped army, adorned with royal insignia, they wondered. The people of Madra, of small stature, were pleased at the approach of Tajibhatta; they became unruly, left their ruler Tattarakhana[66] and came to him, thus causing a division among themselves. Tajibhatta created some confusion in Tattarakhana's country by burning down *masjedas* which had been built by the Khana at Shrigalakota[67] and other places. As Tajibhatta was born of an ordinary[68] family, the people believed he had no worth in him, but nevertheless through his devotion to his master he performed acts which were not expected of him. He reduced the herdsmen of Purapattana, until their power existed in name only, and his own prowess became irresistible like that of the sun.

He reduced many petty chiefs to vassalage, and performed many deeds of courage and of serverity, and thereby inspired terror in the celebrated kings of Dilli and other places. He soon returned to his country with wealth and horses. In the interests of his master a minister sometimes looks on his own son as his foe and shelters his bitter enemy as his son. Deceived by fate, the Mallika disregarded this maxim, and unable to brook the prosperity of Tajibhatta resolved on humiliating his pride.

The minister thought that Tajibhatta was strong on account of the affection which the king bore towards him, and was oppressing all men. He was therefore afraid of Tajibhatta and was angry with him, and caused the king to be jealous of him. At this time the king's little son named Hossana was (taken away from Tajibhatta and) made over to Malleka Nauruja to be brought up. Tajibhatta was returning with his troops when he heard of this disregard of the king's obligation towards him, and he felt his influence diminished. When he arrived with his army, the fickle-minded king, now devoid of affection towards him, did not accord him due honours. The Mallika, however, was unable by his own endeavours to do any injury to Tajibhatta, and he accordinly planned to bring back the Saidas who had left the country. He represented to the king that the Saida had given his daughter to the king, and she had borne him sons, and that the family of his father-in-law ought to receive his protection; and he therefore suggested that the Saidas should be brought back. Bent on pleasing the king, Ahmada despatched encouraging letters to the Saidas in the country of the king of Dilli.

When a person becomes fortunate, his people assert their superiority over others by wicked and evil means. Why do not foolish men grasp this maxim and conduct themselves accordingly, and why do not powerful and prosperous men overcome the whole world by means of good counsel? People ask themselves such questions, and attribute all things to fate. Sagacious men remarked that since the Mallika was bringing the Saidas back after having once done them injury, they would eventually cause his ruin.

## Dread of the Syeds

When Shri Phiryyadamara came to know the purpose for which the Saidas were being brought back, he went to the house of the minister Ahmada, and spoke these sensible words: "Tajibhatta is under your power, he conducts himself towards you like your servant; you should therefore protect him, and subdue his pride by means of good advice. Do not bring back the Saidas, the Turushkas[69] Pushkara, Ashvasa, and others; they are strong and are like thorns to the country; and they have once been expelled with difficulty. You are bringing them back to destroy one man, but when they come all will be destroyed. Should the sacred fig tree be set on fire in order to kill a single young bird? Surely your ruin and that of your sons and servants will follow. It is a misfortune that you propose to bring the Saidas back. The Saidas have been injured once, and you should rather throw a handful of poison in your rice-pot for your own destruction than wish to bring them back. You think yourself wise and do not consider my words as reasonable, but you will bring them back to your mind when I am dead and you are in difficulties." Mallika heard this and said that they could do notking so long as he was alive, that they had once felt his power, and would now become his flatterers. Ahmada thought himself wise, and so he slighted Phiryyadamara. "Be it so", said the latter and went away. After he had gone, the minister did not abandon his project of bringing in the Saidas. He whose sense is lost does not listen to the advice of his well-wishers, but when he finds himself in difficulties he regrets that he did not accept it.

## Syeds return

When the Saidas had thought over the minister's letters, they became anxious to return; they collected their party, and came in like swans. First, their chief Meya Hassana, accompanied by his trusty adviser Nauruja, came to the king. After befitting mutual eulogies, Mallika became favourably inclined towards him, and bestowed on him his own estate Khoyashrama.[70] The same Saida Hassana, who could not even enter the country before, was now, for the destruction of the Mallika, in a position to pass orders on others. Gradually the Saidas entered the country in great numbers, and spread themselves over the kingdom; and the people of Kashmira, those who were in the country and those who lived in the outskirts, became alarmed. And when the minister Ahmada saw the Saidas coming in riding their horses, and moving like waves, and beloved by the king, and when he perceived that the king was influenced by them, on account of the influence which the queen exercised over the king, he and his sons repented. What man would not be happy if the idea that comes to him after a deed is done, came to him before it was accomplished? He could then confide in his friends and defeat his enemies.

At that time the Saidas intended to throw Tajibhatta into prison in order that they might rob his wife[71]. Tajibhatta heard that these people were planning to do him mischief, he became alarmed, and came to the house of the Mallika. By this time the minister had perceived the influence which the Saidas had acquired, and had become alarmed. At this peiod the old Phiryyadamara died. He had performed well the duties of the Pratihara and of other posts, and he alone, at the time of his death, obtained the praise due to worthy acts, such as can be obtained with difficulty in this world or in the next. Urged by the Saidas, the king became angry with Tajibhatta when he heard that he had taken shelter with the minister, and he immediately sent Jona Rajanaka, and other soldiers in order to arrest him. He also ordered that Tajibhatta should be confined in his own house, and his property confiscated.

## Tajibhatta under house arrest

The Mallika gave up Tajibhatta to the soldiers, and he was kept under confinement. It was owing to some residue of his virtue that he spent his days with his relatives, and lived at ease on a small allowance which he received. Though he was confined in his house, he lived with his family like a swan in the Manasa lake. This was on account of the virtue which he had acquired by spending a large amount of money. He who, with the view to acquire virtue, enjoys the pleasure of giving gifts during the time of his prosperity, lives in comfort like Tajibhatta even when he is bereft of that prosperity. In this manner all the powerful men were nearly ruined by Mallika Ahmada who could not bear the welfare of others. Even Jyahangira the Margesha became afraid of the Mallika, because the Saidas had been injured by the murder of their sister's son. Now all the offices of power had been given to men of the Mallika's party and the Pratihara and other worthy men had been sacrificed for his selfish purposes. For these and other faults the king became estranged from the Mallika, and rarely gave him audience; and for the protection of his own life he prudently avoided living in any one place in his kingdom.

Accompanied by the Saidas, the king went to the garden by the side of his palace, to enjoy the sport[72] of flowers, even as Indra went to the garden of Kuvera. After he had enjoyed the sport, he got into a boat and, in the company of the Margesha and Nauruja, gave himself up to drinking. They all became intoxicated, and talked on various topics, and, like the members of the family of Yadu, they hit one another with the arrows of words. When the excitement became great, the king left his turban in anger and went to the house of the Mallika in order to rebuke him. Efforts were made to propitiate him, but the king returned to his palace angry, and grief for the indiscretion of his son (Nauruja) touched the minister's heart. On another day the king, whose heart was estranged from Ahmada, privately told the minister's enemies of his unreasonable determination not to protect any more the party of the minister. The enemies of Ahmada took advantage of this opportunity, and met together to do him injury, even as the diseases meet in the body when they once find an entrance. They advised the king to take away from the minister the charge of bringing up Yosobhakhana[73], and to give it to some one else; for what would the king do, they asked, if the minister set up the prince as the king of the country. The king agreed and soon after he gave the chance of bringing up his child to Jonarajanaka, and thus artfully took away the Khana from the Mallika.

## Clash within the palace

The minister remained in his house on the morning of the day in which he made over the prince to the king, and he said to his wife that he would be revenged on his enemies. In the meantime the Margapati had been sent for by the king and, impelled by the idea of doing some bold deed, he came from his estate to the city, accompanied by his soldiers. When the Mallika heard of the Margapati in the morning, he became angry and went to the king attended by his soldiers, though warned by (evil omen of) the cries of kites to his right. He went on spurring his horse, and the animal's face was bathed with tears as if in sorrow for the impending separation of his master from him.

The Margesha Jyahangira was ordered by the king to enter the court-yard with his soldiers. The sun was then rising, and its beams were reflected on the weapons. At this time the minister also entered the yard of the palace, and there the two met and challenged each other, and the capital trembled in fear of these two chiefs. The king wondered that the minister had entered the palace armed, he became angry and caused Bhangila to support Jyamsara the Margesha. Sent by the terrified king, Bhangila came, and after having barricaded the palace arrived with the Saidas. The victorious Jyahangira had joined Rajanaka, and released Tajibhatta from confinement; and he then marched into the yard of the palace.

The soldiers sent by Tajibhatta were eager for fight and they set the western gate of the palace on fire. The fire consumed rows of houses upto the residence of Hassana Rajanaka within a short time and reduced them to the condition of a burnt forest. The news of the burning of houses, beautiful as the residence of Indra, caused sorrow even to those who were afar. Masses of smoke rose with the flame, and the men in the palace became like live fish in a frying pan on account of the heat. When the affrighted king saw the fire burning in the yard of the palace he was overcome with terror, and his soldiers, though eager for fight, could not engage themselves in it on the heated roads.

## Ahmad imprisoned (1482 A.D.)

When the Mallika saw that on account of his son's haughtiness his followers had deserted and that his son was left alone, he did not know what to do. He wished that his sons should not engage themselves in fight, for the king's government might be crushed in that fight. He had upheld the king for ten years[74]. Why should his government be crushed now in this fight? He again thought of his eldest son who remained indifferent to the quarrel, and who might be overwhelmed with misfortune if engaged in it. He remembered also his son Nauruja who might receive injury in the affray. He would rather that death should come to him than that he should bear a bad name in his old age. Thus he thought to himself and he told his sons not to engage themselves in the contest but to remain there. He felt disheartened and sought the shelter of the king who was in the palace directing the movements of the guards. The king thought of the previous services of the minister and received him with affection; so that those who had sought to do harm to the minister found that the king was on his side. They therefore found no opportunity for commencing hostilities, and went away to Bhutta country. At this time the honourable Jyahangira, always eager for victory, entered the king's yard with shouts by the north gate of the palace; and the metropolis seemed to rejoice at his courage in the echoes of the sound of his battle drum. Jyahangira and other worthy men were pleased to see the king, and they were happy both in mind and in body at the triumph achieved. Urged by these men, the king threw the Mallika with his sons and several servants into prison on the following morning.

Royal fortune returned from the house of the minister to her own residence (the king's palace) as if in fear of incurring superfluous expenditure. The hoarded silver and other metals which the enemies of the king had obtained by oppressing the lower classes of the people and the Kayasthas now came to the possession of the king. And the chief whose influence had been dreaded by Jainaraja[75] and Shri Hajyashaha, and by whose wisdom Hajyashaha's son had reigned for ten years without fear, and Vahramakhana and other obnoxious men had been removed, even that chief was now overcome by the fear of his enemies! Fie to the prosperity of the prosperous! Wealth is soiled by fear, it obstructs progress in the path of virtue, it becomes a source of oppression to the poor, and it is transient as snow. All that wealth which his servants Pherabhatta and others had brought him by oppressing the people, now came to the possession of the king.

The beautiful horses brought from foreign countries, and the clothes which had never been used, were given up to the king, as if they had hitherto been left with the minister on trust. That alone proved to be his own property which he had given away or had used while celebrating his birthdays, which he was ambitious of celebrating like the birthdays of kings.

## Deprived of wealth

Mortals oppressed in mind! You who have obtained great wealth from the king, bestow true gifts and enjoy true enjoyments, for this world is fleeting like the waves of the sea, and wealth cannot always be had. Ye servants of the king, do not boast of your power derived from wealth and known to all, do not boast of the favour of the king. Is there any permanency in the mirage, in the colour of the *kusumbha* flowers, in the love of harlots, or in the favour of a king? While the man proud of his wealth ponders on the speedy acquisition of the highest post and the subjugation of his enemies, on the inexhaust-ableness of his treasury and the obedience of his servants, his adverse fate destroys all these, as if they were but a dream. Jugabhatta saw Ahmada in the prison to tell him to give up to the king, without delay, whatever more he had of gold. Upon this the minister became angry and said: "The avaricious king has taken millions from me and is he not yet satisfied? What shall I say? I have ruined the men of my party for the preservation of the kingdom. I abstained from fighting at the time when my crisis came. I brought back and favoured the Saidas who had once fled from the country. But the king became ungrateful, and they too have turned hostile to me. I consolidated the whole kingdom, and if the king again wants to enjoy it let him maintain peace. He will be glad at my death. Let him for whom I have suffered the cares of the state for ten years in this wretched world, rejoice at my destruction," Thus he spoke, and communicated to the king whatever else he had to say. "Fie to me" he said to himself "that I did not listen to the words of that experienced man, Shri Phiryadamara." He blamed himself everyday and said: "If I be perfectly innocent then let my evil doers, the Margesha, Tajibhatta, and others reap the fruit of their work in a few days." The people soon came to wonder at seeing the result of all this which the minister had exclaimed in his sorrow, while in the prison.

Mallika Ahmada had administered wisely, and when he was thus destroyed with his sons, wicked people acquired influence with the king. The avaricious Tajibhatta[76] and others, and those among the Saidas who held offices, oppressed the people, even as painful diseases oppress the body. On the pretence of taking "flowers of joy"[77] and "dinnara pieces," the Saida officers began to acquire riches at the expense of the subjects. Shri Meya Hassana got the title of Malla which had belonged to the Mallika. and likewise obtained the Mallika's village of Nagrama and his estates. He divided his new estates among his sons and servants, and gave half of the wealth and estates to Meya Mahmada.[78] The Saidas became unruly after their triumph, they placed the king under their control, and they sent messengers and brought in the able Saida Nasira. When he arrived at Panchaladeva by the Surapura road he was attacked with fever, and in that state he entered the capital. He gave audience once to all—his grand daughter, son-in-law, wife's brother, kindred, and the ministers—all the people whom he would not live to see again, for he arrived almost in a dying state, as if only to see them. He passed two days in fever and died in his house. The imprisoned Mallika, alarmed at the banishment of his son, was overpowered by grief, and he fell ill and died. Though the chief minister died in prison, the people gave vent to their sorrow in cries and loud lamentations when they heard of his death.

## Syeds consolidate hold

When great men who have done good deeds die, insignificant men come forward to take their places, even as lamps serve the purposes of men when the sun which lighted the world has set. It was owing to the good luck of their daughter (the queen) that the Saidas obtained wealth and greatness; but they regarded the people of Kashmira scarcely even as grass. The king, bent on furthering the interests of the Saidas, acquiesced in orders, whatever they were, that were issued by them for their own selfish ends. They were busy in creating factions, the king was forbearing and women came to have great influence. It was apparent that some revolution was at hand. Accepting bribes was considered by the officers of the state as a virtue, oppressing the subjects was regarded as wisdom, and addiction to women was reckoned happiness. All opposition ceased. Meya Hassana was proud of being able to accomplish whatever his heart desired, and he oppressed the whole kingdom. Gradually he became more and more powerful, and slowly he spread his influence over the king's country, and as Rahu spreads his shadow, even so did he extend his authority over all.

The Saidas then intended to conquer the little[79] and the great Bhutta country, and ordered Shri Jyahangira and Nasera to march there. The Margapati Jyahangira suggested that if both of them marched together they would be able to accomplish their work but the two Saidas did not follow this suggestion. One of the leaders conquered the country and returned with glory to the capital. The other was struck with panic, his course was arrested, and he saved himself by artifice. Bhuttas fell on the rear of the army and destroyed the soldiers. I have abstained from giving even a brief account of this defeat in consideration of the present *unsuitable time*. The Kechilshyas, Baddharaga and other servants of the old king fell in that Bhutta war even as insects fall into the fire. The Saidas remembered the injury done to them before by Nossarajanaka,* took advantage of this defeat, and prevented him from obtaining an audience with the king. The Margapati apprehended mischief from the Saidas but he was clever in protecting himself. He returned to the king's dominion but avoided coming before the Saidas. Apprehending mischief to himself, he artfully appeared before the king.

## Jahangir's advice to the king

Once when Jyahangira found the king alone, he thus said: "These Saidas, O King! were once exiled but have been brought back. You have yourself brought this curse on this peaceful country. As the son of king Shri Jaina's son, you have a right to the kingdom: but as his daughter's son, Meya Mahammada has also a similar claim on the country. The Saidas have further been encouraged by the Turushakas with hopes of support. Such are the Saidas and they should always be feared. They are ever eager for the kingdom as vultures are for meat. It is not fit, O my master! that you who have many ends to accomplish should devote yourself exclusively to one. Who praises the black bee which is attached to one plant only? All your work, O King! will be accomplished if you avoid placing yourself under the influence of your wife. Do not, therefore, O

* The same person as the Margapati Jyahangira, one of the leaders in the Bhutta war (translator).

master! be influenced by your spouse. I am going away for the safety of your kingdom as well as of myself. The country is ruined, and you ought to save yourself somehow." When the king heard this he said, "So will be". But when he went to his wife at night he was overcome by affection and he told her all that had been said to him. Whereupon the queen, who had espoused the cause of her father's party, became enraged, and like a fearful she-serpent, sought to injure the Margapati. Where a woman, who despises men and supersedes her husband, becomes the master, there the goddess of Royal Fortune does not abide long in her anger. Rising from the side of his beloved, the king became anxious to favour her party and placed the kingdom in their power, as it once was under the power of Mallika Ahmada.

## Jahangir leaves the country

The Margesha feared mischief from the Saidas on account of the hostile queen and he, with his troops, went away by the Karkotadranga[80] road, took away with him all his relatives and property through Bhangila, and went by inaccessible roads but did not lose his patience. Jewels lie scattered in the great sea into which the rivers flow, and the waters are agitated by storm; even so there are jewels in this great and prosperous kingdom in which the armies meet and which is agitated by the mutual quarrel of ministers. When the enemies prosper day by day, and the sovereign becomes infirm in a country, the few who are good follow the only proper course that is left to them — they leave the country. For to remain quiet would be weakness, to make liberal gifts would reduce wealth, to create factions would be a wicked act, to go to battle would cause death to men. The king repented the destruction of the party of the minister; and the flight of the Margapati and of others was to him like salt in a wound. Though the king was attended by all the Saidas, yet without the Margesha he felt like an elephant left alone out of the herd. A few of those who were born of the family of Thakkura, or of the treasurer, were still alive. They had been powerful before on account of their family and of their successes but they perished by reason of unwise counsel and quarrel among themselves. When the Margapati had left the country, the sky suddenly began to scatter snow[81], and thereby left no doubt in the people's mind that he, of all men, was the most fortunate. On account of the heavy fall of snow the inhabitants of the country became withered like trees with broken branches. The soldiers of the Margapati got into caverns covered with *kusha* grass as if they expected that a fall of snow would enable them to lie hidden for a time. He was the delighter of the hearts of all, and the king's court became desolate without him, even as the *kumuda* flower withers in the absence of the moon.

## Women take bribes

The king remained indifferent to the doings of his servants, his mind was influenced by his wife and the Saidas, and his own acts became disorderly and reprehensible. Unable to enforce his orders in governing his own country, he disliked ability in others and liked only to watch the looks of his beloved women. These women were quick in inflicting punishments and bestowing favours on men, and were eager in accepting bribes and they, not the ministers or the servants, became the intimate friends of the king. The Turushkas, Pushkala and Ashvasa, who had given up even the observances of decorum in the enjoyment of pleasures, now gained their own end, not the end of their master. When the people saw the kingdom of their sovereign under the influence of women they felt grieved, and repeated the following *shloka*: "They perish who have no leader, they do perish also whose leader is an infant and they also perish whose leader is a woman, and those who have many leaders perish like-wise."

## Jahangir's message

The king remained in bed day and night and mourned for the Margapati and others for whom he was grieved, but was unable to bring them back. The Margesha had taken shelter in Lohara[81], he was oppressed with anxiety for his master, and he took this opportunity to send the following words of advice by means of a letter. "O king! Jewel among men! Your treasury, which used to gratify the hopes of all, has been removed by the Saidas, and they have brought in abject poverty. Like a drop of quicksilver the Saidas are by nature heavy, restless, and adhere to one another; they do not wish for the company of others. You are, O king! like the green sandal tree, the bestower of all felicity, but you are surrounded by a hissing she-serpent. What sensible man will not leave the kingdom, though it be like a jewel, if there abide in it serpents of deadly poison preventing the approach of others? Royal Fortune is like the flame that burns on the funeral ground, frightful to the sight, and he who serves her must not touch the flame, though he sees it burning. Meya Hassana's mind is under the influence of evil planets, and like Ravana he keeps away from the right path, though advised by his well-wishers to follow it. The woman named Mera[82], who accepts as plentifully as she takes meat, is abiding with you for your ruin, even as Tadaka did with Ravana. Let the Saidas remain with you in the kingdom if you so wish it, but I will go from here to the Turushka chief of Karavinda. There was not one in my family who forgot his devotion to his master or became a rebel to the king. You are my only shelter and I shall remain loyal towards you as if I were at your gate. Our conduct has always been proper, and we are opposed to injustice, and if we adopt evil ways no one will have confidence in us. Who can be at ease in this world, even if he lives to the end of *kalpa*, and acquires wealth, and destroys his enemies? If others be ruined, you should protect them, but if you are ruined, who else is there to protect you?"

When Meya Hassana came to know of this letter, he soon replied in the presence of the king, hissing like a serpent in his anger. "Exiled from his place and deprived of his livelihood, surely the Margapati will be withered by our prowess, even like a lotus torn up and taken from the water; and his servants will not stay with him, even as the birds stay not in the tank which is dried up by the heat of summer and in which nothing is left but mud. What can he do to us, remaining where he is, and receiving the fealty only of the people of that place? My followers will be able to overcome him in battle or drive him from thence. Let me go there in person, or he will join with the Turushka." Then Saida Hassana remembered the previous friendship which had existed between him and the Margapati and said: "Let his confiscated estates be returned to him, and I will bring him back. During the disturbance created by the ministers we swore friendship to each other, and Fate will be adverse towards us if we now seek each other's harm[83]". Determined in his enmity towards the Margapati, Meya Hassana heard this said before the king, and immediately bestowed the estate of Naushahara[84] on his relative Daulatayana. He said that this good servant Daulatayana being stationed outside the country, would do his duty well, and he directed that one *koti* of money be given to him in order that he might collect an army. He then sent on Edharajanaka[85] armed and accoutered but soon caused him to come back, although he had himself supplied him with money.

When Parashurama[86] and others, of the country of the Madras, heard uf all this, they apprehended danger in Kashmira, and asked the permission of the Saidas to depart. But the Saidas said that they would allow them to go after providing them with provisions for the road; they were told to stay a few days, and their salary was promised to them. But when the Saidas returned to their houses, they said to one another that these Madra people were hostile like the Turushkas, and that they should not be allowed to depart.

In the meantime the king felt anxious for several of his servants, and the anxiety made his face like the lotus in the month of Pausha.

The Saidas were fond of hunting, and in the month of Magha they took with them the king in that state of mind in order to destroy animals[87] in the kingdom. Wherever their oppressive army encamped at night, there the cries of the oppressed people resounded on all sides, and wherever the king's army halted encircling some hill, the people complained bitterly against the uprooting of the vines.

## Deer-hunt in winter

The army, bent on destruction, attacked high and pleasant hills with gentle waterfalls, even as wicked men attack the good. On the top of a hill there were some deer whose bodies were covered with snow. They heard the noise and came down in herds in alarm, and the Saidas were glad to see them come with their tongues protruded, and their faces smeared with blood. The animals came to the king with their young ones as if to say "take us who are strong but spare our young ones who are weak." All the people of the place asked the king repeatedly to cease hunting, urging that the gods would be angry at the destruction of the deer of a hill inhabited by holy men; but the king did not desist from hunting, even as a lustful man does not desist from the company of women. The *muni* named Vaishravana[88] had his seat on this hill; he came to the king and pleaded that the place was a pen for the deer and kine of the hermitage, and begged that it might be spared. The female deer struck while crying and weltering in blood, were killed by the relentless Saidas; and the ground was filled with fetuses from their womb.

The king was not satiated with killing some animals; he denuded those hills of deer and, tired in the evening, he ordered the forest beaters to occupy the houses of the villagers. Some of these men, terrible as the servants of death, passed the night in houses where the owner's daughter-in-law and daughter and wife were young and beautiful, and there were wine and meat and fish. The Turushkas were powerful, and strong in archery; they seated themselves in the houses of Brahmanas who had devoted themselves to the performances of the six duties: they ate from the vessels of the Brahmanas the cooked meat of fowls killed as if in sacrificial ceremonies; and they gave themselves up to the pleasure of drinking. The inhabitants of the place were robbed of their domestic animals and rice and wine and other things; and some of the avaricious servants of the Saidas killed the people in their own houses.

## Unsportive hunting

The impotent king heard the people express their wish that he might not come there again, and was grieved on account of the oppression of the people. Hunting is an evil habit, and fie to kings who do not possess the dignity of a king! Certainly, in the present instance, it was killing men under the pretence of killing beasts. If to tie down and kill hundreds of deer, like beasts of sacrifice, be sport, what then is a butcher's work? The skill in taking aim from horseback on running animals is to be coveted, but what praise is due to the practice of tying up animals and shooting them with arrows? Hunting is the vocation of the Kshatriyas, but since the beasts of game live harmlessly on grass, it is not good that one should be greatly addicted to it; for excess in everything is bad. Killing and extirpating the deer in this manner, the king at last reached the hill on the side of the Mahapadma[89] lake. Sin was thus committed which will strike terror into hunters in future times.

## Hunting birds

After hunting, the king returned to the capital suffering from diarrhea. Some said that it was owing to the sin committed in the pursuit of game that the gods were angry, and it was while he was yet in the hunting ground that the disease was first observed. Others said that the Saidas, urged by a desire to obtain independence and the kingdom, and instigated by the Turushkas, did something to the king to cause the illness. Some again observed that owing to the king's separation from his ministers his heart was filled with anxiety and grief, and this gave rise to the illness. No one could ascertain the real cause. While the king was in that state of health he went to the district of Sarja[90] on the first day of the new year with the vain desire of killing birds. As he was going in a boat, that day, a serpent from *Jainavatavihara* crossed his way, and he killed it with an arrow in order to allay his fear arising out of this ill omen. He thus removed the anxiety from his mind but did not remove the illness from his body. A head wind violently opposed him, as if to warn him against setting out, and to lead him back to prolonged acts of virtue. The disturbed lake trembled with its rising waves, as if in sorrow that the people of this country would come to be opposed on the death of the king. Surrounded by the Saidas, the king feasted at the festivity in Sarja, and gave audience to all, as if he would not see them again. He then immediately embarked with his servants on a boat, and during the whole day be killed birds by means of hawks, as if to drive away the anxiety from his mind. The hawks brought down many birds as presents to the king, as if knowing that their master who was sporting with them that day, was not destined to do so again.

## Last days

The king then returned: he left the Saidas, and went to his bed, informing the queen of his illness and telling her that he was not well. The queen herself ministered to his wants, and asked him what he would eat, but the king became void of lustre like the moon during the day time. His chest broad as the leaf of a door; his face fair as molten gold; his waist, thigh, knees, and legs like the petals of a lotus; his two bright eyes, and his forehead adorned with eye brows, all became discoloured by the disease. Once the king privately told Meya Hassana that he would not live long, that his infant sons were not fit for the kingdom, that the son of Vahramakhana who was in prison would not allow his sons to remain safe from harm. "Rather" he said, "bring the son of Adamakhana by some artifice, and coronate him. Or do as your daughter, the queen advises." When Saida Hassana heard this, he advised the king to be patient, and said that he would recover, but the Saida was very much grieved and wept. Then the queen Mera Mukhata when alone with her father, thus said to him: "It is doubtful whether the king will live; what should be done now about the kingdom. Rather coronate the youthful son of Vahramakhana, and make your eldest grandson the heir-apparent. Two or three people whom we hate may be killed, but all need not perish." When Meya Hassana heard this he rebuked her in anger.

## Death of Hassan Shah

The Saidas had no reverence for Brahmanas, and they gave wealth to the Mausulas for the benefit of the king in his final rest. All the females who knew the king went to see him, but they prevented others from going to him, and did not allow those who charm away poison to chant *mantras*. They did not follow the advice of physicians[91] and themselves prepared pills for the king to take. The king exclaimed that some mischief had been done to him, and when these female doctors found his voice and complexion changed they brought in Ruyyabhatta[92] who prided himself as being a physician, a charmer against poison and a man of experience. But when the attendants asked the king why he was gazing on that skilful man, the king, then on the point of death, replied by ordering the removal of that hypocrite[93] from his sight. All then burst out in loud lamentation with tears in their eyes and said that the king had seen the buffalo of Yama and would go to heaven that very day. The king's voice stopped, his eyes watered and rolled, and on that very night he was on the point of death. In the year 60 on the ninth day of the dark moon, in the month of Vaishakha, the king went to heaven after having reigned for twelve years and five days.

The whole night resounded with the cries of the people, and in the morning all the Saidas with their servants placed the body on a conveyance, and with umbrella and *chamara*, conveyed it to the ancestral burial ground. The people were not so grieved at the death of Shri Jaina as at the death of this king, for they were now left without protection. The ministers laid the king, with his turban and belt and bright cap, on a stone within the cavern, and covered the body with cloth; and the people were anxious to see him. They thought of the king, and fancied that he was merely sleeping within the cavern. For seven days the Saidas came there in the morning, and read their own Vedas, mingling their perusal with cries of lamentation. Those who are attached to this world and enjoy youth and prosperity, and who yield themselves to the love of women, to enjoyments and drinking, they all pass away in a few days, bereft of everything, and grieved and sorrowful in mind, even like a lustful man when he leaves the delightful abode of his mistress. A king thinks within himself: this is my country, this my youthful wife, and these are my sons and servants; suddenly death comes to him, and he leaves them all and departs on his long journey, bearing with him only his virtues and his sins. His dominion does not abide with him after his death, though he had gloried in his beautiful kingdom complete in its seven component parts. Thus the people said and lamented in the burial ground, for those who had been kings before had now only a tombstone left to them.

Owing to the *mlechha* law the queen found it difficult to bestow the kingdom on the son of Vahramakhana[94], and thought that the step might lead to evil consequences.

This is the account of Hassanashah's going to heaven.

Here ends the third book, named 'the account of the reign of Hassanashah,' of Jainarajatarangini composed by Pandita Shrivara.

## References

1. Shekandharpura: Hassatt gave up Nauhatta for Naushehra.
2. Mark of sovereignty: The word used is *tilakam*.
3. Haidershah sat on a golden throne.
4. *homa*: Obviously a remnant of the rituals on the coronation of Hindu Kings.
5. Six schools of philosophy: ref. 79/41.
6. Nagrama:.. Nagam.... Dvarpal: Commandant of the guards.... Ikshuka: sub-division to the west of Srgr.
7. Mallas: party of the minister Malik Ahmad.... Tajibhatta (or Tazibhat) had served Haji Khan in Lohar. He was adopted by Malik Ahmad Yatu 'as his son' and married the elder sister of Jahangir Margapati who got a divorce from Syed Nasir. This created him *enmity* of the Syeds. He was a poor lad of obscure origin when unexpectedly he outshone the elite in an archery competition commemorated in the verse: *greh yeti aasi kaasani Shahas/teli maati sapdi Taezbatun kaan* (when the Emperor—God—wards off evil constellations, it is like Tazibhat's arrow hitting the bull's eye).... Ahmed.. Malta: Malik Ahmad (SK).

8. Imprisoned: See pp. 92 and 95.
9. *Karnaha*: tehsil comprising hill areas n. of Uttar Pga.
10. Kramrajyapura: obviously Kupwara
11. Both parties: Z also complained of the disloyalty of officers.
12. Mavari country: the catchment area of the Mavar river, including Handwara.
13. Dulapora: v. Dolipora near Wilagam in Kupwara dt. RNS places it 2 miles s.e. of Shuluru on the way to Sopore... Chakrabhava: pb. some of the Tsaks or Chaks.
14. Was Phiryadamara a Brahmin? The name Phera, from 'Phiryabhatta', was borne by Kashmiri Brahmins till the last fifties. But on p. 184 Phirya Thakura, a barber, is mentioned as having built a *khanaqaha*.
15. desert his elder brother: ref. p. 139... arrow in the face: Adam was killed when an arrow hit him in the face in Jammu. Bah ram was hit by an arrow in the mouth (PH).
16. Z.'s candour.
17. Avatarasiha: mentioned only here.
18. Maliktaja: Malikjaja (SK)... Panchgahvan ref. p. 27.
19. Abhimanyu: mentioned as Zain Padar (PH), Zainvadar (T. Ak.)..., Devsara: in Kulgam t. was a stronghold of feudal barons.
20. sin of him: Bahram's eyes were plucked by Jonarajanaka.
21. Powerful faction: of Malik Ahmad.
22. Gratified: Abhimanyu was a partisan of Haji Khan and opposed to Z.
23. Could not do: this tongue-in-the-cheek comment of Srv. conveys that Abhimanyu had many supporters.
24. Mallika Jada: pb. Nauroz, or even Malik Ahmad himself. A chronological sequence appears to be wanting.
25. Paigamvara: The holy Prophet...., Saida Jyamala: Syed Jamal
26. famed: for all the faults Shrivara attributes to the Syeds they appear to have been brave and skilled warriors.
27. Large estates: Baharupa (Beeru) and other estates (SK) Dillipora: Delhi... adopted: the Muslims of Kashmir had, pb., not discarded the practice of adoption inherited from their pre-Muslim past.
28. Jyahamgira: Jahangir, a prominent army commander
29. Goddess of fortune: allusion to the humble origin of Tazibhatta.
30. Diddamatha: a *matha* or residential quarter built for travellers by Queen Didda (980-1003) below Safa Kadal. The locality has, as a consequence, taken the name Diddamatha or Dedamar. At present known as Maliksaheb. A similar place name of recent origin is *Kaksarai*...solar dynasty: the umbrella architecture is said to have come to Kashmir from the Central Asia.
31. Garuda: regarded as king of the birds and arch enemy of the serpents.
32. Golkhatona: Gulkhatoon.

33. Kuloddnarananga: the palace built by Z. at Pampore... Vijayesha: Bijbehara.
34. garden: another interpretation puts it as 'his garden in the Anekaksh or Anyech Pga'.
35. *masodha... khanagaha*: a mosque with compartments for meditation in solitude.
36. Satipusha: not mentioned elsewhere. Satipura v. is in Pulwama. Lawrence mentions another Satipura in Sonawari t.
37. Kheri: Khur-Naivav (Stein) which is on the route leading to the plains.
38. Kshipitika: Ka'ta' Kol. The causeway cannot be identified with certainty. Pb. it was built from the present Safakadal, left, to Zaldagar. to protect the low-lying Ga'nzkh'od area. On p. 71 a similar causeway is attributed to Damara Kacha.
39. Richika: Rigaka and Noothaka (SK)
40. Karala: Ardhvana or Advani... Kudmadinpuri: refer p. 84/138.
41. Edarajanaka: a descendent of Ramchandra who was assassinated by Rinchena.... native land: pb. Lar....
42. Hayatkhatona: daughter of Meija/Meya Hassan was the principal queen of the Sultan....
    Mrigavata: Mrigavati was one of the queens of Nirjitavarma (921-923 A.D.) but no *matha* in her name is mentioned.
43. Jayarala: mentioned by some as Jaimala, princess of Rajapuri, married to the king.
    Pherathakura: name borne by Hindus and Muslims alike.
44. Suyyabhandapati: either (*i*) Suyya, the chief of the guild of actors, or (*ii*) Suyya, chief superintendent of the king's stores. Should read: 'Suyyabhandapati.... Vijayeshvara, which having strengthened the *Sangha* (church) of righteousness shed iustre on the path of salvation of the Buddhists.'
    Bhimasvami Ganesh: the temple at the south-western foot of the Sharika Parvata.
45. Destroyed: precious books and specimens of art were lost for ever through incendiarism or vandalism-demolition: another form of severe punishment.... woods: Srv. as a lover of trees.
46. Shri Toramana: grandson of Meghavahana, struck coins in his own name.
47. Hindu customs: Srv. has a soft comer in his heart for men or women favouring old customs.
48. any one else: Bhomarakhatun, Mera and Jairala/Jaimala have already been mentioned as wedded to the king.... Shahabadinapuri: Shadipur (p., 44) ....Mahmadakhana: prince, Hassan's son.... year 54: 1477/1478 A.D.
49. Great actors: the lively tradition in acting soon became extinct. According to another version 'great actors... to see the performance

of *Krishna-Chandravali*, obviously a popular folk play based on the love of Chandravali for Krishna...'

50. Pb. Srv. had given instruction to Hassanshah in Sanskrit and music while the prince was campaigning outside the Valley-section: obviously the department had a large faculty.
51. Vahavadena: Wahab-ud-Din.
52. Shikhshakara: pb. the leading musician/conductor.
53. Six tunes: Gauda, Bhangala...tunes are rarely played now...lila: also *sarvalila*.
54. *Bharatashastara*: the ancient Indian authoritative work on poetry, drama and the arts... holy thread: presumably made of gold.
55. Alabhadena: Alla-ud-Din.... Jyahamgira: ref. p. 186,
56. cow market: pb. Gojawara.
57. Paravareshapura: Paravarasena's capita! city 'Srinagar' near Hariparvat.
58. Gulikavadhika: the locality was across the erstwhile Mar canal (SK).
59. *Masjeda*: the Jama Masjid built by Sikander.
60. *Sangaravara*: *tvangsaravar ut tunga tarang*, high waves in the ocean.
61. Friday: 'caused the illusion of people emerging from their graves on the day of resurrection. (RNS)... Panchvasas: five abodes.
62. Khandva forest: a forest in the Kurukhshetra sector which Arjuna reduced to ashes.
63. Surapattana: Pura-pattana (SK), hamlets, habitations, herdsmen's quarters which caught fire fanned by the destructive wind.
64. Seven conditions: refer p. 152/12.
65. Malesa: Mulla Eesa.... pieces: retrospective comment....guardianship: ref. p. 185 and 191-2.
66. Tattarkhan: governor of Panjab on behalf of the Lodhi king of Delhi According to *B.S.* Tazibhatta found Sialkot with no defence as Tattarkhan had led the forces out on an exercise. Tazibhatta subjected Sialkot to plunder, and subsequently Tattarkhan retaliated by annexing part of the territory of Kashmir.... Jyabhadeva: also known as Ajeodev.
67. Shrigalakota: Sialkot.
68. ordinary family: refer p. 208/7... Purapattana : what is meant, pb., is that Tazibhatta reduced many vv, townships, strongholds and communities of herdsmen and Gujjar hillmen.
69. Turushukas Pushkala ... : these are not names of persons but, pb. hordes of mounted foreigners.
70. Khoyashrama: Khoyahama or Khoyahom, the sub-division around the northern shore of the Wular.
71. Rob his wife: who had sought divorce from her previous husband Syed Nasir, father of Merja Hassan.
72. Sport of flowers: *kusumakrida*.

73. Yosobhakhana: the third son of the king, the others being Mahamad and Hussain... Within the palace courtyard Ahmad' is said to have dealt a blow to Jahangir which he narrowly missed. The reader feels some difficulty in following the details of the 'clash within the palace' (p. 195-6). Jamsara/Jyamsar? has been referred to earlier and identified as Sanjermer at 168/23. Since Bhangila estate was granted to Merza (Meya) Hassan, the king's father-in-law, he also plays his role with his Syed followers.
74. Ten years: 1472-82 A.D.
75. Jainaraja, etc.: kings Zain-ul-Abdin and Haidershah.
76. Tajibhatta: Pajabhatia (SK).
77. "flowers of joy": *anandapushpa; naasti mushiq, nazarana, mithaa'i, chaai* are some other euphimisms coined in course of time.
78. Meya Mahmada son of Meya Hassan and Z.'s daughter... half of wealth:
Ardhvana (SK), meaning the estate of Advani... Panchaldeva: crossed the PP mts. .... their daughter (the queen): Hayat Khatoon.
79. Little and great Bhutta country: pb. Kargil and Ladakh.... Other writers have said that the reverses met by the Kashmirians caused a wave of resentment in the V., especially against the power exercised by the Syeds.
Kechilshyas: Jyulshian Bhuta (SK); Bhaddaraga: Bhadoraga (SK). Prose-lytisation on behalf of the Shia divines was already in progress.... treasurer: Hassan Kuchhai (*Koshadiksha*).
80. Karkotadranga: Srinagar-Beeru-Tosamaidan route which was controlled from a watch-station at v. Drang above Beeru. Bhangila: includes Beeru-Gulmarg.
81. Snow: a good omen. Lohara: Loharkotta, a castle in Rajauri.
82. Mera: daughter of Mir Hassan, one of the queens of Hassan Shah (RNS), pb. the same as queen Mera Mukhata on p. 206, or 'Evil Fortune personified' p. 215.
83. Harm: the Syed appears to be more mature in statesmanship. Karavinda: Turushukakargam (SK).
84. Naushehra: about 40 km. S.W. of Rajauri.
85. Edharajanaka: Eidi Raina (SK).
86. Parashurama: It appears a contingent of soldiers raised in Jammu area was engaged in service in Kashmir. According to PH the Raja had taken refuge in Kashmir against Tatarkhan Lodhi of Panjab. According to SSC the following Rajas ruled Jammu during the 15th century:
    1. Maldev (s/o Jodh Dev), 1360-1407, a contemporary of Taimur. Some scholars hold that his rule ended in 1399 A.D. He built the Purani Mandi in Jammu in 1380 A.D.
    2. Hamirdev (s/o Maldev), 1420-23.
    3. Ajeodev/Ajabdeo (s/o Hamirdeo), 1423-1454.

4. Biramdeo (1454-1489).
Sultan Ali Shah is believed to have married a daughter of Raja Maldev. Ajedeo made friends with Sultan Zain-ul Abdin and sent his son to his court in about 1440 A.D. Biramdeo was given a jagir in the Vy. on which his nephew Parashuram settled down.
With his contingent of troops Parashuram played an active role during the civil war in the Vy. following the death of Hassanshah. At the outset of the ethnic hostilities these troops wanted to return to Jammu but the Syeds advised them to wait. They assisted the Kashmiris against the Syeds.

87. *Normal*: deer (SK)...
88. Vaishravana: literally Kubera. The name was borne by Hindus and Muslims alike; ref. p. 159.
89. Mahapadma lake suggests that hunting took place in Lar-Sadarkote area, in the bright half of Chaitra.
90. *Normal*: location uncertain. Z. adorned Sureshvari *kshetra* with *viharas*, including Jainavatavihara, and a serpent may have come across the Dal from that direction. Z. also built a *vihara* at Marisangam, opp. to the present Shergarhi. Hokarsar has been a natural habitat of birds and Jainakote, or Zainakot, is close by. May be the king was being rowed across the Hokarsar lake on the new year's day in spring.
91. Physicians: Haidershah also was not permitted to be treated by physicians.
92. Ruyyabhatta: persons bearing that name have been earlier mentioned as (*i*) an astronomer, and (*ii*) an engineer.
93. Hypocrite: *sanda*. *Sanda* means, among others, a buffalo.
94. Son of Vahramkhana: the Syeds had already rejected the suggestion.

Shrivara's

*Jainarajatarangini*

# BOOK IV
# Beginning of the End

## Mohammad Shah crowned

On the third day the Saidas hastily held a council among themselves and decided to bestow the kingdom on Mahmadakhana. They wished to place the prince on the throne, and were in haste, and had no time to lose. This prince, beautiful as Gonanda, was aged seven years; he was named Mahamadashaha and was placed on the throne. Various things were placed beside the throne, but the king's hand first lighted on a bow, leaving alone the articles of food; and when those who were near saw this unerring sign, they declared that there would be *frequent wars in the kingdom*. The beautiful boy-king looked graceful as he sat on the throne and under the umbrella, and diffused gladness to all, like the young watery moon. The Saidas wore white clothes dotted with red, which gave a reddish complexion to their features, as if they were smeared with the blood of the civil war which has to break out like a disease. Hossanakhana, the king's younger brother, graceful in form, appeared before the boy-king, even as the planet Jupiter appears before the planet Mars. Like the Lokaloka[2] mountains that cause light and darkness to the world, the people on that day felt both grief and joy, owing to the death of the father and the advent of the son. The Saidas looked handsome and happy at the accession of their daughter's son to the throne, and roamed about like black bees in spring, laden with the perfumed juice of flowers. The echoes that rose of the festive music seemed like voices, by which all the directions of the sky blessed the king. The Saidas domed the court-yard of the palace during the festivity, and pleased all the servants of the king with clothes and ornaments.

## Syeds' exclusive power

When nothing but memory was left of the one Hassana (who had created a disturbance), the citizens saw two such Hassanas[3], surrounded by thundering horsemen, come from two directions; and the presiding goddess of the country, who with the seven elements of royal power resided in the king's palace, came like his injured daughter to complain of her discomfiture by her enemies. The captains and the officers of the king came to their sovereign, they rolled on the ground like dogs, but could not enter into his presence. The Saidas neglected men learned in the vernacular and in Sanskrit, and addicted themselves to women inside the house, and to hawks outside it. Haughty in their conduct and cruel in their behaviour, these arrogant men urged by excessive cupidity, oppressed the people, even like the messengers of Death. They were unapproachable on account of their wicked character, and were envious of others, and the servants and subjects of the king became alienated from them. Though some of the servants of the king received benefits from the Saidas, they did not value their acquaintance even as the *kokilas* do not value the acquaintance of crows. Hawks and the servants of the Saidas disturbed the colony of birds on the Sati[4] lake where they had lived in ease and security. These singers whose beautiful voices used to be heard in loud songs now remained dumb before the king, as if in sorrow, even like black bees in the month of Magha. The Saidas took the young king with them, with the intention of killing birds, and went by boat to the banks of the Vitasta, and there they let loose their birds (hawks). They carried their food with them, and were blind in their pride, and they did not behave with due courtesy towards the people of Kashmir a. They massacred the birds in such a manner as if they would never come again to kill birds.

Once upon a time the Saidas assembled their own people and held a council; and when the Kashmirians and the Madras heard that the Saidas had held a council among themselves in the city, they became alarmed. Parashurama and others who had been appointed by the Kashmirians and the Madras met the five Saidas on that day and thought of hostilities. The Saidas worked privately, and their purpose was hid as if by the darkness of their acts, and was not known to any.

## Omens

Now Mera, Evil Fortune personified, the beloved daughter of Mera Hassan, came on one occasion to her father and privately asked him to follow her without delay as there was some work of the king to be accomplished. With this wicked request she led him inside the house. Mera Hassana had dreamt a dream in which he was warned by his father that he would meet with a mishap on Sunday, and he was told not to go to the palace. But bewildered by Fate he went there. At the same time Saida Hassana came in from his own house, and told him that his legs would be cut off on account of his rebellion, so that he might not run away. As soon as he had said so, Mera Hassana's legs were cut at the joint and he fell from his horse on the ground. And it seemed, by the dust that was raised by the Saida horsemen, as if he sighed in sorrow anticipating that the Saidas would not walk in the street again.

## Intrigue against the Syeds

Now Jonarajanaka falsely informed the Madras that a letter had arrived that day from Tattarakhana which would cause them harm; that the Saidas who had spread over the kingdom, but who were afraid of the survived Madras, had, agreeably to that letter, come to some determination, and that the Madras would be arrested the next morning; they should therefore devise some plan of safety. "We will first destroy them" thought the Madras. They knew that all the Saidas had met in a house named Amritavata[5] and they repaired thither. Parashurama and others entered the house armed, directing Tajaka[6] the gate-keeper to keep the door safe. Tajaka informed the servants of the Saidas that their masters were engaged in council, and dismissed them from the place. Tajaka then reported to the Saidas that their servants were plundering articles of food, and on this the Saidas sent away their armed attendants to stop the plunder. At this juncture Jonarajanaka, accompanied by some servants of the king, came hastily from another house by a different route, with the purpose of killing the Saidas. His trusty door keeper Taja also mounted a horse which was before the house and went to another part of the house as desired by Jonarajanaka, with a view to kill the Saidas.

## Madras kill the Syeds

The Saidas were in a room, divided into four compartments, within the house, and when they saw the Madras they became alarmed. Simhadvija[7] saw them approach and angrily asked them why they did not go to their own country when they were allowed to do so; and why they came there into the room. "No passport has been received", they replied, "and why should we go away from you, verily, we shall be revenged on you today," Parashu saw that no one else was there, so he went forward under the pretense of asking for travelling expenses, and in his fury he first killed Simhabhatta. At the end of the room, which was divided into four parts, Simha (lion) fell like a jackal, besmeared with blood which issued from his body. "What treachery is this? What treachery is this?" cried the Saidas, and rose from their seats in alarm. Then all the Madras combined together and killed the Saidas with their swords. Saida Hassana was beautiful and stout, he was leaving the room with no other weapon than his fist, and he perished at the door stunned with a hundred wounds. When Meya Hassana beheld him in that state, he immediately ran away in fear, trying to climb over a wall, but his two legs were cut off. Thus was Meya Hassana killed by some of the Madras, and with Meya Hassana perished also Gadayamin, Yasimaṇmallala, and others with their sons and friends, thirty in number. They raised the cry of *'hala' 'hala'* but the Madras, their hands wet with blood, were busy killing them, and moved about like the servants of Death.

As the Saidas had slaughtered cows in their houses without any compunction for the sin, even so the Madras now felt no mercy in killing the Saidas. As the Saidas used to mutilate deer and other animals, after the termination of a chase, so they were similarly treated in that house[8] by the *diminutive* Madras. They who were accustomed to lie on costly beds, now lay without any apparel, their clothes being robbed by their enemies; and in their helplessness they became the objects of the people's gaze. Haibhatakhana and certain other men drew their daggers, hastily scaled the wall, took to their horses and fled. The attendants of the Saidas did not know' who were being killed in the thick of the combat, they forgot their pride in their alarm and fled, and none of them drew his weapon in the yard of the house.

Called by the son of Malta Jada, Meya Mahammada came from his house and immediately attacked the king's house. The road keeper Noroliaha came to him, but he thought the man to be a rebel, and in his anger he soon caused him to be killed on the king's highway. When Meya Mahammada saw the newly-repaired palace gates closed, and knew that the enemies were within, he reluctantly caused them to be set on fire. The gates thus fell a sacrifice to the fire, as if grief for the tumult, and for the death of their protector. Volumes of smoke rose gracefully and reached the white-washed building, and it seemed as if the goddess of Royal Fortune sighed in grief, not knowing where the wicked people were leading her. In the meantime, when the armed rebels saw the foe, they issued out of the house and came to the yard of the palace. The hero Jonarajanaka came there in anger, and a certain foot-soldier killed two or three in the yard with his sword. Then all the Madras united themselves in a body, mounted the king's horses, and reached the skirts of Mulakanaga[9], and there they held a consultation. "We should remain here" they said "and fight the Saidas; there are only a few of the enemies left, and they will not be able to save themselves." When Jyalala Thakura, well-versed in politics, heard this, he said to them: "This is not the place for fight, let us quickly go by this road and cross the Vitasta, and then let us remain on the other side with our followers. There we will devise plans so that the Saidas may perish of themselves." They approved of his advice, and the brave people crossed the Vitasta by the Juhilamatha'[10] road.

## Meya Mohammad retaliates

In the meantime Meya Mahammada having obtained time, killed the doorkeepers, the brothers Taja and Pajaka in his anger. They were pulled by the *chandalas* from the yard of the palace by a rope tied to the ankle joint, their limbs were besmeared with unholy wine, and they were devoured by dogs. They were miserly from their birth, and had collected wealth by obtaining bribes from villagers whom they had oppressed. At the time of their death they yielded up all their wealth. All that these avaricious men had hoarded by oppressing villagers and robbing others, all their fine silver and other metals, came to the king. People cannot recover from a miser the wealth that once enters his house; like a serpent entering in a hole, it can only be pulled out along with its life. One hundred *Kharis* of rice with sugarcane were taken away from the house of those who had not given even a handful to beggars. Beggars had never received wheat flour from them, enough to make a cake, but now when their houses were robbed, the wheat flour which fell on the road lay like snow.

## Chaotic moves

In the meantime Alikhana came from his house and arrived in an exalted state accompanied by soldiers, and first of all he set fire to the houses in the neighbourhood of the Vatika[11] road in order to occupy it. At this juncture Edarajanaka[12] and others liberated the son of Vahramakhana from imprisonment, and he soon issued through a by-lane. When the son of Vahramakhana saw the soldiers of the enemies before and the fire behind, he was, like a young deer, unable either to advance or to stay. Alikhana knew that the son of Vahramakhana had been released from prison by the enemies in order to do some harm, and he therefore gave the prince an assurance of safety, and then killed him, even as a lion kills a deer. The Saidas blamed Alikhana and said that it was by the advice of Pajabhatta[13] that the queen had set the prince free, in order to give him the kingdom. Others said that the enemies had desired to relieve the prince from bondage, but contrary to their intention, their plan to do him good led to his ruin; for who could outstrip the decrees of fate? Instigated by Alikhana, the wicked Mira and her servants beat the prince until he became unconscious, as the hunters do hares. When Pajabhatta witnessed the calamity, the murder of the prince, he became as one bewildered. He came in after the prince, and was also killed, even as a Rakshasa is killed by the people of his own party.

The trees, as if in sorrow at the sight of the murder of the prince, lamented in the voice of the *kokila*, wondering why the prince, who had never possessed anything in the kingdom, was killed. The plants, moved by the wind, wept, as if in sorrow, pleading against the murder of the prince who had just been released after a long confinement. The trees, moved by the wind, seemed to tremble at those Turushkas who had done the evil deed and committed the heinous crime. The mother of the prince received the dead body of her son who was aged twenty-four years, and whom she had not seen for a long time; she kept the body for three days out of affection and then performed the funeral rites. This widowed and chaste mother of the prince, lady Sobana[14], lived on barley meal, and to the end of her life resided in the tomb of her son.

As if unable to bear the sight of the murder of the prince and the massacre of the Saidas and of the Dvijas[15], the sun departed to some other land, red in its anger. The people saw the bodies of those great men lie naked all around the place, and none could give them a piece of cloth to cover them. The frogs in the tank croaked incessantly all night, as if they lamented for the dead in their sorrow. Those handsome men who had entered the palace, clad in fine garments, causing darkness by the dust raised by their trotting horses, were now sent out of it on two or three carts, clad in torn clothes and bleeding. Thus in the year 60 on the fourteenth day of the moon,[16] in the month of Vaishaka, ruin came upon the Saidas, and it was the cause of future calamities. Surely Yama in the person of Hassana appeared that year before the king's servants, and from him these men received their death. Rather let men be born in the house of a common man where there are many afflictions, than in the house of a king. Several common people sleep on one small piece of coarse cloth, but two kings cannot find room in one extensive kingdom.

Meya Alikhana and others then heard that the rebels who had raised the insurrection had crossed the river; they became angry and followed them. Jyallala Thakkura and others severed the bridge of boats, and with a view to overcome their enemies, united themselves with the Madras and the people of Kashmira. The Saidas clad in armour and supplied with the means of conveyance, pitched their tents of cloth at Vimshaprastha. They had nothing but the capital in their possession, but having made up their quarrel among themselves, they had many horses, armours and swords. Men who never possessed a cowry before, now became possessed of gold and silver and moved about finely dressed. They showered riches on all sides so that even mechanics and cart-men took up arms, and the inferior servants of the king rode rare and fine horses from the king's stable. The Saidas then joined Hassana Rajanaka, and others, and began to devise plans with a view to subdue the people of Kashmira. But having now got themselves free from all obstacles they gave the management of their work to their servants, Meyamattanaracha and others.

## Commotion

In the meantime the very intelligent Thakkuras and others who had crossed the river collected an army at Jaliadraga[17]. When the people heard that the Madras, mighty in their courage, were collecting an army, they armed themselves and came to the town from all parts of the kingdom. There was a commotion in the city, and all the people in the city, in village, and in town became excited and ran about with arms. The people of Shamala, Bhangila and other places, and those who were at Kramrajya turned Sthamartha on the banks of the Kshipitika into a camp. Vaiduryya Bhatta who was at Sthama[18], arrayed himself for battle together with others of Chakkavaka[19], and Darad, and with the valiant warriors of that country. Pammarajanaka and others had collected the people of Nilashva, and in order to reach Sthama near Dugdhashrama[20], they crossed over to the other side of the Sindhu. Heaps of paddy were brought by boatmen from all places, and with it the people of Kashmira paid their expenses of living abroad for want of money. They went by river to two of their own towns but treated them as the enemy's country; some houses they robbed and others they burnt down. In these two towns, situated one on each side of the river, five or seven men died every day in camp by arrows discharged from bows. The Khashas, the petty chiefs on the frontier, men who had a few retainers, they who had no houses, and who had nothing but their name, the Khanas, the strong, the poor afflicted by their poverty, thieves who had committed theft, men released from imprisonment for life, the enemies of the king, the wicked who behaved like dogs, those whose possessions had been confiscated, those who had ability, and such people were glad of this commotion in the kingdom.

## Engagement on the river

They who were on the left side of the river collected all the boats, and those from the bridge of boats at Madavarajya, and used them for their own benefit. A fowler named Deva was the head of the boatmen; he brought about an engagement of boats on the river and thereby caused the death to many good soldiers. Upon this, the Saidas sent some new fowlers, who lived on the shore of the Dalla lake, with boats to fight with those who were at Nandapura.[21] But Meya Vahaka,[22] the superintendent of the town, believed two or three of those men to be thieves and impaled them; and when the fact was made known by beat of drum from Samudramatha,[23] the fear of the people of the town on account of thieves abated.

When the bridge of boats was destroyed, the town became like a fortification unapproachable by the enemies. But the Saidas fearing an attack from the temple of Skanda[24] excavated a moat, measuring five cubits in width, in the vicinity of the yard of the temple. Another similar moat was excavated near the gate where Rajanaka[25] was besieged, in order to guard against attack from the enemies. The servants of the Saidas plundered the houses of their opponents and robbed them of their riches, and caused a terror among the subjects by killing cows. The houses of the enemies were broken into and plundered, and with the wood obtained from them, as with fuel from Rudravana[26], they set fire to Diddamatha. The Saidas through their ignorance needlessly demolished the beautiful houses of their enemies for trivial ends, even as cows are destroyed for feeding dogs! Every day the retainers of the Saidas rode on horses and proudly entered the yard of the palace, well armed, and covered with armour. Rajanaka burnt the houses of Mallamina, of Chunda the Kayastha, and of Hassana in his anger.

Owing to mutual fear the army of the Saidas and that of the people of Kashmira lost their firmness at that time, and misjudged each other's motives. The fearless soldiers hastily crossed the river from one side to another, killed people, cut off their heads and fixed them on poles. When the cavalry on both sides had perished, Pirvajakhana[27] and other Saidas came riding on fleet horses and plundered Padmapura. Jonarajanaka[28] and others heard of this event and crossed the river with their excellent army, and, being angry with the Saidas, they raised a tumult, and set fire to the rows of houses in the village in which he was born. When Jonarajanaka heard of this, be similarly caused fire to be set in the house of Tajibhatta in the Vadavi country.[29] Supported only by his infantry, Jonarajanaka came to Lahara, set fire to the houses and caused the people of Dugdhashrama Sthama,[30] and other villages to flee.

## Syeds *versus* Kashmiris

At this time Jyallala Thakkura and others sent the following letter to Shri Jyahangira the Margesha who was in the fort of Lohara[31]: "Joined by Madras we have ventured to attempt the destruction of the chief through fear of whose power you have left the country with your relations; and we have laid our plans accordingly. His sons Meya Mahammada and others have posted themselves on the right bank of the Vitasta with a view to subdue us, and we on the left. We are trying to secure supremacy and have accordingly spread ourselves over the country of Kashmira; and the Saidas who have only the capital in their possession have been surrounded. Leave aside, therefore, thoughts of delay, and come speedily; for when you arrive, we shall be victorious, and yours will be the glory. In this country you alone are powerful and loyal[32] to the king, so tarnish not your renown by failing to come.[33] After a battle which was not hotly contested, and in which Alishaha was captured, Mahammada the Margesha, the only son of Malla, formed a plan for usurping the kingdom. You should therefore come speedily now, and save the life of the boy king, otherwise the Saidas will not leave him alive in the kingdom."

The Margesha took the letter into his consideration without delay, and anxious for his country, soon came by the road to Parnotsa; and when in two or three days he arrived at Kudmadinapura, the Saidas trembled in their camp, even like a lamp in the wind. They then held a council, and being struck with fear, they wished to establish peace. They accordingly sent Shikhasahava[34] and others with the following letter: "You are the good and principal men in the country! But why have you killed the Saidas? Alas! That you should do a deed that is hated by men. If the son of the late king has been, through the will of fate, established in his place, who among you has lost thereby, and what has he lost, that you have taken measures to destroy all? We are not all against you; make over to us, ye people of Kashmir a, two or three of the foreigners by whom your[35] people have been killed, or drive them out of the kingdom with their followers, and be ye the principal ministers in this country as before. Let each retain the post he had held before, and let all of us enjoy together. Death is destined for the living, and what is decreed by fate must come to pass, no one can prevent it." The Margesha and the leaders considered the contents of the letter and they sent the following reply written in the alphabet of the *yavanas*: "The king should ever be defended, even like a jewel, but through wickedness even such a king was not spared! What was the reason for which the prince, the son of Vahramakhana was killed? Who will, after the murder of Noroloha and others, trust in his own safety in the country? The whole wealth of the infant king of this kingdom has also been robbed. There is but an iron gong left in the king's gate, and it seems to proclaim by its sound that it alone has been left by the Saidas! The troublesome Madras should be removed out of the country by various devices, while you remain happy in your grandfathers' posts!"

## Terms for truce

When the Saidas heard this, they sent an invitation to the Margapati. He, however, did not go but sent a messenger who told the Saidas on his arrival that they should replace in the treasury the wealth of the infant king that had been purloined, that they should without hesitation lay aside their arms before they could be admitted to a conference, that the *people of the country* should as before be allowed to perform the work of the state, that no harm would thereby befall the country, but the defects in the administration would be removed. Those who are gone, are gone from this world; the dead do not come back to life again; and mutual enmity has been expiated by slaughter committed by both parties. When the Saidas heard these words of reason, they became arrogant and, as if consumed by anger, they were roused by the following words which Haibhatakhana uttered: "King, treasure, arms and soldiers skilled in war, are all in our hands, what can our opponents do"? They then made up their minds for battle, and made preparations even as the Kauravas did against the Pandavas.

## Dombas plunder citizens

Then Saiphadhara, Jonarajanaka and others at once crossed over the bridge of boats and came into the city in order to attack the Saidas. They were eager for battle, and did not pay heed to the advice of the Margapati who said that the time was not yet ripe for a battle, and that victory was to be won by strategy. Davoda, the son of the Margesha, was puffed up with pride; he joined the Pratihara and others, and soon entered the city. His troops then entered the city by the way leading to Samudramatha and arrived at Loshta[36] Vihara with a view to destroy the army of the Saidas. But the Dombas and other sturdy soldiers, turned aside from battle, and through their avarice, busied themselves in plundering[37] all within the city. These Dombas and other valiant warriors raised their weapons against one another and hurt one another, and plundered the principal citizens of their property. The citizens had buried their wealth in their houses, but the soldiers dug up the ground with their spears at every step, and took away the wealth as if it were given to them.

## Offensive fizzles out

When the Saida army was first attacked by the Madras, and the Saidas saw human heads lying scattered about, they despaired of victory that day, and retreated speedily as they had come. But when their troops heard of the doings of the enemy, they entered the city and marched to battle discharging arrows as they went. The Saidas found Padmabhata before them, and they killed him in his own tent, and in order to ensure the success of their arms, they painted their foreheads with his blood. Alikhana was there, and alarmed at the approach of the army, set fire to the Labdhabhadva[38] vihara, in order to obstruct their passage. The flames had spread over the road when the heroic Davoda the Margapati arrived, and together with Hosana the Pratihara[39] he engaged in fight. The former moved forward along a difficult path over a causeway, but fell into a moat and died while fighting. There the heroes Ahmada the Pratihara and others displayed their valour in the field of battle, and won the pleasure of the company of the celestial women by their death. Though Davoda is dead, the wives of the citizens still remember his handsome features and declare that they never saw beauty like him. Is it that the gods feared to take so handsome a person to the celestial abode, and therefore left his dead body on earth?

## Syeds gain victory

In the meantime Haibhatakhana and others arrived by another route from behind and destroyed the valiant soldiers in front of the Khanagaha.[40] They obtained victory, but with their uplifted arms they looked like men possessed by devils; and in their anger they killed the citizens who had come that day to witness[41] the battle. What more should be said of them? Impelled by avarice, they killed two or three messengers who had come from foreign countries, and had stayed in the house of Brahmanas, saying that these messengers were Madras. Saiphadamara released several persons from imprisonment, and fought with the army of the Saidas, and pierced the shields of the citizens and the Saidas. The soldiers of the Saidas were angry with the learned physician named Yavaneshvara[42], believing that he helped their enemies, and they killed him in his own house. The Saidas committed barbarous acts; they cut off the physician's head from his body, smeared the body with sandal paste, and left the head in the king's highway. Some of these Rakshasas entered the city that day, and as they were of a relentless disposition, they killed all without discrimination.

When the citizens saw the head of him whose body was smeared with sandal paste, they knew it for certain that the wicked crime had been committed by the Saidas; and who did not blame them? The dead bodies lay in the streets of the city from Mallekapura[43] to Loshtravihara, and were like dried grass used as fuel. They who had reposed on luxurious beds of cotton, reclining at ease on pillows, were now seen lying on the ground, naked and motionless, emitting foul smell, devoured by crows and dogs and wolves, and attacked by worms that fed on fat and flesh.

The Saidas were satisfied with the victory and they celebrated their triumph with music within Vimshaprastha. If those who had fled and those who had retreated had been pursued, many of the survivors would have been killed. But the gods of the country had been plundered, and some of them had been burnt; and the angry deities did not inspire the Saidas with the idea to pursue the enemy. The soldiers who were crossing the bridge of boats, all tried to go in first[44], and the bridge broke under their weight. Thus a hundred men fell that day into the river, and being heavily weighted by their armour, they sank and died in the Vitasta. Surely the goddess Sharada[45] was angry at their sins, and in the form of the Vitasta devoured the two armies. The citizens who had come to witness the scene were killed, and in order to prevent a similar mishap, the Saidas placed heaps of the newly severed heads in their front. They fixed several heads on poles, and in order to strike terror into the people, they placed them like rows of lamps on a piece of wood on the banks of the Vitasta. The corpses became swollen in the river and emitted stench, and drifted down into the Mahapadma lake.

## Another confrontation

In the meantime the people of Kashmira collected the surviving soldiers from all directions and again raised an army. Shri Jyahangira, Jyallala, Saiphadamara and others meditated plans to overcome the Saida chiefs. Under instructions received from a saint[46], Saiphadamara divided his army into sections and placed them both on high and low grounds; and soldiers came to these divisions every day from all sides, well-officered, devoted to their chiefs, and protected by shields, and they received supplies of arrows with wooden shafts and fine feathers, sharp and well barbed. There were tumultuous gatherings on both banks of the Vitasta, and on both banks were mounted, engines of victory, and the two armies met in the great city of Pravarapura[47] once more, and fought in anger. Horses clad in armour galloped forward, and made the army terrible in appearance, and the soldiers rained fire by their strokes; and the hearts of many citizens who had come to see the battle were excited with feelings of heroism. The sound of the battle drum was first heard in the house of the king at night, and then in camps of the Saidas and of the Kashmirians. Many of the citizens' wives who had gone to fetch water on both banks of the river, were pierced with arrows from the engines, and killed. Not a day passed in which two or three heroes were not struck with arrows and carried in a dying state from the banks of the river to their own homes. Every day was terrible on account of conflagrations by fire, destruction caused by soldiers, and other calamities. The soldiers used indecent words and gestures, and said what should not be uttered. They talked of mischief arising out of mutual enmity[48] between the king, the Saidas and the Brahmanas and they abused one another, and used languages which should not be used. They were now surrounded on all sides by Daulatasiha and others from Kashtavata; by the gentle Salhanahamsa[49] and others, sons of king Shahibhanga[50]; by some chiefs from Panchagahvara who were related to the king of Sindhu; by the Khashas; the *mlechhas*, and other people. The people of Kashmira, on account of disunion among themselves, had called in armies from several quarters, but as they did not know the ulterior motives which these armies had in view, they became very much alarmed. At this time a shooting star with many heads was seen conspicuously one evening in the sky, darting in a flame from north to south. When the two armies beheld this wonderful object, they apprehended some calamity in battle, and were beside themselves in terror.

In the meantime Tattarakhana, influenced by a letter from the Saidas, sent a powerful Turushka army in order to obtain possession of the country. When these wicked Turushkas arrived at Shastragalasthana[51] they were met by Bhodanaraja and others, even as insects are opposed by snows. Surely the goddess Kali in the guise of the river Kalidhara devoured them in anger, for the benefit[52] of the Satidesh. The son of Adamakhana was sent with the news of defeat to Tattarakhana, but he was prevented by the Turushka chief from going, and was detained by him. The inhabitants of the place took possession of the horses and the effects of the Turushka, and obtained riches such as are rarely obtained, and looked like Kuvera. And when the people of Kashmira heard of the destruction of the Turushkas they celebrated the event by music, and the faces of the Saidas became sad. Among the survivors of the wicked army which had met with this disaster, two thousand lay dead.

## Anarchy

The rear of the army of the Kashmirians was such as could be relied upon, and so the Kashmirians felt no fear. They became haughty on obtaining an addition to their strength, and with a glad heart determined on battle. They arranged to station the Margesha and others in the centre, outside the capital, and the Rajanaka and the Madras on either side, near Sthamastha. As the number of the Kashmirians was small, they thought that if they were defeated on one side they would all be destroyed, so after consultation, they stationed men both below and above, in the neighbourhood of Sthama. Jonarajanaka then crossed the river by boat and killed five or six men of the Saida army, and caused the rest to flee; and he robbed them of their clothes, horses and armours. Every day the Kashmirians were seen prowling about. What more need be said, the shameless men who were with the Saidas during day time were seen at night in the army of the Kashmirians. The people went over from side to side unrestricted. What disasters ensued because the boy king's orders were not obeyed! The wicked men plundered many houses, and deposited their plunder in large boxes. The country was struck with panic, and the people ceased to walk in the streets. The Saidas and the Kashmirians did not give up their desire for supremacy and the struggle on both banks of the river continued for two months. The *tree of enmity first grew out of the murder* of the Saidas, and gradually unfolded its leaves; and ultimately it shot forth into a hundred branches. When the people beheld the king's treasury on the right and the army on the left, they felt doubtful as to which party would obtain the victory. Then men could not frequent the roads[53], women crossed over the river by boats; and when avaricious and wicked men crossed the river and robbed the wayfarers, the town roads came to be frequented. Two or three of the men who had crossed the river in order to rob, were daily arrested, and in anger impaled.

## Across the river

Once the councillors of the Kashmirians sent the following message to the Saida army: "If you are strong, come and engage in a pitched battle with us, or fix a time, within which we shall expect an encounter. For the people are being daily killed by arrows and are in a state of fright. Let him whom Fortune favours obtain the supreme power." When the Saida soldiers heard this, they cut the rope which the men on the left had placed on the river side in the outskirts of the city, to demarcate their limit. The Saidas understood that the enemy wished to cross the river from the place called Kashtila[54], and became anxious; and they placed Hasanarajanaka and others at Sthama. After the Saidas had cut the tie of the bridge of boats, they made the city as inaccessible as a fort through fear of the enemy. The people of Kashmira then spoke to the Saidas who were on the banks of the river: "Since you have, through fear of us, cut the rope which we had placed, and which held together the bridge of boats, and since you have only the town under your power, come forward now to battle. How long will you consume the plentiful grains and what will you effect in the town"?

When the Saidas heard this, they thus replied in a loud voice through their servants: "We will not depart in fear from this place, for want of food and oppressed with hunger. What objections have the Turushkas[55] to their consuming food? We eat the meat of all kinds, and we will stay here as long as there is plenty of beef[56] and the flesh of male beasts. And when we shall come out in battle, who among you will be able to oppose us?" When Jyallala Mallika and others on the river bank heard this, they were glad, and they all sat down and held a council, and came to the following determination: "At Sthama we will divide our army, and will march crossing at three points: the Saidas too will divide their army, and will thereby be weakened. Otherwise if all on the side of the Saidas held together, they would be unconquerable[57]. We will overcome all of them if they be defeated at one point, and be thereby reduced in number. We are strong, and should not delay" When Jonarajanaka and others heard this, they joined with the Madras, and said: "We will die or conquer." Thus they prepared themselves for battle.

The leaders of the army at Sthama, pursuing the same plan of operations, crossed the river from the ancient place called Takshka[58] and reached a hill. Praulabhatta and others crossed the river by boat from a place called Hastavalika[59]; they were in high spirits, and infused that spirit into their soldiers. When the Gakkas[60] and other soldiers, who prided themselves on their valour, witnessed the coolness of the Brahmana marching to battle, they praised him. The soldiers of Kashmira fixed a twig with leaves on their heads, in order to distinguish themselves from their enemies, so other[61] warriors held spears in their hands, and it seemed as if valour had assumed bodily shape, and was issuing forth from the persons of the warriors in order to destroy the enemies.

When the Saidas heard that the Kashmirians had crossed the river they became alarmed, and they hastily sent Hashima, who was eager for victory, against the enemy. Arrived at Abhivanayurtha.[62] Hashima was proceeding along the banks of the river, when he was seen by those who were on the top of the hill, and they opposed him by throwing stones at him. Hashima was alarmed at the shower of stones; he was thrown down from his horse, and escaped on foot with difficulty from the place where the contest was hot. The Kashmirians captured his horse, like victory incarnate, and the horse was covered with mail with Hashima's sword tied to it. When the Saidas saw that Hashima was defeated, they sent Pirvajakhana and others with fresh soldiers even during the night. At this moment Meya Bhakera and others arrived at[63] Dugdhashrama, and like thundering clouds of the rainy season they came down to Pupamatha. At this time also, the Madras, the Damaras, the Pratihara, and other valiant soldiers joined one another and arrived at the frontiers of the district of Somanovata[64]. On the side of the Saida army, Saida Hossana with Saida Khana and other brave warriors arrived that very morning. The swords of the warriors with their dark blades and points looked like serpents which had issued from the nether regions. A severe battle was then fought between the two armies, and the diminutive Madras, armed with sword and shield, were irresistible in the battle. Purushurama, the chief of the Madras, armed with a battle axe, thus addressed the people of Kashmira at the commencement of the battle: "Warriors! Fight now with a glad heart, and do not turn back. If the relentless Saidas be victorious, they will destroy all of us; but if you win the victory, there is joy for you if you live, and if you die, you will obtain pleasures in heaven by your virtues."

## In the thick of battle

First of all, Pirvajakhana[65] came in front of the battle, he felt proud in joining the combat. Pirvaja the Pratihara went against him, even as Parashurama went against Rama. When the Madras saw that the Pratihara was not skilled in fight, they instantly sent soldiers to cut off the hoof of his horse. The horse reared when its hoofs were cut, and the rider was disconcerted. He held up his spear, but the Gakkas[66] struck him with vigour. His servants, the Shahibhangiyas came with their swords, like black bees with stings, and they pierced the Gakkas in their anger. When the people of Kashmira saw the Pratihara fall[67] in the field of battle, they were rejoiced and exclaimed: "We win the victory today". The Shahibhangiya guards were attacked by the Kashmirian soldiers and the Madras and the guards behaved with their accustomed valour. The soldiers called out to one another saying "come", "stand here," "where do you go?", "you are mine." The setting sun behind the Kashmirians shone on the points of their swords, as if to assure them of victory. Eager for fame, the warriors moved in the field of battle, each trying to go first; even like bees in a garden eager for flowers. Soldiers showed the movements of their bodies by their various postures, even as actors do in a dance on the stage. Jyahangira and others engaged themselves in the front of the battle with their guards[68], and died fighting like heroes.

## Victory for Kashmiris

Arrows poured forth like rain from the cloud-like[69] army whose arms flashed like lightning, and whose sound was like the sound of thunder. Bhakera distinguished himself by his valour; he stood in the front of the battle, sword in hand; the sun shone on his face, and he made himself conspicuous among the Saidas. He rode a spirited horse, and by the movements of his body displayed the postures of a dance as on a stage. Though attacked by all, and wounded, it was not till after a long time that he fell from his mail-clad horse. Possessed of valour, he cast his look on all around, killed two or three soldiers, and then lay on the bed of heroes, and his blood trickled on to his outer garment. Of what use are those worthless men who do not appreciate the valour of heroes determined to die in the field of battle? When Saida Hosana and other chiefs and the Kashmirians[70] who were on the side of the Saidas saw Bhakera and others killed, they left the battle and fled. The leader of the Kashmirian army then smote the followers of the Saidas, even as young birds are smitten on issuing from their nests, when the riverside tree is thrown down by storm. They fled with all their might, and neither swordsmen, nor horsemen, neither bowmen nor spearsmen could see them. The Kashmirians went on plundering and destroying, and even killed those who had taken shelter on trees, and in this way they entered the city.

## The field of battle

The dead bodies lay naked on the road, like heaps of white grass, from Samudramatha to the east[71] of the city. Some were drowned in the canal, and some killed in the field of battle, while some were robbed and left naked, and they fled across the country in their terror. The earth was strewn with the severed limbs of warriors, and seemed like the kitchen of Death about to devour those remains. But none, alas! gives up the love of his own person even after witnessing that men who had lived a luxurious life and had been like Indra in their enjoyments, and like kings in their wealth, now lay naked on the ground, emitting foul smell. "Rather" said Habhebhamera "would I this day meet death in battle, leading to the enjoyment of heaven, then endure the shame of begging a living from my new master?" and he went to battle riding a steady horse, and calmly met his glorious death. Rajanaka Hassana too saw that his enemies were before him, and the men of his party were running away, but he still was intent on fighting, and never thought of flight. Seated on his horse, and accompanied by his followers, he maintained the combat for a time at Sthama at the outskirts of the city, on the bank of the Mari[72] canal, though his finger was cut off. At last he was killed by Serangamera and others. His head, and his hand from which a finger had been severed, were taken by the soldiers and shown to the Margesha and others, in the hope that the sight would please them.

But the Margesha cried, "What is the use of insulting the body of the dead, give it its last rites", and he caused the funeral rites to be performed. He who bad for long time been the chief among all the ministers of the palace, and had held high posts, and whose charity and greatness had been proportionate to his wealth, even he came in the end to a pitiable plight, like ordinary men. Fie to the lust of worldly pleasures which is never satiated with enjoyment! He had received injuries, but had he borne them quietly and remained in his house, all the ministers would have courted him. But longing for wealth, he again took the side of the Saidas; and not knowing what was in store for him in the future, he asked that the lordship of Kampana[73] might be bestowed on him at some future time, and thus he became the object of laughter of the people. Or, it may be that when death is near, one's intellect is perverted. Those who are blinded by pride and have lost their judgement, insult the dead bodies of their enemies in battle. They soon come by a similar end and, people say, they deserve to descend to hell.

Fie to Haibhatakhana, who, though he considered himself to be a warrior, withdrew himself from the battle, and went to Phakuva[74] country in fear. He left his stately horse and wandered about the country in fear, unarmed and bereft of his servants, and he hid himself dressed like an ordinary person. But the soldiers of the Margapati were angry with him because he had killed Davoda Margesha, and they killed him inside a house, even as one kills a thief, and took away his head. The soldiers cut off his head, and in their anger they waved the head before the corpse of Davoda, even as a lamp is waved before an image of a god. This was the consequence of his flight. Had he gone that night to the camp of the Saidas, his life would have been saved; but how can a sinful man keep his judgement clear? The servants of the Saidas had robbed the country and killed cows in the city, and it was for the sins of their servants, I think, that the Saidas came to such a plight. Though Haibhatakhana was the son of a king's daughter[75], and was born in the family of warriors, it was through the sin of his servants that his heart became devoid of courage.

## The aftermath

Thousands of Brahmanas, Rajputs, Saidas, Kashmirians, and others perished that day in battle. It was not possible to take out the body of any particular man from amidst the heap of dead warriors and soldiers. Those who had been handsome and stout, and had lived in the enjoyment of prosperity and pleasures in the kingdom, now emitted a foul smell in the sun, and became the food of dogs and crows. There lay like the red flowers of the cotton[76] tree, the dagger, the knife, the spear, the club, and the mace, all smeared in blood-weapons which once graced the soldiers in battle. The Margapati remembered that the Saidas had burnt Rudravihara, and in his anger he caused Alavapura[77] to be set on fire. The fire issued from houses in dreadful flame, and with intolerable heat, and reduced the town to the condition of a burnt forest. The fire, which rose from the house of illustrious Saida[78] Hamadanakhana, was like the flame of anger for the injury done to the king and to the subjects.

When Bhakera and other chiefs had been killed, and the others had fled, their *chandala* servants began to plunder the city; and in the confusion which ensued, those who had been poor from birth now became rich, and those who had always been rich became poor. Some searched dead bodies wherever they lay, and found valuable articles on them, and became happy even like the mendicants who rejoice in carrying skulls. Fights took place among those who robbed and stored the ill-gotten wealth in their houses, even like the fights of the dogs for flesh and bone. What one man had first purloined was again robbed from him by another, and that was once more robbed from him by a third; and thus they behaved like fish. The current of victory which had flowed alternately in one direction and in another, now steadily flowed on one side only, and uprooted the trees (the Saidas). The rich citizens, among whom were many Brahmanas and merchants, who had been in enjoyment of ease before, were now robbed by the soldiers, and reduced to poverty. The houses of the citizens were consumed by fire, and their minds by constant misery, and many things were burnt down. Low and wicked men violated the virtuous daughters and wives of good families and defiled them. *Kotis* of wealth had been spent in rearing houses in the hope that they would endure to the end of time, but they were burnt down and became dust and ashes.

On the right side of the river the plunderers, emboldened by success, behaved like drunkards; some assailed the people, some yelled aloud, and some plundered property. Those who had not a vessel before to drink wine[79] from, now brought, during the season of festivity, thousands of vessels filled with water from the city. Some were sorrowful for the death of friends, and some for the loss of their hoarded wealth; some grieved over insults which they suffered, as they belonged to the defeated party, and others for lands taken away from them. Many such persons wandered about in grief, only one per cent of the population was happy. Two thousand men died, great and low, including those who perished in battle or of their wounds, and those who died in their homes. Thus it happened that in the year 60 on the first day of the moon, in the month of Shravana, many people died on account of this decisive victory. The *first shoot* of the tree of mutual enmity which gradually brought forth leaves and bore fruits on that day made its first appearance when the Saidas were murdered. The soldiers pillaged the citizens every day of their hoarded wealth, and all the inhabitants were robbed of the fruits of agriculture, and were reduced to misery. In that contest with the Saidas, a destructive fire arose on all sides at Pravarapura, in the houses, the gardens, and among the fruit trees.

In the meantime when Alikhana and other Saidas, who had been defeated by the Kashmirians, heard of this disaster, they remained attended by only a few menial servants. Meya Mahammada killed two or three persons in the city, but returned to his tent as there was no bridge. But when the Saidas heard that Bhakera and others had been killed, they killed two or three men, and determined to fight again, though they were in a state of alarm. Tajabhatta believed that the Margesha would cross over from behind and kill them, and so he proposed to give him battle there where they were. This threw the Saidas into disorder. Meanwhile Ravatra[80] crossed over from the other side of the river, skilfully took the Saidas and sent them to their own homes.

## Kashmiris befriend the king

The ministers hold a council in the presence of the boy-king, who was now freed from the Saidas as the sun is freed from clouds; and the ministers were agreeable to the citizens, as the breezes are agreeable to men. The Saidas relied on sinful warriors and were attached to sin; they were violently against virtue and the caste system, and were bent on war; and they had held the kingdom by wicked measures, and did it harm. The Saidas were like the sons of Kuru who depended on Duryyadhana and were joined by Shalla[81], who were violently against Yudhishthira and were aided by Kama bent on fomenting quarrels, and who grieved

Dhritarashtra by their evil acts. And like the sons of Kuru the Saidas did not win victory in battle. The ministers removed the king's new residence from Padamapura and repaired the burnt houses[82] of the Khanas in Shrinagara. The house of Bhabhasaida[83] Hamadana was erected on the bank of the river, and it seemed as if the unsullied virtues of the ministers towered in the form of that building. Then the ministers confiscated all that had belonged to the Saidas, and exiled Alikhana and other Saidas, with their families, from the kingdom. The ministers of Kashmira were of one mind, and Parashurama and others received men among.... The Saidas had hoped that by bestowing the kingdom on a boy they would enjoy prosperity, and they had accordingly acted in furtherance of their own interests. But now that they were destroyed, others obtained by force the posts of ministers which the Saidas had held so long. Fate is powerful in this world, not man.

## The spoils of power

Jyallala Thakura took possession of Nagrama and the other possessions of Meya Hassana[84]; and his son took Lohara and other places. Sri Jyahangira took Vangila which had once been his own, and then he took Makhaya[85] and other places. Saiphadamara became master of Makshashrama[86] and other places, and gave other villages to his brothers, befitting them. Jonarajanaka was in command of troops, and had become strong and independent, and did not rely on, the help of any one else; and he made himself master of Parihasapura.[87] The powerful Ebhrahima the Margapati took to himself the possessions of the Dvarapaia[88], and gave protection to the servants of the Saidas. The ministers, like the elements which compose all the substance of this world, created new things in government. One Thakkura was of the party of the Margapati, and another Damara was of the party of the Rajanaka: they both became conspicuous like fire. The boy king, who was like a soul without action, was merely a witness to the administration which was conducted by the ministers. They divided the country among themselves as they liked, and made the king write the three letters of sanction on the documents. Oppressive towards others, disliked by the subjects, and sinful through the actions of their servants, they felt themselves happy; they were bent on doing mischief, and they acted as they liked.

Clever in holding their own party together and in defeating the purposes of their enemies, they were like debaters well-versed in discussion. They were exempted from the payment of the king's taxes, and oppressed the country, even as the twelve suns oppress the world with their excessive heat at the end of a *kalpa*. By the plaintive barking of dogs, by the firey meteors, and by frequent earthquakes, the trembling people understood that their calamities had again returned.

## Intriguers busy

The king being a boy, his officers oppressed the people, even as diseases harass the body in the feebleness of old age. A prosperous king is soon ruined When his officers, his chief supporters, quarrel among themselves through jealousy, even as the body is destroyed by its disordered components. Men who were sharp like thorns, and adept in seeking flaws in others, became the favourites of the royal officers even as prickly vegetables are liked by young elephants. Such intriguers moved among the officers, and by their deceit created disunion among them every day, and increased their enmity towards one another. They fabricated out of their own imagination words which were never uttered by any one, and such false words of their servants were pleasing to the officers even like poetry. Thus the pure minds of the ministers, which had reflected one another like mirrors, were dimmed by the deceitful breath of their servants.

## Disaffection against nobles

The other ministers were unable to brook the high position of the Margapati which had descended to him from his ancestors, even as *chakravaka* is unable to bear the high position of the moon. The Margapati heard his attendants say that while he had fled through fear of the Saidas, his attendants had killed them; but nevertheless he had now become the principal personage in the king's court, and boastful. On hearing such remarks, the Margapati became indifferent to the affairs of the king through anger and disgust. Jonarajanaka had rendered himself an object of the people's curse for having plucked out the eyes of Vahramakhana and on account of the supremacy which he exerted by the strength of the arms. And this cruel man became among the ministers even as Rahu is among the planets by his injustice in bestowing rewards, and inflicting punishments. He plundered unopposed the villages in Chhundinika[89] and in other tracts, robbed the people and took possession of their lands, and made himself master of those places. During the time of the mutual disunion among the Saidas he had robbed the people and obtained various articles from different places, and had filled the granaries of his house. This avaricious man forcibly took away the riches which the people had earned and saved by their own labour, as if they were given to him by Brahma. He was not satisfied with destroying men by bringing together his troops; but like the submarine fire, the fire of his oppression was not quenched by the collected waters of the rivers. When he oppressed men in town or in village either through jealousy, or without any cause whatever, no one could save the oppressed from his power. If any one undertook to protect the oppressed out of humanity, he was punished in the king's court by more powerful men than he. Other avaricious officers oppressed innocent men in their homes, even as diseases oppress the body. What evils do not speedily overtake the country where the king is a boy, and his old supporters are independent and jealous of one another and break down the administration of the kingdom?

## Bloodthirsty rivalry

Edarajanaka and Thakkura Ahmada[90] who had been sent to countries outside Kashmira returned to the city on the plea of seeing the Margesha. But the Margesha had heard certain rumours from his spies about these ministers and had become alarmed; he did not go into the city, but went to his house, in fear on account of Saipha Damara, and passed the night in fear on account of the foreign soldiers that had been called in. When the soldiers of whom the Margesha was afraid reached his house, Ahmada Thakkura killed Jonarajanaka in the morning by the advice of the Margesha. Who did not start in fear when he saw the dead body in the house of the Margesha—the blood issuing from the wound caused by the weapon and moistening the ground? Some people remarked that Jonarajanaka had bestowed his daughter on the Margesha and had come to his house under sworn assurance of safety. But nevertheless he was killed. Fie to the lust of enjoyment! Some again said that ministers perish by violence because they are unable to tolerate difference in opinions. Others said that

Jonarajanaka with the Madra chiefs had killed the Saidas, and it was for that crime that he was killed by his enemies within a year. Vainly were guards employed! Not one of the thousands whom he maintained, could save his life at the time of his death. Enemies rob us of all objects in the same way in which we acquire them. Wealth wrongly obtained does not remain long in the house, and when fate becomes adverse, the officers of the king do not distinguish between virtue and vice, strength and weakness, between friend and foe, or between praise and blame. His son had once advised him to give up the post of commander of the army, as he could gain no advantage by means of foreign soldiers; but good fortune had left him, and he did not accept the advice. When destruction comes to a luckless man, he loses a proper regard for his son, and reposes confidence in his enemy. Thus, Jonarajanaka had always considered foreign soldiers as his countrymen, and had believed the heroic soldiers of this country to be cowards and foes. That chief among heroes, Saipha Damara, had at one time been afraid of the prowess of Jonarajanaka, and had yielded up his arms. Even heroism fails at times. Jyallala Thakkura was shut up by his own doorkeepers within the courtyard of the palace. What means are left when fate becomes adverse? Even the sun in the sky undergoes changes day by day, becoming obscure sometimes and bright at other time. What stability then can there be in the strength of man who is subject to perplexities? Strange are the vicissitudes of his power! Masoda Damara and others, who had destroyed the bridge of boats, collected an army as before at Jaladragada. Saliya and other Thakkuras were not attached to Shringarasiha; they went to him separately, but were thrown into prison. No man's prosperity is stable! Jerka a bold servant of Shringarasiha[91] robbed Thakkura Ahlada of his horses inside the city, and went to Rajapuri. Thus the crime of Jonarajanaka's murder was aggravated[92] by the imprisonment of his warriors, even as one's unbearable suffering from a disease in the throat is aggravated if his foot is burnt.

## Fateh Khan

By the time a man gets over one anxiety, fate creates another for him; when the moon has passed through its period of wane and arrives at fulness, eclipse comes in and destroys its beauty! When the Margesha had become free from anxiety and without a rival, he heard of the arrival of the son[93] of Adamakhana. I will narrate the account of this Khana from his boyhood, how he arrived into the kingdom, and how he took it. When his father Shri Jaina died, the helpless Adamakhana went to the Madra kingdom. While he was living there, his son was born on the Shivratri night at a moment which indicated his future royalty and wealth. When the boy's father perished in the battle with the Turushkas, he was brought up in the house of his mother's father, even as the moon is reared in the sea of milk. In time Tattarakhana gave him his protection; and subsequently he went of his own accord to the shrine of Jallandhara[94] and spent there a few years. When Jyahangira the Margesha was living outside[95] Kashmira out of fear of the Saidas, he asked the son of Adamakhana in an artful letter to accept his ancestral kingdom. When Tattarakhana died, his son[96] gave protection for a time to the son of Adamakhana. The latter was courageous enough to undertake bold deeds; he deluded the Turushkas, and came to *grahana country* with numerous retainers. On the other hand, messengers had been sent from Kashmira by the Margesha when Shringarashiha brought him to Rajapuri. The lord of Rajapuri bore ill-will towards the Margesha, and with a view to secure a protector he caused Phatahakhana to be brought to him. Now owing to the murder of Jonarajanaka, the Damaras and Edharajanaka, Thakkura Daulata and others had departed from Kashmira, and had been living at Rajapuri. They now took shelter under the Khana, as the black bees take shelter in a tree, and the Khana obtained great reputation, even as the *son of Vopyadeva*[97] had obtained before.

Masodanayaka had the charge of defending the road, and though he was related by marriage to the Margesha, he went over to the side of the Khana. The message of the arrival of the son of Adamakhana was to the poor villagers, oppressed by many masters, like salt sprinkled on a wound. The guilty, the debtors reduced to servitude, the thieves, the wicked, and the destitute were glad to hear the news about the Khana. Who did not, in village and in town, leave his home and kindred and come to him, fixing his hope on his kingly fortune? The wealthy Khana received many men who had come from the country, and obtained fame, and wished to rival the king. The people from all the kingdoms took shelter with him discarding others, and they exclaimed that he was a worthy grandson of King Shri Jaina. When the thieves and others, who had remained concealed, heard of him, they jumped out in gladness as the fishes do in large tanks. But even as a tree is afflicted by insects, so was the king afflicted by the thought that he had not a large army, that when one foe had been conquered there still existed another mighty antagonist, that the country was besieged by powerful enemies who had won over the servants and spies of the state, that the state horse was unfit for work, and that the officers of the kingdom took no interest in the king's affairs.

Jyahangira who had sent an artful letter to the son of Adamakhana was now glad of his approach, but when he found out the views of the Khana he became anxious. Jyahangira had accumulated great wealth in the country by destroying his enemies, and had wished to enjoy ease, but his ease was disturbed by the tumult that was now created. The people trembled at the news of the approach of the Khana, who was daily coming nearer, even as trees in the weeds tremble in the storm. The Khana was bent on conquering the country, and his crafty and scheming councillors sent a messenger to the Margapati with the following letter: "O Margapati! You have in your pride overcome the valour of all within Kashmir a, and are, like a god, enjoying fair fame. This Khana, O Margapati, is the chief of his dynasty whom you have invited by letter from the country of the Turushkas. Why are you neglecting him now? Why are you repenting of what you yourself have done? Others are enjoying the power of the state by placing a boy on the throne. Why should this person, whose conduct is worthy of his position and whose character is pure, be kept waiting outside the country? Or, if you give him his father's share of the kingdom, then let him stay without and let the king remain within the realm. But what is the use of saying many words if you are not going to acknowledge him? The sin of the death of the soldiers who fall in battle on both sides will be on you."

## Fateh Khan's overtures

When the Margapati had read this letter which was shown to him by the messenger of the Khana, he gave the messenger a letter in reply to the following effect: "O! protectors of the kingdom and enjoyers of kingly fortune, doers of all beneficial acts! Consider what is said in the Purana[98], that Kashmira is Parvati, and know that its king is born of a part of Shiva. Even if the king be wicked he should not be slighted by those who strive for good. Sovereignty is obtained in this country by religious penance, not by valour. Why else did Adamakhana and others of lenial descent fail to obtain? Why did they speedily reap the punishment of their unworthy acts? The present king has come to the throne by inheritance, and how can the Khana, who intends to usurp the king's power, be allowed during the lifetime of the king to enter the country in order to create a disturbance. This boy was coronated by others, and was not set up by me, but who can destroy him at present while I am near? The Khana will be honoured in every way, if he wishes to follow our views; the rising sun receives due honour when he follows the dawn. Fortune obtained by ingratitude does not last long for the enjoyment of men. The pleasure derived by eating bad food causes illness. What more should be said, the way by which the king has been released from the hands of the Saidas, will be open to him again for coming out of the hands of the Khana. This is the will of fate."

## Another confrontation brewing

Jyahangira despatched this letter. He was angry with Masoda on account of his leaning towards the Khana, and took away from him the post of warden of the road. He entrusted the duty of defending the road to Vahramanayaka and others, and sent Shringararajanaka[99] and others without delay to Sthama. The troublesome Masodanayaka was enraged at being deprived of his charge of the road, and he arrived at Surapura following the Khana. Masoda's followers, the Khashas[100], and the Dombas who had been deserted by him, created a tumult in the Madavarajya at every step. On the other hand the king's army harassed the army of the Khana, and the two armies looked like the two rows of teeth of the all devouring Death. The tumult created by the Khana was greater than that caused by the Saidas; it was like a painful disease of the throat, aggravated by the burning of the foot. Travellers were attacked by robbers, the weak were destroyed by the strong and the country was reduced to a miserable plight, as if it had no king. The inhabitants of that part of the country left their houses in fear, taking with them their kine and wealth, and went to Dakshinapara[101] and other villages. The two armies then entered the kingdom of Ksheri which with its woodlands[102] was deserted by the inhabitants, and was devastated by the two armies as by a great fire. On occasion Jerka and others came to know through their spies that the soldiers of the king were asleep, and they attacked their camp. The king's soldiers did not keep themselves awake, nor employed spies, nor had learnt to wield their weapons, and they fled like beasts[103] in fear from the camp. Some relatives of the commander of the king's army were alienated from the king's cause by the enemy. They left the king's army, took shelter with the enemy, and rebelled against the king. When differences[104] arise among the strong and powerful in Kashmira and the government is paralyzed, then the Khashas who live beyond Kashmira begin to rejoice; the people suffer from plunder and conflagration, thieves accumulate wealth, the enemy seeks for riches, and the soldiers, heroic and enduring, desert their cause. When the commander of the army saw those people rebel, and found that the zeal of his troops had relaxed, he was struck with fear and fled from the army; but he was killed by soldiers who came up from behind. The Khana was glad of this first victory by which he obtained everything. It was by the advice of Bhagasiha[105] that the Khana had come unopposed from the Turushka country, but Bhagasiha was killed by some unknown person as he was going away from before the presence of the Khana.

Now the Khana, happy and exulting in his victory, encamped at a place called Mallashila[106] and collected his army with a view to subjugate his enemy. At Karala his soldiers destroyed the powerful soldiers of the king, and robbed and killed the helpless inhabitants. At this time, the Margapati took the boy-king with him and went out of the city accompanied with troops, in order to overcome the enemy. During the disturbance caused by the Saidas, the people had been frequently plundered of their property, and they were therefore now filled with alarm, and they sent away their women from the city to villages. The city was without a king, and its wealth had been taken away from it, and it did not look imposing; it was like a beautiful woman who had been robbed.

The Margapati encamped in a garden at Gusikoddra[107] and his troops cried out against the insolence of the foreign soldiers. But when he heard that the Khana was at Kalyanapura[108], he left the king at Gusikoddara, divided his army into three divisions and came out for battle. When he arrived at the extreme boundary of the village of Drabha[109], in Sakhanamaruga,[108] he found himself in the neighbourhood of the Khana, and he remained there in great anxiety. Vaiduryyabhatta, whose power was irresistible at

Chakravata[110] and other places in Kramarajya, stationed himself on the mountain road on the west. The sons of Gakkarajya, and others, with Privaja the Pratihara, came forward and manoeuvred as on a chess board.

## Battle at Drabhagam

On one side the sons of Masodanayaka,[111] accompanied by the Kashmirian and the foreign soldiers, came out of their ranks in order to fight. The soldiers, armed with sword and shield, approached with shouts, and moved in array, as the swans do across the sky. Ahlada Thakkura's phalanx engaged them as they advanced to the front, but his troops were defeated. Armed men shouted like thunder, and their arms flashed like lightning, and they came out with shields for battle. The field of battle was uneven and muddy, and the roads leading to it were difficult to traverse, but the soldiers came to it as if it were their own home. When the army of Ahlada Thakkura saw the foreign troops, and the waving of their shields, they lost heart, and like sparrows fled afar. Ahlada Thakkura could not stay the broken and the fleeing army, which was like a river that had broken its embankment. Some of them ran crying 'I will flee', 'I will flee', died of the wounds they received, and thus they paid with their lives the wages they had received. Their bodies were besmeared with blood, and lay on the field of the *shali* crop, and looked like beasts that had been sacrificed on fields during some religious ceremony.

## Fateh Khan's 'success'

The army of the Khana which came from the south-west and broke the king's force, even as the wind breaks the trees, was like a tempest that destroyed men. Some Kashmirians perished by the flame-like arms of the foreign soldiers, as if they sacrificed their persons in fire. What is the use of mentioning the names of those who fled to save themselves when they saw the array of troops, reduced to the condition of a herd of animals by fear? The owners of estates who had figured in the royal court were now struck with fear such as they had never felt before, even like men who had never used arms. Only they * * * obtained praise by dying like a hero. Three or four of his followers who wished to go to heaven fell in battle and went there before him. The great army of Khana having routed the survivors, returned and appeared before the Margapati mistaking him to be of their own party. Hassana Mira and other heroes who were determined to conquer sought Masodakhana and were recognized by the soldiers of the Margapati. Nauruja and others, the five attendants of his wife's brother, together with Gaurabhatta were killed in the presence of the Margapati.

## Jahangir's leadership

Fate, that had been long adverse to the Kashmirian army, now became favourable to it, owing to the prowess of the king or to the commendable firmness of the Margesha in this battle. He remained fixed with his troops like a strong and immovable column of victory. Had he retreated but one step from the place, nothing of this Kashmirian army would have remained. As the skill of a physician is observed in a serious disease, even so the skill of Shri Jyahangira was observed in bringing to order the disordered state. In battle, the goddess of victory comes pleased to him who in the hour of danger possesses indestructible energy, genius, skill in devising plans and fearlessness. He circulated the false rumour that the Khana had fallen into his hands and thus, by an artifice, he brought back those who had fled from the battle. The soldiers returned to the battlefield with shouts in the presence of the Margesha and joined their party even as in spring the black bees come to a garden humming on their beautiful wings.

## Fateh Khan defeated

Gakka and others, flushed with victory, killed many men, and plundered the camp of the Khana of articles left there by the Khana after what he had taken away. Evaraima[112] Margesha was in the front of the battle with his attendants; he threatened Masodanayaka and others and caused them to retreat. Shringarasiha and others saw the formidable army and fled without delay from Medavana[113] and reached their own country. All the soldiers of Rajapuri were surrounded by the Kashmirian troops, but Gakka, like Ganesha, gave them assurance, and protected them in the battle. The foreigners left all the ammunitions of war behind and fled, pursued by the Kashmirian soldiers. They were plundered by the Khashas and the Dombas who hung on their rear and greatly harassed them. Some of them lived by eating the leaves of trees in the wood, and they gave back all that they had extorted from the villagers, as if the things had been only deposited with them. Hundreds of foreigners and Kashmirians died, some oppressed with cold and fever, some faint with hunger. Fate is beyond our comprehension; and though it is not really the cause, yet it is considered the strange cause of events. It casts down, all of a sudden, some person in high position, and prospers some who should be cast down, even as the wind does with the trees. The Khana's intention was good, and if his soldiers had been like him, what results might not have ensued? For victory follows virtue.

Thus in the year 61, in the month of Shravana, when Phataha Khana arrived in Kashmira, many natives of the country and foreigners perished, as in the preceding year, by the meeting of the two armies near Kalyanapura. Astrologers found three reasons for this destruction of men in the country: the presence of Saturn in the seventeenth mansion of the moon, the conjunction of Saturn with Jupiter, and the year being presided over by Mars. In the reign of King Shri Jaina, the subjects were devoted to the study of the six schools of philosophy and were attached to their own religion, they were fearless and did not suffer from the six[114] calamities. But the customs of the country were injuriously affected by the base acts of the subjects when that king went to heaven, and so the destruction of men came to pass. This is my opinion. Some merchants, for instance, discarding the custom which befits Hindus, killed a cow within the city and ate its meat. Sons are now fond of the Mausulas, and are ashamed to follow the Shastra which was followed by their fathers and grandfathers. Men of the four castes had graced the kingdom in former days, but latterly the people had gradually adopted blameable practices, and the ceremonies prescribed for special days in the Puranas came to be forgotten year by year. Why should not the people whose custom is bad suffer calamities?

The Margesha heard a false rumour that the king had been attacked by the enemy, and he became anxious. He placed Tajabhatta and others in his post, and went to his own tent. If he had pursued the fleeing and powerless soldiers of the Khana, not one of the retreating army would have survived. But the Margesha was unacquainted with the road, and all his men had accepted[115] payment from both sides. Intending to promote their own interest in this world and wishing misery of their relatives, they induced the Margesha to retire from the battle, and they themselves dispersed. The victorious Jyahangira then took the king and the army with him and, elated with victory, went to Jyamalamaruga.[116] Tajabhatta thought that the people who had been left behind by the Margesha had joined the Khana, and he set fire to the villages of Mangalyanadaga.[117] The smoke which arose from the flames of the burning houses covered the sky and looked like clouds in the rainy season streaked by lightnings. Conflagration and robbery were now witnessed in Kashmira, such as the people of this country had inflicted on other countries, when they had made foreign conquests. Kashmirian invaders in foreign lands had seen the poor and the naked as well as helpless new-born babes, but had not supplied them with clothes. And when the poor of those lands saw their silver and baser metals, their kine and beasts taken away by the Kashmirians, they filled all sides with sighs and lamentations and exclaimed that as the Kashmirians had robbed them of everything without any provocation, so they too would, in their turn, be similarly robbed by their enemies. When Phatahashaha obtained the kingdom, the great sin bore fruit in the sufferings of these persons at the time of their death.

As commotions rose in the country the Margesha returned to his place listening, as he passed, to those and other animadversions. It was owing to the sins of the people that he refused to conclude a peace. He reached the city, accompanied by the king, and began to celebrate a festival on account of his victory; and he punished the partisans of the Khana, both high and low. But he did not oppress *the relations* of those who had gone over to the side of the Khana. As a disease oppresses the body, auspicious Fate sometimes bestows happiness which is enjoyed by all, and sometimes, in its pleasure, it afflicts people with the six calamities. Curious, alas! is the course of Fate in this world; like the course of a planet it brings on good as well as evil on the people.

## Fateh repeats attempt

For a time the Khana was struck with panic and was without any help, and he remained useless like a cloud in the season of drought. At this time he was at Bhairavagala[118], and he received some accession of strength from the Nayaka, so that he again thought of entering Kashmira. After two months he marched towards the country and arrived there supported by excellent soldiers. When he had reached Shurapura[119], Jyahangira issued out of the city, without delay, accompanied by the king; he had numerous troops under him, and much wealth. As before, he remained at Gusika, but he heard that the son of Gakkaraja had fled. When the Margesha was about to mount his horse, the animal took fright. The Margesha understood omens, but had become impatient in his anger, and would wait not for a moment. The son of Gakkaraja had accepted a large sum of money from him, and if he fled, who else would stay with him? This thought made the Margesha anxious, and he returned. He again issued out of his camp in an auspicious moment and thought of creating a division in the army of the Khana. In the meantime Jeraka and other great chiefs came from Shurapura and entered the city at night and liberated those who were in prison. Thus Saiphadamara and others issued from the prison, as from the door of death, and came to Vijyayeshvara. On a previous occasion, when in prison, Saiphadamara had dreamt that some one had severed his two legs by a weapon at night. To keep a great chief, the head of a strong party, in confinement is like covering a fire with a cloth. And so it happened. Why was he brought from the fort of Jayapidapura and kept imprisoned in the city? This imprisonment of Saiphadamara caused harm to the Margapati.

Ebhrahima the Margesha came up from the rear and killed Shamshanayaka and many other people. Thakkura Ahmada, Jerka, the Pratihara Anvaya and others had marched over sixty *kroshas*, and displayed acts of courage. Some people suffer in times of danger, only to achieve a royal station, even as gold is melted in fire and beaten by a hammer in order that it may be formed into a diadem which adorns the head of a king. Set free from the bondage of a prison, like a bird from a cage, the Damara[120] thought as if he was born again. Once before when he had been imprisoned, along with Hodara[121] in the fort of Jyapura[122], he had scaled the walls of the prison by means of a rope, and had come out alone. But he was captured again when asleep, and was kept in the prison of the capital, and his friends felt certain that he would be killed within two or three days. From such a danger he was now set free. In time he came to the Khana and remained with the ministers as was expected. Such was Saiphadamara, and he obtained the fame due to a great man. Had not Rama been decoyed out of his dwelling into the forest by Ravana, and had not Vali aroused the anger of Sugriva, how could Rama have won his victories, marching to Lanka and destroying his enemies? Fate ordains both pleasure and pain for the good of man. The Khana had aspired after the kingdom but was driven from the country; but now he obtained the support of great warriors on his side, and became addicted to pleasures. The Margapati was angry with Saiphadamara, but he came to be ruined and was deprived of his post. How could the Khana have entered Kashmira and obtained it, if he and the Damara had not mutually and of their own accord, come to each other's help. It is by the help of many chiefs that the king obtains glory, and the chiefs obtain it by depending on the king; their union is indispensable, and looks graceful like the golden ornaments on a young woman. The court of the Khana was adorned by the fortunate leaders who joined him, even as the person of a woman is adorned by necklaces of pearls.

## Attempt fizzles out

The Margapati became alarmed by the union of the Khana with the leaders, and he sent Khanashikhavahabmukha who was desirous of establishing peace. Edha Rajanaka, Riga Damara, and Keshavabudha[124] brought the king of Rajapuri to the king of Kashmira with a view to establish peace. At this[125] time the Margapati gave wealth and assurance of safety to Shringarasiha, and alienated him from Gadayaravatra Mukha. The king of Rajapuri took with him the son of the Margapati, and desiring to establish peace, prevented the calamity of a battle between the two armies. Others at this time resolved to get hold of the son of the Margesha, to whom the king of Rajapuri had not paid any special attention, and the ministers became alarmed. When fate became adverse to the king and his subjects, the distress that befalls their party cannot be removed even by a hundred remedies. When one is oppressed by mental anxiety, how can then the disease which has got a firm hold on him be removed by the skill of physicians? The partisans of the Khana alienated the king of Rajapuri from the party of the Margapati, and when that king left the side of the Margapati, a tumult arose which alarmed both the armies. Gakka, Shringarasiha and others were alarmed and went to Rajapuri; and the Khana with his army was struck with fear, and retired as before, without effecting anything. Jerka, Mera and others, who owing to their love for Jyalla Thakkurra, had resolved to remain neutral, went to the Margesha. The confusion which thus arose made the army of the Khana tremble; and it broke up into a thousand parts, even like a river whose embankment is destroyed.

## The Syeds return

When the Margapati heard of this, he pursued the Khana and arrived with his army at Surapura. But his anxiety became great when he learnt from his spies that disorder had broken out at Kramarajya, and that some troops had arrived at Shahibhanga.[126] Leaving the king, he went to Svayyapura, and there, by an artifice, he threw Naurujakhana into prison. This was a wise measure, as Nauruja had intended to plunder Shrinagara on that very day with the help of wicked men, and it was owing to the virtues of the citizens that his cruel intention was not fulfilled. He had expected the arrival of the Margapati from Kramarajya, and he set fire to much property, and reduced it to ashes in his anger. Wealth which is obtained day by day by wicked means and is not given in charity, which is hoarded in pits, and only causes sorrow to the raiser, finds its way at last either to the king or to fire, to enemy or to robbers. Jyahangira arrived in the city with Nauruja, and graced it by his triumph over him. Though the Saidas had been exiled from the country, and though they had killed his son[127], yet Jyahangira wrote to them and brought them back because they were worthy men.

## Salt famine

In the meantime the Khana stationed himself in his exalted position of strength at Janmavata[128], and distressed the Khashas even as the lion distresses the deer; and as he had harassed the twenty- seven districts of Kashmira in his prowess, so did he now harass Sindhuri.[129] His army was strong in good soldiers, and was joined by the Malha[130] chiefs and he plundered the country of the Madras, and alarmed the Turushkas. He conquered the country of the Madras, and gave it to the king of Rajapuri having thus secured a victory, and joined by the king of Rajapuri, he arrived in the house of Masodanayaka in the month of Chaitra. The Nayaka received the Khana in his house as if he were a god; and owing to the Khana's virtues, the Nayaka's devotion to him was never shaken. The sea may overleap its shores, the sun may rise in the west, but a Kshattriya never swerves from his duty towards one who asks his protection. The Khana had now collected an army and was joined by the Chhayilla[131] soldiers and, with a view to overcome his enemies, he stationed himself on the top of a hill. The soldiers were like diseases, and destroyed everything in the houses and the people remained in them with difficulty, even as life remains in a body prostrated by illness. Jeraka, who was in prison with his back fastened to a door, was killed by the Margapati within the city out of fear. When the officers of the king heard of this they all became displeased and spoke ill of the Margesha, for the Margesha had violated the assurance of safety he had given to Jeraka. In the month of Jyeshtha the cruel Margesha heard the evil news, and being distressed, remained at Mallashila with the king. As the Dranga[132] road was blocked, those who had received pay from both parties despaired of reaching the two armies. At that time, the people of this country had to eat their food without *salt*, and who did not hear of this ludicrous Margesha[133] curry? It was with difficulty then that the people in the city bought one and a half[134] pala of rock salt for twenty-five dinars.

## Surprise attack

In the year 62 the Margapati heard that the Khana was anxious to come into Kashmir a, and he adopted a wicked policy. He appointed Eskandharakhana, son of the daughter[135] of the Hajyakhana, to the post of the lord of Kampana, and sent him to Sthama; and in order to protect himself he gave the possessions of Masodanayaka to Yashsharajanaka, and sent him out with an army. When the snow decreased, and with it the happiness of the country decreased also, the Khana came with his army from Rajapuri. When the Margesha heard that the Khana had come within Bhairavagala, he went to Surapura with the king, with a view to obstruct the Khana's way. Now the Khana who was in a high pass was obstructed from entering the country, even as Rahu is prevented for fear of the Chakra from coming in contact with its lifeless trunk. So the Khana went by the Pashupadishta[136] road as in the previous year, and after surmounting a hill issued by the Kachagala[137] hi the month of Shravana. But the soldiers of Tajabhatta and others came like a storm and agitated the sea-like army of the Khana in the field of Gusikoddra. The Khana and his army spread alarm on all sides by the din of the sounding kettle-drums, and agitated the city with panic. The Margapati was astonished when he heard of this, and was struck as if the

Khana had come on his wings, and he hastened with his army and the king to offer him battle. The Damara named Vaga[138], of high rank, was like the immortal Garuda, in valour and beauty, and in the engagement which ensued he graced the field like the fiery Shiva. In that battle, some of the Saida warriors fought against the powerful soldiers; they did not retreat, but died on the field, and obtained the pleasure of the company of celestial females. Many fell into chasms, many died of wounds, and heaps of dead bodies lay on the field. Neither in the struggle with the Saidas, nor in the first engagement with the Khana, did so many soldiers perish as in this battle of Gusikoddara.

## Masodanayaka killed

The proprietors of lands, although high in their position, remained passive witnesses to the battle, and did not display the heroism befitting their rank. The dead bodies of persons killed in the battle or when fleeing, or of those who died of wounds, lay here and there, like the young ones of birds scattered by the fall of a tree. Those who had injured others before in village or in town, were now harassed by stronger men. Masodanayaka was killed by a discharge of arrows and the career of his horse was arrested at the same time. Who can escape what must happen? The Margesha sent his people to fight, but he himself retired to a distant place for safety. Shri Saiphadamara, however, was there attended by powerful warriors. He was rejoiced that the very man who should be sought for had come there of himself, and he struck the Margapati on the head. Alam Shira, and Haidhara, like cruel planets,[139] struck him on the face, arm, and forehead and made him insensible; and the Damara took away the Margapati's gold-coloured, auspicious and indestructible necklace, as if it were the goddess of victory. The Margapati lay there, neglected by his own men, but a horse of noble breed, fleeing from the battle, saved him, and his mind was comforted.

## Khan's bid fails again

When all the ministers direct the helm at the same time, and lean on the same side of the vessel of state, Royal Fortune sinks like a boat though supported on all sides by arms. When the foreign soldiers mutinied at the beginning of the war, Katthavada[140] and others led the Khana out of the country in the same manner in which he had come. Saiphadamara, skilful in battle, was then disheartened by the false rumour that the Khana had been captured in battle by the king's soldiers, and he turned away from the engagement. He went away by the Surapura road, taking with him good horses and other things, but he afterwards joined the Khana. Then for the third time the Khana entered the country; and after having killed many men, he issued out of Mandala[141] and arrived at Parnotsa. The Margesha thought that the time was fraught with calamities, and that all were inclined to rebel. He considered that the king was but a young child, the ministers had become insubordinate, his own men were unruly and were wishing to go over to the side of the Khana, the citizens bore no affection to him, and there was no money in the palace; and he himself was an old man, without any life in him and bereft of all strength. He was moreover oppressed with the pain caused by his wounds, and he spent two months in his own house. Let that man go to the sea who desires to acquire valuable jewels and pearls and corals, and can, at the same time, cast away fear, and can overcome the frightful monsters of the deep by his strength.

## Success at last

In the meantime the Khana came down from the Chatikashara[142] hill, strengthened by the soldiers who went from Kashmira. He arrived into the interior of the country, and the hills clad themselves, as in gladness, in the white garment of snow that fell that day. The Margesha was alarmed at this news, and saw the villagers fleeing. He left Vangila with his army and came to fight. The Khana then came to Bahurupa with a few followers, and joined by the Damaras, arrived in the field of Damodaroddara.[143] The powerful Margapati accompanied by the king came like a gale from behind, and stationed his troops in the neighbourhood of Saatadaivata.[144] But Saiphadamara, who was there with his army preparing for battle, reached near Damodara, arose like Vishnu and routed the army of the Margapati at the close of night. It is strange that by his three expeditions the Khana, though weak in army, accomplished, through the help of fate, what was not accomplished by Haidarashaha. What else need be said? The Khana, though he had a small force, killed, routed, and destroyed the troops of Kashmira, as a lion destroys herds of the elephants. The Margapati retired within the city, fearing mischief from

Saiphadamara as before, and perceiving that he had lost the regard of others. The bridge[145] was destroyed, as during the previous civil war of the Saidas, and the citizens on both banks of the river were harassed, as if they belonged to two separate kingdoms. Pirvaja the Pratihara and others came from Madavarajya, and they left the side of the king and went over to that of the Khana.

The Margapati found that his army was weakened by mutual dissensions and was at a loss to know what should be done; and like the Saidas he spent two or three nights in the temple[146] of Skanda. At one time he had made Meya Mahammada[147] head of all the army, and had joined with Nossarajanaka and risen against his master. What could he not have accomplished had his body been as strong as his mind, and had he not pursued only his own interest. But he sought his own interest, and slighted his nephew the king, and rose against him, and these acts became the cause of his destruction. His army fled, he was humbled and afraid, and he sought shelter with his benefactor Jyalla Thakkura who was living at Kharwashrama[148]. He was reduced to that state to which his opponents had been reduced by his orders. Fie to the uncertainty of prosperity derived from royal power! As the king Bahrama had, under the influence of the seven planets, worn costly and various tinted robes and ornaments seven times, and had then met death like an ordinary mortal, even so it happened with the Margapati. Fie to Fortune! He[149] arrived at the cavern of a saint, and forgot his king and his former prosperity and his attendants. His brother had taken away the king's[150] wife, and for that sin he became unable to escape, and got into a boat with his wife.

## Khashas avenge injury

The soldiers of the Margapati were humbled, they spent their days in the caves of mountains, their complexion turned pale, and their hearts were damped by the rain which fell to their misfortune. Their powerful and unrelenting enemies pursued them; they were robbed of their clothes, dragged and forcibly thrown into prison, and confined like beasts. The wicked enemies, the Khashas, shouted and plundered the country, and men and women left all their property behind, and went about without clothes in fear of them. The weak people were killed on the road by the Khashas who remembered the injury they had received from the Kashmirians. The disorder which then prevailed in the kingdom was like that at the end of a *kalpa*; it was terrible. The condition in the city was miserable; the rich were robbed of everything, the poor became rich, and the rich became poor. The trees which had once been decked with leaves and flowers and fruits, were now withered in winter; the rivers which had once flowed in waves were now dried up; and the *kokilas* which had sung before now became mute. What does not come to pass with the reverse of fortune? When the king's party was destroyed, the beautiful women who were dear to the king, lived only in name!

## Mohammad Shah dethroned

Thus the king, Mahamadashaha, sat on the throne for two years and seven months, and he was dethroned in the year 62, in the month of Asbvina. He was then brought from Vimshaprastha, and given up to the enemies by Phiryapala. The Damara chiefs who had assembled in the yard of the palace and in the residence of the king gave Mahmadashaha a few attendants and a maintenance allowance, and kept him under their protection. He had hitherto lived under difficulties; and as long as he was a king, he had never enjoyed the ease which he now felt through the favour of the king's ministers.

## Khasha robbers at large

The city had been plundered during the slaughter at the time of the civil war of the Saidas, but now, when a new king assumed the royal power, the Khashas robbed thrice as much, but they did not burn it down. Some principal merchants were deprived of the millions they had accumulated; they saved their lives, but lived by covering their bodies with grass. The foreigners bribed the ministers, and the ministers allowed them three days to plunder the city. The foreigners plundered in the same way as the Kashmirians had *plundered foreign countries* when they had marched against those countries. What does not time bring forth? The industrious female bee extends the hive by working with her peers but others come and raise a smoke, deprive her of the hive, and enjoy its sweet honey. For six months the followers of the Khana enjoyed at ease what others had saved in their houses with great care. None, however, plundered the wealth which was hid in the grass and besmeared with blood, mistaking it for the rags of a lying-to room left in a dirty place.

Listen to the truth which we tell you, O ye rich! Make proper use, by gifts and enjoyment, of the wealth which you have hoarded in your houses depriving others of it. Otherwise, riches are of no value during this period of revolution in the kingdom. Some people scatter broken pots and boxes round their houses, pretending that they had been plundered, and thus deceived[151] the Khashas. Some citizens saved their wealth by emptying their houses, and filling grave yards beyond the water with their goods. Holes were dug and heaps of riches were thrown into them, and the earth everywhere became Vasundhara (holder of wealth) in reality as its name implies. The people of Rajanavatika[152] threw missiles and stones with a view to obstruct the road and did many rash acts.

The revolution was to the royal officers what the sound of drum is to the serpent; it was to the old and persecuted servants of the king what the winter is to the lotuses; it was to the king's dominion what the thick smoke is to the hive; and it was to the new court of the king what the spring is to the trees of the garden. It was owing to a change in manners and customs, or to the unjust acquisitions of wealth, or to the oppression of the good, or to the admixture among men of the higher castes, or to the weakness of the boy king, or to the enmity of the ministers, that this calamity befell the people of the kingdom, even like the one in the reign of king Sussala.[153] Let Saipha Mallika, the chief of the Damaras, the meritorious leader among the ministers, the one without a rival, be victorious! He had before, during the war of the Saidas, liberated in battle those who had been captured; he attained prosperity according to the way approved by saints; he conquered the enemies and destroyed them and obtained fame; and he gave an extensive kingdom to the king Phatiha.

Here ends the fourth book named 'the acquisition of the kingdom by Phatihashaha' of Sri *Jainarajataraṅgiṇi* composed by Pandita Shrivara.

## References

1. Shrivara's *Jainarajatarangini* ends with this chapter.
2. the visible and the invisible worlds.
3. Two Hassanas: PH and BS refer to only one, *i,e.*, Syed Hassan. Syed Hassan and Meya Hassan are distinctly accounted for by Srv.
4. Sati lake: Kashmir was originally called Satisar; the people of Kashmir, especially poets and intellectuals (singers), were overawed

by the Syeds... 'Birds' used allegorically Parashurama: ref. p. 212/86. Merya Hassana: Father of Hayatkhatoon and grandfather of the new king, (ref. pp. 155 and 185).
Tattarkhan: Lodhi governor of Punjab.

5. Amritavata: A'anta'bhavan, near Vicharnag. The 'house' must have been well-fortified.
6. Tajaka: mentioned later as Taja.
7. Simhadvija appears to have been a Brahmin in the confidence of the Syeds. It was, pb. he who with Shrivara accompanied Z. when he went round the Vishnupad lake. Simhabhatta and Simha also refer to him.
8. house: Amritavatika or A'antabhavan. Syeds killed included Gadayamin, Kasim, Malazada, besides Syed Hassan and Meya (Mir) Hassan.... 'Diminutive' or mean-looking (*khyudra*) has been used by Shrivara frequently for the *Madras* from this point onwards. But the term 'diminutive' does not appear to be appropriate, for the *Madras*, a community of warriors, were not especially shortsized nor 'mean looking'. Damodargupta, the chief minister of Jayapida (746-81 A.D.), has applied the word *khyudra* to a blackbee in his *Kutinimatam*. (v. 439) Earlier, Subandhu referred through this word to a 'courtesan' in his *Svapanavasvadata* Shrivara also appears to have used the word *khyudra* with sarcasm and bitterness for the *Madras*, in the sense of 'exploiters' and 'parasites'..., helplessness: Srv. appears to be genuinely sad at the murder of the Syeds.... Meya Mahammada: grandson of Z. through his daughter (p. 199-200).
9. Mulakanaga/Muktamulaknaga: the spring at Vicharnag. Sheikh Nur-ud-Din practised austerities near Muktamalaknaga for years. The Madras were allied with Kashmiri leaders like Jonrajanaka, Eidirajanaka and Jalala Thakura. Jalal's wife Lachhma Khatoon had a canal laid out to carry water from Shahkol to Jama Masjid. The canal was named Lachhmakol after her.
10. Juhilamatha: pb. Junimar or the present Zinimar. After he failed to find refuge anywhere in the Hariparbat area, Harsha (1088-1101 A.D.) was deserted by the city prefect at Juhilamatha in 1101 A.D. before the rebels killed him at the nearby cremation ground which was close to the Vitasta.
11. Vatika road: the road leading to A'anta Bhavan
12. Eidarajanka: Eidi Raina (PH). Yusuf, Bahram Khan's son, was, PH states, killed within the prison itself by Syed Alikhan who was a leader among the Behaqi Syeds after the death of Syed Hassan.
13. Pajabhatta: Naji Bhat (PH).... Mira: pb. the daughter of Meya Hassan (text).
14. Lady Sobana: Sobandevi (SK). Sthandevi (PH) Also Sitandevi.
15. Dvijas: It appears that in spite of the bitterness of Shrivara against the Syeds, they had some friends and collaborators among Brahmins.

Simhabhatta, obviously one such, paid the price of collaboration with his life.

16. Moon: less than one month of Mohammad Shah's enthronement.... cause: Srv.. repeats the comment a number of times ....Yama: ref. p. 212/93.
17. Jalladraga: a small place ringed with water: Zaaldagar opp., to the SMHS Hospital across the Kat'a'kol.... Shamala : Hamal in Handawara.
18. Sthama: cantonment or camp (Stein).... Kshipitika: Ka'ta'kol river.
19. Chakkavaka: Chakavada (SK). The Chaks are reported to have come originally from Gurez area, the abode of Darads. During the reign of Jaisimha (1128-55) Alamkarchakra had his castle at Sirashila near Shardhaji in the vy. of the Kishenganga. Chakavada could be taken as a stronghold of the Chaks.
20. Dugdhashrama : Do'darhom near Ganderbal. Nilashva is in the Sindh vy. near Kangan. The verse should read: '... they crossed over to the other side of the Sindhu near Dugdhashrama to reach the camp'.
21. Nandapura: v. on the Mar canal near Rainawari.
22. Meyavahaka: Vafaka (SK): Miyan Wafa.
23. Samudramatha: near Haba Kadal right.
24. Skanda: Stein states that the temple was located 'at a spot near the southern end of the Khandabhavan Mohalla'. Hassan Shah had built a palace at Diddamatha not far from the temple. The verse should read: 'But the Syeds fearing... from Skandabhavan excavated... in the vicinity of the palace yard of the king.'
25. Rajanaka: Rudrarajanak (SK): 'another similar moat was excavated near Rudrarajanaka in the vicinity of the gate.' Rudravihara mentioned on p. 233 indicates that the moat was excavated around it for purposes of defense.
26. Rudravana: there were several forest areas in and around the city, the suffix *van*, as in Taashivan, still indicating a clue. Rudravana forest, pb., existed near Diddamatha. Rathapora, near Idgah, appears to have been founded by Raddadevi, queen of Jaisimha. She also founded the shrine called Rudresvara (R.T. Viii-3389). One of the shrines of Rudra, Rudrarajabhairava, is worshipped near Khandbhavana even now and the temple of Rudrarajanaka is believed to have existed in the same locality.
27. Pirvajkhana: Parvezkhan.
28. Padampura: The road to Padampur was clear for the Syeds on the right hand side of the river and Jonarajanaka crossed from the left bank to strike at the Syeds on the right bank Ovana: Wuyan near Khrew. Vadhavi: Lodhuv near Tulamula.
29. '....set fire to Ovana' (v. Wuyan, near Khrew). As a reprisal the Syeds had the village burnt where Jonarajanaka had taken his birth. At

this Jonarajanaka had Tajibhatta's house in Vadhavi (Lodhuv) set on fire.'

30. Dugdhashrama sthama: pb. the Syeds had posted guards here after the Sindh valley contingent crossed the river (see p. 220.)
31. Lohara: Loharkot.... chief: Meya Hassan.
32. Loyal: both parties pledged loyalties to the boy-king Mohammad Shah.
33. After a battle...should read: After the capture of Alishah, the country was protected against Malik Jasratha by Mohammad Margesha, likewise please come immediately, the Saidas will not leave the boy-king alive in the kingdom.
34. Shikhashahava: Sheikh Shahab-ud-Din (SK).
35. Your: reference is pb. to *Madras*, and 'our' suits the context.
36. Loshta Vihara: Lothikamatha was built by Lothika, daughter of Sangramraja, (1003-28), in Sgr (RT. vii, 120). Lotha and Loshta have been frequently interchanged in RT. Lothika was married to the Superintendent of Diddamatha. It may be presumed that Lothika/Loshtikamatha/Vihara was in the vicinity of Diddamatha. The Syeds being entrenched at Vimshprastha or Idgah, it appears to be plausible that Davood proceeded towards Diddamatha-Lothikavihara to smoke them out.
37. in the course of their invasion of Kashmir in 1947 the tribal raiders lost much valuable time while engaged in plunder and barbarous acts.
38. Labhadhava vihara: pb. Ludrabhatavihara (SK), or Rudrabhattavihara. Pb. Rudreshvara shrine erected by Raddadevi (RT. viii 3389). Refer also to n. 26 above.
39. the Pratihara was an ally of Davood.
40. Khanagaha: pb. the Khanaqah built by Malik Ahmad near Diddamatha (see p. 183), Eidi Rajanaka (Raina) also built one at Baladyamatha (pp. 183-4).
41. Many citizens perched themselves on roofs and sky-lights to witness how fighter planes were strafing the invaders in Nov., 1947.
42. Yavaneshvara; another interpretation is '...cut off from his body the physician's head which was smeared with sandal paste'.
43. Mallekepura: near Zainakadai.
44. first: panic and stampede.
45. Sharada: according to the *Nil-n*, goddess Parvati assumed the form of the Vitasta after Satisar was cleared of water and Jaludbhava killed.
46. instructions saint: *siddhadesha* : 'fruitful advice'.
47. Pravapura: the city founded near Hariparbat by Pravarasena II.
48. mutual enmity: Brahmins appear to have played a significant role along with other Kashmiri nobles in the civil war.
49. Salhanahamsa: Malhanahamsa (SK) Malhana Hamsa was a prominent leader of the Manhas Rajputs of Bhimber-Akhnur area.

50. Shahibhanga: Gandhara.... Tattar Khan : the Lodhi governor of Punjab at the me.
51. Shastragalasthana: Bhimber (PH)—'The site of the Shastra pass'. 'When...Shastragalasthana, a large number of them were killed by Bhodanraja and others, even as...'
52. benefit:...for the good of Satidesha or Kashmir.
53. '...roads:' should read: 'roads.... and crossed the river in boats like frightened women, and when they crossed the river, charlatans and rogues, out of avarice, deprived them of their belongings. A new pathway was adopted for movement through Adhisthana (*i.e.* Pandrenthan area).'
54. Kashtila: Kathil, the area between the Ka'ta'kol and the left bank of the Vitasta a little distance above Habakadal Sthama: encampment, camp.
55. Another interpretation: '...Turushukas have no restrictions in matters of food ....'
56. beef...: the inference is that Hindus in sizable numbers, including those from Jammu, participated in the confrontation on the side of the Kashmiri nobles.
57. unconquerable: the Syeds had, pb., gained in numbers.
58. Takshaka: Puraanatakshaka (SK). The spring at Zevan was known as Takshaknaga. The spot referred to here appears to be near the old capital or Pandrethan...should read: '...crossed the river to the ancient...'
59. Hastavalika : name of a part of the Dal from Nishat to Telbal; at present Astavol. Z. joined the Mar to the Shali canal at Hastikaran (see p. 124 and 128/20). It could lead to the vicinity of Soura. Exact location not clear.... Praulabhatta was obviously a Brahmin.
60. Gakka appears to have had divided loyalties.
61. so other...: Saiphadara and other warriors (SK).
62. Abhivanayurtha: Ayuktamatham (SK) pb. the *matha* build by Shaha, wife of Ahmadayutka, on the road leading to Kheri which was perhaps near the river bank (see p. 183).
63. arrived *at* Dugdhashrama: arrived *from*... Pupamatha: identity uncertain. Meya Bhakera: Mirza Baqir.
64. Somanavata: Sonavar.... Sonavar is at the southern foot of the Shankaracharya hill, also referred to as Jyesthrudra after the ancient shrine Zeythyear near the eastern slope. The contingent that crossed the river near Zevan reached Sonavar.... A gravestone at the cemetery at Baha-ud-Din Saheb bears an eiptaph in *Arabic* and *Sharadha* scripts indicating that the deceased Seda (Saida Khana) son of Aibrahim died in the battle of Justhaludra (Jyesthrudra) in 889 A.H. on Friday, the first day of the dark fortnight of Sawan (9-7-1484 A.D.), in the reign of Mohammad Shah. Saida Khana mentioned in the next sentence is probably the subject of the epitaph.

65. his horse: of Parvezkhan of the Syeds.
66. Gakkas: allied with the Kashmiris for the time being.
67. Pratihara: pb. Parvezkhan Syed is meant and not the Pratihara.
68. with their guards: '...guards, and depicted their valour'; "died fighting.." does not suit the text.
69. cloud-like: the Kashmiris had taken their position on the hillside.
70. Kashmirians: Some Kashmiris were fighting on the side of the Syeds.
71. east of the city: *Purvadhishthanam*, the old capital, *i.e.*, Pandrethan where Kashmiris entrenched themselves first.
72. Mari canal: the battleline stretched along Pandrethan, Sonavar, Dalgate, Sathu and Sadramar (Habakadal).
73. Kampana: the office of the commander-in-chief.
74. Phakuva: the sub-division of Phak including the gardens around the Dal Lake.
75. king's daughter: pb. son of Meya Hassan, and brother of Mian Mohammad.
76. cotton tree: *shaalmani* has red flowers and its fruit yields cotton-like fibre,
77. Alavapura: Alau-ud-Dinpura, near Fathekadal, right, founded by Alau-ud-Din.
78. house of Syed: Syed Hamdan Khanaqaha (SK) now known as Khanaqahi Maula built by Qutub-ud-Din (1373-1389 A.D.) at the site of Pravarasena's temple dedicated to Shri Kalishwari. According to PH no damage was done to the Khanaqah at the time. The Hindu shrine co-exists with the Khanaqah to this day.
79. wine: obviously people resorted to drinking on an extensive scale.... the first shoot: Srv. repeats this observation a number of times.
80. Ravatra: Gadairavatra (SK), a partisan of the Syeds.
81. Shalla: Raja of Madradesh, brother of Madhuri and uncle of her Pandava sons Nakul and Sahdev.
82. houses of...Khanaqah (SK), *i.e.*, Khanaqahi Maula burnt earlier (n. 78)
83. Bhabhasaida...Khanaqahi Maula.
84. Hassana: Nagarama or Nagam was bestowed upon him earlier.
85. Makhya: Khuya (SK), *i.e.*, Khuyashrama or Khoyahom. Jyahangira: also known as Margesha (Margapati), J-Magrey.... Vangila: Bhangil.
86. Makshakashrama: the pga. of Manchahama adjoining Beeru, extended on the east to the Jhelum.
87. Parihasapura: Paraspur, the town founded by Lalitaditya lies to the right of Miragond on the Srinagar-Baramula highway.
88. possessions of Dvarapala: office of the commandant of the Gate.
89. Chhundinika: pb. v. Tsonduin near Shalabug in Anchaar area; Jonarajanaka had taken Paraspur as his estate.

90. Thakkura Ahmada: Ahlad Thakura (SK).
91. Shringarasiha: a chief of Rajauri (Stein).',..went to Shringarasiha by way of Rajapuri. Saliya and other Thakuras, being without any following and having come of their own accord, were thrown into prison....'
92. 'Worse than the massacre of the Saidas was the murder of Jonarajanaka as the crime was aggravated by the imprisonment...'
93. son of Adamakhana: Fateh Khan (Phatihakhana).
94. shrine of Jalandhara: pb. Kangra.
95. outside: in Loharkot.
96. His son: his son Hassankhan (SK).... *grahana*: identity not certain, pb. home country.
97. Vupyadeva: A.D. 1171-81. Lavanyas helped his brother Jessaka to the throne. The reference is, pb, to the. latter's successor, Jagadev (1199-1213)
98. Purana: According to *Nil-n*, Parvati assumed the form of the Vitasta when lord Shiva struck the earth with his trident.
99. Shringararajanaka: Shringarasiha, mentioned as Shangi Raina in Persian chronicles.
100. Khashas: inhabitants of hills girdling the Vy. on the s. and s.w. Khasas created a disturbance after Zulchu departed but were suppressed by Rinchana and Shahmir. They continued to create trouble off and on.
101. Dakshinpara: the territory along the right bank of the Ledar river.
102. Woodlands: Ardhvanam, *i.e.*, Advani, also known in the past as Karala.... kingdom: basin.
103. Beasts: a similar incident occurred when the pretender Bhikshachar opposed Jaisimha during Kalhana's lifetime (RT. viii).
104. differences: History has demonstrated the truth of this observation again and again.
105. Bhagasih/Bhagsingh: pb. a Madra adviser of Fateh Khan.
106. Mallasila: see p. 102/13.
107. Gusikoddara: Gush Udar near Romuh on the Sgr.-Shupayan road.
108. Kalyanapura: now Kalampur on the highway from the P.P. pass to Srg. *via* Shupyan; originally founded by Kalyanidevi, queen of Jayapida.
109. v. of Drabha: Drabhagam, about 5 km. north of Kalampur .... Sakhanamaruga: Khanamaruga (SK). 'sa' stands for proximity (t' *'maraga'* or alpine vy.), here the vy. of Birnai stream.
110. Chakravata: Chakavaad (SK), pb. in Uttar Pga. or the norii.wii areas.
111. Masodanayaka joined Fateh Khan after Jahangir dismissed him while Ahlad Thakur was fighting for Mohammad Shah.
112. Evaraima: Ibrahim Magrey, pb. son of Jahangir Margapati (Magrey).
113. Medavana: Bhedavana (SK), a forest on the route from Kalampura to Rajauri.

114. *six* calamities: excess of rain, drought, destruction of crops by rats, locusts and birds, and the approach of a foreign army. For six schools ref. p. 79/41.
115. accepted... The chronicler repeatedly refers with bitterness to this grievance.
116. Jyamalamaruga: Jamalmarg. According to PH, Raja Rajdev granted to Jaimal Acharya an *agrahar* in a v. which came to be known as Jaimalnagar or, later, Jamnagar. It is in Advani pg., pb. the same as Jamalmarg.
117. Mangalyanadaga: Mangalyanad (SK); A v. by the name of Mangalnar is in Rajauri t. Srv. expresses disapproval of aggression.
118. Bhairavagala: a v. on the western side of the P-P pass below Pusiana, now known as Bahramgala (*gala*: pass); Nayaka: Masud Nayaka.
119. Shurpura: Herapur.
120. Damara: Saiphadamara or Saiphadar.
121. *hodara*: with his brother, or 'he who was imprisoned in the castle of Jyapur and was rescued with the help of ropes'.
122. Jyapur: Jayapidpura or Andrakot.
123. Khanashikhvahabmukha: Sheikh Wahab (SK), 'sent prominent men like Sheikh Wahab...'
124. Keshavbudha: 'and the wise Keshav'.
125. 'At this...assurance of safety to Shringarasiha, but alienated him from Gadairavatra' by offering him wealth.
126. Shahibhanga: in the present context pb. Bangash to the n.w, of the Vy.
127. Son: Davood died fighting the Syeds.... worthy men: Shrivara vents all his gall against their activities towards the end of Hassan Shah's reign!
128. Janmavata (SK), Jammu (RNS). Nauruja: pb. the son of Ahmadayukta.
129. Sindhuri: elephants- pb., 'collected many elephants for a fresh campaign'.
130. Malhas: a Rajput clan; Malhan Hamsas.
131. Chhayila: Chhayil (SK) pb. soldiers of the hill area near Bhimber called Chibal, or Chibs.
132. Dranga road: Karkotdranga. All routes were pb. closed owing to hostilities. The Herapur route was called the 'Salt Road' wherefrom this essential commodity was imported loaded on mules or goats in accordance with the season.
133. Margesha curry: adversity caused by economic blockade in 1947-48 gave currency to similar expressions and doggerel rhymes sarcastic in nature. During the winter of 1947-48, when hostilities broke out between Kashmir and Pakistan, salt was so scarce as to cost ₹ 25 a kg. An official who was suspected of having bungled in the import of salt (by getting jaggery instead) was sarcastically referred to as '*Rab* (jaggery) Saheb.'

134. One and a half *pala*: eight seers equivalent to 160 palas (Stein), the quantity mentioned should be about 70 gms. In Abul Fazal's valuation 100 dinars or 4 *puntshus* were equivalent to 1/40 rupees.
135. Hajyakhana: Haidershah, son of Z.
136. Pushpadhishta road: goat-tracks.
137. Kachagala: Kachagalamarg on the northern slope of the P-P range near Chittapani pass.
138. *vaga*: pb. not a name. Another interpretation has it thus: '..and in the engagement which ensued...fiery Shiva in the Sati Yajna.' (RNS). The attributes in the verse, however, suit Saiphadar.
139. cruel planets: Saturn, Mars and the Sun.
140. Katthavaada: pb. Kaathavaar near Nunar in Badgam which the Khan may have passed in going out of the country. Another v. Kashtwar near Baramulla provides an exit from the Vy. to the west.
141. Mandala: province
142. Chatikasara hill: pb. the Sangisafed pass wherefrom several streams flow to form Chhatskol or the Doodganga. RNS identifies it with Cherahar... Bahurupa: Beeru.
143. Damodaroddara: near the present airport.
144. Satadaivata: Saatadaivata (SK), near Damadarudara.... Haidarshaha: 'Adamakhana' suits the context.
145. the bridge of boats.
146. ...Skanda: Khandabhavan locality in Srinagar.
147. Meya Mahammada: son of Syed Hassan and Z-'s daughter. His sister was married to Hassan Shah, and the king was thus his nephew. Some links appear to be missing in the para.
148. Kharvvashrama: Khuyahama (SK).
149. He: Margapati Jahangir.
150. could it be the present king, a mere boy of nine? *Kokilas*: poets and intellectuals.
151. Deceived: some tribal raiders had similar experience in 1947 when many parts of the Vy. were under their subjugation for two weeks.
152. Rajanavatika: Rainawari. Road blocks are placed even now as an expression of protest.
153. Sussala: ruled Kashmir during A.D. 1112-28 except for a brief interval in 1120-21. A fierce civil war took place during his rule.

**Shuk Pandit's**

*Rajatarangini*

# Chapter I
# The Seesaw

## Fatehshah *versus* Mohammadshah

### Shuka's prologue

I bow to the Great Being, Mahadeva, who assumes the form of the movable and of the immovable, oh whose crown rests the moon, and whose purpose is pure. Let that form, half of Hara and half of Gouri, protect you. At the sight of this form, the king of the serpents twined himself round the bracelet of Gouri, out of excess of devotion. I bow to the sun-like *guru*, the light of whose favour dispelled the thick darkness of ignorance, even of Shuka—and expanded the lotus-like heart of Buddhyashraya.[1]

A good poet should bow to the truthful words of persons skilled in discussion and deliberation, to the *shlokas* graced with good rhythm, thick with alliterations, and beneficial, and conveying various meanings and full of sweetness and thought. It is by the beauty of such sentences that a king's fame is brightened on all sides. When the energetic Shri Jonaraja and the learned Shrivara saw the *Rajatarangini* written by the Brahmana, Shri Kalhana, they, in order to immortalize themselves, composed two beautiful books of kings, bringing the account down to the year[2] 62. Then the poet Shri Prajyabhatta[3], adorned with every good quality and fortunate in having bathed at the shrine of Bhagavati on the Ganges, composed his 'Rajavalipataka' in the reign of king Phatiha, giving an account down to the year 89. Then the poet did not write the accounts of kings, owing to the tumults in the kingdom and on account of the fear of the wicked and the avaricious, even as swans do not feed on the moss in the Manasa lake for fear of the fowlers. I, Shuka, son of Buddhyashraya, am giving an account of kings in this book from that date. I heard the admirable deeds of fame of past kings who enjoyed great prosperity; and I write this book not because I felt a desire to become a poet, but to lighten my mind of the mass of accounts of by-gone kings of great prosperity about which I had heard. What a difference there is between the description of former poets and of my own, I who am of little sense! How can a fragment of brass be taken for gold simply because of its colour? My account of kings is like a desert, but let good men hear and understand my words, and favour me by showering *amrita* in that desert.

King Phataha[4] was like a sprout of the dynasty of the great king Jainashaha, and he became the ruler of the country of Kashmira. The subjects were happy in every way during the time that he ruled; they were given to pious acts and were graced with the virtues of kindness knd simplicity. The king was not addicted to evil habits regarding women, dice or wine; and his chief minister was Somrarajanaka[5], born of the Lunar dynasty. The other chief minister was the Margesha Ebhrahema. He was pious and intelligent, and was bent on doing good deeds, and was born in the family which had produced men who attained greatness from the time of Sropala.[6] The third minister was the Pratihara Hajyameya of great worth, but he died by the will of the gods, and the king gave his son Malleka Jyangira his ancestral villages and estates, and the usual respects due to him.[7]

## Socio-cultural changes

Surely the Brahmana at this time did not do the duties of their castes, and Somachandra was the person to induce[8] them to disregard the performance of their duties. Merashesha[9], the pupil of Shahkasima, was born in the country of Iraka; he knew all the sciences, and became Somachandra's *guru* without giving him religious instructions. According to Merashesha's advice, Somachandra arrested men belonging to temples, confiscated lands of the Brahmanas and gave them to Merashesha's servants, and thus pleased him. Supha and other followers of Merashesha cut down lofty trees on the pretence that they were required for burning incense, but really for the object of obtaining fuel. The gods then deserted their images, for otherwise how could men plunder their temples? All men became alike through the influence of *Kali*, be they of good or of evil habits, be they the learned or the illiterate, or the actors, or the wicked!

## Zainakadal burnt

Now Abdalaka and the other sons of the Margesha were unable to bear the honour and the fame which the son of Somachandra attained, and the sight of the gifts which he gave away. They intrigued against him and alienated Hosarajana from the Pratihara[10], slighted their father who was related by marriage to Somachandra, and broke down the bridge of Shri Jainalabhadena which had towered high as if it were the accumulation of the virtue of that king. This bridge for crossing the river was named Jainakadala; it had stood over the Vitasta for a long time adorning it, and a vast amount of Rajana Somachandra's riches was spent upon[11] it. It was now burnt at night, together with the houses at Mallekapura near Valladhyamatha[12], in order to overpower the enemies. The town and the Kadala presented the appearance of a forest that was burnt; and the wicked men in their plunder did not spare even people's bathing suits. The heat of the fire lasted for a short time, and so did Somachandra's life. He collected his army and stayed at Jaladramgada.[13] Only one per cent of the Brahmana inhabitants had Brahmana spirit in them, and one such Brahmana chastised the Rajana even as one chastises an enemy. Rajana Somachandra gave up his person as an offering to the fire of the king's wrath and to the flame of the burning town. The king gave him a passport to go out of the country within a few days, and he was on the way destroyed by the curses of the Brahmanas, even as the moon is devoured by Rahu. Malekala, and others, Somachandra's sons, fled in fear from the strifes, and the minister Margesha Ebhrahima performed the last rites of Somachandra by the order of the king, and thus pleased his own men as well as his enemies. The illustrious Margesha gave the extensive estate of Siddhadesha[14] to his eldest son Malleka Piruja, and to Abdalaka he gave the authority over the arsenal, and he divided the other estates and gave them to his other sons, Malleka Luhara, and others. This intriguing Margesha also gave estates to Hosa Rajana, Jyangera the Pratihara[15] and to the Damara[16] who dwelt outside the kingdom.

When the minister Somachandra died and his power became extinct, the indomitable Shingabhatris[17] and the Vyadayis became free from all restraint and began to prowl about. Man holds half of a rope in order to cross a river, but adverse fate breaks his rope. It was to destroy Somachandra that these Damaras, who had been living outside the country, were brought in by the king's orders; and they now rose against the Margesha. The Damaras, the Pratihara and others broke the bridge of boats and caused the Margesha to flee and thus drove him out to a foreign country. The Damaras named Utsa Malleka, Daultaya, and others obtained posts in the palace, even like the black bees in the forest. Then the Damara chiefs held control over all the business in the court, and the strong became weak and the weak became strong. The good behaviour of the Shingas did not appear grateful to the Damara chiefs, even as the light of the earth to owls who are fond of darkness; and the Damaras threw Alemera and others, who were the cause of these troubles, into prison at night out of fear of them. But in a few days, Jyahangera Pratihara and Hossa Rajanaka, rose against the Damaras owing to insults that were offered to them.

## Hossa Malik dies fighting

Now a person named Gadayamera[18] struck Gajakhana and Mallekadatta, all of a sudden, with a dagger in their chest as they were seated in an assembly. When Utsa Malleka heard of this, he departed from the presence of the king, and fought with the enemies for a long time. He was called in by the king and honoured. Loud lamentation, however, rose within the capital on account of the murder of the two persons, and the citizens wept and blamed the king. The powerful warrior Hossa Malleka, the Damara, was in Suyyabhoga[19]; he heard of the death of his kindred but did not lose his coolness. This great warrior who was irresistible in battle, fell fighting with his enemies and joined the women of heaven. Then the skilful, the illustrious Khana Ebhrahima, born of the family of Shahabhadena, and a relative of Jyahangira the Pratihara, divided the estates of the kingdom within five or six days, and distributed them in the presence of the king among Hosa Rajanaka and others accordingly as they deserved. He was afraid of Utsa Malleka, who remained with the king, and he led him to an inaccessible house of the Khashas and there confined him. For a month the Damaras enjoyed wealth as great as that of the city of the Gandharavas, and then, like low people, they fled from the country out of fear of Margesha. The account of the act of enmity against Utsa Malleka reached his brother[20] Ravatradevaka, and he marched out and surrounded the house of the Khashas. The Khashas were alarmed, and they released Utsa Malleka from Gangamatha[21] and the two brothers felt great delight in helping each other. They, however, felt anxious on the approach of the Margesha, and oppressed with the sense of danger, they took shelter of the king, even as those who are oppressed with the powerful rays of the sun take shelter of the strong *kalpa* tree. Thus were the Rajana Damaras destroyed in the year 89, between the bright fortnight of the month of Ashadha and the month of Ashvina.

## Kashmir divided

In autumn, the Margesha crossed the frontier and returned from the outer country. He divided the estates in Kashmira and gave something to all. To his sons he gave the posts of authority in the kingdom, and for a short time he lived in his native country like a hermit free from fear. Now in the year 90, Utsa Malleka and Rajana Shringara caused the house of Abdala[22] Mera to be completely burnt down, with a view to subdue him. When the Margesha heard that his son's house had been burnt and his son captured, he went from Bhangila to Hinduvata[23] by the Kshuyya road. Now when the Margesha had fled, his fierce enemies took Malleka Abdalaka to the inaccessible house of Ladda the Khasha. Utsa Malleka and Rajana Shringara came to the king, and at Varahamula intended to divide the country Kashmira into parts. By the orders of the king they brought the men who owned lands in Siddha[24] country, who knew how to divide land and understood the work, and writers, and Kayathas named Budha[25], Hashmisha, Samkhesha, and Jugaka, and by their help divided the whole country into three divisions. One division was given in writing to Phatahashaha[26], another to Malleka Utsa, and the third to Rajana Shringara. The country was now divided among these three great men, even as it had once been divided among Hushka, Jushka, and Kanishka. Then the Rajarajana Damaras came into the city, but they did not lay aside the deep enmity of the hearts, the enmity such as exists between a mongoose and a serpent.

The king gave Utsa Malleka the post of the chief minister, and to Rajana Shringira he gave the extensive estate of Siddha.[27] When Utsa Malleka, the arbiter of all affairs, took his seat in court, people saw the meeting of a jackal and a sheep of which they had only heard before. When the one whose fleece is shorn and the one who howls met, the king gave his orders under a closed cover in order to see how the meeting would terminate. Then came Ebhrahema Margesha, the chief among the ministers, well dressed but full of animosity, and accompanied by Masoda[28] Shahi. His army arrived at Varahamula, and the king's forces, with Utsa Malleka at their head, entered Svayyapura, with the intention to fight. When king Phatahashaha saw the two armies stationed one on each bank of the river, he thus said to Utsa Malleka, the chief minister, "This Margesha, O! Minister, had robbed us of our Royal Fortune, which is to us even like a wife that is married, because he thinks us to be cowards." When Utsa Malleka heard this, he said to the king: "O King! what mischief is not this Margesha doing, finding me friendless and alone? But O Chief among men! it is but seldom that man sees a Chintamani jewel or a flower that grows in heaven, but one never sees a man to prosper who is consumed by the prowess of a king. Arise O King! and fight; fortune is under the influence of fate."

## Battle of Sopore

When the king's soldiers heard these words they marched out for battle. The Margesha marched along the road with his army and came to Bhavatunga[29] while Utsa Malleka with his forces entered Koshanastsa[30]. There the two armies stayed, but soldiers came out from the main bodies which were stationed on both banks of the river, ascended a hill, posted themselves between the two parties, and discharged showers of arrows against each other. There Shirya, son of the Margesha, fought with the enemies, and sacrificed his life, as if thereby he gave a great offering to Padamanaga. When Shirya Margapati fell, the victor (Utsa Malleka relaxed his exertion out of friendship for the deceased. The great warriors and soldiers of the Margesha observed this relaxation and came up by the Khuyashrama road, and pursued the powerful Utsa Malleka who was retreating. When Phatahashaha heard this news, from Svayyapura he took Rajana Shringara with him and went from Surapura to Hinduvata. Utsa Malleka was hemmed in by the pursuing soldiers of the Margesha at the skirt of the village of Nvova[31], even like a lion hemmed in at the mouth of a cavern.

King Phataha fled, after having ruled the *country for nine* years; and Mahmadashaha, who was supported by the Margesha, then got possession of the kingdom.

In order to please the Margesha he made the powerful Seha Eskandar[32] his heir-apparent, though this person had once attempted to murder the king. The Margapati again placed his enemies in prison; and once more graced his sons with kingly fortune. Utsa Malleka lay in prison, secure in the idea that the Margesha would not kill him, having bestowed his daughter on him, and he being thus related to the Margesha by marriage. But the son of the Margesha was hostile to him, and the powerful Utsa Malleka, whose feet were tied with an iron chain, was foully murdered by the son within five or six days. Like Utsa[33] Malleka, Bhattarjuna had fought in the field with the armed enemies; he was now imprisoned, and was the last of the rebels. A deep gloom, like that when the moon is devoured by the powerful Rahu, spreads even over the face of the sun when men are engaged in mutual hostility. The people loudly lamented for Utsa Malleka as if he were their father. Wicked men walked about at night and began to infest the country, piercing the dense darkness with their eyes. In that year the villagers were doubly unfortunate, the ministers who heard their petitions were both deaf and dumb!

## Fatehshah returns

Mahammada reigned for *nine*[34] *months and nine days*. Once he went out of the capital, when Phatihashaha, on receiving encouragement, came in. The king bestowed the post of the minister on the Pratihara Jyahangira, and he gave the great estate of the Siddha[35] country to Rajana Shringara. He had become king by his own efforts, and he gave Kacha[36] Chakra the authority over the arsenal of his own will. Kacha Chakra was strong, and his prowess was like the rays of the sun. Surely Kacha Malleka was an incarnation of Indra and of Vishnu, since throughout his life he was graced with kingly fortune. The heroic Kanchana was born of the Hosana Chakra who was the cause of the battle in Kramarajya, even as Rama was born of Dasharatha.

## Gangabal pilgrims perish

The king's mind was turned to virtuous deeds owing to return of virtue in the people, or perhaps because the king knew that he was to remain in the kingdom for a short time only. He kept his actions under control, as if he were a servant. He prohibited the execution of the inscriptions on copper plates. He ordered the bones of the Hindus who had been dead to be collected and taken to the Ganges[37], so that the outrages of the mlechhas on them might be prevented. The people had deposited the bones in the Ganges[38] and were returning when they were suddenly overtaken by storm and rain on the way, and they perished to the number of ten thousand. But I think that the river Ganges was oppressed with hunger, and as it was after a long time that she had devoured bones, she surely devoured the men also who had carried the bones. Those who had recourse to their legs escaped with but little of their life left in them; they reached home, but perished through the influence of fate.

In the autumn of the year 91 of the Margapati again came from Vangila accompanied by Mahmadashah. Phatahashaha with his army stationed himself at the village of Vangila and his troops marched out to fight with the powerful enemy. The virtuous[39] son of the Margesha was the leader of the army, and while fighting hotly with the enemy in the field, he joined the company of the women of heaven (died). There exists in this world only one part of virtue, out of four, in the Kali Yuga, but the son of the Margesha had made that virtue four-legged in the shape of the great towers of the Masoda (mosque). Surely Karkotanaga[40] had devoured the Margapati in anger so that the Naga might go from and return to Karkota hill every year without any obstruction. The plans of Abdala Malleka, Luhara, and others, sons of the Margapati were discovered by the king, and they fled[41] to different countries.

## Epidemic

As by chance the hand comes across a hole in a cloth and that which was torn but half a cubit before is enlarged, even so misfortunes come upon sinful people. An epidemic which was as it were the wife of Death broke out on all sides, and it caused sickness, tumults, and destruction of men. The number of the dead could not be counted either in villages or in the capital. Men could hardly get a piece of torn cloth at their last moment. Friends did not weep for friends, what of sorrowing for others? Anxious for themselves, some managed to save their lives, for as yet they were destined to live. Now when the epidemic disappeared from the country, through the influence of fate, men heard the news of Mahmadashah's arrival into Kashmira. Mahmadashaha set out from Noushahara accompanied by Luhara, and obtained a large force from Eskandara, lord of Gaja[42]. He wished to take possession of Kashmira, and he came bringing with him the sons of the Margesha, and reached the country of Rajapuri.

All this the king heard from his spy, and though he was alarmed at this bad news, his former enemies and all the ministers wished for the arrival of Mahmadashaha. Kacha Chakesha and Rajana Shringara went to Surapura with their troops in order to wait for the arrival of the new king. The fate of the reigning sovereign began to waver, and his servant Alemara took refuge with the enemy. This man was of Shahibhanga country, a foreigner, and had no one to help him; in consideration of these circumstances the king had prospered him, even as his son, by giving him villages, gold, and other gifts. Phatihashaha set out from the capital in order to give battle, supported by one minister, the Pratihara Jyahangira. When the army of Phatihashaha was encamped at Kroshanaka[43], the keen-sighted soldiers understood the hostile movements of the enemies, and they went to meet them at Surapura and there to fight with them; but they found there the bed of heroes (died). Phatishaha fell from his horse while watching the battle, but he was protected by the ministers, for he was a king, and out of love which they had previously borne towards him. Thus in the month of Ashvina, in the year 92 the king was deprived of his kingdom after having reigned in it for *one year and one month*. Phatihashaha was then driven by the ministers to the outer country of Lohara across the hills of Chatikashara.

## Victory to Mohammad Shah

The fortunate Mahamadashaha, being victorious, felt greatly elated, and re-entered Kashmira with the army of the lord of Gaja. As the powerful elephants, the gifts of the lord of Gaja, ascended[44] the mountains on the way, they appeared as moving hills to the soldiers. The people's cry of victory for the king was redoubled by the neighing of horses, the grunting of elephants, by the noise caused by the flapping of the elephants' ears, and by the sound of drums. Victory be to the great and the wise king, who is like Balarama[45] renowned for the strength of his arm, the beautiful, the merciful, and graceful as the letters of his name. Glorious on account of his powers, prosperous among his countrymen, possessor of extensive territory, his countenance is like the sun, and who by the administration of justice raised the people of Kashmira, who had before been oppressed by injustice. Let victory always attend Mereja Haidhara Mahammada, who, like

Nausharavana, is wise in speech, and who was born on earth to perpetuate the works of former kings which had for a long time lain in a delapidated condition at Satisara.

## Kacha Chakra survives

The king imprisoned Rajana Shringara, and thought of turning out Abdala Margapti from his post of minister. The powerful Chakresha Kanchana accepted the post of the chief minister, by the orders, though Alemera and others had asked the king for it. Having appointed ministers for the administration of the kingdom the king felt himself free. He divided the people who lived in forests into different sections, and went out of the country. Now Luhara Margapati and Rajana[46] Nosaka, bent on hostile purpose, collected an army and entered Nagramakota[47]. The whole country trembled at this bad news beause the king was absent from the kingdom, men suffered from cold in winter, and the ministers were not known to the people. Not knowing what to do, Chakresha soon brought to his help the great warrior Malleka Jyangira[48] who was honoured by a public proclamation. The powerful Luhara and Noska remained at Nagramakota for a month, and then went one morning in anger to the city of their enemies in order to fight with them. The soldiers of Kacha Chakresha also marched towards their foes, and they fought with one another at Jaladramgada. Luhara Margapati retired after fighting, but Rajana Nosaka sacrificed his life in the battle, and enjoyed the company of the women of heaven. Najoka Margapati and others cut off Kacha Chakresha's fingers, but they perished like insects in the fire. The great warrior Devaravatra[49] was retiring from the field when he was killed by Chakra's soldiers on the banks of the Mari river. Kacha Chakra survived this battle; he was like Kama and Arjuna, and all the people knew him as the saviour of the country. This great hero, this minister Kanchana[50] Chakra, whose fingers were cut off in that battle, looked as beautiful as if he were made of gold.

Now the king satisfied the other kings[51*] (who had helped him to conquer Kashmira) by gifts, and honours, took leave from them, returned to his kingdom, and governed it well. Within a year the Malleka Laddabhatta and other powerful men were thrown into prison by the minister Chakresha; and when the king had them thoroughly brought under control, Kacha Chakra was pleased with Malleka Jyangira and gave his intelligent son Khana Ebrahima the possession of the Siddha[52] country. This was done in the month of Shravana in the year 94.

## Brahmins murdered

Now in times gone by Shiryya,[53] a twice-born, had planted * * as it were the creeper of his Karma. On the approach of winter * * it was watered by the good Brahmana Shri Nirmmalakantha. Then at the time of the *mlechha* oppression, Kanthabhatta and others held a council and were able to avert the disgrace which such oppression begat. Khujyamerahmada, on the other hand, by devoting his life to the service of Kacha Chakra and by giving him wealth, induced him, who was alarmed at the work of Nirmmalakantha and others, to give him permission to act against them; and actuated by the *mlechhas* caused them to be murdered. * * O! Brahmanas, where in this *Kali Yuga* are your Brahmanical spirit and practice? It was for want of these that the sorrowful and the affrighted Nirmmalakantha and others were killed. The oppression of the Mausulas which began in the time of the Saidas was made prominent by Somachandra, and was perfected by Kacha Chakra.

## Fatehshah's death

Now in the month of Shravana, in the year 95, the great king Phatahashaha, the moon among sovereigns, died in a country outside Kashmira. Mahmadashaha did not take his meal on the day on which he heard of this event, nor did he sleep, or bathe, but spent his time in thinking of that king. Where could be found a king like him, experienced, truthful, patient, a great politician, a lover of men of worth, and one who loved his servants? The king was born in a country outside Kashmira, and he died there. The work of fate is extraordinary! The corpse was then placed in a litter and was brought here within a few days, by his servants and chiefs, in order to give it its last funeral rites. The king, attended by his ministers, placed the deceased sovereign in the ample burial ground[54] of king Shri Jainashaha and others, where the crystal gravestones lay like images; and performed the rites befitting a king, and laid the body under the ground. What exertions does not a king make in order to preserve his kingdom; and to root out from it men of violent temper, powerful persons, and wicked servants and to support his own ministers? But, alas! When fate forsakes him, he is overwhelmed by a tempest of misfortune, and is overthrown and like a tree he is tossed about, and he falls. Or, why did this king kill his own ministers Saiphadamara and others, and die surrounded with difficulties? Alas! Alas! The vicissitudes of time!

This is the account of Phatihashaha's going to heaven.

Then came the noble-minded Rajana Shringara, and as if out of affection for the king who had gone to heaven, he followed him. Eskandhara[55] the king of the country outside Kashmira, the lord of Gaja, also went to heaven about this time in order to see Indra. On the death of Phatihashaha, Chakra Nayaka became afraid of Malleka Jyangira, Mera Khujyahmada, and others, of Ebrahema Khana, Shringarabhatta, and others, who were of the party of the late king; they were in the capital; and in the months of Vaishakha, in the year 96, Chakra Nayaka[56] caused them to be arrested. Chakrapati gave Sidha and others districts to the noble minded Rajana Hosana, the favoured of fate; these estates had belonged to the persons who were imprisoned. Unable, however, to brook the prosperity of Hosa Rajanakana, Chakresha, the chief among the intriguers, threw him into prison within three months and became free from fear. He pleased his friends Malleka Chakra, Seranga, Tajemera, and others, and fully gratified them by publishing a proclamation of their dignity in the kingdom.

## Dissension, defeat, death

In the year 97, in the month of Jashtha, Maleka Abdalaka and others sons of the Margesha, joined the people of the country. They took Eskandara Khana, the son of Phatihashaha with them, and came with an army from the country outside Kashmira. They desired the prosperity of the family to which they belonged. But when the powerful Chakresha Kacha heard of their arrival, he took the king with him and went to Laulapurroddara[57], with a view to fight with the Margapatis. The enemies had a small force with them, and when they saw the large army of Chakra, they fled in fear of their lives at the close of the night to the fort of Nagrama which was difficult of access. The army of Chakresha followed the Margapatis. Chakresha stationed many soldiers on the ground attached to the fort, and warriors from both the armies came out and shouted in the field of battle, and covered the earth and sky with the discharge of their arrows. At this time Jyahangira Pratihara entered Lohara with his army and accompanied by Gadayamera and Bahadoramera. When Chakrapati saw the enemy's troops together, and both above and below him, he sent his son Masoda Chakra[58] against Luhara. This heroic Mir Masoda, accompanied by Taja Chakra, arrived at the town of Shahabhadena, with the intention to fight with the enemies. When he came in sight, the soldiers of the other side welcomed him to the field of battle, and they fought with him. The hero Mira Gadaya avoided the arrows discharged by Masodamera, which were like the banners of his kingly fortune; and when the son of Chakra fought like the son of Arjuna there was no bowman among the enemies who could stand firmly on his ground. One named Arjuna Rajanaka then thus addressed the soldiers: "Do not, O! Mighty warriors, flee from the battle overcome by enemies, and leaving aside the virtue of heroes, but march forward in phalanx." The soldiers marched forward and entered the battlefield, even as insects enter the fire. After fighting with these great warriors Masoda was returning with his army when Gadayamera received the love of the women of heaven (died); and when these women saw that Pushpassavaka[59], the son of Chakri, had been made a leader of the army, they soon snatched him up from the field of battle. When the soldiers who had been following him saw their leader killed, they ran towards Masodamera and wounded him with an arrow in his eye. Pierced in the eye by the arrow, Masodamera, the chief among the bowmen, the son of Chakri, was killed, and he fell on the ground, and his soldiers dispersed at his death, even as when the central jewel in a necklace is broken the pearls in it are scattered about. Among the enemies, Hosa Rajanaka, Gajamera[60], and Shringarabhatta were captured in that battle, and were killed by wicked men. The army of the Pratihara was destroyed; it entered the town and stayed there for two days, after which it went out of the country in the same manner as it had come in.

The grief caused by the death of such a heroic son, killed in the battle by the enemies, cast a gloom over the mind of Kacha Chakra. When Taja Chakra and others of his relatives saw their leader thus sorrowful, they asked him not to be dejected. Kacha Chakra was not quite overcome with grief for his son, and he issued orders to fight with the army of the Margesha stationed in the fort[61] on the opposite bank of the river. The soldiers of Kacha

Chakra were eager to fight with those of the enemies, but the people of the village in their sorrow did not know how to act. The valour of the Margesha was well-known; but when they saw that the strength of Chakresha was directed against them, they retreated with the Khana. When the army had gone away in the manner it had come, the victorious Chakresha, accompanied by the king, but oppressed with sorrow, entered the capital. This powerful minister saw the hero Daulata, patient, possessed of worth, and foremost among warriors, and he felt no fear, but gave him, who was his brother's son and who was skilful in wielding the bow, all his deceased son's villages and estates.

Now in the year 98, the Margapati took the prince Habheba[62] Khana with them and again came from the Chatikasara hill. By the time they had stationed their forces at Tamasimarugasthana[63], the soldiers of Malleka Kacha Chakra entered Sandapura[64]. As the Margapatis had but a handful of soliders, and as they had once experienced the valour of the Chakris, they did not descend from the mountain road into any village. The soldiers of the Margapatis were less in number than those of Chakesha, and from among them again Eda Rajana, son of Somaraja, came out and took shelter with the army of Chakri. The Margapatis very much felt this treachery of their friend when they came to hear of it, and they cast aside the evil[65] spirit of a hope and returned by the same mountain road. Their army divided itself into hundred different parts at the hill named Mitradroha (treachery of friends), and united itself again at Vahyapalvala[66] and thence it went away. Habhebha Khana was taken ill and died in the way. His followers placed the corpse in a litter and brought it to Kashmira. Last rites were given to it on the burial ground and the noble-minded ministers placed the body in a hollow in the ground by the side of his father.

## Matrimonial alliances

The enemies who could not have been driven away by means of arms, were thus, on the advent of Kacha Chakra's good fortune, expelled by means of finger nails. Malleka Jyangera, who was to the family of the Pratihara as the moon is to the sea, perished by fire in a country outside Kashmira. Chakri then brought the Margapatis Abdala, Luhara and others into the country, and they came for the purpose of forming a marriage alliance. For instance, the Margapati Luhara gave his daughter to Malleka

Kacha Chakra, as if Sachi was given to Indra. Chakresha gave his daughter to Malleka Abdala, but the father lost his affection for his daughter shortly after the marriage. Taja Chakra then married the daughter of Margapati Abdala, as if kandarpa married Rati. Kanchan Chakra raised the dignity of the Margapatis by frequently issuing proclamations in the kingdom regarding them, and by giving them large gifts, and bestowing honour on them; and love between the Margesha and the Chakris became stronger every day. But, impelled by fate, that love was banished by a friend named Riga Chakra.

It was at this time that King Ebhrahema of Hastinapuri[67] was overthrown by Babhora of Kambboja, the king of the Yavanas; but the expectations of the heroic followers of the lord of Gaja, who was besmeared with dust of battle, were never fulfilled.

The harmony that had existed between the family of the Margesha and that of Chakresha was destroyed by Riga Chakra and Alimera who were tale-bearers; even as a lamp supplied with oil is quenched by water. Chakra's mind was inflamed with anger, but it was cooled by the arrest of Riga Chakra, even as fire is quenched by water.

In the year 3, the Margapatis, their affection now alienated from the Chakris and themselves, encouraged by Alemara, encamped at Chiroddara.[68] When the king learnt what the Margesha had done, he consulted Chakrapati and placed his own troops at Jaladramgada with the view to fight with the enemies. The soldiers of the Margeshas were determined to fight, and were not to be brought over by reconciliation, gift, or by any other means, nor could they be brought back from the position they had taken by any person in the army of Chakri. Chakresha fought with them at Shalasthala[69], Palada, and in other places, and for a hundred days he remained without any fear. But one night the king issued from the army of Chakri and went to Yatikatala[70] in Lahara, and Kacha Chakra left Kashmira in fear. This dispute between the Margapatis and Chakresha was like a desert tract in which the wise Alemara caused flowers and young plants to grow. When the angry minister Chakresha had gone to Hinduvata[71], the king reigned in the country surrounded by the Margapati ministers. Chakresha had his army with him, and like Shri Jainashaha, he exacted tribute from petty chiefs with tact. His heroic brothers,

Taja Chakra and others, killed the Muggulas in a fight at Lohara[72] and in other places and performed deed, befitting their youth. Chakresha believed that all this was the effect of the intrigue of the heir-apparent, and like a huge serpent he surrounded Eskandhara on all sides. When the king saw Chakrapati's boldness, he caused him to be brought into Kashmira in the summer of the year 4.

## Sikandar blinded

It is well known in the world that the father, the brother, or the son of a king is his enemy, on account of his desire to take possession of the kingdom. Other enemies can do nothing worse. The Margapatis who knew of this danger of kings went with their army to the country outside Kashmira by the Kichasrama[73] road. But when Chakrapati arrived, bringing with him Eskandara[74] Kfaana who was like a hawk among his enemies, the king became glad, for he thought that his kingdom had now become free from danger. Eskandara was not destined to see the world again: he was carried into the palace by the servants of the king and his lotus-like eyes were put out. Cruel men extracted the eyes of the prince, by the order of the king, even as the hawks do of the deer. And even as the cranes behave towards the deer so did they behave towards the prince. The pain which he then felt could not be described; but the curse of the prince's parents, or it may be of the prince himself, was realized on the relentless servants of the king who had acted with great cruelty towards the prince.

Chakresha knew that the Margapatis were stationed at Kirtyashrama, he therefore went from Varahamula and entered Shrinagara. He then crossed the river, and the two armies met, as if to see who gains and who loses the battle in which many men perished. Malleka Daulata, son of Chakri's brother, arrived at night after crossing the hill, and drove out the chief of the Margapatis from the country. Meya Mera, the chief of the Margapatis, was unable to travel by the road, and some armed soldiers perished in the way. Thus when the Margapatis had fled in fear, and were perishing, Mahammada Shaha, surrounded by the Chakris, went into the city.

A foolish man feels happy when his enemy is destroyed, even like a fire that is quenched; but it sometimes happens that a great fire bursts out from his house. King Mahammada Shaha was to be deprived of his kingdom by his own son! O strange are the works of fate!

## Mohd. Shah dethroned

The king had placed his son Ebrahima Khana as a hostage in the house of the lord of Gaja.[75] But there scattered by the tempest of a battle with the Turshukas, the soldiers of the prince escaped with their valuable lives, as by a boat in a sea. It was because the prince was destined to obtain a kingdom hereafter, that he escaped with his life from that battle. He grew in the affection of his father and came to Kashmira. In the meantime Chakrapati intended to usurp the kingdom, and his evil design afflicted the king even like cholera; and as a physician treats a difficult disease by strong measures, even so Chakrapati in anger cast the king's confidential persons Malleka Laddabhatta and others into prison. Now Alimera had been confined in the house of Taja Chakra; but one night Alimer's followers deceived the guards, took him out of the prison, and removed him to a distance. Chakra became angry with Mahammada Shaha on account of his ill-behaviour and harsh and abusive language and set him aside in a few days, even as Rahu obscures the moon during eclipse. Thus was king Mahammada dethroned after reigning in Kashmira for *eleven years ten months, and ten days.* The pain which the Khana had endured on his being blinded was now borne by the king on his being deposed. Virtue bears fruit in time, but the effect of plucking out the prince's eyes was seen without delay. Chakri then sent the king to a place named Gaggoda[76] in the country of the Khashas and kept him in the custody of his trusted but stern guards under Nyayka Suyya.

Thus the dethronemet of Mahammada Shah took place.

## References

1. Buddhyashraya: Shuka's father.
2. Year 62 or 4562 of the Kashmiri calender corresponding to 1486 A.D. 4589: A.D. 1513.
3. Prajyabhatta, it appears, feared persecution from people in power for recording events as he saw them. Jona. and Srv. obviously lived in more liberal times.
4. Phataha: Fatehshah.
5. Somarajanaka: Mossarajanakachandra (SK). Mosa Raina of the Persian chroniclers and, pb. a descendant of the Chandra clan of Lar.
6. *Sropala: Asropala* (SK) pb. meaning 'in abundance', not a name.
7. (Omitted in the translation): 'Rajanaka Shringara, well-trained in diplomacy, became, along with his brother, a favourite of Mosachandra. His son was for friends as life-giving rain to fields

and for foes he was like famine. Seekers found him warm like the sun. By nature the Margapati would tilt himself to one side or the other like the beam of a balance. But he was a steady friend of Mosachandra.'

8. Obviously a circuitous euphemism.
9. Merashesha: Mir Shamsha who came from Iraq (SK): Mir Shamas-ud-Din Iraqi under whose influence Mossarajanaka or Mosa Raina adopted the Shia faith.... *Kali*: the Iron age.
10. Pratihara: Jahangir Malik, son of Haji Mir. Should read '...alienated ... from the Pratihara, and the Chaks, slighted .....'
11. Spent: the chief minister had pb. repaired and improveed it.
12. Mallekpura near Valladhaymatha : Balladhyamatha has been placed near Nawakadal, right, by Stein, but the present context points to its location near Mallekpura in the Zainakadal-Maharajganj area.... bathing suits: the traditional bathing suit was not much more than a fig-leaf.
13. Jaldramgada: Zaldagar. literally a small place girdled with water.
14. *siddhadesha*: issued orders that control over the arms and ammunition, etc., be given to his eldest son...
15. Pratihara: Malik Jahangir, J- Padar of the Persian chroniclers.
16. Damara: pb. Saif-ud-Din; Utsa Malleka, Daulatya: Utsa Malik, Daulat (SK), Malik Usman and Datti Malik (PH). Margesha also gave permission to Hosa Rajana, Jahangira Pratihara, the Chaks and the Damara, who dwelt outside the kingdom to stay in the country.
17. 'When the minister died... the indomitable people of Shinga (Chingas) with golden (dark brown) hair prepared to rise up in arms.' Chingas is on the western slope of the Pir Panchal. The entrails of Jahangir, the Moghul king who died on his way back from Kashmir to Delhi, were interned here.
18. Gadayamera...: pb. the same as Gadaya Ravatra (Rather), Ghazi Khan and Datti Malik.
19. Suyyabhoga: Soyabug, a village a short distance to the west of Sgr.
20. brother: foster-brother Ravatradevara. Utsa was the son-in-law of the Margesha.
21. Gangamatha: Pb, Gangabug now Sharifabad, on the outskirts of Sgr. Gangapora, Badgam t. is another alternative.
22. Abdala Mera or Abdallaka was the son of Ibrahim Margesha.
23. Hinduvata: see n. 16, p. 93. .. Kshuyya road, *i.e.*, Khoyahom on the northern bank of the Wular where Jalala Thakur was living. Rajan Shringara is named as Shangi Raina in Persian chronicles.
24. Siddha country: not a place name... 'Under orders of the king they brought the men who owned lands and knew...'
25. Budhaka, Ashvisha and Jugaka (SK).

26. Phatashaha: the reigning king....Vushkor (Baramula left), Zukura (near Nasimbag) and Kanispora are named after the three Kushana kings respectively.
27. Siddha: '..Vast powers were given to R. Shringhara....'
28. Masodshahi: should be Mohammadshah.
29. Bhavatunga: obviously Botuing near Sopore.
30. Koshanastsa: Keshanastsa (SK) could pb. be: Kunas, No. 56. Bandipura. Padmanag is, of course the Wular lake. Shiryya: Ali Sher.
31. Nyova: Nyuv is a v, in Pulvama t. Pb. Utsa reached there in his flight towards Herapur.
32. Seha Eskandar: son of the king's cousin, the daughter of Haidershah, who was earlier C-in-C of the forces... A son of Fatehshah bore a similar name. (p. 274)
33. 'Like... Bhattarjuna ....armed enemies; he was now imprisoned by Shamschakri, and his armed companions were fought with. He was rebels.'
34. nine months: five months only (PH).
35. Siddha country: under orders of the king a high office was bestowed on Rajana Shringara.
36. Kacha Chaka/Kanchana Chakresha: Kaji Chak of the Persian writers.
37. Ganges: Gangabal Lake in the lap of the Harmukh mtn. The Hindus immerse the bones of the deceased in the lake on the bright eighth of Bahadun. It appears they had not done so for several years because of disturbances.
38. Storm: According to PH the pilgrims were misled down a crag by a goblin and died. This is confirmed by the chronogram: *gole gufta tabahi panditan.*
39. Virtuous son: pb. Malik Feroze who built a mosque with four towers.
40. Karkotanaga: one of the several mtn. tarns in Bhangitgil. supposed to be the abode of Karkotnaga. Kakodar in the pga. is named after it. It is mentioned in the *Nil-n* and is different from the Karkota Naga in Uttarasu.
41. Fled: pb. Magrey with his sons Feroze and Abdai died at Bhangila (PH).
42. Lord of Gaja: Sikander Lodhi of Delhi (1488-1518).
43. Kroshanaka: Troshana : (SK) Harshana (PH), pb. Tranj in Shopayan Tehsil. A village named Tranj exists in Bhimber also (Ref. 169/42). PH states that the two armies met in Bhangila.
44. '....ascended the Kalidhara mtns...' near Bhimber. The name Kalidhara applies to the mtn. as also to the river nearby (ref. p. 227).
45. Balarama.... this and the next three verses are not in the text edited by SK.

46. Rajan Nosaka: Nusrat Raina (PH).
47. Nagramakota: the fortress at Nagam in Chadura Tehsil.
48. Jyhangira: Jahangir Pratihara (Padar).
49. Devaravatra: also mentioned as Ravatradevaka.
50. Gold: pun on the word *Kanchana* meaning 'gold'.
51. kings: the Lodhis of Delhi.
52. Siddha.... was invested with authority under orders of Kaji Chak.
53. Shiryya: Shri Bhat, who persuaded Z. to improve the lot of the Brahmins of Kashmir, '....planted good deeds....*karma* and watered it with nectar. The Persian work *Baharistani Shahi* provides further information on the topic. It states that when Musa Raina was in power, all the 'depraved heretics' in Kashmir had been converted to Islam. But sometime later reports prejudicial to the 'infidels and pluralists' were made to Mir Shamsuddin Iraqi who desired Malik Kaji Chak to take disciplinary action against the community of the idolators according to the provisions of the *sharai*. During *Ashure* in H. 924 (SS 4594 or A.D. 1518) seven to eight hundred 'infidels' were accordingly put to death. This is one of the major achievements of Malik Kaji Chak, concludes the author.
54. burial ground: Fatehshah was buried at Sa'hyar, Sgr. close by the grave of his father Adam Khan (PH).
55. Eskandara: The Lodhi king of Delhi.
56. Chakra Nayaka: Chak leaders.
57. Laulapuroddara: the upland of *Laulapur* or Lalpur, near Beeru. Some, however, believe it to be Lalgam near the airport.
58. Masoda Chakra: son of Kaji Chak, also mentioned as Masodamera.... town of Shahab-ud-Dina: Shadipur.
59. Pushpassayaka: love-god son of Chakri: *svasreye*, sister's son, named Dattanayaka.
60. Gajemera: Ghazi Mir Chak.... Pratihara : Jahangir.
61. fort: pb. the fort at Nagam.
62. Prince Habhebha Khana: son of Fateh Khan.
63. Tamasimarugasthana: pb. Tosamaidan on the incline of the P-P range.
64. Sandapura has phonetical resemblance to Sandha Sharmal v. in Shopian. Another Sundipora is near Badgam.
65. the evil spirit: halucination.
66. Vahyapalvala: 'the spring of Balpalvala'. Because of the treachey of friends they divided their army into a hundred parts near a hill and re-united further
67. Ibrahima...: Ibrahim Lodhi of Delhi. Babhora of Kambhoja: Babar of Kabul.
68. Chiroddara: Tseravudor, now Jwalapur near Badgam (PH).... year 3: 4603 or A.D. 1527.

69. Shalasthala: Halathal in Yechh pga. Palada: Palar near Badgam.
70. Yatika: identity uncertain. The original is *Yatika talam*, with the First 't' as in 'two.' A suggestion has been made that the original is '*vatika talam* in Lahara' meaning the sylvan surroundings or groves of Lar.
71. Hinduvata (outside Kashmir): Sindhuvata. Ref. n. 23 above.
72. Lohara: Some Mughals entered the Poonch-Rajauri area with their troops but were stopped by Kashmiris at Naushehra.
73. Kichashrama: Kitsahom, 6 km. below Baramulla. See also p. 291.
74. Eskandhar Khana: obviously the heir-apparent who was the king's cousin. He died in prison soon after he was blinded. (PH).
75. Lord of Gaja: the king of Delhi.
76. Gaggoda: Lud (PH), a stronghold amidst hills.

Shuka Pandit's

*Rajatarangini*

# Chapter II
# Mirza Haider's Invasion

I bow to Mahadeva who is the cause of the creation, the preservation and the destruction of the universe; who is the bridge by which to cross over our sea-like worldly existence; and who is in himself Brahma, Vishnu and Rudra.

## Ibrahim Shah

Kanchana Chakra then raised the son of Mahammada to the kingdom, and named him Ebrahim Shaha. He took possession of the money derived from taxes, and with it he undertook to manage the kingdom. He gave the estates of Nagrama and others, which were worthy of kings, to Taja Chakresha, Meyya Mera, and to his other younger brothers.

## Babar assists Margesha

Now in the country outside Kashmira, the angry Margesha Abdala went in search of service to Merja Babhora, king of Dilli and the chief of the Muggulas. This king of the Turushkas observed the external and the mental emotions of the Margapati, heard what he had to say of his work, and for a short time held down his head in wonder. He understood the worth of that chief minister, and gave him one thousand valiant soldiers. In the month of Vaishakha, Chakrapati, who shone in his own valour, heard of this news which had spread itself in the country of Panchamahayana[1]. The Chakris were in enjoyment of the pleasures of heaven on earth when the great Margapati warriors Malleka Abdala, Margesha Luhara, and others crossed the mountains, and soon came within Kashmira from Bangela, accompanied by the Muggulas Shikhala[2] Bhega, Mahmoda Khana, and others. They united themselves together, placed Najoka[3] son of Phataha Shaha at their head, and halted in the desert of Pratapapura[4] well prepared for battle. When Chakrapati heard of this, he stationed his soldiers at Nilashva[5], and the warriors came out' from the two armies and displayed their devotion to their masters. As birds spread themselves over the sky, even so did the enemies and the *mlechha* soldiers cover all sides, so that Chakrapati, though supported by his army, could not move a step. At this time a messenger arrived and conveyed the following message of the Margesha to Chakrapati: O Chakrapati! I have for my help brought in these followers of king Meraja Vabhora who by his own valour has made the petty kings in foreign countries his tributaries, and who has killed the illustrious and powerful Ebrahim, the lord of Gaja, surrounded as he was by five hundred thousand soldiers; now gather up your strength for battle". When the letter-carrier had thus said, Chakresha replied as follows: "Dilli[6] is not your country neither are we the inhabitants of Kashmira. You will derive no benefit from the country of the powerful Muggulas."

## Death of Taja Chakra

Now the heroes and the strong and powerful men who wielded bows, Ebhrahima Khana, Seranga[7] Mera, Malleka Tajaka, as also Malleka Luhara and others on the side of the Margesha; and Riga Chakresha Malleka, and the *mlechhas* Shikhi Bhiga, and others were determined to show how the battle of the Kuru-Pandvas was fought. The heroes proud of the strength of their arm issued out for battle. The great warrior Riga Chakresha hurled a spear against the enemies but it was broken by Taja Mera, a man of uncommon prowess. Mera Seranga struck with his sword, but his enemy Luhara Mera felt it as it were a blow caused by a flower. Thus the great warriors fought with one another in this great battle; they filled all sides with valour even as musk does with sweat scent. At this time Taja Chakresha with his soldiers joined the battle, his banner fluttering in the breeze as if challenging the enemies. The battle between the armies of Chakresha and the Margesha raged round him, and as the combatants fell, there arose the cries of "come", "kill", "stay". When Margapati Luhara saw Taja Chakra in the midst of the battle, he came up to him and said: "Fight on, what else can you do, what else can man do than serve his master?" When Malleka Taja heard this, he fought with the heroes for a long time, and then lay on a hero's bed graced by the women of heaven. When his career had ended, Meyya Malleka, Seranga Mera, and other brothers of Chakri joined the Muggulas. Chakresha saw the destruction of his army and, overcome with fear and grief, he went to the house of a Khasha with a few soldiers.

## Nazukshah enthroned

The Margapatis, Malleka Abdala and others, gave assurance of safety to the people who were overcome with fear, and entered the city. All the Margapatis then went to the yard of the king's palace, and there they bestowed the royal insignia adorned with umbrella and *chamara* on prince Najoka Shaha. He then ascended the throne of his father, and all the people, high and low, were filled with joy. The ministers then went to Jamala[8] Maruga, and at that place a division of land into four parts was made, one for Malleka Abdalaka, one for Alemera, one for Margesha Luhara, and one for Riga Chakra.

## Battle of the Vitasta

When the kingdom was given to Najoka Khana, Dauluta Chakkaka could not enjoy it, because he assigned it to another. When the people, who used to tremble at the *mlechhas*, saw this new king begin his reign they were as glad as those who trembled in winter are always at the advent of spring. The people began to prosper when Najoka Khana accepted the kingdom, even like the lotuses at the rising of the sun. Those who were quarrelling with one another were reconciled; but on account of the division of villages enmity began to grow slowly among them. Ederaina and other servants of Merja Haidera[9] remained at Sadashivapura[10] because of their quarrel with the Chakra clan. Chakkaka Dauluta and others arrived at the banks of the Vitasta and remained at Samudramatha[11], and thence fought with their enemies by means of firearms[12]. After fighting for a month with firearms and arrows, the party of Dauluta Chakra obtained the victory.

## Release of Mohammadshah

Then the great men of the country sent a messenger who verbally delivered to Chakrapati, who was in the house of the Khashas[13], the following message of the Margesha: "O Chakrapati! It was by wicked ministers like you that the devotion due from the ministers to the king was withheld, even as the moonbeam is by a choud. The ministers used to wait with clasped hands before the boy king during his reign in accordance with the duties they owed to government; but why has that been imprisoned by you? What fool can by a pitcher shade the sun?" When Chakrapati heard these words from the mouth of the messenger, he released the king. Mohammada Shaha then came to Lohara and exacted revenues and other taxes from towns like the former sovereigns of the country. This wise king then consulted the Margesha and gave leave to the Mugulas to depart. He honoured the Margapatis and gave them their posts. The Turushkas passed over Lohara and reached their homes; and Alimera received Mahammada Shaha, his old master. Here the Mera passed the winter, and then, as advised by the Margesha, he took the king, who was like the season of spring, to the gardens of Kashmira. Najoka *after having reigned for one year*, received from king Mahammada Shaha the post of heir-apparent, in the month of Jaishtha, on the tenth day of the bright moon. It was in the summer of the year that Mahammada Shaha was released from the house of the Khashas, and was congratulated as being born again, and was crowned by the ministers. At this time Meraja Vabhora[14] went to heaven, leaving his possession to his two sons Homaya and Kamarana.

## Mughals invade Kashmir

In the year 7 Kacha Chakrapati intended to fight with Margapatis and he moved out with his army from the village of Maurvvara to a distant place: and a comet appeared on the west, when he had departed, as if the west had been his wife and had held the comet on her head in anger on being deprived of her love. Mahroma, the general of Kamarana, came in the bright fortnight of the month of the Karittika, to conquer Kashmira. He was accompanied by Shikhala Bhiga, Mahmoda Khana and other Muggulas; and they filled all sides with their strong and thundering army. When Mahammada Shaha heard of this, he, by means of the Margapatis, soon called in Chakrapati with proclamation for his help, and honoured him. The *mlechhas* entered the city with thousands of cavalry, and the Kashmirians placed their soldiers within forts. The citizens went out by different ways to the caverns of mountains in fear, and as the *mlechha* soldiers outnumbered the Kashmirian warriors, the latter were destroyed. The Muggulas who had plundered Kuduadina[15] found the beautiful capital empty, and in anger set fire to the houses and the palace. The warriors now came out of their forts with a view to fight with the Turushkas, and they willingly sold their lives, and they all obtained fame. The cruel Turushkas, the destroyers of the Juluchyas[16], killed thousands of people in villages, in the capital and in the kingdom. Then the Kashmirian warriors–the Margesha and the Chakris–made peace[17] among themselves, and drove the Turushkas away, even as the sun's rays drive away darkness.

Thus the ravages of the Turushkas took place.

The warriors now relieved of their desperate task lived in their own homes. Kacha Chakra was afraid of the coldness shown by the Margesha towards him, and he went out of the country. He came again from Shurapura, in the summer of the year, but finding that his force would meet with resistance, he went out in the same manner as he had come.

## Mirza Haider's invasion

In the month of Agrahayana in autumn, Mereja Haidara and other leaders of Kaskara[18] troops of King Shri Saida Khana, came to this country with twelve thousand cavalry in order to subdue the people of Kashmira, even as the hawk comes to prey upon other birds. They came from Kota to Gagana hill,[19] and thence they entered the capital. The good people were distressed when they heard of this news; they considered the ravages of the Kaskaras as being of greater magnitude than those of the Turushkas, even as the eclipse of the sun is than that of the moon. All living creatures left the place, and the rows of houses looked like heaps of corpses, breathless and frightful; and these incendiaries conquered the town of Sekandhara[20] in order to burn it. Hundreds of thousands of low houses were burnt, and the city that had been populous before now became like the ground for burning the dead, fearful to look at with its charred wood. Where will kings get two such capitals in which millions had been spent in lime[21], wood, brick, and painting? Shri Jainanagara and Diddamatha, which had stood like images of the virtues of kings, were deserted on account of fire. Surely the Muggulas[22] had evil sprites under their command, for they discovered the hidden treasures of the citizens in their houses.

## Houses burnt

The leader of the Kashmirian army took shelter in the king's lands which were covered with water[23], in fear of the *mlechhas*.

When the people of Chiroddara[24], Angakotta, and Chakradhara[25] in Hajya country heard of the acts of the *mlechhas*, they spent three months in fighting with them. The Khasha Dainyarupa fought like demons with the Kashmirians who were stationed near Chakradhara hut without any effect. The Turushkas robbed the crops, killed the villagers in anger, and made Madavaraja unapproachable. Those persons, young and old, who reached the level tract of Khuyashrama, lived at ease, for they had yet a portion of their destined life to spend. It was owing to the evil deeds of sinful men that calamities had before now visited this country, such as the ravages of the Juluchyas, and the battle of Kajjala.

The Margapatis headed by Chakesha joined the king, they came from Chakradhara, crossed over from the left side of the Ledari, and pitched their tents near Bhimadevi[26], with a view to fight. In the battle which there took place Eskandara[27] Khan a, Merja Haidara, and other great warriors united themselves together and went against the Kashmirians; and Mallekalaka, Hosana Mera, Shikhala, and Kamala Mera, in the two armies sacrificed their lives at the foot of Marttanda. Some Kaskarian warriors made a good use of their lives in the contest with Mallekala and others and went to heaven. Alimera perished in the battle with the Muggula chiefs, in the cause of the country. O fools! look at that death and ever serve your king, and leave aside all fleeting riches of the world. The Kashmirian soldiers fled like Vidura when Alimera died, though cheered by Chakresha and the Margapati chiefs. The headless dancing goblins, the Yakshas, men, sprites, and Rakshasas were eager to devour human flesh in this field of battle, which looked like a palace crowded with the followers of a bridegroom. The survivors returned to their places of shelter from the field of battle where men had been drunk, as in a garden, with warriors' wine. Then in accordance with the orders of the king, Chakresha and the Margesha, great on account of their valour, held a consultation, and established peace with the Mugulas.

## Truce effected

The Muggulas took nine[28] pieces of cloth, and a green coloured letter marked with the words '*Katephasohasaglata*' in Mausula character and language. They returned from the presence of the king, exulting with joy; they carried some idiotic men and woman in the van of their army, but Hassana Mera took pity on the idiots, released them, and brought them back to the neighbourhood of Pushyat. Then in the year 9, in the month of Jyeshtha[29], the Muggulas returned to their country, taking with them by force the wealth of the people, and by treaty the daughter of the king. In this way calamity befell the sinful people in the Satisara country, and a comet was seen continually in the sky on the east and on the west.

Thus the ravages of the Kaskarians took place.

## Famine

Stars fell from the sky on the fields where the full harvest of rice was ripening, and a comet became again visible. Even as a Rakshasa devours a king so did this calamity devour the grains; and there occurred a great famine, the destroyer of food. When Famine entered the kingdom, his powerful soldiers, hunger and thirst, the oppressors of the people, stalked about. One *khari* of grain was then bought for ten thousand pieces of *nishka*,[30] and none but the rich could get it. Men and women wandered about in hunger in order to save their lives, casting aside their love for husband, for son, and the service due towards their parents. The hungry people ate twice or thrice or four times during day, and yet again wandered about like sprites in quest of food. Abdala Malleka and others were bent on doing acts of virtue at this time: they cooked a large quantity of grain and fed the people every day.

Men died of hunger and thirst in villages, in the city, and in the king's highway, and lay like sprites, and uncounted. Some people saved their lives by selling their stores of silver and base metals, and by living on herbs, walnuts, and heart-peas. The calamity caused by the famine was greater than the ravages done by the enemies, even as a bad boil is more troublesome than the disease of the throat or of the eye. The famine became more severe at the end of the month of Jyeshtha, in the year 10, than what it had been in the year 9, and spread itself all over the country. Then a good season, like the minister of King Food, brightened all sides with small seed as with lamps, and came to struggle with Famine. As wheat grew on stalks and rose from the ground, and looked like a terrace, its grains welcomed, as it were, the survivors. It seemed as if when King Food saw his army overpowered, he came himself to conquer the powerful famine which was like a mighty Rakshasa. He spread out his great army of vegetables and rice and coarse grain, and the walnuts were the stones he shot from his machines. He conquered Famine, and then took his rest. The lean creatures were nourished by the produce of King Food, and they always thought that they were born again.

Thus took place the ravages of the famine.

Now Kanchana Chakresha, by the orders of the Margapati, graced the place of minister before the king, and stayed at Jainapura. Called by the *chandalas*, Chakresha went to Madavarajya, but there he experienced indifference from the Margapatis and he imposed a fine on the land. All this time the men who lived at ease in their houses grievously oppressed this great country, even as a vile disease oppresses the body. It was owing to the sin of these oppressions and through the force of fate that the king Mahammada Shaha fell ill in the later part of Chaitra in the year 13. When the king found himself attacked by illness, and exhausted, he thus said affectionately to his minister Malleka Laddabhatta: "Though our body is nourished according as we acquire virtue or vice from the performance of our kingly duties, yet it is universally true that the body is subject to destruction. Our ancestors, Kings Shamsadena and others, and Shri Jainollabhadena were great in our family, and I am born in their dynasty. My mind had always been anxious to know who would be obedient to me and to what extent; and today that mind is being consumed by fever."

## Death of Mohammadshah

When the king had said this and remained quiet, Margesha Abdala and others who were present saw his condition, and with tears in their eyes, thus spoke to him: "It was owing to oppression caused by us O king! or owing to the misfortune of the subjects, that you are afflicted with this bodily torment, even as the soul is afflicted for the sin of being born." When the king heard their words he said: "You should always protect our children, we are now going by a road which is remote from here." When the men heard these words of the king, there arose cries of lamentation in the palace. That day the king gave one *koti* of coins to be spent for religious purposes, for when the month of spring had arrived, the liberal-minded king, oppressed with pain, believed that he would die in a dark fortnight[31]. On Thursday, the first of the month of Jyaishtha, in the bright fortnight, this virtuous sun among men set after having reigned a second time *for five years*.

When the king had ascended to heaven, the people lamented for him, and thus said in their grief "Whose protection should we now seek when thou hast gone to heaven? O! Beautiful like the moon, and powerful like Karttikeya! O King! without thee who shall protect us in our times of difficulty? Where wilt thou go, O King Mahammada! leaving this earth." Thus loudly the people lamented as they stood at the gate of the palace and it seemed as if the tears from their eyes served the last offering of water to the deceased sovereign. The ministers then placed the corpse in a litter, and bore it on their shoulders to the great grave-yard, and laid it within the ground beside his father. What a difference there is between a king lying on his bed soft as the moon and befitting a sovereign and one lying in deep darkness within a hole in a gravely ground? That day the people remained dumb with grief, and their sighs only were perceptible. No smoke was seen rising from their houses, for they did not cook their food that day.

Thus Mahammada Shaha ascended to heaven.

Mahammada Shaha's son whom the Margesha wished to have as king, was, in the midst of applause of all, crowned by the minister under the name of *Sharnsa* Shaha[32]. All the wicked and powerful favourites of the late king were glad to see a young sovereign begin a new reign. Sharnsa Shaha arrived at the palace, accompanied by his younger brother, and heard the blessings of the people on the way saying: "Let him remain long in his ancestral kingdom." After the king had seated himself firmly in the kingdom, the powerful Kacha Chakrapati to whom Riga Chakra had held out some hopes, came to the city from Jainapura. When Margesha Hossana saw that hero come, he joined Utsabhatta and went to the Margapati at Kichashrama. Kacha Chakra, the destroyer of his enemies, entered the beautiful city, and he was honoured by the king with his affection. Kanchana Chakresha knew that his enemies were at a distance, and in order to subdue them he encamped with his army at Gardhasoddara[33]. When the Margapatis heard that their powerful enemy lay very near to them, they soon placed their troops in the neighbourhood of Jalagada. Then the noble minded Riga Chakresha went to Kacha Chakra and to the chief of the Margapatis, and by despatching messengers tried to establish peace between the parties. "Let Kacha Chakresha" he said "remain in the city, and the Margapatis in Kramrajya, and I am inclined to both." Thus he established peace between them.

Then the hero Kacha Chakresha brought over to him his friends Zaita Chakresha, *Mallaka* Dauluta, and Ebrahma Khana from among the army of the Margapatis, and triumphantly went up to the city, and lived in the house of Riga Chakra. In the illustrious Kanchana Chakrapati his name has its full significance, on account of the gifts[34] of gold that he gave; we have actually seen the marks of petals of a lotus in the palm of your hand which indicate your charity. Let your left hand continue to do good to others for a thousand years! O chief of the Margapatis! the king of the seasons (spring) has seen your white fame, and with a view to serve you in every way, has joined the lord of the zodiac (sun) celebrating your triumph with garlands of jasmine and *manjhari* flowers, and of the karnikara buds; and with the hum of the black bees and the voice of *kokilas*. All are happy at every act of yours. Let the season of spring afford you objects pleasant to you!

So long as Kacha Chakra, the arbiter in all things, remained with the king, the strength of the powerful was, owing to his prowess, found in the weak. Riga Chakra came and spent a few days with him; but finding that Kacha Chakra loved him but slightly, he returned. He went to the Margesha whom he knew to be like a strong malady to Kacha Chakra, and told him of the purposes of Chakresha; and he brought together the officers of the king's vanguard and consulted with them. There were celebrated ministers in the land of Kashmira, *Malleka* Shri Dauluta, Gaja Khana, Chakresha, and others. They were wise in council, and were like Bhima, Arjuna, and Drona in the field of battle.

## References

1. Panchmahayana: Panjab.
2. Shikhala Bhega: According to HP one Sheikh Ali Beg was killed in a confrontation with the Kashmiris at Naushehra during the reign of

Mohamadshah. He mentions the arrival of another commandant of the same name at the head of 20,000 Mughals.

3. Najoka: Nazukshah.
4. Pratapapura: now known as Tapar, below Patan. Founded by Pratapaditya, father of Lalitaditya.
5. Nilashva: Kalhana mentions Nilashva more than once and it may be placed in the Sindh valley SK identifies it with Najwan Nilah near Kangan. In the present context another village of a similar name is to be sought near Tapar, pb. the v. is Nilah near Ninalpur, not far from, Tapar itself.
6. Dilli....: 'Delhi is not your country nor are we its inhabitants...'
7. Serangamer: Sarhang Mir.... Shaikh Bhiga: Sheikh Ali Beg.
8. Jamalumaruga: Refer p. 261/116.
9. Mirza Hydera: this para does not appear in the edition of SK.
10. Sadashivpura: near Purshayar, Habakadal left.
11. Samudramatha: near Somayar, Habakadal right..
12. fire arms: use in a battle mentioned for the first time.
13. Khashas: pb. in Kishtwar. Maurvvara, (p. 286) may be Marv Wardvan. According to PH. Kaji took shelter with Gakkhars.
14. Mirza Babar, Humayun, Kamran, respectively.... Year 7: 1531.
15. Kuduadina: Qutub-ud-Din Pura, Alikadal left... sold: a local expression in a different garb.
16. Juluchhiyas: 'The Turushukas or Mughals killed thousands of people in the manner of Zulchu'.
17. peace: according to PH a battle took place at Athavajan between Kamran's Mughals and Kashmiris.
18. Kaskara: Kashgarhi: .... twelve thousand: fourteen thousand (PH).
19. Kota to Gagana hill: RNS identifies Kota with Chitra Kot in the mtn. ranges of Ladakh. Gaganger is in the Sindh valley.
20. town of Sekandhara: Sikandarpuri, Nauhata.
21. lime, wood, brick and painting mentioned.... Diddamatha: many palaces and splendid mansions had been erected here during the reign of Hassan Shah.
22. Mugulas: Said Khan had close kinship with Babar.
23. ...water: Zainalank in Wular (PH).
24. Chirrodara: Tsera Vudar, now Jwalapur, near Badgam.
25. Chakradara: Tsakdhar, not far from Bijbehara. PH states that Kashmiris were stationed at Athawajan. 'After an interval the people fought the *mlechhas* at Chiroddara, Angakota in Hajya country and Chakradhara and they spent three months in fighting with them'. Angakotta: Hajyangkota (SK) or Hanjyak. Identity of Hajyangkota with the v. Hanjura has also been suggested.
26. Bhimadevi: should be Bhimadevipa, Bumuzu, as Bhimadevi was worshipped at Bren, near Chashmashahi.
27. Eskandar Khan: son of Sultan Said Khan of Kasgarh.

28. 'The Mughals took nine pieces of cloth: *katepha, sopha, galata* etc., and made a present of these to the king. They returned to their camp exulting with joy, carrying a letter from the king in Mausala characters. The Mughals carried some low class men'... Pushyat: *Pushyatantimkan* (SK), goat tracks.
29. Jyestha: Hassan records the date of departure as the 10th of Har., 1588 B.S. (22/23-6-1533 A.D.)
30. *nishka*: supposed to be the equivalent of a *dinar*.
31. Bright fortnight: many people in Kashmir felt, and still feel, there is some merit if death takes place in the bright fortnight.
32. Shamsa Shaha: son of Mohammadshah.... Gardhasodara: Giradaar (PH).
33. Kichashrama: Kitsahom. Kicchashrama in the text records a stage in the transformation of the name (and others) from the original Krityashrama to the *modern* version Kitsahom. Krityasharamavihara was built at the place by Jaluka at the suggestion of a witch (RT i. 133-47).... Jalagada: Zaldagar.
34. Gifts of gold: Kacha Chak resumed proselytization to swell the number of Shias (PH). Some of these lines are not found in the edition of SK. Kacha and Kanchana are variations of the name mentioned as *Kaji Chak* by the chroniclers in Persian....left hand: Kaji's fingers on one hand were slashed (p. 272).

## Shuka Pandit's
### *Rajatarangini*

# Appendices*

## *Appendix A*
## Kashgaris Reappear

Margesha Abdala had invited the Mereja[1] to come to Kashmira, but in fear of Chakri he had thought that he would not be able to obtain possession of the country. Now Malleka Kacha Chakresha went to Hinduvat[2] and there died, and the minds of the Kashmirians who lived outside their country became darkened. The great Mereja Haidhara heard of this event, and he took possession of the kingdom of Kashmira as if it had come to him from his ancestors. The Muggulas, at the death of Chakresha, spread themselves over the kingdom without fear ot dread, like goblins at the shrine of Sharada; and their people came from foreign countries to Mereja Mashugola[3], who was in Kashmira, like bees to a hive full of honey. When their number increased they, instigated[4] by Mashugola, seized lands from those who had possessed them for years before, either by plunder or by gift. By virtue of writs given in the *Mausula* character by the Devana, the mlechha leaders of troops took possession of lands in this affrighted kingdom, and thus deprived the people of their income.

### Influence on dress, food etc.

Thus in the month of Shravana of the year 22, the country witnessed the poor people almost dying, and like a chaste woman

* "The verses mentioned below not being in a chronological order have been placed in 'Appendices' by the translator as also in the Hoshiarpur edition of the text.

trembled in fear. But owing to the victory which the people of Kashmira then obtained, the Muggulas fled from the country, and the people again were eager to get possession of lands in order that they might acquire wealth. It was on account of the association of the people with the Turushkas that they did not give up their fondness for dress, land, and food, the last of which brought in punishment on them, in as much as they had to place themselves hereafter under medical treatment. Even when the wealthy people saw the effects of sumptuous easing, they did not give up their evil desire for food, even as great physicians do not give up their treatment of patients in accordance with the *Shastras*.

## Earthquake

In the month of Ashvina of the year 30, there occurred frequently earthquakes on account of the wicked acts of the king, as if the earth suffered from flatulence. The planet which causes calamity is assuaged by various acts, by gifts of land to independent people, by giving back to men their properties, which had been robbed, and by like deeds. Now there occurred an earthquake at the second watch of night when all men were asleep, and it destroyed many people. It caused holes in the ground, and travellers going on their way were misled at every step. Houses fell into these holes at night and the people, anxious to get out from their houses in the morning, issued by breaking through the roof. On this occasion many wooden houses fell into the water of the Vitasta, and when they had floated down for seven *kroshas*, the people who were in them awoke and came out.

The confusion caused by the earthquake in the two towns of Hassanpura[5] and Hosainapura, situated at some distance across the river can be seen even to this day. Pitiable cries of lamentation of the much afflicted people were then heard calling out "O father"! "O mother!" "O friend!" "O brother!" in different places, which made the heart feel as if it were struck by a thunderbolt. At this time the sky appeared terrible with claps of thunder, the movements of the stars were stopped, and the land was agitated like a gourd on the waves. The mind of the people became troubled with the fear of the earthquake, and they felt no affection for sons or friends or wives or for good men or for kind hearted people or for any object whatever. It was owing to the glory of the holy shrines of Vijayeshvara, Martanda and Varahakshetra that fears and apprehensions from earthquakes were not felt by the inhabitants of these places. The earthquake continued for several days, occurring several times every day, and all the people lived under canvas.

When some time had elapsed, and all men had returned to their home, Dauluta Chakkaka governed the whole country with a strong hand. Once he obstructed the passage of water which flowed through a goblin ground with a view of diverting it to a corn field where he lived. For this act, the angry goblin threw stones into his house at night, and heaps of stones thrown by unseen gods lay scattered during night near the palace gate, and the people wondered at them. In their wonder they asked one another who it was that showered stones every day. Now there lived a very wise and a very pious devotee named Abhimanyu in the village of Tulamula. Dauluta Chakkaka one day went to his house and asked the saint how this great kingdom could be freed from the alarm. When thus asked, the saint replied: "Cease, by my order, to levy the annual tax from Brahmanas, and thus you will obtain your end." When the saint had thus said, the chief of the *mlechhas* replied: "Listen attentively, O great saint! to what I say. I will even now bestow on you the village of Tulamula, but how can I, who am a *mlechha*, cease by your order, to levy tax[6] on Brahmanas?" When Dauluta Chakka had said this, Abhimanyu came agitated with rage; and as the tax on the Brahmanas was not forthwith withdrawn by the Chakkaka, the saint in anger cursed him saying that so far as he was concerned, the sun and the moon would fall and sink into the sea. Dauluta Chakkaka, on account of this curse, became bereft of prosperity.

At this time Homaya[7], whose feet were brushed by the crowns of kings bowing to him, became the emperor of the world. He had quenched the great fire of a civil war, but poverty, like jungle fire, oppressed the hearts of his people, and it was not quenched. This king had an enemy named Ajahomaya[8] who meditated taking shelter in an inaccessible country and he thought of coming to Kashmira; for here Homaya would not be able to assail him. Now when with this intention king Ajahomaya came to Kashmira he had to fight a battle with the people of this country on the top of a hill; and the Kashmirians who dwelt on the mountains totally destroyed his army. This king Ajahomaya was, at the time when Najoka ruled the country of Kashmira, like a living fire that surrounded all sides.

## *Appendix B*

## Ghazi Chak dethrones Habibshah

Then king Habhebha[9] reigned for one month, when Gaja Khana, out of cupidity usurped the throne. Let the great warrior, the victorious Gaja Shaha, the ornament of the world–he who had distressed the enemies, who had in battle held the sword of death–the great leader, the life of the world, the giver of good to the humble, the accomplished, who looked graceful in the kingdom, the beaming, the one versed in literature, and the benefactor of the people, be always triumphant!

In the bright fortnight of the summer month of the year 37, Najoka Shaha joined Kara Bahudhara[10], the son of king Homaya, the chief of the Muggulas, and the leader of the army of Akvara; and with a view of conquest arrived in the Pashanda[11] country. When Gaja Shaha[32] heard of this attempt made in the country outside Kashmira, he held a council and sent Malleka Hosa Chakresha to the outer country. This high-minded Hosa Malleka encamped at Surjala[13] with the chief minister Laula Malleka, Chakresha Pijya, Haibhata Khana, Khujya Phatiha, Meralaka and others, and with ten thousand warriors and infantry, and innumerable tents. The country outside was covered with the great Mughula army, even like the pure heart of a good man with darkening sin. First the army of the chief of the Muggulas and then the troops of Pashanda, who had neglected[14] before, covered the whole of the Rajapuri country.

### Confrontation with Mughals

When the king of Kashmira heard of this he became angry and set out with his army from Shurapura to Hinduvata[15], in order to overthrow his enemies. When the *mlechhas* saw this great and powerful army of Gaja Shaha, they melted away, even as a mass of snow in the rays of the sun. Phatte Mallika and Luhara Malleka soon came up to the powerful army of Gaja Shaha. Now when the way to the fort was closed, Phatiha Khana and others raised their battle cry and distressed the large army of the Muggulas. The king of Rajapuri, in fear of Gaja Shaha, made peace with Khujyabhajya, Yosopha Chakra, and others who were with the Muggulas. While Shaha Najoka stayed at Naushahara, the Muggulas established a truce, and employed their time in constructing fortifications and other works. King Gaja sent a messenger of rank who went to the assembly held by Kara Bahudhara and thus said: "Why all of a sudden, O chief of the *mlechhas*, have you come with a large army, not knowing the prowess of the king, and confiding on whom? Have you forgotten the battle of Shailshahi? Yours will be the sin of the destruction of men in the two armies.[16] If you have strength, where is the use of works of fortification? Man enjoys what Fate gives him. Chakri Rajanaka and others will take a portion of this country, what then will become of this land, or of the Muggulas, or of Khujyabhajya?"

When Shasanamakura[17] the letter-bearer had thus said, Khujyahajya replied as follows: "I am under the Muggulas. The chief of the Chakras is liberal, and a man of worth; he is the chief among bowmen, and is upright like Nausharaovana; how can we sufficiently praise him? If you give to the *mlechhas* a portion of the land which belongs to the Kashmirians, as a reward, you will gladden the heart of the king of the Muggulas. Or, what is the use of dividing the country? All know that heroes perish in battle, and none was seen or heard of or remembered like Gaja Shaha who has now come out of his country to fight." When the king heard these words from the messenger when he returned to him, he descended in anger and in surprise from the top of the hill, but ascended to the summit of great renown.

The king of Kashmira encamped near the forces of the enemy. He was graced by the presence of his sons Shri Shringara Malleka, Ale Malleka, Khana Ahmada, Yospppha, Ebha Shaha, and by Khana Shahibhaja, and by the ministers supported by their armies. He was also attended by thousands of cavalry and swift horses, and by hundreds of thousands of infantry in compact masses furnished with bows, swords, clubs, bearded-darts, lances, iron maces and with weapons named *uphakas* used in *nagarandhras*[18] and *ashmarandhras*. As the two well-arranged armies approached nearer and nearer to each other, the troops of both banks of the river began to adorn the field of battle. Surrounded by a thousand infantry, Gaja Shaha commenced the battle; and by the laughter and the sound of kettledrum, by the flapping of the elephants ears and the neighing of horses, and by the roar of *ashmarandhra* he terrified the enemy. When some of the Muggulas saw that hero approach, they became disheartened and slowly issued out for battle. The soldiers in the front and before the king, out of devotion to their master, severed[19] the heads of the *mlechha* warriors in battle, even as the earthen covers are removed from the pots. Haibhatta Khana was wounded with five arrows, and yielded up his life and immediately espoused the women of heaven.

## Mughals repulsed

The surviving Muggulas reflected on the heroic determination of the soldiers in the front, and on the uncommon valour of the king, and they returned in the same manner as they had come. The chief warriors in the two armies wielded their arms and sacrificed their lives, and they obtained great fame and went to heaven. The king beheld the unparalleled valour of the infantry, and gave them silver and other metals which the troops in the front had acquired from *mlechhas*. The Muggulas saw the reduction of their own army and the increase of that of their enemies, and went away even like the sons of merchants when they are paid. Strong in his valour, Gaja Shaha was accompanied by the king of Rajapuri, and he now made the Pashandas tributary to him, and returned to his country. As he entered Kasbmira he heard the blessings of the people saying: "Long reign, O King! Lord of the empire, and always victorious." Though drenched by the tears of the weeping women of the enemies, the houses of his foes were burnt by the strong fire of his prowess, as by forest fire; and when that fire had consumed the houses grass began to grow watered by the tears of the female relatives of his enemies.

The king saw conflagration in different directions, and there occurred earthquakes, and so he took council of the soothsayers who thus said: "In this country O King! a great battle will be fought, and a river shall flow with rapid current even through the field of battle; or it may be that the distress of the people caused by famine shall everywhere prevail; therefore rule the country wisely."

## Qara Bahadur repulsed

Now Kara Bhaddora, a servant[20] of Merja Haidara, came again with his army, with the object of conquering the country. When Gaja Shaha heard this news, he set out with his horses, at whose trampling the rocks resounded and were powdered into dust. The king sheltered himself at Rajavira[21] and ordered the infantry, which was on its way, to fight. The two kings met at Rajavira, and the people, who had been frightened at the very idea of the meeting of two kings, became alarmed. When Kara Bhaddora saw the skill with which the infantry marched into battle, his heart trembled like the wind, and he became alarmed. Then when he saw the Kashmirians discharge their arrows, he became enraged. He fled from the country at the sight of the infantry, even as darkness flies at the sight of the rising sun; and the people came out of their houses when he had done. As a family prospers when the serpent leaves the house, even so the glory of the king now increased, and the world glowed in his glory.

The king's prowess increased like the sun's in the summer season. But alas! at this time Habe[22] Chakka and others, whose hearts burnt with rage, entered the city. When the enemies had encamped at Sadashivapura[23], the king stationed himself near Diddamatha with a view to fight with them. At this battle of Hataka, the Vitasta flowed between the two armies stationed at Svamipura and at Sadashivpura, as if it forbade the parties to fight. The king crossed[24] the river, fought a great battle, and killed Habhe Chakka in the water of the Sita[25] river.

After a long time the chief of the Muggulas, instigated by Nossi Chakka, came with the desire to conquer Kashmira. His name was known to the world as Shaha Abdolamali[26]. He entered Kashmira accompanied by many men and surrounded by a large army. And the king came to Parihasapura[27] when he heard of his approach; a battle was fought there with various tactics, and the enemy's soldiers were captured, and Shaha Abdolamali turned back his way. Many *yavanas* perished in this battle and *yama* was pleased to receive the souls of men in the semblance of the stream of blood. The heads of the dead men were brought into the town from the field of battle, and the king hung them up in the buildings of the city.

## Draconian justice

Once upon a time the king became devoid of mercy, and cut off without delay the hand of a boy of seven years of age who had stolen a fruit. A certain thief had once stolen a fish belonging to some villager, and the king forcibly took two hundred pieces of gold coins from him. Within a short time the king killed his youthful and powerful son Haidera[28] because Haidera had intended to kill his own mother's brother; the people lamented that the wicked king should have acted thus. This heir-apparent had eighteen sons, and like a Rakshasa the mad king killed them.

The king robbed even the neighbours of those who had committed a fault, and he killed one hundred men every day. He imposed heavy fines for slight offences, and gave nothing to worthy men, but bestowed his gifts on the unworthy. He ordered his servant Jaita to kill the prince, his son, but that servant, out of affection, did not kill him. The prince was afterwards murdered by Delavara Khana. The people became alarmed and they thus exclaimed: "What will be thy condition in the next world O! sinful king? Hadst thou no pity even on thy own son? Why does thou kill thy servants without any fault?"

## Death of Ghazi Chak

In the course of time the king was attacked with a severe leprosy and was deprived of his beauty, even as the moon is by eclipse. Itching was caused by worms in his body, and pus and blood came out of it; and sights that are seen in hell appeared during his life-time. Worms drank of his pus and blood and ate of his flesh and he suffered pain during life-time greater than that of hell. Who was not grieved to hear him cry out "O father! O friend! O son! my sufferings have come?" Thus oppressed in body by a severe leprosy that was visible to all, the king was deprived of his life, and with it his lust for worldly prosperity. Hosaina Khana, the brother of the deceased king, dug a hole in the earth, and performed the rites due to the dead. The earth at that place was suddenly lighted up by the fire of hell, and smoke rose from it, which astonished the people. The smoke was, as it were, the breath of the king tortured by Death. It arose on all sides and was seen by all; and all men who had gone to that place heard the sound of chastisement with which the servants of *yama* tormented the king. The people wondered and said to one another that he was gathering the fruits according as he had sown the seed. Gaja Shaha governed the kingdom darkened by his sin, and died within two years, reduced by leprosy. Alas! how that king committed sin day and night and was in the course of a short time cut off from many years of his life.

## Hosain Chak

When the king went to heaven, his brother Hosaina Khana accepted[29] the kingdom, even as when the moon goes down, the sun rises on the eastern hill. After having taken possession of the kingdom, the king relieved the subjects from misgovernment, even as the cloud in summer quenches the fire of the forest. He attained prosperity by always attending to the complaints of the people, and by giving gifts to every one who asked for it. His fame spread afar. The king drank new wine, sported with women, and enjoyed pleasures which even Indra did not enjoy in heaven. Prosperity, as if bound by his merits, did not go elsewhere but remained in his house; but fame finding prosperity so bound went after, as if in fear. He had come to claim his ancestral property, but when he arrived at his house, his desires were fulfilled to such an extent that he did not claim the property he had come for. People always bowed their heads low at his lotus feet; they were now devoid of sorrow and they attained great prosperity. When such a king ruled Kashmira, the land became full with abundant crops of fruit and flowers. The king dispelled the fear from famine, from thief, and from foreign potentate, and the people believed the kingdom of Kashmira to be equal to heaven. Whenever he sat in judgement, there the occupation of thieves was gone. He did not feel uneasy when he distributed his gifts, his fame therefore spread itself abroad.

One named Khanojamana[30] was the minister of the king; and when once the king went out of the city, the minister sucked the town dry within a short time. But king Hosaina returning immediately destroyed the troopers of the minister, even as the sun destroys darkness in the morning. The subjects wondered at this act of the king who protected them according to laws, and himself enjoyed various kinds of pleasure every day. He plucked out the eyes of Mamada[31] Khana and others who were the king's antagonists, were inimically bent towards him and had come to subdue the country.

## Popular festivals

When all the people had met at Sharikasthana[32] and the king had arrived at the hill of that place, he held a great festival on the day appointed to celebrate the season of spring. The people besmeared themselves with saffron, aloes, camphor and sandalwood paste on that day, and looked beautiful. The king fixed a mark so high that it could not be easily seen, and then he gave an elephant, a horse and wealth to his servant who succeeded in shooting it. Again, on the day of Shripanchami[33] the king saw the people collect on the hill of Jyeshtharudra[34]. Some held bouquets tastefully made of beautiful flowers to their noses; some who were intoxicated became uneasy when women, strangers to them, smiled; some drank wine and adorned their persons with flowers; thus all the people amused themselves on the Shripanchami day and then dispersed themselves. Many a time the king witnessed the dances of beautiful women, and looked at their youthful beauties, and heard their songs and gave them clothes of gold and of silver, and then embarked on a new boat. Gradually the king was attacked with epilepsy, which was like the stain on the bright moon. Even as the moon is attacked by Rahu, so was Hosaina Shaha attacked by epilepsy, and the people became uneasy in fear of misrule as of darkness. King Hosaina bestowed the kingdom[35] on his brother and, as if out of curiosity, went to heaven which he had attained by his gifts. He went to heaven after reigning for seven years, which had always been pleasant, as if to see what the heaven was like. The goddess of wealth, though insulted by large expenditures, went with him; and how could his fame remain among men when urgently called away by the goddess of riches.

## Alikhan Chak

All the people became happy when Ali Khana received the kingdom, even as the lotuses are when the sun appears over the eastern hill. They saw the country of Kashmira well governed by the king, and they were happy; they even slighted heaven which had once been destroyed by the chief of the Daityas. Wicked men disappeared when the king sat in judgement, even as owls do when the sun rises on the eastern hill. Thieves became alarmed and uneasy at that time, and hid themselves like rats in holes at mid day. Attended by the great council the king judged the people, and the enquiries which he made to ascertain the truth were always effective.

## Famine

The king showed kindness to the timid, and his subjects amused themselves at their ease. But suddenly the sky became red on all sides, like the fierce fire that will appear at the end of the world; it prognosticated destruction by famine. The world showed symptoms of a calamity and trembled, as if unable to bear the weight of a famine. Heaps of dead bodies lay during famine in rows in every street, like the war drums of *yama*. There was no necessity then for gold or silver, and the vessels for preparing wine became as rare as the *chintamani* jewel. A certain housewife, who had become gaunt. Hung aside her affection for her husband, drove away her son to a distance, and used to eat in secret. Though the son remained hungry, the daughter begged for food, and the husband was dying, the woman ate alone.

Once an elephant died at the gate of the king's palace, and many people hurried there in haste, to be beforehand, and cut out pieces of meat from the carcase and took them away. A manufacturer of iron utensils killed a barber's boy for food, cooked the human flesh and sold it. The people were anxious to save their lives, and they went out to other countries, leaving behind their houses, their wives and sons. A storm came on at this time which uprooted trees, and the people who experienced it talked about it, and were afraid that the destruction which would happen at the end of the world had come. The storm raised dust that covered the sun, and mid-day appeared like midnight. While the storm was yet blowing, a fire arose from the Sadashiva[36] forest, and it suddenly blew into a flame, as if it had come to meet its friend the storm. The fire followed the direction of the wind, crossed the Vitasta, and burnt the whole town together with Samudramatha. The burning town was reflected on the Vitasta, and it looked as if it had plunged itself into the water in order to quench its flame. Though the stars in the sky were hidden by the smoke, the numerous sparks of fire looked like stars, and appeared double in number. It seemed as if the stars which were concealed by the smoke, saw the flaming fire and fled away in fear.

## Yusufshah crowned king

The king went to heaven after having enjoyed pleasures for nine years, as if to convey there the tidings of the troubles which arose from famine. His son then accepted the kingdom, whereupon Abdala Khana, the brother of the new king's father, became angry and sent a messenger to his nephew with the message saying that it was the practice of the family that when a brother died a brother took his post, why then should he aspire to the kingdom. After Abdala Khana had sent the messenger he fought a battle with Yosobha Shaha at Sekandarapura, in which he destroyed the army of his enemy, and then went to heaven, as if out of curiosity to see his brother. King Yosobha then took possession of the kingdom, and gave such rich gifts to the people as to make them forget Karna and Mandhat of ancient time.

Then Momara Khana[37] came from a distant[38] country to fight, as if invited by a combination of king's misfortunes. Mahmada Khana, a servant of king Yosobha, fought with him near Diddamatha. The flames from the firearms flashed amidst the great mass of dark dust and looked like lightnings playing among the clouds. Mahmada Khana fell and his men became bereft of glory, like lotuses when the sun sets in the evening. The moving horseman reflected on the water of the Vitasta seemed as if they were fleeing into the nether world, alarmed at the defeat of Mahmada. The king retreated by the difficult and inaccessible road leading to the country of the Khasha people, after having enjoyed the kingdom for *two months and a half*.[39]

## Seeks help from Akhar

King Yosobha fled in haste when Momara Khana obtained the kingdom, so flies the moon when the sun rises in the morning. He went to obtain a shelter[40] at the feet of King Jyallaladina (Akbar) who was the ruler of the whole world. Mutual enmity gradually arose among the men of Momara Khana, even as the forest fire arises by mutual friction. Momara Khana was imprisoned by his opponents after he had enjoyed the kingdom for one[41] and a fourth of a month; and he lived in a temple.

Chakka Haidara and others defeated Momara Khana and set up Lahvara[42] Chakka to the throne. The villagers, during the reign of this king, suffered from the depredations caused by lions[43] on all sides. Men in every village who went out of their houses at night were killed by lions which were like devouring goblins.

## Yusuf triumphs

Now king Yosobha was happy to see the effect of King Jyallaldina, and returned[44] to Kashmira after a year. He took shelter in the village of Sayyapura, even as the sun takes rest on the eastern hill. This village was difficult of access owing to the water of the Vitasta. King Lahvara then issued out of the city, accompanied by many men, even as a lion issues out of the cavern of a mountain. Haidara Chakka knew that the village of Sayaypura was difficult of access owing to the water of the Vitasta, he therefore marched without delay by another[45] road. King Yosobha learnt of these attempts of his enemy, he crossed[46] over the water of the Vitasta, and fought with Lahvara. Abdala Mera the minister of Lahvara, fought a great battle which struck terror to all living creatures, but he perished in the battle. King Lahvara fled, and king Yosobha was joined by his own troops and thus his army increased, even as the ocean is increased by the waters of the rivers. Lahvara took refuge at the feet of Yosoba Khana, and the latter soon put out the eyes of Lahvara and of his brother. Haidara Chakka learnt of this act of king Yosobha, and, with a view to fight again, he took shelter of a forest tract. A battle took place between king Yosobha and Chakka Haidara in a forest[47], where a stream of blood quenched the forest fire.

Haidara Chakka went to Jyallaladina in penury, even as the moon, devoid of rays, approaches the sun. After his departure, king Yosobha ruled the country, even as the sun rules the lotuses when darkness departs. When the king began to rule the country, Indra sent rain in due measure, the breezes that gave pleasure to all blow, and the sun god shone in person. His fame spread over the world, but his prosperity stayed in his house bound by his merits, and did not stray anywhere else. The king had many good qualities, but his only fault was that he sheltered prosperity, which was fickle, in his house, and sent out fame which was steady. The moon is well-known to be a foe of the meritorious, and how could he equal the king who was a friend to worthy men? Yosobha ruled Kashmira, but he felt very angry towards Habhebha[48] and others, and he plucked out their eyes.

## Yaqub returns

The king of Kashmira sent his son Yokobha to King Jyallaladina in order to serve him. Yakobha accordingly made his preparations. But when king Jyallaladina saw the presents given to him by Yakobha, he felt a desire to subdue Kashmira. And when he felt that desire he gave the necessary orders to Bhagavaddasa and other kings. Yakobha came to know of this, and he left the service of the king, and returned unperceived to his own country of Kashmira by another route. When he came to his father he felt himself free from anxiety, and thus said to him: "O adorable! The king has sent Bhagavaddasa against us. If a great man has no strength in him, his greatness becomes useless; the lion kills an elephant huge as a hill." They then settled their plan to defeat the enemy, and ordered all the people of the mountains to turn out under fear of penalty. The king then came forth and the soldiers were arrayed and the banners which dwarfed the trees looked beautiful. King Yosobha took shelter in the shrine of Varaha[49], and there he remained; his ministers advanced to the front with a view to fight.

## Yusuf prepares for surrender

The king then thus addressed the ministers: "You should not fight, we will take refuge at the lotus feet of Jyallaladina that we may serve him. How can the weaker of the two have the strength to overcome the mightier? The storm has not the strength to uproot a mountain." When all the ministers heard this they said to the king: "Why do you think thus? One never accomplishes a religious act he wishes to perform if he does not obey the good advice of his religious preceptor; a patient who disregards the advice of the physician never recovers; and the elephant never acquires skill if it does not follow its driver; and a king who neglects the words of his ministers never attains prosperity." When the king had heard this, he said to those ministers: "You have not seen the army of King Jyallaladina; Indra reigns in the east only, Yama in the south, the god of water in the west, and the god of gold in the north. But why do they feel proud–they who rule in one direction only? King Jyallaladina is the lord of all around. Victory be to him! No one was so liberal as Akavara, and no one shall be; he bestows gifts on the learned men even if they be his enemies. Karna attained fame by the gift of gold, Bali by that of land; but this king, by gifts of all things. Though Kuvera is rich, he is miserly in many ways; though the moon is pure, yet it bears a stain from day to day; though fire is powerful, it is always darkened by its uprising smoke; but all of these have been surpassed by this king in gifts, fame and power."

King Yosobha was bent on serving Jyallaladina, and the ministers thus made him a fitting reply: "The life of that man is useless whose desire it is to serve the feet of his enemy, but he who fights with his foe deserves praise. Stay at a distance and we will accomplish your work; we will take shelter of a forest tract and continue to fight day after day. The powerful sun with its thousand rays cannot destroy the darkness of a cavern, so the emperor, bent on destruction, will not be able to destroy those who would take shelter in a forest[50]."

When the king had heard these words spoken by the ministers, he, as if to extinguish their fire, thus addressed them in a nectar-like speech: "Cast aside your fear, obey my words, I shall take refuge at the lotus-like feet of Jyallaladina. He is an ornament among kings, and Cupid is of no use so long as his person exists. I bow to him out of my own will, and feel proud of it. How can I act inimically towards the emperor? I will serve him, and there shall be happiness in my country. None ever existed like this king, nor now exists, nor will exist, and in saying this I feel a pride every day and at all times. My ears have become restless at listening to the merits of this emperor, and even Karna would run away if he heard of his liberality. Men whose foreheads have been marked for poverty fall at his feet to wipe away the writings of fate. It is rarely that the dust of his feet can be had even by great men; and that dust befits the heads of kings even as an ornament; and as a charm to secure prosperity.

"The emperor worships the sun, the real and the visible god; and his difficulties fly away from him owing to his devotion to this luminary. The intelligent emperor Jyallaladina thought to himself that the different Vedas varied in their views, that the realm of the chief of the gods was once assailed by the Asura chief, that the pride of the Gandharvas was also humbled. Indra and the other gods were much subject to fear, and Brahma, Vishnu and Shiva turned towards the sun with clasped hands; he therefore bows to the sun, the visible god. How can my troops cope with those of King Akbara when they arrive? How useless is it to try to repel the waves of the sea when they break over the land, by means of a winnowing[51] fan? What harm befalls the sun, the visible god, should an owl vilify him?" The king resolved to do what he had said, and went over to Bhagavaddasa in order to take refuge at the feet of king Jyallaladina.

Thus having enjoyed prosperity for eight years, king Yosobha went to serve King Jyallaladina.

## Yaquhshah

When King Yosobha went over to the army of Bhagavaddasa, his son Yokobha took possession of the extensive kingdom. He pleased all men by spending for military purposes all the treasure which had been acquired by his ancestors and hoarded in the treasury. And when Bhagavaddas had departed from the country with king Yosobha, king Yokobha looked as beautiful as the sun emerged from the clouds.

There are four different factions in the Mausalas and there arose a quarrel among the people owing to the difference that existed in these doctrines. Shamsa Chakka became jealous of the king and constructed a fortification at Sadashivpura with the intention to fight. King Yakobha then fought a great and tumultuous battle with him near Diddamatha in which Shamsha Chakka took with him Alamashira and Malleka Alaka. It was by the advice of Malleka[52] Alaka that Shamsha Chakka then went to the village of Svayyapura, situated in the midst of the water, and occupied it. As the rising sun speedily destroys the darkness of night by its rays, even so Yakobha sent the soldiers of his enemy to Yama by arrows discharged with his own hand. Alamashira Khana fled after he had fought awhile and the king besieged Shamsha Chakka within the town. Yakobha obtained the victory, but from that time he always apprehended danger from the king of Madhyadesha[53].

## March of the Mughal army

The desire of King Jyallaladina, sovereign of Madhyadesha, to conquer Kashmira prevailed again and with this view he sent there Kasema Khana who was served by Chakka Haidara. Anxious to conquer Kashmira, the king ordered twenty-two leaders of army to march; and these leaders of great glory promptly issued by his orders from the city of Lahora[54]. Wells were dried up, tanks were drained to the mud, and hills were levelled by the march of this army. Lines of tents were adorned with lofty banners, and it seemed as if the tents stretched out their necks to see the hills of Kashmira. Such a mass of dust was raised by the marching army as to strike terror to the sun in the sky, even as from Rahu. Their infantry, their cavalry and their elephants could not be numbered, even as the dust in the road.

The soldiers covered with dust in their long marches reached the Chandrabhaga[55] river in a few days, even as the chakori reaches the moon. There the men who had soiled themselves with the mud of tanks, washed their clothes, drank the pure water, and enjoyed themselves as they liked. The horses shied on the banks of the Chandrabhaga, being afraid to bathe, at which men who were near them became frightened and agitated, while those who were at a distance jested at them. An elephant was loosened for bath, and though placed behind a female elephant became struck with terror and alarmed the men and threw them into confusion.

In a few days the army crossed the Chandrabhaga in its march towards Kashmira, and reached the neighbourhood of the mountains. The infantry felt greatly exhausted in ascending and descending the hills, which they did on their knees, ankles and feet. The way over mountains is like the way to *Yama*; there are waterfalls at some places, and in others water is scarce; in some places exhaustion is caused by puddles, and in others there is fear of being struck by stones; some places are always cold and some are always hot, being exposed to the rays of the sun. Bullocks, elephants and horses ate in these mountain tracts the new and tender shoots of grass which was grown by copious rain.

These men from Madhyadesha beheld the arrangement of the mountains, made enquiries about the trees they met in villages, and they were greatly filled with wonder. When the troops had ascended the top of a hill, they looked like *yama* at the end of a *Kcalpa*, They smothed passages over impossible tracts, by means of boulders of stone, they alarmed the elephants which were in groves, they cleared the groves and made torrents of water flow over table-lands. The inhabitants of these mountains were struck with fear at the prowess of the emperor, and at the sight of his army, and they came to Kasema Khana bringing him presents of goats and citrons. As men catch birds by giving them bits of meat, as fish is caught in water by means of hooks, as skilful men induce animals to come near by throwing corn at them, even so did Kasema Khana overcome the inhabitants of the country by distributing wealth amongst them. His army was in want of a person to show them the road to Kashmira, and Haidera Chakka offered to do this act of enmity towards Yakobha.

## Qasim lavishes gifts

At this time Bahrama Nayaka was incharge of defending the road to Kashmir. He felt uneasy on account of fear for Yakobha; he stationed his men in their places and went alone to the army of Kasema Khana. Kasema Khana was well-versed in work of every kind; he gave dresses, ornaments, and wealth to the Nayaka, and thereby he greatly honoured him. Other people who were at Panchanila[56] hill had also disregarded Yakobha and had given the kingdom to Hosaina Khana, and when Hosaina Khana heard that Kasema Khana, a foreigner had come within his territory, he became angry. Now Yakobha reviled Hosaina Khana, and marched towards the Panchanila hill. But the soldiers whom he had sent, turned away from the work of their master, and made peace[57] with Hosaina Khana on such terms as they liked. When king Yakobha heard that his army had joined Hosaina, he blamed his fickle-minded men, such as steal wealth in times of prosperity and act inimically in times of danger; they are difficult to be kept under control, even as the thieves are.

Yakobha released Mera Mahmada and Shamsha Chakka[58] from prison, and went to Kashthavata. Spoiled of their glory, these two servants did not pay their respects to Yakobha nor serve him; monkeys play with the *chintamani* jewel as with a ball! The soldiers disbanded themselves when Yakobha went away, even as the pearls scatter themselves when the string of the necklace is torn into two. Some went to Kashthavata, some lived in the city, some went to foreign countries, some came to an agreement with the Muggulas. Shamsha Chakka snatched the kingdom from Hosaina Khana, but in fear of Kasema Khana he retired to the top of a mountain. He heard of the approach of Kasema Khana, made up his resolution, and took to the mountains which were difficult to be approached by men. He was at that time attended by a handful of men, while the other was attended by many. Kasema Khana placed Haidara Chakka in front of him, even as Rama had placed Sugriva, and fought a great battle.

## The Mughals enter Srinagar

When the Kashmirian troops saw Chakka Haidara they all fled away, even as the darkness of night flies at the rising of the sun in the morning. As a great mass of dust is driven away by the slightest wind, even so the Kashmirian troops were driven away by those of the Muggulas. The former fled, and the latter became victorious and the women who had husbands and children raised loud lamentations when they heard of this news. They had lived like lotus plants, their hands had trembled like lotuses, and so also their eyes under locks of hair, even like blue-water lilies under black bees. Then when the calamity came in like darkness, the eyes brightened, like the blue water lilies, but the lotus faces shrank. Tear drops fell on the breasts of these women, as if to quench the fire that was burning within their heart. The soldiers entered the city on Sunday, the second lunar day of the bright fortnight of Karttika, in the Shaka[59] year 1509. The city was full of grapes and walnuts, and was adorned with flowers and saffron, and the *Yavanas* who entered it fully confessed that it was like heaven. All the Muggulas who received presents of grapes from the cultivators and tasted them, acknowledged that they were superior to the nectar from the lips of their wives. The Muggulas adorned their heads with flowers and saffron, and extolled their valour over their wine.

## Yaquh returns from Kishtwar

Even the people of Kashmira entered the service of Haidara Chakka when they saw Kasema under his guidance. But when Kasema found that Haidara Chakka was attended by many men, he became alarmed, and threw the Chakka into prison; whereupon the people of Kashmira who had followed him retired to a distant forest. They then all united themselves together, reproached themselves, held a council, and resolved to fight. Their *ary* was full of men, but did not look graceful without a king, even like a woman without a husband, or like a night without the moon. Thus thought they who had been defeated by the *yavanas*, and they promptly caused Yokobha to be brought. Kasema Khana heard that Yakobha had arrived in person, and he sent Momara Khana to vanquish him. Now when King Yakobha heard that Momara Khana was approaching, he put on his armour in order to fight a great battle; but his ministers asked him who this Momara Khana was, a servant of his servant, that he should fight with him. Whereupon the king left alone Momara Khana, who was stationed at Vijayeshvara and marched towards the city by another road. At this time the sun, which is full of the knowledge of the three Vedas, set, as if in pity for the destruction of men which was about to take place in the impending battle. As the day declined, twilight lingered for a short time, and then, as if afraid to be alone, went away to obtain the company of the day. When the moon saw Yakobha, terrible in appearance and with two swords in his two hands, and remembered that both he and Yakobha were kings, he went, as if in fear, to the place of setting.

## The city on fire

At this time Yakobha, whose army was tired after having marched from a great distance, attacked the city without delay near Sadashivapura. It was at night, at the time when husbands were kissing and embracing their wives, and when Cupid was cruelly discharging his arrows that the cry, like the roar of a lion, rose at the place of battle. Yakobha killed many *yavanas* in the streets and within houses, and followed by a large army, he set fire to the gate of the palace[60]. Kasema Khana lay hid in his own house, like a black bee enclosed within the petals of a lotus, wishing for the arrival of the morning. Phatiha Khana, the Muggula, had collected an army, was well clad in armour, and was at Sekandharapura. The whole city was burnt, to the terror of the *yavanas*, and the people of Kashmira fought by the light of the flame. When Kasema Khana saw the troops of Kashmira, he, in his anger, killed Haidar Chakka who was in prison. Yakobha abstained from his night attack in the morning, and his soldiers departed after plundering houses, elephants, and clothes. The king had completely chastised the wicked at night during which the sky had displayed its stars, even as a trader displays his jewels; but when the powerful sun forcibly opened the petals of the lotuses in the morning, the sky perspired dews in the effort to hide its jewels in a hurry.

When the morning came, the moon set, and the sun drove away darkness in an instant, all the Muggula people collected together, and Yakobha became very much alarmed. He then withdrew from the city in the morning, and the *yavanas*, whose hearts were inflamed with anger on account of the night attack, plundered the capital. Kasema Khana knew that Yakobha had departed, but he saw his own army broken, and still he was anxious to achieve a victory; he therefore marched by the way by which Yakobha had gone. One named Alamashira Khana accompanied by many men bowed at the feet of Kasema Khana. Alamashira was an inhabitant of Tailagramma[61], and he and his friend Shamsha Chakka had once fought with each other Phateha Khana, a Muggula. remained at Sekandharapura with a large army for the protection of the city. A fierce battle was then fought between king Yakobha and Kasema Khana in which the Kashmirians hurled stones, arrows, and iron clubs; but a quarrel again arose among themselves, attended with the cry of "I am the king." "I am the king." When king Yakobha learnt of this quarrel, he, at the advice of his friendly brother[62], went again to Kashthavata. Yosobha Khana and Mera Mahmada then concluded a peace with Kasema Khana, a peace which the latter had sought. Kasema Khana then sent Yosobha Khana and others to the feet of king Jyallaladina who always honored them by giving them wealth, and they bowed at his feet.

## Yaqub's stiff resistance

Now the winter season, like another invasion of the Muggulas, came to Kashmira, and many people suffered on account of the rigour of its cold. Snow fell on the houses of the *yavanas* after they had achieved the victory like showers of flowers from the sky. Then came the season of spring adorning all the roads with abundant flowers, as if to advise the assiduous King Yakobha to begin hostility.

He returned from the country of Kashthavata accompanied by many men, with a view to overcome the Muggulas. When Kasema Khana heard of this, he too, with the object to conquer the enemy, marched out with horses and elephants which made the earth tremble. A great battle was fought between them in the country of Kshetra[63]. and the day was clouded with arrows and stones. The Muggulas pressed on king Yakobha, but he, unperceived by them, went towards the city, took shelter in an almost inaccessible hill[64] near the paddy fields, and came up suddenly against the Muggulas.

The sun reflected on bright swords and armours which lighted the dark caverns in the wood. The turbans were filled with blood issuing from the bodies of the many who were slain, as if they were the wine cups of *yama*. So many were the stones hurled, breaking down trees, that it seemed as if the Kashmirians were unable to bear the sight of lofty hills. The waters of the fountains were mingled with the blood of the dead. Was it that the sportful *yama* played with red powder dissolved in water? Thus the war continued between king Yakobha and Kasema Khana; and for a month none of them was either victorious or defeated. Now Adula Khana was sent by Kasema Khana, with an army to fight with the Kashmirians who were stationed on the hills. And when the battle was about to be commenced, the mountains became covered with clouds which brought a storm and, as if with it, the last night of *kalpa* for the *mlechhas*. Thunders pealed in the clouds, and the quick succession of its lightnings looked like the quivering tongue of *yama*, as if he was devouring something. The clouds poured forth torrents of rain as the army of Adula Khana marched and he ascended a hill up the way towards the sky. There was one named Shriranga, a prince, a servant of Jyallaladina; he also went to fight, ascending up the way towards the sky. When the Muggulas had entrenched themselves at Sadashivpura, the Kashmirians took shelter on a hill near Jyeshtharudra[65]. Streams of blood flowed in the battle which then took place, and ran into the Vitasta.

Merja Adula, the servant of the emperor, came with a view to commence hostility, but at that time a battle was being already fought between the followers of Yakobha and of Alamshira Khana, the Kashmirian. But when Adula arrived, the followers of Yakobha saw him and exclaimed, "Here the Muggulas have come"; and they left the soldiers of Alamshira Khana, attacked Adula, and fought with him. But Alamshira Khana's men helped Adula Khana and fought against Yakobha. Adula Khana was pleased with Alamshira Khana and acknowledged that he had helped the emperor. Shriranga entered into a relationship with Raya Simha. He had with him forty Rajputs, whom, when it began to rain, he ordered saying "Retreat, O Rajputs! I have become a cripple and have not the strength to go." But they replied: "It will not be so, the habit of running away does not exist in the Rajput tribe, the emperor honours the Rajputs, and we will, therefore, continue to defend Lanka."[66] Those Rajputs did not retreat.

Many perished in the battle thus fought, and the men of Kasema Khana were struck with panic. The Kashmirians saw that the *yavanas* were defeated and broken, and they rushed on them suddenly.

## Yaqub isolated

King Jyallaladina heard the news of this war and ordered Saida Yosobha[67] to subdue the country. When king Yakobha heard of this, he went against Yosobha Khana, even as a jackal goes against a lion knowing him by his roar. Kasema Khana had come to Kashmira led by avarice, but remained their blockaded by Yakobha, even as a black bee that comes to a lotus is imprisoned there by the approach of night. He was full of fear and could not stir out. He was, however, relieved of his fear within a short time by the arrival of the sun-like Yosobha Khana, and he issued out in triumph. The news about Merja Yosobha alarmed Shamsha Chakka and others who wandered about like pigeons when the hawk is on its wing. Kasema Khana was freed from his fear when Yosobha Khana arrived, even as the chakravaka is freed from its position of separation from its mate on the rising of the sun. Mahmada[68] Mera joined some *Kashmirians* and always placed himself at the service of Yosobha Khana who sent many people of Kashmira to the feet of king Jyallaladina.

## Loses heart

Now king Yakobha came from Kashthavata with the desire to overcome the Muggulas, even as insects come out of madness to a flame; and Merja Yosobha Khana sent Hajya Mera with Mahmada to subdue him. The king's and the Muggula armies remained on their grounds unmoved, as if Fate examined strength by holding both of them in a balance. The *yavanas* occupied the land on the south-west[69], and the Kashmirians on the top of a hill, and none could advance towards the other. The shouts, like the roar of a lion, rose from the two armies, as if the noise issued from the teeth of *yama* eagerly crushing men. A great and tumultuous battle was then fought terrible to the gods and the *asuras* and a touchstone to test the worth of great warriors. The Kashmirians hurled stones which shook numberless branches of trees, as if the arms of those trees trembled in fear at the might of the battle. In the never ceasing shouts of the great warriors it seemed as if the hills cried out in fear. The arrows discharged by the warriors covered the trunks of large trees and looked as if their hairs stood upon their bodies at the sight of the tumultuous battle. The Muggula army fought in diverse ways, and felt satisfied; but Yakobha saw his army broken, and became uneasy[70] with fear. He thus said to himself: "I believe that my soldiers have been devoured by the *yavanas*, even as the moon is devoured by Rahu; how can I alone cope with the *mlechhas* in this sea like battle?" He then retired alone from that place, and came to Kashthavata, feeling humiliated day by day.

Now Yosobha Khana returned to Jyallaladina in order to serve him, and his brother Merja Baddhaka took possession of Kashmira. All men felt happy when he sat on his seat of judgement, even as the *chakra* bird feels happy when the moon ascends the eastern hill. Once upon a time a merchant killed a person in the merchant's house; a piece of the corpse of the murdered man was thereupon tied round the merchant's neck, and he was taken round with the proclamation that "any person who becomes so devoid of sense as to kill another will surely get similar heavy punishment". Once a *yavana*, intoxicated with wine, killed a Kashmirian without any fault. The murdered man was kept hidden under water, and the *yavanas* declared that he had murdered none. When Merja Baddhaka was informed of this by the relatives of the murdered man, he at once asked the *yavana* why he had killed a Kashmirian; but he asserted that he had killed none. "If a person is killed", continued the, *yavanas* "where is his headless trunk?" The yavana said this in a firm tone, whereupon Merja Baddhaka ordered men to look in the tank. When the tank was stirred up, the headless trunk appeared, and the *yavana's* guilt for having murdered a man was established. Merja Baddhaka found the *yavana* guilty and ordered his punishment as it is laid down in the *shastra*.

Asked by Jyallaladina, Yosobha Khana, with his head bent down, thus spoke about the countless excellent things of Kashmira: 'The Creator has created Kashmira like a second heaven; and even the king of serpents, with his two thousand tongues, cannot describe the glories of that country. There the amorous men leave aside the grapes whose sweet juice does not last long, and drink the nectar which exudes from the lips of their beloved women, There the faces of the women, with their quick moving eyes of flirtation, look graceful like the lotuses on which the black bees move busily about. But there, alas! the snow gives constant trouble, and as if pretending to feel cold, the women, with their both hands trembling before their husbands, express their love." The other ministers then thus said to the sovereign of the world: "O Emperor! The glories of Kashmira are innumerable. There the glorious morning, noon, and evening indicate themselves by the ebb[71] and flow of water. There is the celebrated god Amareshvara[72], the living snow which grows and diminishes in the bright and the dark fortnights. There is the glorious living[73] fire which remains always ablaze, which requires no fuel, and leaves no charcoal behind."

## Akbar's first visit and Yaqub's surrender

When king Jyallaladina heard of the excellencies of Kashmira, he issued from the city of Lahora in order to see that country; and on the fifth bright lunar day of Ashadha, arrived with his army in the capital of Kashmira. On the seventh[74] bright lunar day of that month he pleased the Brahmana boys with gifts of gold, and they blessed him. He then went to Martanda, and gave cows adorned with pearls and gold to Brahmanas. He was glad to see Kashmira with its vines and walnut trees and high champing woods of *tali* trees[75]. He stood on the banks of the Vitasta and saw the position of the city and was greatly astonished. He saw the tank[76] near Jyeshtharudra adorned with various kinds of flowers, and was greatly surprised. Even Yakobha came to take refuge at the feet of Jyalladina, by whose generosity Yakobha was honored. Yakobha took refuge[77] with the king as he had purposed to do, and the king made him an attendant of Manasimha. Yakobha remained at the feet of Manasimha, he went out of the country and enjoyed the delights which the emperor bestowed on him. King Jyalladina saw the kingdom of Kashmira, bestowed it on Yosobha Khana, and went away.

Merja Yosobha Khana was well-skilled in serving the king. He ruled the whole country well according to the king's orders; but Jyalladina became angry with him, and gave the possession of Kashmira to Kaji Ala. When Kaji Ala sent the annual revenue to the king, the servants of Merja Yosobha were deprived of their possessions, and they became like guests in their own homes. The Kaji gave nothing to any one, nor enjoyed anything himself, but collected a large quantity of gold by robbing others, even as mice collect paddy. Menaced by Kaji Ala, Yosobha Khana's men went about hungry, even like tanks in the hot season. The people of Kashmira came to rob the heaps of paddy when they saw it amassed by Kaji Ala; and the wealth hoarded by this wicked Kaji caused a quarrel among the Muggulas themselves. Merja Yadgara,[78] brother of Yosobha Khana, joined the people of Kashmira with the intention to kill Kaji Ala. The Kaji fought several times with him, and then fled. His horse perished in ascending a hill, and he also went to heaven. Hasana Bhiga, a servant of Jyalladina, fought heroically and returned alive from the battle. The people said with a loud laugh and without feeling any grief that the riches which the Kaji had hoarded by dishonest means were consumed by his enemies. Alas! Why did he hoard them! Merja Yadgara gave to his own people all that had been accumulated by depriving the cultivators.

## Yadgar's revolt

Merja Yadgara turned aside from serving the feet of King Jyallaladina and assumed the sovereignties of Kashmira. The inhabitants of the country, when they saw this, became apprehensive of another war and were grieved. When King Jyallaladina heard of this conduct of Yadgara, he marched without delay, and in his anger, he spread his army on the ridge of a hill, and passed through an almost impassable mountain road. He then sent Shikha Phareda[79] ahead with many men to subdue the Merja. The Shikha ascended the top of a hill called Hastivanja[80], even as the chariot of the sun ascends the eastern hill. At this time Merja Yadgara arrived at the village of Shurapura, but he was killed by his own servants who rose against him. When the people saw him lying dead, and eaten by jackals and dogs, they spat on the ground and at once said that he was "a rebel against his master", and remarked that he had thought that he should pay his respects, now that the glorious emperor had come, in more than one way, and so he sacrificed his life, and thus paid his respects and with them, presents and devotion. Shikha Phareda came within the city after *Merja* Yadgara had been killed by his own servants. He governed the city himself, and the thieves could not then go about, even as the owls cannot in the morning. Now Jyallaladina came to see the kingdom of Kashmira adorned with saffron, walnut, fruits, and flowers. The wives of the citizens hastened to see the king. One woman pointed out the king to her beloved female friend who was anxious to see him; another exclaimed with a flutter that she had seen that leader of the army; another woman, with threats to her child (who wanted to drink of her milk) covered her breast and went (to have a view of the king). After the people of Kashmira had seen the sovereign, a continuous festivity[81] was held in every house.

Formerly, the kings of the house of Chakka used to exact an annual fine from the Brahmanas, owing to their animosity towards the people of that caste. In every house a Brahmana of good family and character who maintained his own caste, used to pay an annual tribute to the king. For the preservation of his sacred thread a Brahman annually paid a tribute of forty *panas* to the king. The good Brahmanas had left the country which was polluted by the *mlechhas;* those of the middle class had become shameless; and the low Brahmanas had given up their caste. When the *mlechhas* remained like clouds in the country, and obscured it, the Brahmanas went to other countries, even like swans that go to Manasa lake.

## Brahmins' disabilities removed

Now when king Jyallaladina learnt of the condition of the Brahmanas, he repealed the practice of levying fines on them, which had prevailed since the time of the kings of the house of Chakka. He announced that he would without delay reward those who would respect the Brahmanas in Kashmira; and that he would instantly pull down the houses of those who would take the annual tribute from them. The Brahmanas, versed in the Vedas, whose fear of the payment of an annual tribute was removed by this order, blessed the king, saying that let king Jyallaladina who had repealed the annual tribute live for 10,000,000,000 years. One thousand cows used to be killed every day, without any opposition, under the orders of the kings of the house of Chakka, and for them. The Brahmanas had been overpowered by the *mlechhas*, even as by darkness. They were unable[82] to see their friends and like lotuses they mourned at night. The means of their livelihood were consumed by the *mlechhas* who were even like the forest fire; they did not remain in the country, even as deer do not stay in the forest which is burnt. As they left the country, they sometimes, like jackals, felt alarm in the way and sometimes they were the objects of laughter and of reproach.

Ramadasa[83] who always served Jyallaladina was a great benefactor of the Brahmanas. This celebrated person saw their condition and gave them gifts of gold and silver, and he was like a second Karna. The cloud rains nectar, but that benefit is dismissed by its thunders; but in the heart of king Ramadasa who always gave gifts, there was no pride. Where art thou now, O Mandhata? Inferior to him in liberality. Stop thy ear O Karna! that thou mayest not hear Ramdasa's praise. Feelest thou no shame O Jumutabahana? In what art thou strong? Truly O Vikramaditya! I know of no lasting benefit that has been attained by thy fame. Ramadasa always distributes his gifts wisely and skilfully.

## Gifts

Ramadasa, the servant of Akavara, gave one hundred pieces of silver, and also pieces of gold to every house of a Brahmana.

He distributed fifty thousand pieces of silver among the poor Brahmanas.

O Ramadasa, the *kalpa* tree of the world! I think there exists as much difference between thy gifts and the gifts of others, as there exists between a gift and no gift. Nirmmala[84] and all other Brahmanas versed in the Vedas, and the Panditas blessed him and returned to their homes. On another day, Prahlada, Nirmmala, and all of them were honoured by the speech of this king, which was as sweet as nectar. Even the illustrious Jyallaladina gladdened the Brahmanas who were recommended to him by Ramadasa, even as the moon gladdens the *chakaras*. The emperor bestowed villages on the Brahmanas, and they looked graceful, even as the forest that had been burnt by fire does when the clouds begin to rain. Aditya[85] knew well how to serve king Jyallaladina; he was always employed by the king in distributing lands; but being blind on account of his affection for his relatives, Aditya overlooked such men of merit as were his enemies, and prospered such men without merit as were of his own party. As the nectar rose from the sea churned by a hill, even so the gifts of land issued from the king's palace moved by the words of Ramadasa. But, alas! Aditya, like Rahu, disappointed the learned men, and gladdened his wicked *daitya*-like friends by gifts of land. Jyallaladina himself was a sea of kindness, and he satisfied the mendicants by his gifts of gold and silver.

The emperor then ordered Shikhaphaija[86] to take one thousand pieces of silver and to distribute them among Brahmanas and beggars who dwelt in villages and in woods and in other places.

King Jyallaladina then bestowed the country again on Yosobha Khana, and went away. The people felt happy when Yosobha Khana took possession of the kingdom, even as the lotuses are when the sun ascends the eastern hill. An annual payment was fixed from the cultivators in every village, and soldiers were forbidden from entering it, lest they create disturbance again. Yosobha knew how to distinguish the cultivators from the soldiers, even as a swan knows how to separate milk from water.

## Begar

Merja Laskara, Yosobha Khana's son, took possession of the country when his father had left it in order to serve Jyallaladina. He was without a blemish, a jewel fit for the head of all men; his person was like nectar, and he looked graceful like the youthful moon. Now one of his *yavana*[87] servants went to the banks of the Vitasta, and there harassed the people by ordering them to lift loads of wood. Merja Laskara himself saw the *yavana* harassing the people and said to his minister: "See how he is killing the men. Alas! do my servants oppress the people of Kashmira? Why do they not fear King Jyallaladina? How strange it is that there is no robbery, no fear from thieves or from wicked men, that merchants pay no tax either in village or in town, that clouds rain, the earth becomes fruitful, and the cultivators keep their annual grain, and the country suffers no loss when emperor Jyallaladina rules." He then ordered the *yavana* to be promptly arrested, and the minister immediately hurried to seize him. But the *yavana* fled in fear, whereupon the minister reported that the man had run away. Merja Laskara then said: "Now that the man has fled, do what I say: take the boats laden with wood into the middle of the Vitasta and burn them in such a manner to strike terror to the people." The minister did as he was ordered, and when the *yavana* saw the boats in flame they became almost dead with fear. Any *yavana* who would so lose his sense as to oppress the people of Kashmira would soon obtain the fruit of his guilt.

## Saffron blossoms

Now the saffron shoots sprang from the ground, as if the king of the serpents had reared his heads in rows in order to behold the season of autumn. The buds of saffron flowers issued slowly as if through bashfulness, from the spotless cover of their rinds; and when the people saw the village of Padmapura rich with the beauty of these saffron flowers, and with grapes and walnuts[88], they deemed even heaven inferior to it. The cultivators who in the month of Shravana had sown one *khari* of saffron seed in the ground, now plucked half a *khari* of flowers, and they plucked them morning, noon, and evening, and at each time they collected them in the same quantity. From the time that Takshaknaga[89] taught the cultivation of this flower, there had not been such a plentiful crop as now. People had no rest at this time on account of the large crop of saffron. Some were busy in plucking flowers, some were conveying them in carriages, the heads of some were bent with their weight, some were sleeping in boats (laden with saffron), some were constantly occupied in weighing, and some were guarding the crop.

This is the account of the saffron harvest.

When eight years had passed away, King Jyallaladina took the country from Yosobha Khana and bestowed it on others. On the arrival of Asaha Khana, Merja Yosobha's troops were scattered like the dust at the time when the wind prevails. Then the illustrious Jyallaladina sent his two servants Ahlada Khana and Soltan Mahamada[90] Kula Khana. Asaha Khana knew them to be the servants of jyallaladina; he gave them the possession of the country, and went to the feet of his master. These two officers drove away injustice from Kashmira, even as the sun and the moon drive away darkness from the earth. They ascended a hill near Sharika in the neighborhood of Pravarapura, and there, under the orders of King Akavara, built a fort with the inappropriate name of *Naganagari*.[91] Men after performing various kinds of religious austerities go to heaven in their second birth after death; but when the people saw this Naganagari they did not attempt to ascend to this heaven.

## Cantonment for troops

At this time the houses in the city were occupied by the king's soldiers, and the inhabitants suffered thereby. The merchants saw this distress of the people and informed the king of it; whereupon the king removed the difficulty by the following arrangement. The king's followers stayed in the new town, and any one of them who harassed the people was made guilty of an offence. The Muggulas, after King Jyallaladina had thus ordered, lived in the new town. It was whitewashed with lime and was situated on the Sharika hill, and it looked as if it jeered at the old capital in its neighbourhood. When the *yavanas* had gone out of the old city, the people held a festivity; they always blessed Kings Jyallaladina, and were happy. Now all of a sudden, at midday and within a short time, the old town built at Alabhadina, with its two thousand houses, was in a flame, as if in sorrow for its separation with the Muggulas whom it saw depart in order to live in the new town. This extensive city, adorned with many paintings[92], and with its houses and buildings, was soon reduced to ashes. When the old city was burnt, the new one looked beautiful, even as when a co-wife dies, the other feels happy.

Here ends the description of the acquisition of Kashmira by the emperor, Akavara Jyallaladina.

## References

1. Mereja: Mirza Haider, nephew of Mirza Abu Said of Kashgarh.
2. Hinduvat: referred to a number of times as situated outside Kashmir, pb. lies on the western side of the P-P mtns. PH states that Kaji died at Thana after he failed in effecting the ejectment of Haider's Kashgarhis in spite of a series of confrontations at Wathanar, Giradaar, Kohtar, Wahathor, and Gulmarg, even with the assistance of Sher Shah Suri's troops. Referred to also on PP. .... 267. One reference (93/16) indicates it could be reached by the Khuyya (*i.e.,* Khuyahama) road which could place it in the basin of the Indus, or even in the Kishenganga vy. See also n. 15 below.
3. Mashugola: Haider (Madhugola) goblins: allusion, if any, forgotten.
4. instigated: having been instigated through diplomacy by their chief when their numbers increased, they seized lands... Devana: of the emperor of Delhi.... year 22: 1546 A.D.
5. Hasanpora ...' two vv. on the Vishav, near Nandimarg in Advani pg. PH states that the cultivable land belonging to the first was found shifted to the second and *vice versa*, and the consequent cross-cultivation continued till his own time. The incident is recorded in appendix of the edition of SK.
6. Tax: obviously Daulat Chak was afraid of the reactionaries. The well-known shrine of *Khirbhavani* is in Tulamula. The original verses of the next paragraph are given on p. 363 of SK's edition.
7. Homaya: Humayun who had recovered his throne.
8. Ajahomaya: Ajmahomai (SK) identity with Shah Abul Moali of Kashgarh has been suggested.
9. Habebha: Habibshah, son of Ismail Khan was dethroned. The following para is a translation of the verses on p. 418, Appendix D (S.K)...year 37:1561 A.D.
10. Qara (Kara) Bahadura : nephew of Mirza Haider, not a son of Humayun.
11. Pashanda: pb. Pusiana. The Mughals approached Kashmir from Rajauri and reached Bahramgala (PH).
12. Gajashah: Ghazishah Chak who usurped the throne of Habibshah.
13. Surjala: Suyal (SK) pb. the v. Suyal Sai in Rajauri t. 20 km. from Rajauri. Also spelt Sialsui.
14. 'The Mughal army, to whom the troops of Pashanda paid no heed earlier, covered the whole of Rajapuri.'
15. Hinduvata: presumed to be on the western slope of the P-P. mtn. According to PH the confrontation took place at Bahramagala across the P-P pass below Pusiana.

16. Shailshahi: Shahi (SK) refers, pb. to an earlier engagement at Hanjivera. Sialsui appears to be phonetically close to Shailshahi.
17. Shasanamkura: Kabhra (SK).
18. *nagrandhara* : cannon
19. '...severed the heads...': they were promised one gold coin for each head (PH).
20. servant: nephew....Pashandas: pb. people living around Pushiana.
21. Rajavira: Rajauri.
22. Habe Chakka: Habib Chak.
23. For Sadashivpura see n. 36 below.
24. As the king crossed the river, the battle was probably fought near Bahukhatkeshvar shrine, tri-junction of Doodganga, Kutakol and the Veth (left). Hataka and Svamipora are one as Hatakasvamipora (now Chhatabal). RNS places the Hataka shrine near the temple of Mata Rupabhavani. If that were so, Ghazishah stationed at Diddamar would not have to cross the river.
25. Sita river: One of the seven rivers mentioned in the *Nil-n* (V. 621-22) as worthy of worship. Probably Doodganga is meant on account of the implication of the purity in milk (Dugdaganga), whitishness (Svetaganga).
26. Abdolmali: Mirza Abul Ali Maula, a relation of Humayun.
27. Parihasapura: capital of Lalitaditya Muktapida on the Vitasta, left, a short distance below Srg.
28. powerful son: According to PH a servant of the prince once picked some grapes from a shop without payment. The vendor complained to the king who had the erring hand chopped off. The prince was furious and complained to his uncle Mohammad. When the latter advised patience, the prince was mad with rage and killed the uncle. As a consequence the king had the prince, his own son, hanged at Idgah.
29. Hosain Khan managed to occupy the throne even while Ghazishah was alive (PH).
30. Khanojamana: Khan Zaman.
31. Mamada Khan: Mohammad Khan (SK) Mohd. Magrey son of Abdal! (PH).
32. Sharikasthana: Hariparbat. The festival was held till recent times, but without the competition in archery, during the first week of bright Chaitra.
33. Shri Panchmi: the fifth of the dark fortnight of Baisakh, generally in April. Shrinagara is the mystic city of the supreme goddess dominating the Srichakra.
34. Jyeshtharudra hill: close to the Shankaracharya hill.
35. According to Persian chroniclers Hosain Chak was shocked when Akbar expressed his resentment against him by rejecting a princess offered to his son. His health was shattered, he abdicated in favour of his brother Ali Khan and retired to Zainapora.

36. Sadashiva forest: Sadashivpura was near Haba Kadal, left. The Vitasta is no barrier against fire which in the past often crossed from one side to the other. Samudramatha: locality on the river near Haba Kadal, right. Also see 257/26.
37. Momara Khan: Pb. Mubarik Khan Behaqi, a descendant of Meya Hussain, father-in-law of King Hassanshah. PH states that the confrontation between Yusufshah and Syed Mubarik was the outcome of a misunderstanding.
38. Distant country: Mubarik Khan son of Syed Ibrahim had pb. gone away for want of patronage and returned on the eve of Yusufs enthronement, or a little earlier Diddamatha: Idgah (PH)
39. Two months: one year and two months (PH).
40. Yusuf took shelter with some hill chieftains close to the Vy. (pb. the Khashas), fought another engagement with his enemies at Idgah, was defeated and finally went to Agra (PH).
41. One....six months and two days (PH).
42. Lahvara: Lohar Chak, nephew of Hosain Shah Chak and a cousin of Yusuf Shah. According to PH it was Abdal Bhat who sponsored his enthronement.
43. Lions...Persian chronicles state that foodgrains were cheap and abundant in his reign and a loaf of bread weighing 2½ lbs., nicknamed *loharmond* (Lohar's cake) was sold for 1 pice.
44. Yusuf gave a slip to the escort provided for him by Akbar and returned to Kashmir, after eleven months, at the head of a force of his own which included Mohammad Bhat and other Kashmiris (PH).
45. Another road: Khuyahama road.
46. Crossed over: at Delina, 5 Km. below Sangrama on Sgr-Bla road.
47. forest: in Banihal Hills (PH)
48. Habhebha: Habib Chak, a rebel leader.
    Bhagavaddasa: Raja Bhagwandas Kachwaha, father of Raja Mansingh... people of the mountains: their role has often decided the fate of the V.
49. shrine of Varaha: at Baramulla.
50. forest: an excellent strategy in the face of the superior resources of Akbar.
51. winnowing fan: commemorated in the Kashmiri saying *yupis shup....* went: Kashmiris coined a chronogram: *nyov giriftar gav* (he has been taken and placed under custody) A.H. 993, *i.e.*, A.D. 1585. Yusuf was obviously tired of dissensions amongst Kashmiri leaders, and frequent defections that Yaqub, who continued to revolt, had to face to his cost to confirm it.
52. Malleka Alaka: Ali Dar (PH).
53. Madhyadesha: the central region, Delhi. Jalaluddin, king of...'
54. Lahora: Lahore, capital of Panjab (now Pakistan).

55. Chandrabhaga: the Chenab, pb. near Wazirabad, now Pakistan.
56. Panchnila hill: pb. P-Panchal mtn. is meant. Kashthavata: Kishtwar
57. Made peace: according to PH prestigious Kashmiri leaders including Sheikh Yaqub Sarfi and Baba Dawood Khaki sought the audience of Akbar and entreated him to conquer Kashmir to deliver the people from the chaotic misrule of Yaqub Chak.
58. Mohd. Bhat and Shamsi Chak were set at large by the defecting nobles including Yusuf Behaqi, Alamsher Magrey and Zafar, son of Shamshi Chak, in order to fan the flame of internal revolt when the Mughals were already at the threshold. (PH).
59. Saka year 1509: A.D. 1587.
60. palace...: Yusuf Shah laid out a garden stretching from Fateh Kadal to Dalhassanyar flanked by the Vitasta and the Kutakol. Kasem Khan was staying in this palace.
61. Tailagrama: v. near Pattan; another locality of the same name has been placed in the Kishenganga vy.
62. Friendly brother: pb. Ibrahim Chak, son of Yusuf Chak.
63. Kshetra: the battle was fought on the Dagvan hill (PH) in Volur pga. (Avantipur-Tral). Kshetra obviously refers to Vyjayakshetra, the sub-division of Bijbehara.
64. Hill: precise location uncertain.... The Mughals later entrenched at what is called Shivpora today.
65. Jyeshtharudra: Zeethiyer. The battle appears to have taken place near Badamibagh. The next para is a translation of the verses given as a footnote on p. 400. Sadashivpora: the present Shivpora.
66. 'Lanka' suggests an island-like configuration to land, as at the river bank near Shivpora.
67. Saida Yosobha: Syed Yusuf Khan Razvi.
68. Mohd. Mera: Mohammad Bhat, a former prime minister. He surrendered to the Mughals, along with many Kashmiri nobles.
69. During the civil war between the Syeds and the Kashmiris the latter had taken a similar position.
70. According to PH the Kashmiris were disheartened when an arrow struck their commander in the eye. They, however, fought another engagement near Hanjyek.
71. ebb and flow: pb. Trisandhya spring in Anantnag dt. Otherwise also, the flow of water is maximum at nightfall.
72. Amreshvara: at the cave of Shri Amarnath, beyond Pahalgam.
73. Living fire: *svayambhu* agni, natural flame at Svayam in Kupwara dt. According to I largopal Kaul, the flame had a diameter of fifty feet in 1877 A.D. (*Guldasta Kashmir*).
74. The seventh day; sacred to Martanda, the sun god. Kashmiri Pandits make *rangolis* in coloured powders, representing the sun, on the seventh of the lunar Ashar. The place mentioned here is Matan.
75. Appendices trees: deodars.

76. Tank: the Dal.
77. refuge: after offering stiff resistance to the Mughals, Yaqub found his Kashmiri allies defecting to the enemy, and finally he surrendered himself.
78. Yadgar: Mirza Yadgar, nephew of Yusuf Khan, the previous Mughal governor (PH).
79. Shikha Phareda: Sheikh Farid Badakshi Begi (PH).
80. Hastivanj: a spur on the old route across the Pir Panchal wherefrom an elephant slipped down while Mihirkula was on his way to Kashmir. The painful grunting of the tusker pleased the Hun. The well-known orientalist Jarrold gives the place the name *Hastibhanj* at the suggestion of Radha Krishen Kaul, governor of Jammu during the last quarter of the last century.
81. Festivity: Akbar ordered the Vitasta to be illuminated with lamps, floating or fixed on boats, on the 'birth anniversary' of the river on the lunar thirteenth of Bahadun (August). Large numbers of people were also feasted. For celebration of the same festival by Z. refer to p. 109.
82. Unable: Brahmins were pb. denied freedom of association by some Chak rulers.
83. Ramdas: pb. the same person mentioned as Mathra Das in *Akbarnama*. PH refers to him as Satradas. Other persons referred to are celebrated in the classics for their munificence.
84. Nirmmala: prominent among those Brahmins who having left the Vy. in the earlier chaotic times returned to Kashmir attracted by the patronage of Akbar.
85. Aditya: Rajanakaditya (SK), pb. a local man.
86. Shikha Phaiji: Sheikh Fyzee, of the court of Akbar.
87. *yavana*: pb. a Mughal soldier.
88. almonds, apples, etc. are not mentioned: *Khari*: about 77 kg.
89. Takshaknaga: with his abode in a spring at Zeven, a v. close to Srgr., Takshaka was one of the principal *nagas* who sought shelter in Kashmir against the predatory Garuda. According to local folkore it was Takshaka who gave a saffron bulb as a gift to a physician who cured him of an ailment.
90. Sultan Mohd. Ali Khan Turkman (PH).
91. Naganagari: Naagamagar of Persian chroniclers, the rampart round the Hariparvat area, was built under the supervision of Khwaja Mohd. Husain, an erstwhile slave (Bates), to create avenues of employment for the people who had suffered in the disorder of the Chak regime. The fort on the crest of the hill was built by Sardar Atta Mohammad Khan, a governor of the kings of Kabul, in 1811. Under orders of the emperor a palace and other mansions facing the east were constructed at the foot of Hariparvat washed by the Dal. The emperor rewarded an engineer with a necklace, thus creating

the family of Kanths (from *kanthi*). The citadel afforded protection to the Mughals against unforeseen uprisings and also served as a cantonment. According to an engraved tablet displayed on the lofty gateway facing south, the citadel was completed in 1597 A.D., in the forty-fourth year of the emperor's reign....inappropriate: the word *nag*, 'a' short as the vowel sound in 'nug' stands for a wide range of objects including a 'mountain', a 'gem', a 'tiger', the 'sun', a 'serpent' and is also an epithet of Indra. *naganagari* was, pb., meant to be interpreted as the 'City of Indra' but somehow came to be referred to as the City of Serpents—*Kohi Maran*—by many Persian speaking people and, later, chroniclers. Hence Shuka's grouse.

92. Paintings: because of frequent outbreaks of fire, little evidence of the glorious paintings and other arts has been left.

# Kings of Kashmir

## (1155–1587 A.D.)

| | | |
|---|---|---|
| 1. | Jayasimha | d. 1155 A.D. |
| 2. | Paramanuka | 1155–1164 |
| 3. | Vantideva | 1164–1171 |
| 4. | Vopyadeva | 1171–1181 |
| 5. | Jassaka | 1181–1199 |
| 6. | Jagadeva | 1199–1213 |
| 7. | Rajadeva | 1213–1236 |
| 8. | Sangramdeva | 1236–1252 |
| 9. | Ramadeva | 1252–1273 |
| 10. | Lakshmanadeva | 1273–1286 |
| 11. | Simhadeva | 1286–1301 |
| 12. | Sahadeva | 1301–1320 |
| | *Invasion of Zulchu* | |
| 1. | Rinchan Shah | 1320–1323 |
| 2. | Udyandeva | 1323–1339 |
| 3. | Kota Rani | 1339 (six months only) |
| | *The Sultans* | |
| 1. | Shams-ud-Din (Shabmir) | 1339–1342 |
| 2. | Jamshed | 1342–1344 |
| 3. | Alau-ud-Din | 1344–1355 |
| 4. | Shahab-ud-Din | 1355–1373 |
| 5. | Qutub-ud-Din | 1373–1389 |
| 6. | Sikandar | 1389–1413 |
| 7. | Alishah | 1413–1419 |

| | | |
|---|---|---|
| 8. | Zain-ul-Abdin | 1420–1470 |
| 9. | Haidershah | 1470–1472 |
| 10. | Hassanshah | 1472–1484 |
| 11. | Mohammadshah | Ap. 1484–Oct.1486 |
| 12. | Fatehshah | 1486–1495 |
| 13. | Mohammadshah | 1495–1496 |
| 14. | Fatehshah | 1496–1497 |
| 15. | Mohammadshah | 1497–1509 |
| 16. | Ibrahimshah (s/o Mohammadshah) | 1509 |
| 17. | Nazukshah (s/o Fatehshah) | 1529 (one year) |
| 18. | Mohammadshah | 1530–1535 |
| 19. | Shamsashah (s/o Mohammadshah) | 1537 |
| 20. | Habibshah | 1560 (dethroned) |
| | *The Chak Dynasty* | |
| 21. | Ghazi Chak | 1560 |
| 22. | Hosain Chak | 1562 |
| 23. | Ali Khan Chak | 1569 |
| 24. | Yusufshah Chak | 1578 |
| 25. | Momara Khan | 1578 |
| 26. | Lahvara Chak | 1578 |
| 27. | Yusufshah | 1579 |
| 28. | Yaqubshah | 1587 |
| | surrenders to the Mughals | 1587 |

The above schedule of succession has several gaps, especially during the period 1486–1560 A.D., but some other historians have presented the following account:

| *Sr. No.* | | *A.D.* |
|---|---|---|
| 12. | Fatheh Shah | 1486–1493 |
| 13. | Mohammad Shah | 1493–1505 |
| 14. | Fateh Shah | 1505–1514 |
| 15. | Mohammad Shah | 1514–1515 |
| 16. | Fateh Shah | 1515–1517 (dies) |
| 17. | Mohammad Shah | 1517–1528 |

| | | |
|---|---|---|
| 18. | Ibrahim Shah (S/o Mohammad Shah) | 1528–1529 |
| 19. | Nazuk Shah (S/o Fateh Shah) | 1529–1530 |
| 20. | Mohammad Shah | 1530–1537 (dies) |
| 21. | Ismail Shah (married to the daughter of the Prime Minister Kaji Chak) | 1538–1540 |
| 22. | Nazuk Shah (s/o Fatehshah) | 1540–1551 |
| 23. | Ibrahim Shah (s/o Mohammadshah) | 1552–1557 |
| 24. | Habib Shah | 1557–1560 (dethroned) |

Shuka mentions the death of Fateh Shah in 1519 A.D. The Chak Dynasty: as above.

# Index



---

Note 1. Figures indicate the page numbers. Where two numbers have an oblique sign (/) in between, the former indicates the page and the latter the serial number of the 'note' in the relevant 'References'.

Note 2. The chroniclers have often given a number of variants of the same name, *e.g.*, Jugaka/Jugabhatta, Ahmadayukta/Ahmadamalla/Ahmadamallekka, Andrakotta/Androtta/Androta. It is often difficult to identify such variants. But all such entries have been recorded in the Index, even though many duplications may have occurred in the process. In some cases prevalent names have been given in brackets also.

## C



## D

## E

## H

## I



## J

## M

## N

## Q



## R